A RIVER FLOWS FROM EDEN

A RIVER FLOWS FROM EDEN

The Language of Mystical Experience in the Zohar

Melila Hellner-Eshed

Translated from the Hebrew by Nathan Wolski

STANFORD UNIVERSITY PRESS
STANFORD, CALIFORNIA

Stanford University Press
Stanford, California

A River Flows from Eden was originally published in Hebrew in 2005
under the title *Ve-nahar yotzei me-ʿEden* ונהר יוצא מעדן.
©2005 by Am-Oved—Alma.

Printed in the United States of America on acid-free,
archival-quality paper

Library of Congress Cataloging-in-Publication Data
Hellner-Eshed, Melila.
[Ve-nahar yotzei me-ʿEden. English]
A river flows from Eden : the language of mystical experience in
the Zohar / Melila Hellner-Eshed ; translated from the Hebrew by
Nathan Wolski.
p. cm.
"Originally published in Hebrew in 2005 under the title
Ve-nahar yotzei me-Eden."
Includes bibliographical references and index.
ISBN 978-0-8047-5939-7 (cloth : alk. paper)
1. Zohar. 2. Cabala. 3. Mysticism--Judaism. I. Wolski, Nathan. II.
Title.
BM525.A59H4513 2009
296.1'62--dc22   2009007193

Typeset by Bruce Lundquist in 11/16 Bembo

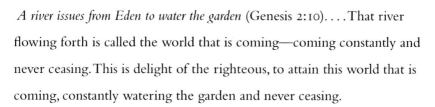

A river issues from Eden to water the garden (Genesis 2:10). . . . That river flowing forth is called the world that is coming—coming constantly and never ceasing. This is delight of the righteous, to attain this world that is coming, constantly watering the garden and never ceasing.

Zohar 3:290b (Idra Zuta); transl. Daniel Matt

In loving memory of my father, Moshe,

and with great love to my mother, Leah,

who both planted within me love for life and Torah.

Contents

Acknowledgments

Now that the work is complete and this book is seeing the light of day, I find myself filled with gratitude toward many people. The Zohar is a great teacher of thanksgiving, and I hope I have succeeded in learning from it the delights of praise.

"Your eyes shall behold your teachers." I wish to thank my beloved teacher Yehuda Liebes for opening my heart to the love of the Zohar. I thank him for guiding me through its dense mysteries for many years. He continues to reveal before my astonished eyes precious gems mined from the radiant quarry of the zoharic corpus. His wisdom and vast knowledge are embedded in every page of this book.

I am grateful to my dear teacher Moshe Idel, who expands my horizons and understanding. In being somewhat of a magician when it comes to the domain of the temporal, Moshe always found time in his ever-so-busy life to sit with me to discuss various matters related to this book. He kept me from pitfalls and encouraged me with his unique humor all along the way. His thoughts, inspiration and wise counsel are present throughout this work.

I also wish to thank my friend and colleague Daniel Abrams. His willingness to publish (in Hebrew) select chapters of my work-in-progress encouraged me greatly.

This book was translated into English by my dear friend Nathan Wolski. His rendering is that of a true Zohar connoisseur. Working together gave me the delightful privilege of living in his Australian home in a family of Zohar lovers—Nathan and his wife, my beloved friend Merav Carmeli, and their daughters.

For reading, reflecting and editing this manuscript, I thank my teachers, colleagues, and friends Daniel Matt, Arthur Green, and Elliot Ginsburg—for their unwavering support and for being my *Ḥevraya*; my friend and teacher David Blumenthal, for being among the earliest to read my work and for encouraging me to translate it into English; my mother, Leah, and my friends Orna Triguboff and Sara Meirowitz, for carefully proofreading the drafts of the translated manuscript; as well as my friend and colleague Joel Hecker, for reading the manuscript with a keen eye and for making important suggestions.

Without the support and generosity of my soul friend Tirzah Firestone this translation would not have come into reality. Thinking of Tirzah, I am filled with joy and gratitude.

Thanks are also due to Ina Tillman for her encouragement and for being the first to make a donation toward the translation; and to my friends Yonatan Benarroch, Judy Margolin, and Laura Bowman, for their vital final touches in preparing the manuscript for print.

I am also thankful to Stanford University Press for publishing this book; to the editors Norris Pope and Mariana Raykov and especially to David E. S. Stein for his outstanding editorial work; and to Rob Ehle for the beautiful cover design. I offer deep thanks to Itiel Pan for generously permitting me to use his father's beautiful artwork, which adorns the cover of the book you are now holding.

I wish to acknowledge the Memorial Foundation for Jewish Culture, the Jewish Studies Enrichment Fund of Emory University, and the Department of Jewish Studies at the Hebrew University in Jerusalem, for their support of the publication of this book.

Heartfelt thanks to my friends and colleagues at the Shalom Hartman Institute for their good questions and intellectual inspiration; to my friend and mentor Rachel Cowan and to our colleagues at the Institute for Jewish Spirituality, for keeping my heart open as I did this work; and to the many friends and students in the study groups of which I have been a part, both in Israel and in North America. This book is enriched by the thoughts and insights you sparked in me.

To my beloved husband Dror: Your support of my work ensures that we all stay sane, and your humor keeps me from taking myself too seriously. To my most beloved children Hallel and Yotam: May God bless you and watch over you always!

Finally, I am deeply grateful for wondrous moments of awareness that the river from Eden is forever flowing.

Jerusalem 2009

A RIVER FLOWS FROM EDEN

Introduction

When I was twenty years old I received as a gift, in honor of my forthcoming overseas trip, a copy of Gershom Scholem's *Zohar, The Book of Splendor: Basic Readings from the Kabbalah*. Sitting in distant Norway, I read in English a passage from the Zohar's opening to Genesis. I did not even know then in what language the Zohar had been composed. All I knew was that I wanted more. Since then—and now for many years, both within the gates of the Hebrew University and without—I have been blessed with the opportunity to study the Zohar with wonderful teachers and students alike. Like many other readers across the generations, I too have been seduced by the charm of this book. Indeed, as the years go by, I have become more and more attuned to the music of the wondrous world that emerges from its pages.

The Zohar is the jewel in the crown of Jewish mystical literature. It is unparalleled in terms of its acceptance, sanctity, and influence on the consciousness of generations of Jews—and all this despite its apparently sudden appearance toward the end of the thirteenth century. Its mysterious style, and the unique mystical-religious dimension it offered Jewish life, quickly captured the hearts and minds of its readers. The mythical-erotic creativity that burst forth from its pages turned the Zohar into a world unto itself. Its surprising interpretations of biblical verses resonated in the souls of many, along with its deep insights into the human psyche—in both joy and grief.

Yet perhaps above all else, it was the worldview of the Zohar—through its establishing a reciprocal relationship between the world of humanity and the world of divinity—that left an indelible impression on the hearts of its readers. In this ever-changing, constantly evolving relationship, the divine flow seeks to be revealed and to saturate the world of humanity; and humanity, for its part, seeks to attain, to take part in, and to cleave to the divine world. Indeed, the Zohar created a view of reality that bestows upon humanity the ability and the responsibility to rectify, constitute, and beautify over and over again the figure of the Godhead—and in so doing, itself and the world.

The Zohar invites the reader on a journey through diverse secret worlds, a complicated game of hide-and-seek—pleasurable to be sure, yet requiring from the reader great effort to reveal its moves. Indeed, this invitation accounts in no small part for the Zohar's charm. The hero of the composition—Rabbi Shim'on bar Yoḥai—became, both in the consciousness of the Zohar's readers and in Jewish popular consciousness, a mythological figure. His image as the great teacher, the mysterious man of God who reveals the light of secrets to the world, has served as a source of inspiration for creative minds, and for lovers of Torah and God alike.

The Structure of This Book

This book seeks to understand the special mystical dimension of the Zohar. *Mysticism* is a general term used for phenomena found in all the world's religions (and indeed outside of them). It refers to the human endeavor to develop ways of life and special practices in order to make present in one's life the unmediated experience of the holy or of God. In mystical documents from different religions, we encounter the conscious effort to experience dimensions of reality unattainable through the ordinary states of consciousness in everyday life. These modes, and the experiences that accompany them, are not usually the norm in the religious culture to which the mystic belongs. Jews who live according to the norms of their religion—like Moslems, Christians, or Hindus—are not obligated by this more intensive form of religious life; the decision to adopt this life has been the heritage of individuals alone. In the Jewish tradition, this trend is known as the "secret way," the "way of truth," and it is hidden under the shroud of mystery. Yet Jewish literature has bequeathed us testimonies, from the Bible to our own day, about special people who in their lives fulfilled the desire for a special intimacy with the divine, and who left us accounts of their experiences.

The Zohar is not a theoretical book about the essence of Jewish mysticism. Rather, the Zohar *is* a mystical composition, parts of which were surely written in heightened states of consciousness, and parts of which seek, to my mind, to awaken the reader to a change in consciousness. The Zohar does not present us with a systematic presentation of mystical consciousness and mystical language. No invisible hand appears to guide the reader systematically through the chambers of divine wisdom. Nor can a teacher direct the new reader to a particular page of the zoharic text so as to learn "the mystical teaching of the Zohar." The mystical aspect of the Zohar is made manifest among a collection of literary forms and expressions. It shines among them. In order to enter gently into the zoharic world—unparalleled in its richness and complexity—this book is divided into four parts, each of which endeavors to answer one of the following questions:

1. Who are the heroes of the Zohar?
2. What do they do?
3. Why do they do it?
4. What is the nature of their mystical experience?

Part I presents the world of the heroes of the Zohar—the great teacher Rabbi Shim'on bar Yoḥai and the circle of students around him. Together they are known as the Companions—in Aramaic, *Ḥevraya*. These chapters explore the way in which the Zohar depicts them, and also the way that they understand themselves as figures who together constitute the ideal mystical society.

Part II describes the life of the Companions and explores their distinctive life-style. Here we encounter the fact that in the Zohar the mystical dimension transpires and is experienced in the context of a group—not of a lone individual. We also analyze the Companions' two main spiritual practices: walking together on their way, with the special scriptural exegesis that accompanies such travels; and also the creative Torah study undertaken from midnight to dawn. Additionally, we explore the meaning of the appearance of wondrous characters as a means of generating mystical experience, and the collective journey of the entire mystical circle into different dimensions of reality and consciousness.

These first two parts, taken together, familiarize us with the heroes of the Zohar and with their unique life-style and practices. Only then will it be possible to turn to the major questions that this work seeks to explore.

Part III deals with the heart of the zoharic enterprise and with its essential aims. Three main issues are discussed here:

1. *The "secret" and its diverse meanings in the zoharic world.* Here we explore the structure of the zoharic homily that grants access to the "secret" dimension, and the nature of creativity from within this dimension.

2. *Awakening and arousal.* The greatest wish of the Zohar is to awaken the sleeping consciousness of humanity, and to arouse it to a more expansive and divine perception of reality. Such awakening in the Zohar is presented in various terms: as erotic arousal, as a longing to know the divine reality and to take part in (and to influence) this reality, and as the founding logic of the interrelationship between the human and divine worlds. Here we describe the means employed by the Zohar, both implicit and explicit, to call the reader to awaken.

3. *The zoharic understanding and interpretation of one biblical verse, "A river flows from Eden to water the Garden . . ."* (Genesis 2:10). This verse, I suggest, is a zoharic code, encapsulating a conception of the dynamic structure of divinity and consciousness. The purpose of this code is to signify to the reader how to awaken the special consciousness that the Zohar seeks to generate.

Part IV focuses on mystical experience itself and the language of its expression in the Zohar. Here I offer a detailed exposition of the language of mystical experience, the emotional and physical phenomena accompanying such experiences, as well as powerful testimonies of these extraordinary events. I discuss the main forms, metaphors, and symbols employed by the Zohar to describe mystical experience, the sources of this descriptive language, and their place and function within this experience. This analysis focuses on the expression of the experience as well as a discussion of its essence, out of the assumption that language and experience influence each other in a dynamic way.[1]

This part builds to a climax: a model of the three main states of consciousness that underwrite zoharic mysticism and language, and that constitute the building blocks for the Zohar's experiential world.

I conclude the book with two chapters on related themes. One chapter explores the (im)possibility of expressing in language a personal encounter with aspects of divinity. The last chapter engages the zoharic dialectics around the question of writing, and on the constraints when moving from an oral world of mysteries into writing.

Methodological and Personal Reflections

The Zohar's literary style shuns systematic and didactic presentation. The authors of the Zohar chose to take existing kabbalistic ideas and experiences, already crystallized by their time into stable concepts and terms, and to melt them down anew—through a special mystical poetics—into a multivalent, flowing state. My exploring the mystical language of the Zohar, however, necessitated a process of isolation, classification, and definition of the different categories within this language. At times, this process aroused within me a sense of betrayal vis-à-vis the unique qualities of my subject matter. If indeed this flowing quality of mystical poetics characterized the Zohar (and it was this quality that aroused my deep fascination with the Zohar), then this research was likely to find itself working against the grain of the text! In order to avoid this pitfall, the words of Michel de Certeau, the well-known researcher of sixteenth- and seventeenth-century Christian mysticism, were never far from my mind:

> The color overflows its designated space . . . [and] mocks my efforts to delineate, in the thicket of our data and analytic apparatus, the sequence of a narrative account whose subject is Christian mystics in the sixteenth and seventeenth centuries. Nevertheless, a demarcation is necessary, if only so that what overflows its borders may become visible. . . . The organization of a space, though necessary, will be seen to be unable to "stop" the subject matter. It places mystic speech within a set of codifications that cannot contain it. It is a form whose matter overflows.[2]

In this work, I have indeed isolated sparks and crystals from the zoharic river, but only to then allow them to be reintegrated into this river's flow, hopefully without losing their original vitality. I hope that I have succeeded in this endeavor.

My attempt to explore the mystical language of the Zohar required that I pay particular attention to the way in which the Zohar expresses its daring world of religious experience in its own unique language, and without the use of terms from the fields of religion and philosophy—such as mysticism, theosophy, theurgy, phenomenology, and ecstasy. I present the results of my research both in terms of the internal language of the Zohar and in terms of the language of the critical research of mysticism, both Jewish and general.

From a methodological perspective, I have been aided by phenomenological and historical models in translating the concealed concepts and encoded language of the Zohar. In so doing, however, I have sought to maintain a level of caution so as not to fall into the trap of reductionism by imposing existing models on my subject matter.[3] The difficult task before me, therefore, was to find the appropriate language, which on the one hand would illuminate the text using conceptual tools derived from critical research, yet on the other hand would neither violate nor conceal the Zohar's unique language—whose power is derived precisely from its enigmatic form.

An additional task that lay before me arose from my desire to mediate the zoharic text—not merely to engage in interpretation. The Zohar invites mediation; its structure frustrates any who would seek out a coherent teaching. Further, Aramaic, the language of its composition, is unknown to most people. Even with the help of Hebrew translations, the reader still finds herself before a complex structure of expressions and difficult-to-decipher symbols. One who is well versed in reading the Zohar knows that it speaks in a coherent manner, yet this is often concealed from the unseasoned reader.

In much of this book, I have sought merely to translate into contemporary language that which the Zohar conveys in its own words much better than I ever could. It was by no means easy to mediate the Zohar without adding description or interpretation to excess, especially considering the Zohar's invitation to taste—and drown in—its honey. This book reflects my attempt to understand and describe the zoharic text not merely as the carrier of ideas, but also as a work of art. In my endeavor to convey that which is hidden in the Zohar, the words of the essayist Susan Sontag were particularly inspiring:

> The aim of all commentary on art now should be to make works of art—and by analogy our own experiences—more, rather than less real to us. The function of criticism should be to show *how it is what it is, even that it is what it is,* rather than to show what it means. . . . In place of a hermeneutics we need an erotics of arts.[4]

The desire to mediate the Zohar also informed my decision to quote many zoharic texts in the body of this work, and to present them so that the reader may encounter them in a clearer fashion than via the Zohar's standard printed editions.

Years of careful Zohar study have led me to be amazed at the manner in which its heroes read the Torah. The complex and subtle play between the close reading of verses on the one hand, and an unbridled mystical, interpretive creativity that knows no bounds on the other, has no peer in the Jewish tradition. Sometimes, after reading a zoharic interpretation of a particular biblical verse, my understanding of that verse—even in its original biblical context—changes completely.

The question of how the Companions read the Torah, what they saw in it, what they heard from among its pages, and perhaps above all, how they gave themselves the freedom to interpret from its verses the ever-changing world of divinity, was always before me. In order to better understand the zoharic art of reading Scripture, one must develop a broad and deep familiarity with the storehouse of Jewish literature preceding the Zohar: with the philosophical and kabbalistic thought of the Middle Ages, and more importantly with classical rabbinic literature—in whose form the Zohar is written, and which the heroes of the Zohar seamlessly assimilate into their own world. The reader of the Zohar must, however, be able to identify when the Companions are creating a standard kind of rabbinic midrash, and when they are boldly opening new paths of their own, in order to return afresh to view the words of Scripture from within their own unique horizon.

My desire to mediate the Zohar raised a particular problem with the syntax of my work. In addressing the density of Zoharic style, Moshe Idel has pointed out that the Zohar is a *symbolic composition* rather than merely a work that uses symbols,[5] and Yehuda Liebes has shown how the relatively limited vocabulary of zoharic Aramaic contains a vast range of meanings functioning in diverse ways in different interpretive registers.[6] I often found myself writing long sentences filled with secondary clauses, as I sought to highlight and explain the multiple realities represented by a given zoharic symbol. The endeavor to unfurl the zoharic map of symbols and referents revealed itself as nearly impossible. Perhaps this is how it should be. The syntactical awkwardness of parts of this work, therefore, reflects the inherent difficulty in clearly articulating the simultaneous multiple fields of meaning encoded in the Zohar's words.

My analysis of the self-reflexive dimensions of the Zohar, and the search for clues that might shed light on the world of its authors, necessitated a hypercritical reading of the text. If at times I may have looked for hints where none were to be found, I did so with a view to exploring one of the Zohar's most seductive aspects, its self-reflexivity. It seems to me that more was gained in this endeavor than was lost.

All researchers have a personal and intellectual biography and cannot but speak from within their own horizon—a horizon that greatly influences their relationship to the subject matter. The history of academic research in the field of Jewish Thought attests to this fact.[7] Not only do I not assume the possibility of a "pure objectivity" between researchers and their subject matter, but rather I am deeply interested in the way in which researchers' personal and intellectual worlds are revealed between the lines of their scholarship. I therefore feel compelled to outline some of my premises regarding my object of study.

I have a deep, personal interest in mystical experience and the hidden potential of human consciousness. The extraordinary endeavor of mystics across the generations to seek out an enhanced human consciousness—experientially, sensorially, and emotionally—has long inspired me. I am particularly interested in the attempt to document mystical consciousness as it is expressed in the language of the Jewish tradition. The Zohar is a spiritually inspired work of the highest order, and to my mind the world it describes is neither closed nor lost nor confined to the Middle Ages. I experience its insights as a living invitation to a special religious consciousness as well as to exegetical, cultural, and religious creativity. In the Zohar I find spiritual possibilities that are capable of redeeming aspects of the Jewish tradition—of which I am a part—from fossilization.

Both as a woman and as a Jew who does not live according to *halakhah* (traditional religious practice and law as interpreted by Orthodox rabbis), I am excluded from the possibility of harmoniously—and uncritically—integrating into the world of the kabbalists. I am aware that this prevents me from hearing aspects of the Zohar's musical rhythm, yet I have found this "limitation" to be fruitful in important ways. My stance vis-à-vis the text enables me to choose those elements of the Zohar with which I identify and reject others entirely. The texts I research are not authoritative in the sense that they require me to adopt a particular ideological position or necessitate any particular action on my part. In other words, I stand outside the boundaries of the "traditional participant" in this body of knowledge. I am free from having to submit to the power of the Zohar's traditional authority.

I am well aware that the Zohar was written—as most Jewish cultural documents have been—by Jewish men for Jewish men. Yet, I find in it deep human wisdom that transcends boundaries of time, religion, and gender. I have tried to approach the world of the Zohar on its own terms. That is, I give precedence to its voice over what I, from the standpoint of my contemporary worldview, might sometimes wish it would say. Only then have I wished to draw out, and carefully so, its contemporary relevance.

I engage the Zohar with great love and respect, yet I acknowledge that the historical-cultural horizons within which it was created are not my own. I come to the flowing river of the Zohar; and to use a biblical expression, I hope that I am bringing forth "living waters."

The Basic Structures of the Composition and Its Performative Aspects

An essential feature of the Zohar is its desire to awaken a mystical-religious consciousness, more intense and different in kind from ordinary religious-spiritual experience. Even in those parts of the Zohar where we encounter detailed theosophical expositions on the structure of divinity and its dynamic being, such knowledge is not presented as theory alone. Rather, it is intended to enrich the life of the mystic.[8] The desire to awaken such a mystical-religious consciousness is not directed solely at human beings for their own sake; rather the broader purpose of this awakening is to affect readers' influence on the divine world, and to increase within this world the qualities of harmony and peace. This theurgic tendency—namely, the conscious intention of the human being to influence the world of the divinity through deeds and consciousness—works for the mystic in several ways at once:

- to satisfy a personal longing to actualize unmediated experiential contact with the divine;
- to fulfill a desire to participate in the great work of rectification (tikkun*) of the world of humanity, and its redemption through the rectification of the divine world; and
- to satisfy an ambition to increase the fullness of divine light in the world.

---

* In the Zohar, the abstract Hebrew noun tikkun spans a range of meanings: adorning, arraying, garbing, installing, healing, rectifying, and restoring. The Companions' expositions are often referred to as tikkunim (plural of tikkun).

Indeed, in the Zohar the language of experience invites the reader to join the way of life that enables the mystical-religious experience described in its pages.

The Zohar is unique in terms of its complex literary structure. On any single page the reader will find a number of different styles, structures, and schemes interwoven with one another. Familiarity with the main features of the composition, therefore, enables an orientation vis-à-vis the text and assists in its illumination.[9] It is possible to identify four channels, interlaced and juxtaposed, that constitute the Zohar's fundamental structure:

Scriptural exegesis (midrash)   The printed edition of the Zohar, as it is presented to the reader, has been edited according to the order of the weekly Torah portions* and is essentially a midrash on the Torah.[10] The Zohar's authors view the Torah as divine revelation, and in that light they interpret its portions, verses, words, and even letters. Their relationship with the Torah is the relationship of one subject to another subject, or perhaps more accurately, the relationship between lover and beloved; it is not merely the relationship of an interpreter with a text. For the Zohar's authors, the Torah is *the* object of desire, and its interpretation the mutual courting of the Torah and her lovers. According to the Zohar, it is through studying the Torah and interpreting its verses that one discovers the secrets of divinity, attains the secret of mystical faith, and encounter the divine dimensions that radiate within the Torah.

The zoharic epic: The story of Rabbi Shim'on bar Yoḥai and the Companions   On nearly every page of the Zohar one can find the stories of the adventures, experiences, and *ḥiddushei Torah* (innovations of Torah) of the mishnaic sage Rabbi Shim'on bar Yoḥai and his circle of admiring disciples. All ten companions are named. Some of them—like Rabbi El'azar (the son of Rabbi Shim'on), Rabbi Abba, the most senior of the disciples, and the young Rabbi Ḥiyya (perhaps the heir of Rabbi Shim'on)—are portrayed

---

* The "weekly Torah portion" is the late medieval standard division of the Pentateuch into 54 sections for public recitation, enabling. a complete reading of the text in each given year.

as complex figures whose personality and viewpoints are broadly discernable, while others are presented in only the most schematic way. In many of the stories, a wondrous figure—old man, child, or donkey-driver—appears as a bearer of profound divine wisdom. Some of them are known to us by name; others are anonymous, marginal, and eccentric.

The stories present an intense mystical circle centered on a remarkable teacher. It is the intensity of the group's spirit that enables daring innovations of Torah. The existence of this group, with Rabbi Shim'on at its center, radiates blessings to the world and heals the generation in which it dwells.

Zoharic stories come in many forms: short stories of only a few lines, story fragments, and long units spanning more than ten pages with complex development that requires detailed analysis. These stories have their own internal language and poetics, as well as structural, linguistic, and stylistic coherence; the seasoned Zohar reader has no difficulty identifying the world of the zoharic story upon encountering it.

This epic layer, however, has no apparent linear, narrative development in the usual sense of the term. In the different printed editions as well as in the Zohar's manuscripts, stories are interlaced throughout all the different parts of the composition. Nevertheless, the stories contain many intertextual references among them. For example, some of the Companions die during the course of events, and their deaths are referenced in other accounts. And in the printed editions, and perhaps earlier as well, the Zohar culminates in the story of the death of Rabbi Shim'on bar Yoḥai, which is interwoven with interpretations of the story of the death of Moses near the end of Deuteronomy.

The stories of the Zohar are the literary space in which mystical language and ambience are constituted, in which mystical experience transpires, and through which we readers gain access to that experience. The Zohar's stories are, therefore, crucial for accessing its mystical-experiential world. As Yehuda Liebes has shown, they are not merely a frame for the teachings expounded therein. They are rather the Zohar's heart and bestow upon the composition its unique character.[11]

Kabbalistic interpretation and reading strategies   The Zohar is filled with interpretations of biblical verses employing the assumptions, concepts, and exegetical techniques drawn from kabbalistic literature, as they had developed up to the time of the Zohar's composition. The Zohar assumes that its reader is familiar with descriptions of the structure of the divine world as they had crystallized in the circles of the first kabbalists in Provence and Gerona, beginning at the end of the twelfth century. These teachings assume the existence of an infinite, abstract divinity termed *Ein Sof*. From it emanate ten *sefirot*, constituting the world of active divinity.★ They are able to be comprehended in different ways. The sefirot are qualities or modes of operation of the divine outside its incomprehensible and indescribable mysteriousness. They are characterized as masculine or feminine, and the relationships between them are dynamic and (hetero)sexual.

The kabbalistic myth depicts the active divine world, the world of emanations, as dynamic. Its interactive qualities are described in human terms such as jealousy, rejection, sexual union, and love. In the Zohar, these teachings about the world of divinity and this picture of reality are wholly internalized. Also taken as givens are kabbalistic conceptions of the Torah, the structure of the soul, evil, and the power of the human being to influence the divine world. Interestingly, in the Zohar, we do not find the widespread use of kabbalistic technical terms. In fact, the words "sefirot" and "Kabbalah" never appear in the main corpus of the Zohar. This, it seems, was the authors' conscious choice. There is no doubt, however, that kabbalistic language is thoroughly embedded in the Zohar's poetics and mysticism. We have before us a work that draws upon a great reservoir of prior kabbalistic interpretations. It should be stressed, though, that the Zohar is also an innovative composition.

Strategies of awakening and performative aspects   The Zohar employs a variety of structures, forms, and strategies whose purpose is to awaken the reader to mystical consciousness—to transform everyday, regular consciousness to an enhanced state, so as to access otherwise unreachable dimensions of reality. Specific conceptual, stylistic, and linguistic forms recur in different con-

★ In Kabbalah, each "sefirah" (singular of "sefirot") is a particular expression or face of the divine as it operates in reality.

texts throughout the Zohar, especially in the narrative layers that describe the adventures of Rabbi Shim'on and his circle, as well as in the *Idrot* (the accounts of the two mystical assemblies), perhaps the Zohar's literary and mystical climax.

Analysis of these forms and their specific contexts, both within the Zohar's narrative units and in zoharic homilies, has led me to conclude that we have here a specialized language displaying a high level of internal coherence, even though it may be the creative fruit of a number of writers. This specialized language is the medium for imparting the Zohar's most fundamental motivations and interpretive meta-assumptions. In my opinion, it serves to awaken the reader to a change in consciousness and as an invitation to mystical-conscious activity.

The Zohar's call to the reader, and the implied assumption that it is indeed possible to awaken human consciousness, is directly connected to some of the Zohar's fundamental attitudes regarding human consciousness, its limits, and its hidden potential. The Zohar repeatedly states in different ways that most human beings exist in a state of slumber. As a consequence, people do not see the ultimate being of reality—infinite and divine. Meanwhile, the Zohar also repeatedly presents its view that human beings are created in the image of God, and are in possession of a divine soul, and therefore all of them are potentially able to perfect their divine essence. The person who longs for such perfection can develop these abilities so as to be exposed to the flowing dimensions within reality, usually concealed from beings of flesh and blood. In the language of the Zohar, the human being has the capacity "to inherit the earth," namely to experience the divine dimension termed "earth."

The most prevalent metaphor employed by the Zohar for human consciousness is sight.[12] The Zohar invites the readers—sometimes explicitly, sometimes implicitly, sometimes subtly and sometimes boldly—to enhance their visionary capacity and to look deeply into reality and into the narratives of the Torah to discover the divine light concealed within. This intensification of vision allows the viewers to see hidden lights and causes them to shine with a great radiance. The verse from which the Zohar's title is taken attests to this desire: "And the enlightened will shine like the radiance (Heb. *zohar*) of the sky, and those who lead the many to righteousness will be like the stars forever and ever" (Daniel 12:3).[13]

The Zohar's main strategy for strengthening this visionary capacity is through the use of special hermeneutical practices for reading Scripture. These include an intensive reading of the biblical text with two central foci: on the one hand, a reading directed at the text as an object to be interpreted, and on the other hand, an interpretive stance that seeks to develop forms of reading capable of leading the reader from text to experience. These two foci are nourished by the rich reservoir of exegetical tools of the ancient Rabbis as well as those from medieval interpreters—philosophers and mystics alike.

The reading practices of the Zohar, however, are mainly fueled by the authors' intense longing to touch the divine through the Torah's words. This longing to enhance the capacity of sight and the desire to touch the divine are perhaps the fire that melts the biblical text. Such fire transforms it from a frozen picture that captures one conception of reality into a window through which one glimpses fluid dimensions of being—profound dimensions that one can experience, participate in, and influence.

The uniqueness of the Zohar lies in the fact that the different structures or channels outlined above are not presented one after the other or side by side, but rather are interwoven one with another without separation. It is this interweaving, as opposed to the formal structures themselves, that makes the Zohar dazzle. In this interwoven structure, the Zohar reenacts the practice attributed to the sage Ben Azzai; in the words of the midrash, he would "bead" the words of the Torah to those of the Prophets, and the words of the Prophets to those of the Writings.[14] Through this beading, the midrash continues, the words of Torah became "as joyful as in the moment of their being given" and the divine fire descended from heaven. Indeed, when the Companions gather for the special study vigil on the eve of the festival of Shavuot that marks the celestial bride's adornment prior to the wedding ceremony of revelation at Sinai, they explicitly state their intention to decorate the bride with adornments created by their beading words of Torah, Prophets, Writings, Midrash, and mystical teachings.

It is this beaded finery that shines on the bride (the Assembly of Israel), the Companions, and throughout the entire Zohar.[15] The stories of Rashbi's Circle and the homilies expounded within them are masterfully linked one with another. Together they create and constitute the zoharic texture. The biblical verses expounded by the Companions become part of their stories and shape them, and the Companions' associative interpretations draw on aspects of their adventures. Different images are juxtaposed as the Zohar displays an array of allusions to stories and interpretations scattered throughout the composition.

As a literary, religious, and mystical composition, the Zohar is characterized by its daring *ars poetica* reflexivity. It is not uncommon for the Zohar's protagonists to pause from time to time and reflect on their own hermeneutical acts. They characterize, evaluate, and compare their own interpretive efforts, both explicitly and implicitly, with the worldviews and interpretive forms that preceded them, from the Bible to the rationalist philosophers of the Middle Ages.[16] This self-reflexive gaze is directed toward their own mystical ends, as well as to the very fact of the Zohar's composition as a written work. The Zohar reflects on its own enterprise, offers evaluative comments on this enterprise, and compares itself with other spiritual endeavors.

Both in terms of its reflexivity and literary composition, the Zohar, it would seem, has no peer in the Jewish tradition. Analysis of the self-image of the Zohar is therefore crucial for understanding the meaning of a composition that chooses to present itself as the product of the tannaitic world of the Land of Israel, while at the same time being saturated with the distinct world of the Middle Ages. This new world, which shines through the guise of the old, reveals new concepts about divinity, theology, and interpretation. The Zohar engages with what may be termed a renaissance consciousness, while displaying clues, both explicit and implicit, about the circle from which it emerged. On nearly every page, the reader encounters comments—sometimes subtly absorbed into the body of the interpreted scriptural verses—whose focus is self-reflection or comparison between the companions of the Zohar with the world of the Bible, the world of medieval Spanish Jewry, and perhaps even the world of other mystical groups.

The Internal Coherence of the Zohar's Language

Familiarity with the Zohar's key structures and assumptions is critical in order for the reader to distinguish how the composition imparts its profundity. A systematic analysis of that kind is one of the aims of this book. However, at no point does the Zohar offer the reader a systematic introduction to its own meta-assumptions. It is only through the act of reading the text and exploring all its layers that these begin to emerge. The zoharic text is neither systematic nor didactic, which seems to have been the conscious choice of the authors. Rather, it is associative, impenetrable, surprising, multivocal, and polysemic. These characteristics bestow upon the text its unique power and quality.

Thus the analysis of individual passages, in order to draw out specific teachings and conceptions, would seem to run counter to the Zohar's unique style. After all, in the Zohar we encounter the reverse process: systematic ideas that had already crystallized in earlier kabbalistic circles are rendered into raw poetic-religious material, becoming a dynamic force in a daring literary-religious world.

The absence of a systematic, didactic approach does not, however, imply chaos or the absence of internal syntax and grammar. The act of reading the Zohar, especially the literary or narrative layer known as the main corpus of the Zohar or the epic layer, reveals a high degree of internal coherence in terms of the deep structures of the composition. Despite the great array of diverse forms of expression, there is no arbitrariness or chaos, as may seem at first glance. Rather, the Zohar is characterized by a deep order, a total language unfolding in its myriad forms before the reader. Well-versed Zohar readers who, like me, have passed through the frustration of the inaccessibility of the Zohar's Aramaic, and through the confusion of the Zohar's intricate symbolic structure, who have navigated the difficulty of understanding the complex interconnections between the stories and the scriptural interpretations, and who know and love the zoharic text, find themselves in a complex, rich, mysterious, and intriguing world. Through this thicket, at least occasionally, is revealed a unique clarity. The symbols, which at first seemed impenetrable, reveal their meaning—and even the impenetrability itself becomes a familiar part of the soul-syntax of the composition. The ear identifies the tones, the eye learns to observe the images, and the soul accedes to the spirit and wisdom that arise from the Zohar's pages.

In order to account for the linguistic coherence, we turn briefly to the question that fascinates all Zohar researchers, namely, how the Zohar was composed.[17] (The comments presented here are merely footnotes to those researchers who have thoroughly explored this grand question, and whose insights appear in this book.)

The poetics, the musical imagination, as well as the intricate symbolic network and the unique religious spirit that resonates among the zoharic texts I have studied, have led me to discern in it the hand of a single author. At the same time, the world of the Zohar is clearly dialogical and group-centered, so it is difficult not to believe in the "actual" existence of the Companions. Furthermore, the structure of zoharic stories, which in many cases is fixed and formal, tips the scales in favor of the proposition of a single author, even if different hands later edited his words. Following my teacher Yehuda Liebes, we can, I believe, posit the existence of a circle of mystics in Castile in the second half of the thirteenth century, which gathered around the figure of a charismatic teacher who attracted a diverse group of creative students. There is no historical evidence for the existence of this circle, nor do we have any idea how often the members of this group might have met. As Liebes has shown, however, we can identify via their own writings some likely members of this circle, such as R. Moses de León, R. Joseph Gikatilla, and R. Yosef ben Shalom Ashkenazi. Liebes even posits the possible historical identity of the teacher upon whom the character Rabbi Shim'on bar Yoḥai is based: the kabbalist Rabbi Todros Halevi Abulafia.[18] It is possible that the author of the main corpus of the Zohar was a member of this group, or perhaps another similar group—in which transpired something original, fascinating, and exciting, unlike anything before. The magic perhaps lay in the new creativity generated by the innovative Torah study of the group, and perhaps also in the spiritual character of the mystical experience within the circle. It should be stressed once again, though, that we possess no testimonies or evidence about the meetings of this group.[19] However, even if the members of this group did not meet many times, the intensity of the experience of meeting others in whom the mystical spirit resonated, and the intensity of the experience of creativity within the group furnished the impulse to create a literary framework (perhaps not originally connected to Rabbi Shim'on and his disciples) in order to describe via narrative and exegesis something of the life of this circle. It is possible that one person, whose historical identity today cannot be determined with certainty, is the unique genius whose hand is found throughout the epic layer of the Zohar.[20] This great writer took upon himself the monumental task to narrate, perhaps from a distance of many years, through the power of memory and artistic imagination, and with literary-mystical sensitivity, the life of this group. The Zohar is then a gift of memory to those moments in which the wellsprings of the heart were open to the world of the circle, and when the world sparkled with secrets revealed.

The Zohar is, to be sure, not a historical record of the life of this group. It is rather a free, literary reworking of its spirit, a spirit that left its indelible imprint on the author's soul. In the words of Ḥayyim Naḥman Bialik: "How much does the inspired artist need to enable him to create? Merely a little raw material, enough for the spirit to lay hold on. If the material is poor, he will enrich it from his own store; if it is dead, he will quicken it from the fountain of his own life."[21] It is this unique interweaving of the memory of the real mystical group with the force of the creative imagination of a master-mystic that perhaps accounts for the high level of coherence of the deep language of the Zohar. This special language is characterized by dialogical intensity, extraordinary eros, and a "realistic" quality that has served as a source of inspiration and model of imitation for later groups of Jewish mystics.

Definitions of Mysticism

Before delving into the Zohar's experiential-mystical world, we need first to clarify whether it is indeed appropriate to define the Zohar as a mystical work, and to reflect on which definitions of mysticism best suit our subject matter. In his lectures on the origins of the Kabbalah and on the book *Bahir*, Gershom Scholem began his attempt to define mysticism with the following words:

> In coming to define the concept mysticism, I should say that no one knows what mysticism is. The number of definitions for the concept mysticism in philosophy or comparative religion is like the number of sages who have written about it. Everyone has their own definition. . . . Even so I will say how I use the term mysticism or mystery in Hebrew. Mysticism is knowledge through which the human being comes into contact with God or foundational knowledge of the world. . . . Not every foundational knowledge is mysticism: mysticism is an experiential endeavor pertaining to God and the foundations of ultimate reality to which the human being connects. Sometimes this endeavor includes knowledge, and other times it exists beyond knowledge in the rational sense of the term.[22]

Scholem's caution is pertinent, as are his remarks that all who engage in the study of "mystical" phenomena ought to explain their use of the term. In this study I adopt a broad definition of "mysticism" that includes not only experiences of mystical union, but also all religious phenomena in all forms and expressions whose aim is to bring the human being into contact with the divine—a contact, in the words of Moshe Idel, "differing from the common religious experiences cultivated in a certain religion both in its intensity and in its spiritual impact."[23] Following this definition, there is no doubt in my mind that it is appropriate to define what is found in the Zohar—its collection of experiences, techniques, forms of expression, and type of Torah study—as mysticism.

In seeking to elucidate the Zohar's mystical characteristics, it is important to be familiar with the state of research in the academic study of mysticism in general. At present, two conceptual approaches can be found, each with their own explanations for the variations apparent in mystical experiences as reported in different cultures and religions. The first school comprises those scholars who view mystical experience as a universal phenomenon, essential to the human *qua* human. These scholars understand the differences in reported mystical experiences as due to culturally determined linguistic and ideological "garments" that clothe (mediate) personal experience. The foundations of this approach were laid by William James and Mircea Eliade. In his classic work *The Varieties of Religious Experience*, James sought to present a phenomenology of mystical experience as an essential human phenomenon. Eliade later drew on Jungian assumptions concerning the universality of key symbols and archetypal structures of the unconscious. To this school might be added Robert Foreman, who has investigated the concept of "pure consciousness," assuming the universal existence of such consciousness.

On the other side of the spectrum are those scholars who adopt a contextual approach to mystical phenomena. These scholars oppose the idea of an independent existence of mystical experience as a universal phenomenon, and emphasize instead the culturally constructed and contextually dependent aspects of the experience. The most extreme advocate of this view is Steven Katz, who claims that those aspects of mystical experience that are determined by culture, place, and context are not "outer garments" of the experience, but rather constitute its very essence.

Between these two poles are many scholars espousing different intermediate positions. In this work, I have drawn in the main on the approach of Jess Hollenback, who argues against the existence of pure mystical experience disconnected from the cultural and religious context of the mystic. The interpretive and cultural dimensions, he argues, accompany the experience from the very beginning. Indeed, they color the experience.[24] At the same time, I have been greatly influenced by the intermediate position outlined by Elliot Wolfson in the context of Jewish mysticism. Wolfson highlights the particular intertextual nature of the Jewish tradition, in which readers actively live out texts from earlier historical periods and engage in dialogue with them. The texts thus shape their consciousness, beliefs, language, and experience. Wolfson presents a model of mutual dependence and fertilization between Jewish mystics' experience and the cultural texts they interpret.[25]

In his comprehensive book on mysticism, Hollenback outlines characteristics that in his opinion define mystical experience. These distinctions, gathered from a range of religious cultures, greatly enriched my endeavor to define the mystical dimensions of the Zohar's religious experience.[26] Hollenback established seven features that, when found together, distinguish mystical experience from other human experiences:

(a) A radical change in the state of consciousness of the individual occurring in a state of wakefulness.

(b) A state of consciousness enabling the individual access to knowledge of those things considered as ultimate truth in the cultural context to which he or she belongs.

(c) An experience granting access to special knowledge of soteriological significance (that is, pertaining to redemption).

(d) An emotionally charged experience.

(e) An experience of enlightenment, both sensorial and meta-sensorial, as well as metaphorical.

(f) An experience that is amorphous by nature and whose content is historically and culturally determined.[27]

(g) A prior conscious act of heightened concentration on a particular subject, causing a quieting of the continuum of thought characteristic of ordinary consciousness.

Hollenback established these characteristics based on analysis of sources documenting mystical experiences in monotheistic faiths, Eastern, and tribal religions, and they serve as a successful diagnostic tool for comparison with the mystical experience found in the Zohar. His decision to base his definition on a broad range of characteristics, rather than to offer a narrow and radical characterization of mysticism (like those who restrict mysticism to the experience of union with the divine) seems to me appropriate for the diverse world of the Zohar—a world that as we have seen is not based on systematic or univocal teachings.[28] This model thus furnishes us with an array of descriptive characteristics appropriate to our endeavor to characterize the mystical experience in the Zohar, without having to adopt one of the polarized stances that characterize scholarship of mystical experience today.

Overview of Zohar Research

Over the generations, the Zohar has attracted many researchers who have gazed and expounded, explored and weighed, and who have illuminated many facets of this diamond. Among its readers were those who saw in the Zohar an ancient document, written with divine inspiration, the product of the hands of the tanna Rabbi Shim'on bar Yoḥai, who lived in the Land of Israel in the second century of the Common Era. At the same time, already from the moment of its appearance in the last decade of the thirteenth century, there were those who were suspicious of the Zohar's antiquity and sensed that the source of its spirit did not lie in the ancient world. Some, like Rabbi Naḥman of Bratslav, dedicated many years to its deep study, and for them the Zohar became the very foundation of their creativity; and some dedicated their lives to expounding the Zohar and to imitating the Companions' lifestyle, like Rabbi Moses Cordovero and Rabbi Isaac Luria. Others imitated the work in their own writings, like Rabbi Moshe Ḥayyim Luzzatto; and still others saw in the Zohar the essence of their Judaism, so beautifully expressed in the famous saying of Rabbi Pinḥas of Koretz, "who was wont to praise and thank God for not having been born while the Zohar was still unknown to the world, 'for the Zohar has kept me alive.'"[29]

In the twentieth century, too, the Zohar attracted unique readers. Hillel Zeitlin was one such reader, who out of his great love for the work, conceived the monumental enterprise of translating the entire work into Hebrew, a project cut short by the Holocaust. Zeitlin's deep identification with the Zohar led him, in great despair after the First World War, to write letters in zoharic Aramaic to the Jewish press, calling for the establishment of a circle of spiritual activists who would be able to draw forth light into a world engulfed by darkness.[30] Rabbi Yehudah Ashlag, another great twentieth-century reader of Zohar, dedicated his life to interpreting, translating, and spreading its teachings, out of an intense messianic urgency—viewing the project of translation as spiritual resistance to the evil forces of Nazism that were annihilating European Jewry, and as a foundation for the renewal of the Jewish spirit in the Zionist movement.[31]

In academic circles as well, the Zohar has attracted much attention from researchers who have illuminated the work from a range of perspectives—historical, philological, literary, bibliographical, linguistic, and phenomenological. Gershom Scholem, the founder of the modern academic study of Jewish mysticism, generated great momentum for the study of the Zohar. Scholem engaged in detailed research and broke new ground regarding the date of the Zohar's composition and its authorship, through analysis of its central ideas. The chapters on the Zohar in his work *Major Trends in Jewish Mysticism* are rightly considered classics of historical and philological research, written with literary, religious, and mystical sensitivity. Scholem identified the Zohar as a pseudepigraphical composition—a work deliberately attributed by its authors to someone else, namely Rabbi Shim'on bar Yoḥai. He established the date of its composition to the period between the mid-seventies and late eighties of the thirteenth century. After much agonizing, he concluded that the Zohar was the fruit of a single spiritual-literary genius, Rabbi Moses de León, who lived in Spain. Scholem solved the mystery of the different literary units within the Zohar by suggesting that they ought to be understood as arising from different periods in de León's intellectual development. Scholem saw in the Zohar a mythical, innovative composition that burst forth from the core of rabbinic Judaism. He emphasized its daring originality more than its relationship to earlier literary traditions or its overall call for religious and spiritual renaissance. Scholem established a central place for the Zohar in the field of Jewish thought. In so doing, he attracted and guided many students who extended his research in different directions.

Isaiah Tishby relied mainly on the key assumptions of Scholem's research. His monumental work, later translated into English as *The Wisdom of the Zohar*, combines his own precise academic research with the bold aim of bringing the treasures of the Zohar to the modern Hebrew reader, versed neither in the text nor in its language. Tishby's great contributions lie in his classification of the Zohar's central topics, and in his scholarly, detailed, and systematic introductions to those themes. Additionally, and arising out of his endeavor to trace and elucidate the systematic teachings hidden in the Zohar, Tishby translated into Hebrew (together with Fischel Lachower) many select texts from the Zohar to illustrate the subjects he explored. His comprehensive introductions and his illuminating translations are invaluable to the general reader and scholar alike.

Yehuda Liebes, my teacher and mentor, has dedicated years to the study of the zoharic corpus, exploring its many dimensions. In his seminal article, later partly translated into English as "The Messiah of the Zohar," Liebes explored the figure and messianic character of the Zohar's hero, Rabbi Shim'on bar Yoḥai, together with the messianism of the entire composition. In that article he also explored zoharic myth and composition; the place of eros and sexuality in the Zohar's unique language; the world of the Companions; their two central mystical assemblies, the Great Assembly (Idra Rabba) and the Small Assembly (Idra Zuta); different uses of the term *tikkun*; the Zohar's influence on later Jewish mystics, and much more.

One of Liebes's central insights is his observation that the narrative layers of the Zohar and the homilies contained therein are thoroughly interlaced, and thus one must analyze the zoharic story as an essential component of the text, constituting a key to the text's uniqueness—and not as a mere frame for the homilies. (While being a work of bold academic research, this article's brilliance lies also in the zoharic quality that runs through its pages, in its creative power and multiple meanings.)

In his article translated into English as "How the Zohar was Written," Liebes reopened the question of its authorship and composition. He points to a range of content, conceptual, and stylistic factors, which challenge Scholem's view of a single author creating the Zohar out of the power of his imagination alone. Liebes refocused attention from the question of "who wrote the Zohar" to the more subtle question of "how the Zohar was written." He sought to trace the historical circle of kabbalists responsible for the Zohar, whose origins he identified with the Gnostic kabbalists in Castile, whose works were characterized by a distinct style of pseudepigraphic kabbalistic writing. The later zoharic circle, Liebes argues, was heir to these esoteric traditions; and it was characterized by the creative reworking of these traditions, the composition of new works, and the personal freedom of each participant to create according to his own style and worldview. Liebes attempted to sketch the figures of the companions in the Zohar against the background of the real experiences of the historical group. This article is based on an analysis of the differences apparent in the varied layers of the Zohar in terms of literary style and theoretical and speculative stances, as well as an analysis of the psychological motivations of different parts of the text. It swings the pendulum in favor of the claim that the Zohar is the product of a circle of mystics and not the work of a single creator.

Another of Liebes's articles, "Zohar and Eros," focuses on the place of eros as the vital force in the Zohar, which bestows upon the composition its unique place in Jewish literature. Here, Liebes explores the "renaissance" character of the Zohar, seeing its creative thrust in the desire to tap and revive creative chapters in Jewish religious culture as well as its attitude toward innovation, and the place of eros and sexuality in religious language and experience. Liebes does not seek to find a systematic exposition of ideas hidden in the Zohar's disorder. Rather, he seeks to characterize those domains that resist categorization and systematic exposition, bestowing upon the composition its unique character.

Liebes has extensively researched the subject of myth and has explored the nature of Jewish myth from its earliest manifestations in the Bible and in classical rabbinic literature, through its historical and conceptual transformations, and especially the uniqueness of kabbalistic and zoharic myths about the divine. He has demonstrated the way in which zoharic myth and mythopoeia have influenced later mystics and writers, like Rabbi Isaac Luria, Rabbi Naḥman of Bratslav, and even the modern "Canaanite" poet Yonatan Ratosh. Liebes's published Zohar research, together with all that I have learned from him over the years, informs nearly every page of this book. As to my many questions regarding the Zohar, in the words of the Companions: *le-kula ka atina mar*—I have come to the teacher for all.

In his seminal work, *Kabbalah: New Perspectives*, my teacher Moshe Idel, one of the most productive and creative Kabbalah researchers of this generation, explored the spiritual and intellectual characteristics of the kabbalistic climate in which the Zohar was produced. He claims that the circle of mystics responsible for the Zohar came into being out of the creative processes of a "secondary elite" of spiritual leadership. Idel distinguishes between *primary* elites, comprising those scholars and rabbis who assumed central leadership roles in the community, and *secondary* elites, whose leadership was characterized by the freedom to choose an innovative path without seeking the approval of the halakhic and spiritual authorities of the time. His book *Absorbing Perfections* focuses and extends his detailed research in the field of kabbalistic hermeneutics, in which he explores the nature of the kabbalistic and zoharic symbol, and the uniqueness of the Zohar's symbolic-dynamic interpretation. Idel has also researched the connections between zoharic literature and kabbalists like Rabbi David ben Judah He-Ḥasid and Rabbi Joseph of Shushan.

Elliot Wolfson has devoted much of his research to the Zohar and emphasizes the centrality of mystical experience in kabbalistic and zoharic creativity, while presenting a critical analysis of earlier approaches to the relationship between theosophy and experiential mysticism in the Zohar. His major claim is that an understanding of the Zohar's world necessitates an appreciation of the fact that the Zohar is not merely a speculative or theoretical work, but rather presents practical means for attaining ecstatic states of union with or participation in the divine. Wolfson has also extensively researched issues of gender and sexuality in the Kabbalah in general and in the Zohar in particular, and has argued for the centrality of male sexuality in both mystical experience and exegetical process in the Zohar, as opposed to the secondary status of the feminine.

Daniel Matt is currently working on the monumental enterprise of producing an annotated English translation of the Zohar based on a critical Aramaic text that he is reconstructing from numerous Zohar manuscripts. As of 2008, four volumes have appeared, covering the Zohar's commentary on Genesis and about half of Exodus. The complete translation, entitled *The Zohar: Pritzker Edition,* is projected to comprise nine volumes. (Arthur Green recently published a popular introductory volume for that edition.) In his research, Matt has also highlighted the tension between innovation and traditionalism in the zoharic consciousness. Further, he has explored the way in which the Zohar as a whole understands itself as representing a Jewish culture alternative to that of classical rabbinic culture.

This book is a translation of my Hebrew book that came out in 2005.[32] Many important scholarly works have been written since then. I regret that this translation does not systematically account for all of them.[33]

From this cursory overview of Zohar research, the great wealth of complex issues explored by researchers and interpreters begins to emerge. In this book I draw and build upon their great contributions with the hope of illuminating additional aspects of the Zohar's splendor.[34]

T H E   Z O H A R ' S   H E R O E S

Rabbi Shim'on bar Yoḥai and the Companions

The world of mystical experience in the Zohar transpires amid the adventures of its heroes: Rabbi Shim'on bar Yoḥai and his circle of students. Through these figures and their stories, we are acquainted with the religious-emotional spirit that motivates and arouses them to create, expound, and act. In order to understand this world of experience, we first need to be familiar with the composition's heroes, and with the way they understand themselves and their destiny. This is the subject of Part I.

Chapter 1 focuses on the radiant star of the Zohar, Rabbi Shim'on bar Yoḥai—"the holy luminary," who reveals the secrets of divinity found in the Torah and in the world. We examine his persona as portrayed in the composition, his self-image, and the way in which he is described by his students. In this context, we compare the figure of Rabbi Shim'on with the figures of Moses (the hero of the written Torah) and of Rabbi Akiva (one of the great heroes of the oral Torah). We also explore his role as the master teacher, the experience of being in his presence, and the sense of terror and loss surrounding his death.

Chapter 2 focuses on Rabbi Shim'on's circle of students, the Companions, the manner in which they are portrayed in the composition, and the different epithets they use to describe themselves—through which we learn about their self-perception as a circle of mystics.

Chapter 3 examines the three generations in Jewish history whom the Companions view as possessing a special religious-spiritual consciousness, and with whom they identify.

The Figure of Rabbi Shim'on bar Yoḥai

Whoever separates from Torah is like one who separates from life, and one who separates from Rabbi Shim'on is as if he separates from all. . . .

Woe to the generation when Rabbi Shim'on departs! For when we stand in the presence of Rabbi Shim'on, the wellsprings of our heart open in all directions and all is revealed. And when we withdraw from him, we do not know anything and all the springs are closed.

Rabbi Ḥizkiyah said, "Corresponding to what is written: *He held back some of the spirit that was upon him and put it upon the seventy men, the elders* (Numbers 11:25)—like a lamp from which many lamps are lit, while retaining its vitality. Similarily, Rabbi Shim'on son of Yoḥai, master of Lamps, illumines all, yet light does not depart from him and he retains vitality. This is the meaning of what is written: *He drew (va-ya'atsel) upon the spirit that was on him and put it upon the seventy elders* (ibid.), like a lamp from which are kindled many lamps, yet it remains intact. So Rabbi Shim'on bar Yoḥai, the master of lights, illumines all, yet the light does not depart from him and remains intact."[1]

Zohar 2:86b; Matt 2004–2007, vol. 4, p. 487, adapted

Rabbi Shim'on bar Yoḥai is the central hero of the Zohar. Often referred to by the acronym "Rashbi" (= Rabbi Shimon bar Yoḥai), he appears as a colossal figure, at once human and divine, who touches and influences the upper and lower worlds. He is the great radiance, the great light of the world and the Torah, the complete man, the perfect mystic, a powerful shaman, master of Torah, and the great teacher. Rashbi teaches his students the essence of the hidden, mystical world as well as the appropriate boundaries between the disclosure of the mysteries of ultimate reality and their concealment. He teaches his students; and through them, he teaches us readers about the possibility of revealing and innovating mysteries in order to take part with him in the *tikkun* (rectification) of reality, and in the drawing-down of blessings throughout the divine and human worlds.

The mystical dimension of the Zohar is created and revealed amid the stories of Rabbi Shim'on bar Yoḥai and his disciples. In order to trace the Zohar's experiential world, therefore, we must first familiarize ourselves with the world of its heroes and with the way in which they understand themselves and their destiny in the world.

In the Zohar we encounter a myth, or a mythical epic, about Rabbi Shim'on bar Yoḥai, the hero of the composition; his disciples (the Companions); wondrous figures from his generation; as well as descriptions and numerous characterizations about the generation in which they all live. This mythical epic bestows upon the composition unique qualities and also implicitly and subtly reflects its authors' understanding of themselves and their generation, as well as their motivations for writing.

The narratives that appear in the main corpus of the Zohar are not linear, certainly not according to the order in which they appear in the printed editions.[2] Yet if we examine them in their entirety, we find that this narrative weaving displays a high level of internal coherence, from which emerges the stable and continuing presence of the Companions. The members of this circle are known to us by name; some are more important than others, like Rabbi El'azar (Rashbi's son), Rabbi Abba (the master student), and Rabbi Ḥiyya (the youngest member of the circle and possibly the heir of Rabbi Shim'on). The life of the circle unfolds with a deep and abiding awareness of the presence of the teacher, who represents the ultimate key for the total illumination of the events that the Companions experience, as well as the biblical verses that they expound. He is, in short, the personality through which the Companions understand the true nature of reality.[3]

We shall begin, therefore, with an exploration of the figure of Rabbi Shim'on bar Yohai. There is no limit to the praises showered upon Rashbi in the Zohar. In the many homilies discussing his praises, he is presented not only as the crown of creation and humanity but also, in pathos-laden descriptions, as possessing divine qualities:

> The blessed Holy One engraved the image of Rabbi Shim'on above and his voice ascends ever upward, and is crowned with the holy crown, until the blessed Holy One is crowned with him in all the worlds and is glorified through him. About him is written: *And he said to me, "You are my servant—Israel, in whom I glory"* (Isaiah 49:3). . . . From the day that the blessed Holy One created the world, Rabbi Shim'on bar Yohai was present before the blessed Holy One and was with Him; and the blessed Holy One calls him by His name. Happy is his portion above and below! About him is written: *Your father and your mother will rejoice* (Proverbs 23:25)—*your father*, this is the blessed Holy One; and *your mother*, this is the Assembly of Israel.[4] (Zohar 3:61a–b)

Rashbi appears here as a figure who has existed since the very beginning of time, and as one who shares a deep intimacy with God. Rashbi's status as the son of the blessed Holy One and the Assembly of Israel (also known as Shekhinah) establishes a myth whereby the divine powers ruling over reality are understood as the father-god, the mother-goddess, and the beloved son—the chosen man, Rabbi Shim'on bar Yohai.

Rabbi Shim'on is the earthly representative of the divine sefirah *Yesod* (Foundation). *Yesod* occupies the ninth position in the kabbalistic system of the ten sefirot emanating from *Ein Sof* (Infinity). The full appellation for this sefirah is *tsaddik yesod olam*, "the righteous is the foundation of the world" (Proverbs 10:25), the cosmic righteous one who is the pillar upon which the world stands, and the conduit that connects the divine and human worlds. *Yesod* draws into itself the flow of the divine world in all its different modes, and it guides this flow into the sefirah *Malkhut* (Kingdom).

The sefirah *Yesod* represents the qualities of transmission, fertilization, and masculine sexuality and eroticism. It is the dynamic, erotic quality in divinity of appropriately timed gathering, storing, and discharging, as well as disclosure and concealment, and is thus symbolized by the male sexual organ.

The power of Rashbi's teaching, as well as the power of other great teachers after him, is understood as an expression of the quality of *Yesod* in the world.[5] The *Idra Zuta*, the section of the Zohar that describes the occasion of Rashbi's departure from the world, tells of his ecstatic and erotic transformation from a human being into the attribute of *Yesod*.[6] Indeed, even in his life, and not only on the occasion of his death, we find Rashbi identifying with this divine level. For example, in the story narrating the mystical experience of Rashbi and the Companions that appears in the Zohar's commentary on the Torah portion *Aḥarei Mot*, we find described the ecstatic moments in which the qualities of the sefirah *Yesod* are made manifest through his person. In zoharic language, Rashbi is "crowned with the crown" of this sefirah:

> *While the king was on his couch, my nard gave forth its fragrance* (Song of Songs 1:12; transl. NJPS). This is *Yesod*, which brings forth blessings for the intercourse of the holy king with Matronita [Shekhinah] [through this level]. Then blessings are given in all the worlds, and the upper and lower worlds are blessed; and now, behold, the holy luminary [Rashbi] crowns himself with the crown of this level. (Zohar 3:62a)

Just as Rabbi Shim'on represents the most masculine of divine qualities, he at times represents the sefirah *Malkhut*, the most feminine of all the sefirot. Before discussing our hero further, let us pause to consider the characteristics of this particular sefirah:

- *Malkhut* is the tenth and last sefirah in the emanatory system. She represents time and movement; the dynamics of birth, growth, and death; differentiation and duality; and the characteristic of containment.
- This sefirah is represented by a rich array of symbols and associations connected with the feminine—motherly, erotic, sexual—both divine and demonic.
- She is the sefirah that receives into herself the river of the divine flow, via the sefirah *Yesod*.

- She is the queen of all reality below the world of emanation, the matrix of the physical world in which we exist. She is also responsible for the just distribution of the divine flow within her domain.
- *Malkhut* is also Shekhinah, the feminine, motherly divinity that dwells among human beings in this world through their loving interrelationships—especially when they share words of Torah. The human beings who experience the serenity of her presence are those who direct their deeds to support and aid her.
- In the zoharic world, the sefirah *Malkhut* merits the most extensive and intensive attention of all the sefirot. She is the object of the kabbalists' speculation, as well as the object of their emotional, religious, and mystical longing.[7]

In the Zohar, Rashbi is described as "the mouth of Shekhinah" or "the mouth of God," with some meriting the opportunity to kiss him.[8] He is also the divine face, "the face of the Master, God," which refers to the face of Shekhinah, as we learn from another passage: "Rabbi Pinhas went out and kissed him [Rabbi Shim'on] and said, 'I have merited to kiss Shekhinah. Happy is my portion!'" (Zohar 3:59b).

In another story, in which the expression "the mouth of God" is explained as meaning the mouth that "rules over all," Rabbi Pinhas ben Yair, depicted in the Zohar as Rashbi's respected father-in-law, comes and kisses him and says: "I have kissed the mouth of God, perfumed with the fragrances of His garden" (Zohar 3:201b).

These passages highlight Rashbi's great versatility, at once capable of appearing as an expression of the masculine quality of divinity, as well as an expression of the divine's feminine aspects. An additional example, drawn from the words of Rabbi Abba, illustrates somewhat humorously the divine qualities of Rabbi Shim'on bar Yohai: "One day Rabbi Shim'on was going from Cappadocia to Lydda, accompanied by Rabbi Abba and Rabbi Yehudah. Rabbi Abba was weary, running after Rabbi Shim'on, who was riding. Rabbi Abba said: *They will follow YHVH, roaring like a lion* (Hosea 11:10)" (Zohar 1:223a; Matt 2004–2007, vol. 3, p. 340).

An additional divine aspect associated with Rashbi is connected with his being the bearer and distributor of light. In the biblical book of Daniel, God is described as the locus of light: "He reveals deep and hidden things; he knows what is in the darkness, and light dwells with him" (Daniel 2:22; transl. NJPS). In the Zohar, this divine light is attributed to Rashbi himself.

Perhaps the most common epithet for Rashbi in the Zohar is *botsina kaddisha* (the holy luminary),[9] which is found along with *botsina di-nhora* (the light that illuminates), *botsina de-alma* (the light of the world), and also their combination, *botsina kaddisha de-havei nahir alma* (the holy light that illuminated the world).[10] Two examples of such terminology will suffice. "Rabbi Abba raised his voice and said: 'Rabbi Shim'on is like the light of a lamp that burns above and burns below; and with the light he kindles below, the whole world is illumined. Woe to the world when the light below will ascend into the light above! Who will illuminate the light of Torah to the world?'" And similarly: "Rabbi Yitzhak said: '[Rabbi Shim'on,] the master of light—the man who cleaves to the devouring fire every day. Behold, the light dwells with him!'" In short, Rabbi Shim'on is the great luminary. He is the lamp that illuminates—from the light of the upper worlds—the reality of human beings, and who reveals the Torah's light to the world.[11]

In quoting the above-cited verse from Daniel, the Zohar applies additional divine attributes to Rashbi: the ability to discover deep and hidden things, knowledge of mysteries, and knowledge of darkness and evil. Rashbi is sometimes presented as the presence of the Tree of Life—the grasping of which, like the grasping of the Torah, assures access to true life. Thus, in the words of the Zohar, "whoever withdraws from Rabbi Shim'on is like one who withdraws from all."[12]

The Companions describe Rashbi with a panoply of additional images: He is the one who prepares sweet dishes,[13] the lion, the hero, the rainbow (the sign of the covenant between God and His people),[14] the master of Torah, the one who illuminates the light of Torah, a free king, the one who prepares the coming of the Messiah, "in the image" of Moses and of the

High Priest, among others. In some places, he is described as a potent shaman, with power over death and the forces of judgment.[15]

Another interesting feature of Rashbi's portrayal in the Zohar is the
amalgamation of characteristics used to describe him. Thus, in his person,
we find that different images used in rabbinic literature to describe the
talmidei ḥakhamim (the disciples of the wise) are blended together.[16] He is
the master of wisdom "like old wine settled on his lees," while simultaneously being an "overflowing spring" and "the river that issues from Eden."

Rabbi Shim'on, Moses, and Rabbi Akiva

Alongside the divine aspects of Rabbi Shim'on, which as we have seen are
sometimes presented in a stark and daring manner, Rashbi is also described
as the earthly leader of the world. His image as leader is characterized by
his courage and daring in the realms of revelation and innovation. From
this vantage point, Rashbi parallels the two greatest leadership figures in the
Jewish tradition—Moses and Rabbi Akiva.

Rabbi Shim'on and Moses   The parallels drawn by the Zohar between Rashbi
and Moses are based on numerous characteristics. First and foremost, both of
them are considered as those who "give" Torah. Just as Moses gave the people of Israel the written Torah at Mt. Sinai (and just as the tannaim began the
enterprise of assembling a new Torah, namely, the oral Torah), so the Zohar
daringly presents Rashbi as one who gives Torah.[17] He is described as a "free
king" who bestows upon the world the secret, esoteric Torah hidden within
the Torah's garments; and indeed, in the consciousness of later generations,
he was valorized as the author of this wonderful work, and as the bestower
of the new Torah that fills its pages.[18]

According to rabbinic literature, Moses and Rashbi are the only human
beings who ever merited experiencing the divine through the *ispaklarya
ha-me'irah* (the speculum that shines). This concept, it seems, designates a
kind of clear spiritual vision through a mirror or illuminating glass, un-
dimmed by the materiality of earthly reality. In the Zohar, the "speculum
that shines" also symbolizes the sefirah *Tiferet* (Beauty). Rashbi and Moses

are understood as those who attained a particularly high level of divinity, characteristic of the great mystics alone. Beneath them stand those who attain the divine grade designated as *ispaklarya she-einah me'irah* (the speculum that does not shine), which in the Zohar symbolizes the sefirah *Malkhut*.[19]

The Zohar presents both Moses and Rashbi as God's elect, as standing in an intimate relationship with Him, and as those who bring the people to a new level of consciousness as members of the Covenant and as students of Torah.[20] Biblical verses describing Moses are interpreted by the Zohar as referring to Rashbi, for example: "About him [that is, Rashbi] Scripture says: *With him I speak mouth to mouth, in a vision and not in riddles*" (Numbers 12:8)."[21] The Zohar, however, is more far-reaching; it argues for the superiority of Rashbi over Moses.[22] He is superior to Moses in courage, in revelatory daring, and, most importantly (as we shall see below), in his acute self-awareness as opposed to the biblical leader's naiveté or lack of reflexivity. Thus we read that a voice was heard saying: "Happy are you, Rabbi Shim'on, for your Master desires your glory more than the rest of mankind! About Moses is written: *And Moses entreated (va-yḥ al)* (Exodus 32:11), meaning that trembling (*ḥalḥala*) seized him. And you, Rabbi Shim'on, decree—and the blessed Holy One fulfills; He decrees—and you annul."[23]

In *Ra'aya Meheimna* and in *Tikkunei ha-Zohar*, sections of the zoharic corpus probably written at the beginning of the fourteenth century and that already relate to the Zohar as a written and well-known composition, we find an interesting development in the presentation of the relationship between Rabbi Shim'on and Moses. In these two sections, the literary arena is transferred from the world below to the world above, and there alongside Rabbi Shim'on bar Yoḥai we find Moses, "the faithful shepherd," the two of them together constituting the heroes of the composition.[24]

Rabbi Shim'on and Rabbi Akiva   According to rabbinic literature, Rabbi Shim'on bar Yoḥai is one of the outstanding students of Rabbi Akiva and continues his master's path as expounder and interpreter of the Torah.[25] In the rabbinic corpus, Rabbi Akiva is considered a trailblazer who forged a new path in Jewish life. He symbolizes the creation of the oral Torah and the great freedom that characterizes this enterprise. He is described as a hero of his times and as a master of esoteric lore.[26]

Rabbi Shim'on bar Yoḥai of the Zohar is similar to the classical depiction of Rabbi Akiva in many respects—and echoes and extends the latter's enterprise. Rabbi Akiva is described by the Rabbis as the great revealer of mysteries: "Akiva, about you is said: *He dams up the sources of the streams, so that hidden things may be brought to light* (Job 28:11)—things that were from eternity concealed from humankind, Rabbi Akiva has brought to light."[27] In the Zohar, Rashbi is presented in similar terms: "[Rabbi Shim'on said,] '. . . we walk after the blessed Holy One, and we know matters; and behold, this word has been revealed by us—what had not been revealed to the former ones. . . . holy words, until now unrevealed, I wish to reveal in the presence of Shekhinah'" (Zohar 3:287a–b *Idra Zuta*).

Like Rabbi Akiva in rabbinic literature, Rabbi Shim'on bar Yoḥai is portrayed as the revealer of a new path in religious life, dependent on love and the pursuit of the divine in all the details of Scripture. His image is that of the royal hero.[28] Like Rabbi Akiva, Rabbi Shim'on is portrayed as the mystic elect, who has developed new ways to interpret Scripture—including the crowns and coronets of its letters; as one who describes his God in anthropomorphic imagery without fear; and as the one whose love for God and for the Torah is infinite.[29] Around both of them we encounter the myth that from the moment of the creation of the world, they were present as God's chosen ones.[30]

The figure of Rabbi Shim'on bar Yoḥai in the Zohar is therefore constructed out of a conscious comparison with the figures of Moses and of Rabbi Akiva. It should be noted, however, that such daring in comparing historical personages from Jewish history with the great figures of the Bible is not a zoharic innovation. Already in rabbinic literature, Moses and Rabbi Akiva are presented alongside one another as the great spiritual leaders for all generations. In tractate *Menaḥot* of the Babylonian Talmud,[31] we find the famous legend in which, through the stratagem of time travel, Moses (the hero of the "old" world of the written Torah, and indeed the giver of that Torah) and Rabbi Akiva (the hero of the "new" world of the oral Torah, and the great expounder and lover of Moses' written Torah) meet. Moses and Akiva come together in the *beit midrash* (house of study), the new cultural institution of rabbinic Judaism. The story describes Moses' experience in Akiva's *beit midrash* as a combination of embarrassment and dismay in light of his inability to comprehend the "new world" of the *beit midrash*. The tale presents him as recognizing the greatness of his successor and heir, Rabbi Akiva, as expounder of Torah. This legend is a quintessential example of rabbinic reflexivity. It expresses both the paradigmatic differences as well as the deep connections between these two "worlds" and how they view the meanings of Torah and religious experience. In this legend and in other places as well, the masters of the oral Torah stand with all their innovative vigor and face their biblical counterparts head-on, as heroes and not as "donkeys in the presence of angels."[32] Indeed, the Rabbis even celebrated Akiva's superiority over Moses: "Things that were not revealed to Moses were revealed to Rabbi Akiva, as it is said: *His eyes behold every precious thing* (Job 28:10)—this is Rabbi Akiva."[33]

The daring and presumptuousness of the Rabbis in examining their own cultural enterprise in such a reflexive manner against the world of the Bible was a precedent for the radical self-consciousness of the zoharic world. As Yehuda Liebes has shown, at the heart of this world lies the desire for a renaissance of the wellsprings of religious creativity of the tannaitic period.[34] It is out of a deep identification with the past and out of the innovation and self-consciousness characteristic of a renaissance culture that we ought to approach the Zohar's depictions of itself and of its heroes as standing on the shoulders of giants, attaining new heights in spiritual striving.

The Zohar admires the figures of Moses and Rabbi Akiva, and in the zoharic compositions focusing on the *Heikhalot* (divine chambers, which the Zohar describes as dimensions existing beneath or parallel to the sefirot), the two of them are vouchsafed the highest rank as the elect "residents" of the uppermost chambers. Moses sits in the sixth chamber called "the chamber of desire" or "the chamber of Moses," where he and God embrace with kisses of love. The spirit of this chamber contains all the rare souls who possess knowledge of the great secret: how to simultaneously arouse the great love of the divine worlds (*ahavah rabbah*), as well as the lesser love of this world (*ahavah zuta*). Together with Moses, the soul of Rabbi Akiva also resides in this highest of all chambers.[35]

One of the main characteristics of Jewish literature is the ongoing conversation, real or imagined, among different texts in the tradition. Analysis of the figures of Moses and Rabbi Akiva, as described across the ages, reveals an evolving arc of archetypal hero and leader images. The Zohar's discussion of these figures and their relation to the figure of Rabbi Shim'on attests to the composition's reflexivity and to the conscious, if at times veiled, comparison between the hero of the Zohar with Jewish tradition's most exalted heroes.

The question arises as to why Rabbi Akiva was not chosen to be the hero of the Zohar. It may be that the complex figure of Rabbi Akiva had been so highly developed and well articulated as a hero in rabbinic literature and in the *Merkavah* corpus (the mystical-magical literature of the amoraic period), that it was no longer possible to draw upon him as the hero of the Zohar and as the figure heralding a new, renaissance "canon." In formulating their unique Torah, therefore, the Zohar's authors needed to look elsewhere. The enigmatic figure of Rabbi Shim'on bar Yoḥai in rabbinic literature—the ascendant/elect one (*ben ha-aliyah*), the one who gazes through the "speculum that shines," the zealous one, he who dwelt with his son El'azar in a cave for thirteen years, the miracle worker—better suited the Zohar's authors in their desire to freely create the figure of their hero. Boaz Huss has extensively explored this question and has convincingly argued that Rabbi Shim'on was chosen because of the comparison between him and Moses that appears in the Talmud, where both of them are described as gazing through the "speculum that shines"; and because the zoharic authors preferred Rashbi's high self-esteem to Rabbi Akiva's humility. In fact, according to Huss it was Rabbi Akiva's modesty that led the Zohar to privilege Rabbi Shim'on, who as we will see is far indeed from modest and humble.[36]

It is important to note, however, that Rabbi Shim'on does not play the role of the hero in all the literary layers of the Zohar. In *Midrash ha-Ne'elam* (the concealed midrash), a layer of the Zohar with its own unique characteristics and considered by most scholars to be its earliest stratum, we find many heroes alongside Rabbi Shim'on bar Yohai. It is possible that we have here testimony to the process of searching for a hero for the composition before the final decision to adopt Rashbi as the work's central hero. Indeed, in the different midrashim in *Midrash ha-Ne'elam*, the hero is Rabbi Akiva and sometimes Rabbi Eli'ezer ben Hyrcanus ("Eliezer the Great"), who is depicted in rabbinic literature as an extraordinary scholar, connected to the divine, and possessed of supernatural powers—and therefore a most suitable candidate for the role of zoharic hero. Perhaps Eli'ezer was rejected because he was already "taken," being the reputed author and narrator of the midrash *Pirkei de-Rabbi Eli'ezer*, one of the Zohar's chief sources of inspiration.

As we have seen, the unique figure of Rabbi Shim'on bar Yohai in the Zohar is constructed through the superlative praises lavished upon him by his students and the composition's other heroes. However, in order to fully understand the Zohar's hero figure—and the Zohar's own self-consciousness—it is insufficient to examine Rashbi's portrayal only through the eyes of his students. We must explore the way in which Rashbi presents himself, in his own words, as the composition's hero.

Rabbi Shim'on in His Own Eyes

The foundations for Rashbi's self-image in the Zohar are found in rabbinic literature. In the rabbinic corpus, Rashbi presents himself as the paradigmatic *ben aliyah* (the ascendant/elect one) upon whom the world stands, and as a "sign" of the covenant between God and the world: "Hizkiyah said in the name of Rabbi Yirmeyah who heard from Rabbi Shim'on bar Yohai: I can save the entire world from divine judgment, from the day that I was born until now"; "I have seen the elect and they are few. . . . if there are two, then they are my son and I"; "The world cannot endure with less than thirty righteous people, like our father Abraham. . . . if there is only one, then it is me."[37] His self-certainty regarding his singularity and the importance of his role in the world is one of his key distinguishing features. Humility and modesty are not part of his personal makeup, and in this way (as Boaz Huss has highlighted), he is different from Moses and his teacher Rabbi Akiva.[38] In rabbinic literature, Rashbi proclaims himself as the defender of the generation; when harsh decrees are issued, he arises and declares before the Master of Judgment, "Rabbi Shim'on bar Yoḥai is present in the world!"[39] So too in the Zohar: "I am present in the world, I am the sign of the world, for in my lifetime the world does not dwell in suffering and is not punished by judgment above" (Zohar 1:225a; Matt 2004–2007, vol. 3, p. 352).

In the Zohar, Rabbi Shim'on is portrayed and indeed presents himself as a singular, messianic figure whose task is to rectify all reality and pave the way for the Messiah's arrival at the end of days. (This aspect of Rashbi's character has been explored in depth in a seminal article by Yehuda Liebes.[40]) Rashbi is also portrayed as the complete *tsaddik* (righteous person), an image with antecedents in the rabbinic corpus. In tractate *Ḥagigah* in the Babylonian Talmud, the Sages ask the philosophical and mythical question: on what is reality founded? After a range of suggestions, the final answer suggested is that "the world stands on one pillar, and its name is *tsaddik* (righteous one), as is said: *And the righteous one is the foundation of the world* (Proverbs 10:25)."[41] The Zohar develops this myth of the cosmic *tsaddik* and identifies Rashbi as its archetype—with him as the pillar upon which the world stands. In the opening of the *Idra Rabba*, Rashbi laments the difficulty and loneliness of this solitary existence; he expresses a desire to transform his disciples into additional pillars upon which reality might endure.[42]

In the zoharic narratives, Rabbi Shim'on is depicted not only as the elect mystic, in intimate contact with the divine, and not only as the greatest expounder of Torah, but also as possessing the miraculous powers of a potent shaman and magician.[43] Rashbi is the *tsaddik* whose decrees are carried out by God: "he decrees and the blessed Holy One fulfills."[44] The secrets of nature, knowledge of the future, the inner recesses of his disciples' hearts, and the designs of evil forces, all are known and revealed to him. The angel of death fears him. He brings the rain, eradicates demonic serpents, and subjugates the forces of evil. The narratives describe Rashbi's shamanic characteristics in terms of his ability to enter and operate in alternate dimensions of reality, and he presents himself in similar terms.

Sometimes these shamanic characteristics are presented in a tangential, marginal manner. In my opinion, we have here a deliberate representation of the hero as someone whose mastery over the forces of nature is negligible—compared with his being the master teacher of mysteries of Torah and divinity! Rashbi's mastery over the generative forces of reality is presented as for him a mere trifle. For example, in the story appearing in the Zohar's commentary to the Torah portion *Vayeḥi*, in which Rashbi sends away the angel of death and saves Rabbi Yitsḥak's life, he is described as immediately returning to his studies, as if to suggest that the preceding drama was for him a brief interruption between the lines of Torah he was reading.[45]

A similar idea is conveyed in the wondrous story about the bringing of the rains, which appears in the commentary to the Torah portion *Aḥarei Mot*. (We shall return to this story again in different contexts.) In this tale, a fascinating plot unfolds, focusing on the process of bringing rain—the drawing down of the divine flow to the world—by means of an ecstatic act of mystical interpretation among the Companions. At the beginning of the story, the Companions approach Rashbi and request that he act to bring the rains, just as their ancestors in antiquity turned to the righteous and miracle workers in years of drought. Rabbi Shim'on answers them: "If for this [to bring the rains] you have come to me, return [to your place], for today I have seen that all will be restored, to be aligned face-to-face. But if for Torah you have come, stay with me." To which they promptly reply: "We come to the master for all!" (Zohar 3:59b). Even so, Rashbi's implication is that rainmaking is a trivial task when viewed against the great task of drawing down the divine flow into the world through interpretations of Torah and through accessing and healing the world of divinity. It is thus his mastery over Torah—and not over the rains—that marks Rabbi Shim'on as teacher and leader.[46]

Just as the Zohar depicts Rashbi in comparison with Moses and privileges him over Moses, so Rabbi Shim'on understands himself as being at once in the image of Moses and superior to him; indeed he expounds biblical verses about Moses as referring to himself, for example, "I dwelt on the mountain forty days and forty nights."[47] In the opening of the *Idra Rabba*, Rashbi proclaims that unlike Moses—who called heaven and earth as his witnesses in the Torah portion *Ha'azinu* (Deuteronomy 32:1)—he, Rabbi Shim'on, has no need for their testimony: "To heaven I do not say, 'Listen!'; to the earth I do not say, 'Hear!' For we are the pillars of the worlds!" (Zohar 3:128a).

The excerpts examined so far serve only as an introduction to one of the most important passages for understanding Rabbi Shim'on's self-image in particular and the Zohar's creative enterprise in general. This passage appears in the *Idra Rabba* (the Great Assembly), which tells the story of the disciples' assembly together with their teacher in their endeavor to attune their human consciousness to the ancient and undifferentiated aspect of the divine known as *Arikh Anpin* (the Long Face, the Patient One), in order to rectify the disharmony in the divine and human world. Rabbi Shim'on proclaims the absolute singularity of the occasion: "For behold, this event will not be again until King Messiah comes." He describes his and his students' intensified state. He experiences his face shining like the light of the sun at the end of days, and the expositions of his students as attaining cosmic significance. In this dramatic moment in the *Idra*, Rashbi distinguishes between himself and Moses. Moses, he says, descended from Mt. Sinai without being aware that his face was shining, whereas he—Rabbi Shim'on—shines and is aware that this is so:

> Rabbi Shim'on said, "All you luminaries, companions who enter the holy circle:
>
> "I call to witness the highest heavens and the highest holy earth that I now see what no man has seen since Moses ascended Mt. Sinai for the second time.
>
> "For I see my face shining like the powerful light of the sun that in the future will emerge to bring healing to the world.
>
> "As is written: *But for you who revere My name, a sun of victory shall rise to bring healing* (Malachi 3:20).
>
> "And what's more, I know that my face is shining, whereas Moses did not know, nor did he contemplate, as is written: *Moses was not aware that the skin of his face was shining* (Exodus 34:29)." (Zohar 3:132b)

Rashbi sees no "likeness," not even a likeness of God. He sees, rather, his own face shining like the sun at the end of days. How is it that he sees his own face? Through which lens is his face reflected that he should know how he looks? Do the faces of his disciples reflect his face? Is he reflected in the face of Shekhinah, or in the face of the angels who have come to listen to the secrets of the assembly? Does the luminous "sun of victory" radiating from his face illuminate all reality? Or is it perhaps the Zohar itself that reflects the radiance of Rabbi Shim'on's face?

The importance of seeing as a motif in Rashbi's description is particularly significant. This seeing, so central to the Zohar's consciousness, comprises experience, understanding, and knowledge.[48] Rashbi's words distinguish between a religious, mystical experience attained without intent, as in the case of Moses, and a structured mystical mode in which the approach to the divine and the experience of the divine presence are the explicit *telos*. This acute self-awareness distinguishes the entire experiential world of the Zohar. It also sets apart the tannaim (sages) of antiquity from the thirteenth-century Spanish authors of the Zohar, who clothe themselves in tannaitic garb. Expressed differently, this is the great difference between antiquity and the Zohar's renaissance quality, and it is the difference between inhabiting a given cultural-historical reality and the conscious choice to retrieve certain elements from the historical and mythical past in order to fashion from them a new delicacy.[49]

Cognitive and cultural propositions are intertwined here. Rashbi's comments reflect the Zohar's radical stance that argues for the possibility of a person's being immersed in experience, while at the same time being aware of the fact that he is experiencing it. Reflexivity here is not viewed as preventing the possibility of experience. On the contrary, while the experience remains central, it is considered as attaining its peak and is intensified precisely when accompanied by the ability to reflect on the experience while it is occurring. On the personal and cultural level, we have here a strong argument in favor of sophistication and self-awareness over simplicity and naiveté.

This passage also contains an implicit literary statement about the Zohar, at once radiating through its words and aware of its own radiance. The

Zohar does not innocently present its world and experiences to the reader, leaving history to judge and evaluate its worth. The Zohar's authors display an extreme self-assurance that their creation (whether this be according to its fictional or historical origins) heralds something profoundly new, thrilling, and singular in religious experience; and that it is fitting to proclaim this to all who can hear—rather than hide behind a veil of modesty, which has no place in an event of this magnitude.[50]

According to Boaz Huss, the self-assurance of the Zohar's authors is expressed in the very choice of Rabbi Shim'on bar Yoḥai as hero of the zoharic corpus, and in his zoharic portrayal as superior to Moses. Huss argues that this view, which is connected with the claim that the Zohar completes the Torah and indeed surpasses it, expresses the desire of the Zohar's authors to attain canonical status and the wish that their work be counted as a classic in Jewish literature.[51]

It is appropriate here to recall the parable that prefaces *Sifra de-Tseni'uta* (the Book of Concealment) in the Zohar about the man from the mountains who would eat only raw kernels of wheat. Upon reaching the city and tasting all the delights that can be made from the kernels, he praises himself in that by eating the kernels he in fact eats of the essence of all those delights. Rabbi Shim'on responds: "Because of that view, he knew nothing of the delights of the world; they were lost on him. So it is with one who grasps the principle and does not know all those delectable delights, deriving, diverging from that principle" (Zohar 2:176a–b; Matt 2004–2007, vol. 1, p. xxv, adapted).[52]

Rabbi Shim'on and his circle see no shame in sophistication and self-awareness, and their perspective is usually anti-fundamentalist. Truth is not found solely in pure essence or in a pure source, but rather in the delights that one can develop from such a source. This is the definition of a culture that celebrates innovation and complexity—and is unapologetic about it. It is this affection for sophistication and reflexivity that accounts for the Zohar's complexity as a work of art. The Zohar does not create a simple world, a kernel of wheat. Rather, it is characterized by complexity, refinement, sophistication, and depth—the secret of its great charm.

Yet even here in this dynamic tension between the power of innovation and the longing for the source, we encounter a characteristic ambivalence. Alongside the Zohar's delight in innovation, and its elevation of innovation as a central value, we find also the apparent wish to return to the primal source. This wish is expressed in the literary choice to don a tannaitic identity, and also in the mystical desire to unite especially with the ancient deity, the divine oneness prior to its separation and differentiation. The ability to hold fast to the kernel of wheat that is the *peshat* (the original, simple meaning), and at the same time to taste spiritual delights through innovative exegesis, is one of the key meanings of the term "new-ancient words" that the Zohar uses to describe its path.[53] The words of the Zohar are indeed new and at times exceedingly daring, but they are always connected, in one way or another, to antiquity and to the archaic source—to the antiquity of the holy text, the tradition, the depths of the soul, or the divine itself.

While it is true that Rabbi Shim'on appears in the Zohar as a most self-reflexive character, the crown of reflexivity belongs to the wondrous figure of the old man in the literary unit called *Sava de-Mishpatim*. In my opinion, this old man, like many other wondrous characters in the Zohar, is a kind of shadow image of Rashbi, or Rashbi in disguise.[54] In the midst of his discourses, the old man occasionally stops to reflect, laugh, or even weep about his words. He simultaneously weaves and unravels his words and brings the zoharic enterprise to its dramatic, reflexive, and poetic peak—and to its most amusing moments.[55]

Note the great license taken by the Zohar's authors in developing the stern and zealous figure of Rabbi Shim'on as he appears in rabbinic literature. With a healthy dose of zoharic eros, Rashbi is transformed into a teacher whose severity is tempered. The Rabbi Shim'on of the Zohar is an enigmatic teacher, possesses a great yearning for the Torah, is full of mystery and humor, loves his disciples, and prepares them to continue his path both in Torah and in the mysteries of divinity. It is not that he lacks the severity that characterizes his figure in rabbinic literature, but rather that in the Zohar these qualities are transformed into pathos. The eroticism in his zoharic portrayal is also new and unique: Rabbi Shim'on is not merely the expression of the sefirah *Yesod* in its single, sterile, zealous aspect, but he is also its fertile, erotic, and joyful expression, as he brings the divine flow to his students and to the world.[56] Rashbi's appearance as the presence of Shekhinah in the world, and his desire (in the two *Idra* sections) to undergo *tikkun* (self-rectification) through the divine and perhaps even the earthly feminine, as well as his preoccupation with Shekhinah and expanding her expression in the religious-experiential world, constitute a softening and feminization of his stern and misogynous image in classical rabbinic literature.

The figure of Rabbi Shim'on bar Yoḥai in the Zohar is the product of a unique interweaving of the figures of Rabbi Shim'on in the rabbinic corpus, of Moses, both biblical and rabbinic, and of Rabbi Akiva as drawn from rabbinic literature and the *Heikhalot* corpus. To all of these have been added features of the mystical hero, beloved of God, as he was imagined by the Zohar's authors—their impression of a messianic figure—and perhaps also features of a historical figure from the world of the zoharic circle in the Middle Ages, whose true identity has been blurred, perhaps deliberately.[57] Out of this arises the complex figure of Rashbi—the great hero who awakens the soul to the hidden world, possessing freedom and courage to arise and reveal that which is concealed from the world.

> Happy is the generation in which Rabbi Shim'on abides! Happy is its portion in the upper and lower worlds!
>
> About him is written: *Happy are you, O land, for your king is a free man* (Ecclesiastes 10:17).
>
> What is *a free man*? [A man] who lifts his head to reveal and interpret things and does not fear, like one who is free and says what he pleases and doesn't fear.
>
> What is *your king*? This is Rabbi Shim'on bar Yoḥai, the master of Torah, the master of wisdom! (Zohar 3:79b)

This passage depicts the breaking of the seal of esotericism in the world of the zoharic companions.[58] Esotericism is no longer a self-evident strategy. Now is the time for disclosure—and the zoharic hero, Rabbi Shim'on, is the great revealer of secrets; and a life lived with him brings blessings to the world. In his persona as the great revealer of secrets, particularly in the two

Idra sections, one hears echoes of the way Maimonides portrays himself and his own motivations for writing and revealing secrets in his great work, *The Guide of the Perplexed*:

> We have already made it clear that the chief aim of this Treatise is to explain what can be explained of the *Account of the Beginning* and the *Account of the Chariot* . . . and you know that [the Sages], may their memory be blessed, blame those who divulge the mysteries of the Torah. . . . only the chapter headings may be mentioned. This is the reason why the knowledge of this matter has ceased to exist in the entire religious community, so that nothing great or small remains of it. And it had to happen like this, for this knowledge was only transmitted from one chief to another and has never been set down in writing. If this is so, what stratagem can I use to draw attention toward that which may have appeared to me as indubitably clear, manifest, and evident in my opinion, according to what I have understood in these matters? On the other hand, if I had omitted setting down something of that which has appeared to me as clear, so that the knowledge would perish when I perish, as is inevitable, I should have considered that conduct as extremely cowardly with regard to you and everyone who is perplexed. It would have been, as it were, robbing one who deserves the truth of the truth, or begrudging an heir his inheritance.[59]

Both the Zohar and Maimonides are acutely aware of the significance and transience of their historical moment, and both see themselves as having attained a never-to-be repeated manifestation of understanding and clarity, fated to disappear with their passing. Both explain their (ambivalent) decision to reveal secrets as a response to crises in the Judaism of their day, and both understand their revelation of secrets as an "emergency situation," citing the biblical verse "It is time to act for YHVH, they have violated your Torah" (Psalms 119:126). (This verse was already cited in the Mishnah in order to justify innovation; and in the Zohar, Rabbi Shim'on uses it in the dramatic opening of the Great Assembly, to justify his urgent call for change.) Both are of the view that if they cannot infuse new meaning in their religion, or expose its true meaning, then Judaism will have become seemingly irrelevant or obsolete, and both feel that if they will not reveal their secrets to those in need, they will be guilty of "withholding the good from one who deserves" (Proverbs 3:27).[60]

The secret of Rabbi Shim'on bar Yoḥai's charm in the Zohar, therefore, lies in the extraordinary complexity of his character: divine-like and human, stern yet humorous, ecstatic, and erotic. The Zohar evokes in the reader a sense of enigma, in which the figure of Rabbi Shim'on seems absolutely real, yet at the same time, so perfect and divine-like that it is impossible to imagine him as actually existing in the world. Rashbi's intense self-awareness of his unique capabilities and personal qualities, and his way of reflecting upon his own experiences, greatly enhance his wondrous image.

In the Master's Presence

Familiarity with the world of the Zohar's heroes requires a special discussion about the Companions' account of being in their teacher's presence. This is vital for understanding how the Zohar explains the experience of interpretive and exegetical freedom and the extraordinary creativity of the Companions' discourses, as well as the unique status of the generation of the Zohar and the disclosure and innovation of Torah secrets.

The Zohar widely reports on many dimensions of the experience of the teacher's presence. Such descriptions are found in the Companions' sayings in the presence of their teacher, and also in remarks made in his absence, though with an intimation of his spiritual presence. The terror surrounding his death and disappearance from the world and the meaning of his passing for the Companions are also crucial in understanding this dimension of the Zohar.

In Jewish literature from the Bible to the present, the relationship between teacher and student is portrayed as being unique, poised between the parent-child relationship and the relationship between two lovers. Biblical stories about Moses and Joshua, or Elijah and Elisha—stories about the relationship between a prophet and his disciple—furnish the narrative and linguistic paradigm. The sages of the Talmud placed the teacher-student relationship at the center of the processes of religious-cultural production. Indeed, rabbinic literature is filled with a rich tradition—both aggadic and halakhic—exploring this unique relationship.

In the biblical stories, the bestowal of inspiration represents the most precious gift that a teacher can give the student. Both Moses and Elijah bestow their "spirit" upon their outstanding pupils. In rabbinic literature, the institution of apprenticeship (*shimush*) among the sages presents us with a deep, complex relationship in which all aspects of the life of the teacher— his teaching, method of study, personal attributes, and way of life—consti- tute the body of knowledge for the student. In the literature of the rabbis we encounter characters who sing the praises of their teacher, as in the case of Rabbi Yehoshu'a, who would kiss the stone upon which Rabbi Eli'ezer sat and then say, "This stone is like Mt. Sinai, and he who sat upon it is like the Ark of the Covenant."[61] Indeed, in the world of the sages, which is the storehouse of inspiration for the Zohar, we find a great diversity of teacher figures: the gracious and sensitive Rabban Yoḥanan ben Zakkai; the strict and stern Rabbi Eli'ezer ben Hyrcanus, possessor of magical powers; the enigmatic, charismatic, and mystical Rabbi Akiva; and the aggressive Rabbi Yoḥanan, also described as possessing supernatural abilities. It is with these teacher-student threads that the oral Torah is woven.

The Zohar uses the bold language of revelation to describe the experi- ence of being in the teacher's presence. These descriptions, recurring in many different forms, present this experience as one of opening, revelation, abundance, enlightenment, love, vitality, and flow. The student experiences contact with the teacher as contact with life itself, with the divine, and with the source of the divine plenty.

> When Rabbi Shim'on would speak the secret of this verse, the eyes of all the Companions streamed with tears, and all the things that he said were revealed in their sight, as is written: *With him I speak mouth to mouth, plainly and not in riddles* (Numbers 12:8). (Zohar 3:79a)

> When we stand in the presence of Rabbi Shim'on, the wellsprings of our heart open in all directions and all is revealed. And when we withdraw from him, we do not know anything and all the springs are closed.
>
> Rabbi Ḥizkiyah said, "Corresponding to what is written: *He held back (va- ya'atsel) some of the spirit that was upon him and put it upon the seventy men, the elders* (Numbers 11:25)—like a lamp from which many lamps are lit, while retaining its vitality. Similarly, Rabbi Shim'on son of Yoḥai, master of Lamps, illumines all, yet light does not depart from him and he retains vitality."[62]

Rabbi Shim'on here is the essence of everything, and the experience of being in his presence is one of opening the wellsprings of the heart. That which is sealed, hidden, and covered is now revealed, flowing, and illumined. Indeed, the emphasis on the powerful emotional experience of opening the wellsprings of the heart recalls the Zohar's definition of the mystic as *ḥakham lev* (wise of heart), as we shall see below. In the preceding passage, the circle of Rabbi Shim'on is depicted as emulating and seeking inspiration from the wilderness generation. Rabbi Shim'on represents Moses, with his students representing the seventy elders—the leaders of the generation upon whom the spirit of God dwells, enabling them to judge and lead the people in more minor legal matters. With the emanation of Rashbi's spirit onto them, the Companions are infused with the holy spirit.

Note here the use of the verb *atsal* (to emanate), so central to the kabbalists' dynamic conception of reality. The world of the ten sefirot, emanated from *Ein Sof* via the sefirah of *Keter* (Crown), establishes reality through a unique flow of divinity that does not diminish its source. The Companions understand their being endowed with the holy spirit in a similar fashion. Rabbi Shim'on is the source of this spirit—his light rests on them without diminishing anything from the infinite wellsprings that reside in him.

The Death of the Master

The converse to the experience of being in the teacher's presence is the terror surrounding his death and absence. The Companions repeatedly wonder what purpose there will be to their lives—and indeed to the entire world—when Rashbi will be taken from them. The account of the death of Rabbi Shim'on, and stories occurring after his death (in which the Companions discuss life in a world without him), together allow us to sense the enormity of their dread and fear. In all the passages dealing with the death of the teacher, we find a bitter awareness of the transience of all things. The Zohar's composers are clearly conscious of the fleeting nature of their own generation and understand that the period of grace that enabled the unprecedented creativity characteristic of the Zohar will not continue forever. As Moshe Idel has noted: "Innovative Kabbalah, as reflected in the Zohar, had a splendid but short life."[63] These passages are of great importance for understanding the work's self-image, as well as for questions as to its process of composition. These passages also raise questions concerning the centrality of Rashbi as revealer of secrets and bearer of the ultimate meaning of reality: Is religious creativity possible after the teacher's disappearance? What are the limits of democratization in the mystical endeavor? And above all: who is Rabbi Shim'on bar Yoḥai in the Zohar? What is the meaning of his portrayal as a figure at once historical and earthly yet also heavenly and divine? Does death have dominion over his life and teaching? Or do perhaps people of his stature continue to live, and to guide the world, even after their deaths?

The epic logic of the Zohar juxtaposes the death of Rashbi (revealer and imparter of esoteric Torah) with the Torah portion about Moses (revealer of the written Torah) creating his poetic ethical will at the end of his days.[64] We thus find the *Idra Zuta* juxtaposed with the Zohar's commentary to the Torah portion *Ha'azinu*. Furthermore, Rashbi is the hidden subject of a series of zoharic commentaries about the patriarch Jacob. The Zohar's commentary to the Torah portion *Vayeḥi* is an extraordinary interweaving of midrashim about the life and death of Jacob with stories about the life and death of Rabbi Shim'on.

Questions concerning Rashbi's death or immortality are most intensive in the *Idra Zuta*, which means "the small assembly," and which describes Rabbi Shim'on's departure from the world after he initiates his students into the secrets of divinity. In moment-by-moment detail, almost in slow motion, the Zohar describes Rashbi's ecstatic passing, his union with Shekhinah, and his total transformation into the sefirah *Yesod*. In this way the Zohar bestows upon Rashbi a kind of immortality: As a person with a body he has indeed died, but henceforth his presence endures with every manifestation of the sefirah *Yesod*.[65]

We turn now to some Zohar texts dealing with the death of Rabbi Shim'on.

And in this generation in which Rabbi Shim'on bar Yoḥai abides, it is the desire of the blessed Holy One for the sake of Rabbi Shim'on, that the sealed things should be revealed by him. But I am astounded by the sages of this

generation, how they can forfeit even one single moment of standing before Rabbi Shim'on to study Torah while Rabbi Shim'on is still alive in the
world! Nevertheless in this generation, wisdom will not be forgotten from
the world. Alas for the generation when he departs and the sages diminish,
and wisdom will be forgotten from the world! (Zohar 2:149a)

Rashbi himself intensifies this same fear in speaking about the world after
his death:

"I am present in the world, I am the sign of the world, for in my lifetime the
world does not dwell in suffering and is not punished by judgment above.
After me there will not arise a generation like this one. The world is destined
to lack anyone who can protect it, and all kinds of impudent faces will haunt
above and below. . . . Inhabitants of the world will one day cry out, and no one
will care about them. They will turn their heads in every direction and turn
back without a remedy." (Zohar 1:225a; Matt 2004–2007, vol. 3, pp. 352–53)

In these and similar passages we sense the great distress surrounding the
bitter future of the world in the teacher's absence. As we have seen, for
the Zohar, the teacher's presence is tantamount to the experience of revelation. The teacher's death, however, heralds the cessation of the flow of
divine plenty, the darkening of the light of revelation, and the blurring of
the clear understanding of reality as it was refracted through the pristine
lens of the teacher's consciousness. To explore these themes, the Zohar offers a surprising interpretation of a verse from Genesis.[66]

It has been taught that Rabbi Yose said, "From the day that Rabbi Shim'on
emerged from the cave, words were not concealed from the Companions
and supernal mysteries were revealed among them as if they had been given
at that moment on Mount Sinai. Once he took his final sleep, it is written:
The wellsprings of the deep were dammed up, and the sluices of heaven (Genesis
8:2), and the Companions would mouth words uncomprehendingly." (Zohar
1:216b–217a; Matt 2004–2007, vol. 3, pp. 306–7)

The Zohar's commentary to the Torah portion *Vayeḥi*, in which Jacob's
death is discussed, contains a fascinating account of the experience of ter-
rible loss that overcomes the Companions after Rashbi's death. The story
takes place on different planes of reality—in a waking state, in a vision, and
in a dream—with the loss of Rashbi experienced differently on each plane.

The experience is mythical and deals with the sealing up of the river of divine plenty that Rashbi constituted for his students. For the students, this blockage creates a sense of losing the way, a lack of understanding, unreality, dryness, confusion, horror, a wish to die, and a sense that with Rashbi's death, all contact with the reservoirs of knowledge has ceased.

The story tells of a dream that Rabbi Yehudah has, in which he sees Rabbi Shim'on ascending on the wings of celestial beings, carrying in his arms the totality of all knowledge: the Torah scroll, all the books of wisdom, the aggadah, and the deeper secrets of Torah. The sum total of divine knowledge is ascending heavenward and is disappearing from view! Rabbi Yehudah then relates the dream to Rabbi Abba, who joins him in mourning the loss of their master. Rabbi Abba, the most senior of Rashbi's students, is the one who regains his composure and instructs the other Companions to stop their tears and their mourning. Below we shall see Rabbi Abba's special role in ensuring the transmission of the Zohar's unique consciousness as a work for the ages.

In this dramatic scene, we sense the slender hope, emerging through the veil of fear and terror surrounding the teacher's death, that even after Rashbi's demise, something of his presence will remain in the world. Consolation for Rashbi's inevitable passing is found in the knowledge that his words will illuminate the world until the coming of the Messiah. Indeed it is possible that we find here the beginning of the Zohar's self-perception as a written work. In the passage below, Rabbi Abba offers a vision of the continued presence of Rashbi in the world even after his death.

> Rabbi Abba raised his hands upon his head and wept. He said, "Rabbi! Radiance of Torah ascends now to the highest heaven of the supernal Throne. Afterward, who will illumine the radiance of Torah? Woe to the world that will be left orphaned! However, words of the Master will shine in the world until King Messiah arrives, for of then is written *The earth will be filled with knowledge of YHVH as waters cover the sea* (Isaiah 11:9)." (Zohar 2:68a; Matt 2004–2007, vol. 4, p. 376)

A more mythic conception of Rashbi's death is revealed by Rabbi Ḥiyya. In a particularly emotional passage, Rabbi Ḥiyya turns to the earth and dust that have enveloped his teacher, and in an outburst of helpless rage bemoans death's utter incomprehensibility. Rabbi Ḥiyya protests the brazenness of the earth. The "Lamp of Hearts" now lies submerged, recalling the sorrowful lament of rabbi and poet Judah Halevi, "The light of hearts has come into the earth, and the earth knows not what lies within."[67]

> Rabbi Ḥiyya prostrated himself on the ground, kissing the dust and weeping. He cried out, "Dust, dust, how stubborn you are, how impudent! . . . The Holy Lamp who has illumined the world, majestic ruler, prince whose merit sustains the world, decays in you. O Rabbi Shim'on, radiance of the lamp, radiance of the worlds, you decompose in the dust, yet you subsist and guide the world!"
>
> For a moment he was shocked, and then exclaimed, "Dust, dust, do not boast! The pillars of the world will not be surrendered to you. Rabbi Shim'on has not decayed in you." (Zohar 1:4a; Matt 2004–2007, vol. 1, p. 20)[68]

What is unique in this account is Rabbi Ḥiyya's ability to simultaneously utter the paradox of absence and presence. Rabbi Ḥiyya offers three conflicting statements about the experience of Rashbi's death. Each statement nevertheless honestly expresses his state of mind. In the first instance, he protests the brazenness of the dust for its apathy in having enveloped his teacher—Rashbi here has indeed died and lies decaying in the earth—"The Holy Lamp . . . decays in you."

Rabbi Ḥiyya's second statement is directed to Rabbi Shim'on and declares a paradox—"you decompose in the dust" yet "subsist and guide the world."

The third statement, directed again at the dust, negates its, or perhaps death's, power to be victorious over the pillar of the world: "Rabbi Shim'on has not decayed in you." Decomposition of the body does not mean total annihilation. Rashbi can continue to serve as a source of inspiration and guidance even after his death. Indeed, if we pause and consider the extent to which Rabbi Shim'on bar Yoḥai has served as a source of inspiration for succeeding generations of mystics, there is much truth in Rabbi Ḥiyya's declaration.[69]

Rabbi Ḥiyya's final statement is radical, perhaps bordering on messianic, as he suddenly understands that Rabbi Shim'on will not go the way of all flesh. Are these merely the defiant, dramatic words of a mourner and thus not worthy of serious consideration? Or are they, rather, suggesting that

Rabbi Shim'on is not subject to the laws of death and decay?[70] Or do they perhaps mean that as long as the consciousness of Rabbi Shim'on illuminates the world, the earth's power of obliteration cannot defeat him? Stories occurring after the great teacher's death illustrate that by preserving Rashbi's teachings, the Companions can, as it were, in fact bring him back to life.

> Come and see! I [Rabbi Abba] saw him [Rabbi Shim'on] in a dream, and I asked Rabbi Shim'on.... he said to me ... [the secret of *A river flows from Eden to water the garden* (Genesis 2:10). After he answered,] I held and kissed his hand. I awoke in this state of delight, crying and smiling. For three days I did not eat a thing out of joy, and also because I did not merit to see him on another occasion. And with all this I became bound to him always, for when a teaching illumined me I would see his visage appearing before me.[71] (Zohar 2:123b)

That a person lives on through his heritage or his spiritual presence is a commonplace familiar to all. In this way our departed loved ones remain with us. In the Zohar, however, we encounter a more mythical and less metaphorical approach to the meaning of the death of important persons. In this regard, the figures of Jacob and Moses, and more specifically conceptions of their death, are critical for understanding the death of Rashbi. Both Jacob and Moses are the earthly embodiment of the sefirah *Tiferet* and are thus the mythic figures that constitute the paradigm of the image of Rabbi Shim'on as the sefirah of *Yesod*.

> Rabbi Shim'on said: "Moses never died. If you should say, however, 'Behold, it is written: *And Moses died there* (Deuteronomy 34:5),' [I would answer:] in every place of which it said of the righteous that they died, what is this death that is referred to? It is called death from our perspective." As we have taught: Rabbi Shim'on said, and so taught, that whosoever is in perfection, in whosoever resides holy faith, death has no sway over him and he does not die—as was the case with Jacob, in whom resided perfect faith. (Zohar 2:174a)

The death of Moses, the great sun, symbolizes the ingathering of the light. This light, however, is not entirely absent. Rather, it serves as the nourishing power of our reality, governed as it is by the indirect light of the moon. Moses represents the sun, and his student Joshua, as is known from the sages, represents the moon. Even in death, therefore, Moses continues to illuminate the world through his heir. In terms of sefirot, Moses' death is an expression of the inevitable ingathering of the light of the sun—the light of the sefirah *Tiferet*—in order to enable the independent existence of the moon, the sefirah of *Malkhut*. Whether this view is great or small consolation, it lies at the heart of the Zohar's approach to death, and to the life of the soul after bodily death. Thus we read: "Rabbi Hizkiyah said: 'The blessed Holy One said to Moses: Even though you will lie with your ancestors, behold you will endure forever to illuminate the moon, just like the sun: even though it is gathered in, it does so only to illuminate the moon—and so illuminates the moon in its gathering.'"[72]

In order to more fully understand the radical meaning of the ingathering of this light, we need to explore the Zohar's approach to the death of the patriarch Jacob. The Zohar adopts and extends the rabbinic idea that "the patriarch Jacob never died."[73] Jacob, like Moses, is the earthly embodiment of the sun, the sefirah *Tiferet*. According to Scripture, the earthly Jacob does indeed die. In the Zohar, however, his death represents a departure from this world in order to unite with the moon, the sefirah *Malkhut*. Jacob's union with Shekhinah fills her with light. The enlightened Shekhinah, now attractive and desirable, arouses the passion of the moon's true partner—the divine grade of *Tiferet*—to come and unite with her. Rabbi Shim'on adds that in every generation, there is an aspect of this act of arousal.

> [Rabbi Yehudah said:] "Jacob did not die—for regarding him, death is not mentioned, rather: *he expired, and was gathered to his people* (Genesis 49:33). See what is written: *He gathered his feet into the bed* (ibid.)—for he was gathered to the moon. The sun does not die, but is gathered from the world and goes toward the moon.
>
> "Come and see: When Jacob was gathered, the moon shone and desire of supernal sun aroused toward her; for as the sun ascends, another sun arouses, one cleaving to the other, and the moon shines." . . .
>
> [Rabbi Shim'on said:] "Jacob was gathered to the moon, generating fruit within her for the world. There is no generation in the world lacking fruit of Jacob, for he stimulated arousal above, as is written: *He gathered his feet into the bed.*" (Zohar 1:248b–249a; Matt 2004–2007, vol. 3, pp. 527, 529)

Here we encounter the mythical-linguistic complex so important for understanding the other dimension of Rashbi's death—where his death stands for the total antithesis of annihilation. In the *Idra Zuta*, Rashbi experiences his death as passage into true life. This is the occasion of his transformation into the sefirah *Yesod* at its full potency in union with Shekhinah. Death is therefore the transition into life in the world of divinity. To be sure, this transition is not merely metaphoric, it is mythical and mystical. As Yehuda Liebes has shown, the event described in the *Idra Zuta* is Rashbi's great personal *tikkun* (rectification) through his complete union with Shekhinah. Such a death also represents the greatest theurgic *tikkun* attainable to man.[74] Like the patriarch Jacob (according to the Zohar), Rashbi does not die. Rather, he leaves this world in order to enter the divine feminine, Shekhinah.

Ecstatic death of this kind, at the apex of divine union, activates the seductive powers of the male aspect of divinity, the blessed Holy One, to come and redeem His beloved—and thereby His people and His world. Seen in this light, there is no greater messianic act than the death of Rashbi—an act whose entirety is aimed at expanding circles of redemption. From this perspective, Rashbi's death is indeed a celebration (*hillula*) in which he merits to fulfill his desire for personal rectification (*tikkun*) and in so doing to restore all reality. Rashbi unites with Shekhinah as the sefirah *Yesod*, thereby facilitating the grander union between the divine male and divine female.

Rabbi Shim'on bar Yoḥai was a real historical figure and indeed we know a great deal about the world of second-century Palestine in which he lived and taught. But if we assume that the Zohar was composed in Castile in the last third of the thirteenth century, we must ask: who is this Rabbi Shim'on who emerges from the quill of the Zohar's composers? Do we perhaps not sense, through the veil of spectacular praises lavished upon him, the fictitious, ahistoric nature of this figure? Does not his depiction, at once perfect and divine, stem from an absence, a lack, and a longing, rather than from the live experience of a real historical personage? Or do we perhaps have here a legendary embellishment and a mythical retelling of a real historical person, whom the composers of the Zohar merited to meet? Was it perhaps the longing for that which was now absent that led to the creation of this uniquely ideal figure?

There are of course no easy answers to these questions, and perhaps this is as it ought to be. These questions, however, assume a particular poignancy after an examination of those passages in the Zohar dealing with the Companions' fear of abandonment and their preparations for a time when the brilliant light of Rashbi will have disappeared. How are we to explain the intensity of these passages, reflecting as they do the awareness that to every wonder there must be an end, if we do not posit that it was the real experience of a great presence that created this sense of loss? Is it possible to assume that all the emotional intensity surrounding issues of presence and absence is the product of the authors' imagination? Who is this personality, whose presence is the great symbol for creativity and revelation, and whose imprint is so firmly stamped on every page of the Zohar? And who created the work that tells the story of the Companions and their teacher?

There are no clear-cut answers to these questions and this book does not seek to explore them in depth. However, following Yehuda Liebes,[75] my sense is that there was indeed a real historical teacher around whom a group of creative students gathered. The members of this circle enjoyed the profound experience of the presence of their teacher, as well as wondrous moments of grace in the life of the circle. In historical reality, the teacher and the group ceased to be. One of the members of this group, perhaps Rabbi Moses de León, assumed the freedom to turn history into art, to transform the life of the circle into epic, and the teacher into a mythological figure. Removed from the actual experience, with the darkness of absence already having descended, this author found a way to breathe new life into the sparks of radiance that remained from the original light that had now disappeared. Perhaps there were others, who like him, also managed to enliven and animate the past in their own way and to continue the work of the first author. The success of this endeavor—the portrayal of their experience—is attested to by the fact that starting with the first generation of readers of the Zohar as a written work, many have experienced the world they encountered in its pages, and the figure of its central hero, with such intensity that this world became for them ultimate reality, and they saw themselves as its ongoing spiritual heirs.

The Companions of Rabbi Shim'on
in Their Own Eyes

Surrounding the figure of the great teacher is the intimate circle of the Companions—the circle of Rabbi Shim'on. The Companions (*Ḥevraya*) bask in his divine light and are the first to be influenced by their teacher's divine plenty. The existence of this circle is dependent entirely on the teacher's being. The Companions are able to attain the holy spirit (*ruaḥ ha-kodesh*) only by virtue of their proximity to their great master. As one of Rashbi's students attests: "As for me, who gave me the arousal of the holy spirit (*ruaḥ ha-kodesh*)? Through my being in the company of faithful prophets, the students of Rabbi Shim'on bar Yoḥai, for whom the upper and lower worlds tremor" (Zohar 2:154a).

The character of the circle emerges through narrative accounts in the Zohar, usually figuring only two or three of the Companions, and also through stories describing special occasions in which the entire circle, including their master, Rabbi Shim'on, assemble together—the most famous of these being the Great Assembly (Idra Rabba) and the Small Assembly (Idra Zuta). We also learn about the character of the circle through the Companions' sayings about themselves and through Rashbi's remarks about them. Through these descriptions, the requisite characteristics for membership in the circle are also defined. The different portraits of the Companions also provide the reader with an image of the ideal mystic according to the Zohar's composers. If we accept the hypothesis that a historical circle of mystics served as the source of inspiration for the Zohar's writing, then these images may shed much light on the self-perception of this otherwise unknown group.

The Companions are described with a panoply of images: They are the ones who entered and emerged; members of the Matronita's palace; the enlightened who shine like the *zohar* (radiance) of the sky; those who understand with understanding of the heart; the wise of heart; those who contemplate by themselves, from themselves; lovers and knights of Torah; the open-eyed; those who are aroused by the Torah; those who walk after the blessed Holy One; pillars of the world; masters of the secret of faith; those who turn darkness into light; and many others.

We will now explore some of the central images used to describe the circle.

*"Those who entered and emerged" (*man de-alu ve-nafku)

The Companions are described as "the ones who entered and emerged." This epithet immediately connects them to the foundational story of Jewish esoteric literature, "the four who entered the orchard (*pardes*)," which describes the ascent of four rabbinic sages into the world of divinity.[1] In all versions of this story, three of the four suffered. The first died, the second was injured, the third "cut the shoots" —usually understood as designating heresy; only the fourth, Rabbi Akiva, "entered in peace and emerged in peace."

The Companions, like Rabbi Akiva, are unique precisely in their ability to enter the world of divinity and the divine orchard of biblical exegesis and emerge unharmed.[2] Like Rabbi Akiva, they view themselves as lovers of God; and like him, their love of God is expressed through the special form of their love for the Torah. They meditate therein day and night. They believe that in every word—and indeed, in every letter—one may find supernal secrets.

The Companions' relationship with God and with the Torah has an intensely erotic character.[3] In this way too they demonstrate their fidelity to Rabbi Akiva, who, in famously claiming the superior sacredness of the Song of Songs over all other sacred writings, made way for interpreting that book as describing God's relationship with *Knesset Yisrael* (the Assembly of Israel). His remark was the inspiration for establishing kabbalistic language in general—and of the Zohar in particular—as the language of the young lovers in the Song of Songs.[4] Within this matrix of love, the Companions sometimes understand themselves as males vis-à-vis the female aspect of divinity, and sometimes as females vis-à-vis the male aspect of the divine.

Perhaps it is their ability to experience themselves as both male and female that further strengthens the Companions' identification with the mystic Rabbi Akiva, who, while quintessentially male, also displays feminine attributes in his relationship with God. Following his emergence from the *pardes*, the verse "The King has brought me into his chambers. Let us delight and rejoice in your love" (Song of Songs 1:4) is used to describe the erotic delight in God's inner chamber, with Rabbi Akiva presented as God's lover.[5]

In the erotic syntax of the Zohar, the epithet "those who entered and emerged" is also used to refer to those who have entered the secret of sexuality, to those who have been measured and balanced on the oscillating cosmic scales of the masculine and the feminine, the *mitkala*. On the simple earthly plane, "those who entered and emerged" refers to married men who have endeavored to bring children into the world. The unmarried are "those who have not entered," and the Zohar views self-imposed bachelorhood as a serious sin. For example, Nadab and Abihu, the ill-fated sons of Aaron (Leviticus 10:1–2), are described as "those who entered but did not emerge," in that they were not married and were not appropriately balanced between male and female—and therefore did not know how to minister to the female aspect of divinity.[6] On a deeper level, "entering and emerging in peace" also alludes to the encounter with dangerous or satanic sexuality and the ability to withstand its seductions—with entrance into this dimension being a prerequisite for perfection. It is along these lines that the Zohar reads the story of Jacob's departure from Beer-sheba toward Haran (*ḥaranah*; Genesis 28:10) as describing his encounter with the "other" (*ḥarna*) and therefore dangerous sexuality of the "woman of whoredom," and his subsequent emergence, a necessary part of his initiation into perfection.[7]

> Jacob had entered this gateway to faith. Adhering to that faith, he had to be tested in the same place his fathers had been tested, entering in peace and emerging in peace. Adam entered but was not careful. Seduced by her, he sinned with that whore of a woman, the primordial serpent. Noah entered but was not careful. . . . Abraham entered and emerged, as it is written, *And Abram went down to Egypt.* . . . *And Abram came up from Egypt* (Genesis 12:10, 13:1). Isaac entered and emerged, as it is written, *Isaac went to Abimelech, king of the Philistines in Gerar.* . . . *From there he went up to Be'er Sheva* (Genesis 26:1, 23). Jacob, having entered into faith, had to continue and probe the other side. For one who is saved from there is a loved one, a chosen one of the blessed Holy One. (Zohar 1:147b; Matt 1983, pp. 76–77)

In a more specific zoharic context, the expression "entered and emerged" refers also to the members of the circle who were present at the Idra Rabba, or at other previous gatherings in which awesome mysteries were revealed, and yet survived the experience intact.[8] Thus Rabbi Shim'on said: "All these *tikkunim* (expositions/adornments) and all these words I wish to reveal to the masters who have been measured by the measure, and not to those who have not entered (nor those who entered but did not emerge); rather, only to those who have entered and emerged" (Zohar 3:141a, *Idra Rabba*).

The Zohar explains the significance of the expression "those who entered and did not emerge." At the Great Assembly (Idra Rabba), the ten companions assemble for a once-in-a-lifetime event of disclosure of mysteries, at the end of which the souls of three companions depart. Regarding the nature of their deaths, the Zohar informs us that they died because at a previous gathering "they entered and did not emerge." Such language is the opposite of that used in the tannaitic account. It may be that like Ben Azzai in the *pardes* story—about whom it is said "he gazed and died"—these three companions entered the world of the divinity and met their death. It is also possible that "entered and did not emerge" refers to their not having left the previous gathering in a state of spiritual well-being, their souls more closely bound to divinity than to their bodies, perhaps paralleling Ben Zoma—about whom it is written "he gazed and was hurt."

The question arises, then, as to whether the Zohar ascribes a positive or negative value to those companions' deaths. If, as seems logical, Rabbi Akiva represents the ideal, then it is surely his emergence from the *pardes* that is a mark of his greatness, as opposed to those who did not merit to do so; and indeed, the Zohar raises the possibility that these companions did not emerge because of an improper or excessive disclosure of secrets.[9] If, on the other hand, non-emergence points to their great cleaving to the upper worlds, then their failure to emerge from the gathering is in fact a positive expression of the total and final cleaving of their souls to the divine: death by the kiss of God. Death by divine kiss is viewed by the Zohar as a mark of great esteem. Such a death, as we have already seen in our discussion of Rashbi's departure from the world, constitutes a theurgic act of awesome power. The ascending soul becomes an arousing, erotic agent for the sefirah *Malkhut*, and thereby arouses the male aspect of divinity toward her, until the longed-for union between the two is achieved, bringing *tikkun* (rectification/healing) for God and for all reality.[10]

Positive interpretations for this kind of ecstatic death notwithstanding, the Zohar prefers mystical practitioners who know the secret of "entering and emerging" from the mysterious world of divinity in peace. The following passage describes the special qualities reserved for the mystic who knows this secret.

> Happy is the portion of the one who enters and emerges, and who knows how to contemplate the mysteries of his Master and to cleave to Him! Through these mysteries a person is able to cleave to his Master, to know the perfection of wisdom through the supernal mystery.
>
> When he worships his Master in prayer with desire and with intention of the heart, then his desire will cling like the flame to the coal, to unite those lower firmaments of the side of holiness, to adorn them with one lower name—and from there beyond, to unite those upper, internal firmaments so that all should be one. . . .
>
> While his mouth and lips are still moving, he should direct his heart; and his desire shall ascend ever upward to unite all through the mystery of mysteries . . . through the mystery that abides in *Ein Sof*. . . . at night, he shall imagine himself as though he has departed this world, and his soul will leave him and he will restore it to the Lord of all. (Zohar 2:213b)

The continuation of this homily describes the nocturnal journey of the one who "enters and emerges" that takes place while the body sleeps. According to the Zohar, at night the soul ascends to the upper worlds, where it encounters various celestial officers. If deemed worthy, the soul passes to the secret place of the point (*Malkhut*) that comprises all the souls "as if swallowing something, becoming impregnated like a woman conceiving." Thereafter this point gives birth to the renewed souls that descend to awaken in the morning in their respective bodies.

From this homily it becomes clear that the epithet "enter and emerge" is not applicable to someone who has had a one-time experience of the divine, but rather is used to describe he who is familiar with, and lives according to, the sublime mysteries of divine unification. In this way the soul is able to experience divine worlds every night—through which it can be renewed and reborn every day.

The epithet "enter and emerge" beautifully conveys the intimacy between the mystic and God, insofar as it is the mystic who comes and goes from God's palace and innermost chambers as though he were a member of the family.[11] In the above homily describing the *kavvanot* (intentions) of the worshipper, "the one who enters and emerges" refers to the mystic who has learned the supernal secrets of existence without losing his grip on reality: "While his mouth and lips are still moving, he should direct his heart; and his desire shall ascend ever upward to unite all through the mystery of mysteries . . . through the mystery that abides in *Ein Sof*." Be it in prayer or in the mysteries of Torah study from midnight to dawn, the companion must know both how to enter the supernal secret that ascends to the Garden of Eden or to *Ein Sof* and how to return to this world in peace.[12]

"The wise of heart" (Ḥakhmei ha-Lev)

Another epithet employed by the Zohar to describe the companions is *ḥakhmei ha-lev* (the wise of heart). This designation is of particular interest because of its fascinating artistic, prophetic, and mystical resonances. In the Bible, the terms "the wise of heart" and "wisdom of the heart" are connected with artists and artisans. The tabernacle and all its vessels and the priestly garments are all made by people so described (Exodus 28:3).[13] In the Zohar, Rashbi interprets this "wisdom of the heart" as a form of prophecy and divine inspiration.

> Rabbi Shim'on said: *And you shall speak to all the wise of heart, for I have filled him with the spirit of wisdom* (Exodus 28:3).
>
> It should have said "I have filled *them*," but *I have filled him* [or: *it*] is written. This refers to the heart.
>
> *Whom I have filled with the spirit of wisdom*—as is said: *The spirit of YHVH shall alight upon him, a spirit of wisdom* (Isaiah 11:2).
>
> *And you shall speak to all the wise of heart*—since they do not do anything until the holy spirit speaks within them and whispers to them a whisper, and then they begin to act. (Zohar 2:179b)

In the Bible, the "wise of heart" are the builders of the material tabernacle; in the Zohar, they are the creators of the spiritual tabernacle. The "wise of heart" know the secret of the indwelling of the divine presence in the world, and their gift is their ability to give expression to hidden and supernal divine worlds, usually concealed from this world: "From the beginning of the world to the end of the world, those 'wise of heart' speak of those hidden levels, even though they are unknown" (Zohar 2:137a).

In the same vein, Rabbi Yose interprets the verse "And let all among you who are wise of heart come and make all that YHVH has commanded" (Exodus 35:10), also dealing with the construction of the tabernacle to highlight the unique qualities of "wisdom of the heart." He explains: "*Wise of heart* precisely! Wise in the heart and not in another place, for it [wisdom] abides in the heart" (Zohar 2:201a).

According to the Zohar, certain mysteries can be revealed only to those who possess "wisdom of the heart." The mysterious secrets of emanation, for example, are revealed to the heart alone, and not to the intellect;[14] so too the deeper recesses of divinity, the sefirot of *Binah* (Understanding) and *Hokhmah* (Wisdom), are accessible only through the discernment of the heart, "for the heart knows and understands [these things], even though [they are] not seen."[15]

The most poetic instance of this epithet is found in the parable of the beautiful maiden in *Sava de-Mishpatim* (see below, pp. 149–50). Here, the "wise of heart" is the lover, who out of his great love walks around the palace of his beloved, and in return for his perseverance finally merits to enter and become her (the Torah's) lover. This parable firmly establishes the connection between man and the Torah (Shekhinah) as rooted in love. Such love, according to the parable, awakens and arouses the lover's heart and soul. Indeed, in this parable, it is the mind and intellect that are confused— only the heart knows its true purpose.

The decision to view the *heart* as the locus of mystical wisdom—and not, for example, the mind or the intellect—establishes for the mystics the foundations of religious life in *love* rather than in *knowledge*, as was the case with Jewish philosophers. It is also possible that the use of the term "wise of heart" is the result of the influence of Sufism, which saw the heart as the seat of religious worship—such influence being well documented in Baḥya ibn Pakuda's *Ḥovot ha-Levavot* (Duties of the Heart) and among the circle of Jewish Sufis to which Abraham the son of Maimonides belonged.[16]

"Initiates of Matronita's palace" (Bnei Heikhal ha-Matronita): The Bridesmaids

The members of the circle are also described as "initiates (or sons) of Matronita's palace." In Aramaic, *matronita* means "matron, queen, lady." In the sefirotic system, Matronita designates the sefirah *Malkhut*, the tenth and final sefirah in the emanatory system—that is, *Knesset Yisrael*, Shekhinah, the partner of the blessed Holy One.[17] As the divine grade with which the human being must first come into contact—and as the precondition for ascent to the higher contemplative levels of mystical experience—Shekhinah is one of the central preoccupations of the Companions. She is quintessentially feminine, and the kabbalists' relationship with her is akin to that of a queen, a mother, a lover, and a wife.

As we shall see below, *Malkhut* is also designated as the state of consciousness and spiritual attainment known as "gazing through the speculum that does not shine," "dwelling in the house of God," "dwelling in the garden," "inheriting the earth," "standing at the opening of the eyes," and "entrance to the gate of God," among others. The state of consciousness that characterizes the sefirah *Malkhut* is dualistic, dynamic, verbal, erotic, and feminine; and in this state, higher states of consciousness and the higher levels of divinity are experienced as the reflections of light in a mirror, one of the chief symbols of *Malkhut* consciousness.[18]

In zoharic literature we find a range of prerequisites for preparing the human being for contact with this divine grade:[19] First and foremost, if the initiate is a Jewish male, he must be circumcised. Circumcision initiates the Jewish male into the covenant established between God and Abraham.

Under the influence of rabbinic and post-rabbinic conceptions, the Zohar understands the removal of the foreskin as inaugurating the transformation of the one undergoing the circumcision to a state of completion, wholeness, and worthiness of experiencing divine revelation. The Zohar frequently hails circumcision as a precondition for experiencing Shekhinah through its interpretation of "And your people, all of them righteous, shall inherit the earth for ever" (Isaiah 60:21). According to the Zohar, the word "righteous" refers to those who have been circumcised, and the word "earth" refers to the sefirah *Malkhut*.[20]

The person seeking access to *Malkhut* must also possess the appropriate balance of fear and love; he must be lawfully married and—by virtue of his wife—have gained knowledge of the world of eros and sexuality; and he must be stringent in upholding the Covenant, meaning that he must maintain a life of sexual purity.

What is common to all these preconditions is their association with qualities characteristic of the sefirah *Yesod* (that is, *tsaddik*, the cosmic righteous one). In order to know how to enter the feminine grade of the divine and behave appropriately there, the male must first perfect his masculine attributes—so that they resemble the attributes of the righteous one (*Yesod*).

Another means of joining with Shekhinah is through the act of imitating or resembling her. Shekhinah is understood by the Zohar as a feminine entity, poor and fragile, wandering from place to place, whose special time is the night. Thus, the mystic resembles and imitates her through choosing a life of poverty, through embarking on journeys and walking, and through being awake from midnight until dawn. This *imitatio* (to use the Latin term employed by scholars of religion) is an act of conscious identification; it contains also an element of consolation for, and aid to, Shekhinah as God's presence in the world. He who acts appropriately vis-à-vis this grade will enjoy and benefit from her goodness; furthermore, he will not be harmed by her. In zoharic mysticism, the "initiates of Matronita's palace" are those who are able to awaken and experience this state of consciousness.

The epithet "initiates of the palace" recalls the biblical verse "One thing I ask of YHVH, only that do I seek: to live in the house of YHVH all the days of my life, to gaze upon the beauty of YHVH, to frequent His palace (*heikhal*)" (Psalms 27:4), in which the kabbalists of the Zohar find the expression of numerous aspects of their mystical desire. The Companions attain this special rank of "initiates of the [bride's] palace" by employing a range of strategies, especially through studying Torah at night, as we shall see in detail below. The colorful myth of nightly Torah study and the mystical experiences associated with it are of great significance both for understanding zoharic self-perception and for appreciating the influence of the composition upon later generations of kabbalists.[21]

In the zoharic myth, the Companions take an active part in the life of Shekhinah, and in this connection the epithet "initiates (or sons) of the palace" also connotes a sense of intimacy. The mystics are members of the household, perhaps in a certain way even its heirs. They are neither strangers nor visitors but rather seek to dwell constantly in the palace. The sanctuary is often understood in the Zohar as the palace of Matronita, that is, Shekhinah.

In the Zohar's commentary to Lamentations, a profound elegy describes the experience of loss by *benei Tsiyyon* (the children of Zion), *benei ha-heikhal* (the initiates/sons of the palace), who are portrayed as little children searching for their mother among the ruins of her destroyed palace, the Temple. In this unit, the term *benei ha-heikhal* refers to those who live in the Land of Israel, the "children" of the blessed Holy One and Shekhinah, who together reside in the palace, the Temple, or in its ruins; those children are distinguished from their Diaspora brethren in Babylonia as a family member is distinguished from a servant.[22] The palace here is unmistakably the palace of the mother, the palace of motherly divinity, rather than the palace of God the Father.

In terms of their gender identity, the members of Matronita's palace are sometimes male and sometimes female. Sometimes they appear as bridesmaids, beautifying and adorning the bride, providing her with companionship, and finally escorting her—in all her radiance—to her beloved, the King.[23] In the story that appears in the Zohar's commentary on the Torah portion *Vayakhel*, the verses describing the convocation of the community and the request for donations for the tabernacle's construction are expounded in a most extraordinary manner. It includes the passage below, which describes the mystics as the generous of heart who bear the gift (*terumah*)—namely, Shekhinah—and raise her up (*leharim*) as a beloved bride to her husband, the blessed Holy One. The mystics are daringly described here as the maidens of the bride Shekhinah; without their help, she is unable to come to her husband.

> Come and see: When the desired time arises before the blessed Holy One to unite with the upper (alternative reading: lower) chariot, so that all will be one, then a voice emerges from that sublime, holy place called Heaven, and assembles all those holy ones from below, and all those holy mighty ones and the supernal camps, so that all are ready as one, as is written: *Moses convoked* (Exodus 35:1)—this is the secret of Heaven.
>
> *The whole Israelite community* (ibid.)—these are the twelve holy, supernal camps.
>
> *And said to them* (ibid.)—what did he say? This is the matter *Take from among you gifts* (*terumah*) (35:5)—prepare yourselves to raise up, and take upon yourselves, the glory of the holy throne, to raise it upward. Give from yourselves, honored ones, supernal, mighty ones, to raise up that gift (*terumah*), the secret of the holy throne, so that She will unite with the fathers (alternative reading: Her husband). For behold, Matronita is not fit to come to Her husband, except with those young women, Her maidens, who come with Her and escort Her until She reaches Her husband, as is written: *Maidens in her train, her companions* (Psalms 45:15). And what need is there for this? To bring Her to unite with Her husband. (Zohar 2:197b)

The mystics, however, are described not only as maidens. Indeed, they are also described as the (male) knights of the Matron, whose task is to erotically entertain and delight their queen, and in so doing, to arouse the passion and jealousy of Her husband.[24]

There are, then, two modes in the mystic's relationship with Shekhinah. The first involves standing opposite her as other, to complete her, as her erotic, male companion. The second involves devotion to and identification with her, typically through imitating her condition as a woman, friend, or intimate attendant.[25] This fluidity between masculine and feminine in the eros of the Zohar's kabbalists, as well as their ability as a group of men to identify sometimes as males and sometimes as females, reflects the same quality in the world of divinity and in the dynamic symbolic structure of the Zohar in general, in which maleness and femaleness are often characterized as dependent on context.

Often in the Zohar, maleness and femaleness appear as descriptions of states or situations rather than signifying the essential identity of things.[26] In the language of the Zohar, the feminine and the masculine are understood as states that are found, or ought to be found, in hierarchical, positional, erotic relationships—the "female" state designating the state of the bride, gathering and accepting; the "male" state representing kingship, control, giving, and influence. To give three examples:

- The sefirah *Malkhut* is female as she receives the divine flow from all the sefirot above her, yet she is male in her capacity as the divine ruler of the world.

- The sefirah *Binah* is female in that it is in her that the upper worlds (sefirot) gestate, having been fertilized by the seed of *Ḥokhmah*, while as the active source of the sefirot beneath her, she is considered "the world of the male" (*olam ha-zakhar*).

- When Rabbi Shim'on stands in the middle of his circle of students at the opening of the *Idra Rabba* to reveal and impart secrets, he is male; yet when he craves to give himself over to God through his interpretation of "I am my beloved's and his desire is for me" (Song of Songs 7:11), he has assumed a feminine state.[27]

The feminine and the masculine are therefore states of relation. (A later kabbalistic formulation, which speaks more of bestower and receiver than of male and female, perhaps blurs the erotic force of these variable states.)

It is difficult to overstate the religious significance of the Companions' self-designation as "initiates of Matronita's palace." The Zohar here defines the essence of its mystical endeavor in its turning toward the female dimension of divinity. Unlike the pietistic miracle workers of early rabbinic literature, who are always understood as sons of the King (*benei Melekh*), in the Zohar, it seems, God the Father has departed and vacated His place, with religious life now being conducted in relation to the divine presence remaining in the world, namely, God the Mother.

It was the Rabbis who had created the myth of the Shekhinah as the divine Presence that forever accompanies the people of Israel in all their exiles and in all their troubles. This attests to a profound religious creativity, through the creation of a divine figure with whom it would be possible to identify even in times of great crisis—the destruction of the Temple, the loss of national sovereignty, and the hardships of exile. In a most extraordinary way, the Zohar develops that mythic idea further, so that the destruction of the Temple now signifies the tragic moment when the cosmic harmony between masculine and feminine was lost. The Temple's destruction then signifies the destruction of the mythic partnership between God the Father and God the Mother in their home, the Temple, and in their bedroom (the Holy of Holies), with this separation causing the departure of the active presence of the divine male—the husband and father—in the world.

The kabbalists, nevertheless, find alternative ways to connect with the male Godhead and bring about His presence in the world—typically during moments of grace and reconciliation between Him and His beloved, Shekhinah. Even so, the center of gravity of religious life and worship has now moved to Shekhinah, exiled with Her children, whose compassionate yet wrathful presence never leaves them.[28]

The meaning, then, of the term "initiates of Matronita's palace" is identification with the female dimension of divinity, now present in the world, including the assumption of responsibility for her well-being.[29] And this idea took root in the consciousness of later kabbalists, finding expression in the thought of Moses Cordovero:

> The main intention of Rabbi Shim'on bar Yohai in writing the Zohar was this: Because Shekhinah is without *shefa* (abundance)—without support, with no one to help Her—he wanted to make a support for Her, to unite Her to

some degree (*yiḥud me'at*) with Her husband by virtue of the composition of the Zohar, in which he and his companions engage in the mysteries of the Torah—which brings about the unification of the blessed Holy One with His Shekhinah.[30]

*"The enlightened ones" (*Ha-maskilim*)*

The verse from Daniel that gave the Zohar its name, "And the enlightened (*maskilim*) will shine like the radiance of the sky; and those who lead many to righteousness, like the stars forever and ever" (Daniel 12:3), occupies a central place in the self-image of the Companions. In different parts of the Zohar there are unique and daring interpretations of this verse.[31] They will help us explain the significance of the Zohar's choice of the term *maskilim* as an appellation for the Companions, and its place in their self-perception. Here is one such interpretation:

> *The enlightened will shine*—who is enlightened? The wise one who contemplates from himself, by himself, words that human beings cannot mouth.
>
> *Will shine like the radiance of the sky*—which sky? The sky of Moses that stands in the center; this radiance (*zohar*) of his is concealed and not revealed. (Zohar 2:23a; Matt 2004–2007, vol. 4, pp. 79–80, adapted)[32]

The "enlightened" (*maskilim*) here, like those "who entered and emerged," are described in terms derived from the talmudic tractate *Ḥagigah*, in its attempt to define the requisite characteristics of those worthy to receive the secrets of *Ma'aseh Merkavah*—the corpus of mysteries pertaining to the divine realm: "One does not expound . . . about the *Merkavah* before a student unless he is wise (*ḥakham*) and understands by himself."[33] The *maskil* is a wise man, distinguished from and indeed superior to the prophet:[34] while the prophet sees and speaks by virtue of his connection with the sefirot *Netsaḥ* (Endurance) and *Hod* (Splendor, the seat of prophecy), the mystic stands above them and attains the divine reality through the divine grade of *Yesod* or the combination of *Yesod* and *Tiferet* (symbolized by Moses, the bestower of Torah).[35] The *maskilim*, then, are those who understand "by themselves" (the Aramaic of the Zohar might also mean "from themselves, through themselves, through their bodies, via their emotions, with all their being"—not merely involving their minds) things that ordinary language cannot describe or express. They understand these things and know how to speak about them.[36]

But what are these things that the *maskilim* know by and from themselves that cause them to shine? Different places in the Zohar convey the sense that they possess secret knowledge about reality; they are the "knowers," the "gnostics"; and their radiance is ascribed to their shining with the "secret of wisdom," namely, supernal wisdom.[37] According to the Zohar, there exists a non-worldly wisdom—a supernal, divine wisdom that is the inheritance of the *maskilim* alone. The radiance of the *maskilim* (like Moses) is the radiance of "the sky of Moses," which in zoharic symbolism usually represents the sefirah *Tiferet*. On the cognitive level, this sky is a state of consciousness or an aspect of reality whose light is concealed from ordinary states of consciousness.

Yehuda Liebes has drawn attention also to the following passage, in which the distinctiveness of the *maskil* is characterized not in terms of his possessing certain knowledge—that is, not in terms of his gnosis, but rather in terms of his ability to create and shine. In my opinion, this passage speaks not only about the *maskil's* power of creating, but also about his ability to employ a special kind of seeing. A homily in the *Tikkunim* section of *Zohar Ḥadash*,[*38] it explores the similarity of the Hebrew words *maskil* and *mistakel* (to see). It suggests that the *maskil* knows how to look within the Bible in such as way as to gain access to the mysterious secret world, to the dimension of reality known as "the world that is coming" (*olam ha-ba*). It is this unique form of seeing that crowns the *maskilim* with a special radiance shining upon them from the world of the mysteries of the Torah.

> *And the enlightened will shine*—who are the enlightened ones? Those who know how to look at the glory of their Master and know the secret of wisdom, [how] to enter without shame into the world that is coming. These shine like the supernal radiance.

---

* *Zohar Ḥadash* is a volume of zoharic materials that were not part of the Zohar's first printed editions in the mid-16th century. Rather, they were compiled by the kabbalists of Safed and printed for the first time in Salonika in 1597.

And it says *the enlightened* (*maskilim*) rather than *the knowers* (*yod'im*)—indeed, for these look at the concealed, inner secrets, that are not disclosed or transmitted to any person. Whoever merits to look at them with this understanding, shines, [for he] sparkles with the crown of the most supernal radiance. There is no radiance that shines like this. . . . this is the radiance of Torah, this is the radiance of the masters of wisdom who inherit that world that is above all. These exit and enter all the treasures of their Master, and there is no one to prevent them. All are overwhelmed [lit. ashamed] by their radiance. (*Zohar Ḥadash* 105a)

Another aspect of the term *maskil* emerges through the Companions' special connection with the sefirah *Malkhut*. The *maskilim* are called "pillars of the pavilion." In the Song of Songs (3:9), we read of the pavilion made by King Solomon from the trees of Lebanon. The Zohar interprets this verse as describing the perfection and completion of the sefirah *Malkhut* through all the sefirot above her with the help of the sefirah *Yesod*, a process that renders *Malkhut* into a perfect pavilion.[39] Seen in this light, the epithet "pillars of the pavilion" is similar to the epithet "initiates of Matronita's palace," insofar as the task of the *maskilim* is to take care of the particular and changing needs of Shekhinah.

This task also emerges through the Zohar's interpretation of "Happy is one who considers the poor" (*Ashrei maskil el dal*) (Psalms 41:2), where *dal* (poor) is interpreted as referring to the sefirah *Malkhut*, who in the sefirotic system possesses nothing of her own;[40] and *maskil* is interpreted as referring to one who takes upon himself a moral responsibility to study the ways of poverty, to recognize Shekhinah, to identify with her, to know her needs, and to support, adorn, and complete her.

This idea is not confined to the cognitive or spiritual domain. Identification with the needy of this world, and providing for their support and well-being, are among the chief obligations of the kabbalist. Furthermore, the Zohar cautions against the erroneous conception that it is possible to have authentic mystical experience that is not fostered by real physical acts in the material world of action. In discussing the supernal guests (*ushpizin*) who visit one's sukkah during the festival of Sukkot, the Zohar pours its fury upon he who would entertain the supernal, spiritual guests

without also generously tending to the material needs of the poor of this
world.

> *The enlightened will shine like the radiance of the sky*—these are the pillars and
> sockets of that pavilion. *The enlightened (maskilim)*—supernal pillars and sock-
> ets, contemplating in wisdom everything needed by that *pavilion* and its sup-
> ports. This mystery accords with what is said: *Happy is one who considers the
> poor* (Psalms 41:2).
>
> *Will shine*—for unless they shine and radiate, they cannot contemplate
> that *pavilion*, looking out for all its needs.
>
> *Like the radiance of the sky*—standing above *the enlightened*, of whom it is
> written: *An image above the heads of the living being: a sky like awesome ice* (Eze-
> kiel 1:22).
>
> *Zohar, Radiance*—illumining Torah. *Zohar*—illumining the *heads* of that
> *living being*. Those *heads* are *the enlightened* who constantly radiate and shine,
> contemplating that *sky*, the radiance flashing from there, radiance of Torah,
> sparkling constantly, never ceasing. (Zohar 1:15b–16a; Matt 2004–2007, vol. 1,
> pp. 117–18)[41]

Interestingly, in this passage the words "will shine" from the verse in Daniel are interpreted not as a prize or trait awaiting the *maskil* because of his
special qualities, but rather are inherent in being a *maskil*. He shines so as to
be able to fulfill his destiny. In order to care for and support the pavilion, he
needs an intensified seeing, a particular radiance, that strengthens his powers
of distinction connected to *Malkhut*.

In this passage, as in many other interpretations of this verse, the radiance
that shines among the *maskilim* is the radiance of the Torah. In Rabbi Moses
de León's *Shekel ha-Kodesh*, we find an interesting parallel:

> For He (may He be blessed) made manifest the mystery of His being and
> emanated the radiance of the *ispaklarya* (speculum) that He drew forth from
> His light. And even so, the worlds could not endure Him, until He created
> light for His light, and created worlds; and this light is called garment. . . . and
> it is true that the mystery of these matters He gave to the wise who know
> religion and law, to gaze at and contemplate the supernal matters, for the
> mystery of His being, He (may He be blessed) made manifest to sustain the
> worlds. . . . and no one can apprehend His truth (may He be blessed), only a
> fraction of the paths of being that He made manifest. In sum, when the wise
> *maskil* arouses himself to investigate and to know the nature of truth, he may
> apprehend only a small fraction of the truth of His being.[42]

In the words of Rabbi Moses de León, who frequently employs the epithet *maskilim* to describe the kabbalists of his own day, the task of the *maskil*, as in the Zohar, is to reflect on and contemplate supernal matters. Contemplation (*iyyun*) and gazing (*histaklut*)—cognitive terms derived from seeing and vision—are the traits of the wise and the *maskilim*. The secret that has been transmitted to them comprises means of employing this capacity of gazing and contemplation—not only in matters pertaining to this world, but also to the supernal world—so as to attain some part of the truth of God's being, and not merely the paths of His being. The significance of this passage from *Shekel ha-Kodesh* lies in the fact that the *maskilim* described therein refer not to mystical masters from the ancient world, but rather to real figures from de León's own day. In Moses de León's consciousness, mystical enlightenment did not cease in the tannaitic period, but rather is alive and flourishing in his own day.[43]

> *And the enlightened will shine like the radiance of the sky*—these are those who engage Torah and contemplate words of Torah with desire and murmuring of the heart.
>
> *The enlightened*—who contemplate, yet do not contemplate only the matter (or: word) itself, but rather contemplate the place on which that matter depends, for there is no matter that is not dependent on another supernal mystery. And they find in that matter another matter of supernal mystery. From within the speculum that does not shine, he will find and see the mystery of the speculum that shines.
>
> And your sign: *He who broods (maskil) over the matter (davar) will find good* (Proverbs 16:20).
>
> *Matter (davar)*—this is the speculum that does not shine.
>
> *Will find good*—this is the speculum that shines.
>
> It is written *broods over the matter* and not "on the matter," rather *over the matter*, for he seeks to gaze at that which is above. And this is the meaning of *like the radiance of the sky*—the sky that is known, above the creatures below. For from within this sky he will gaze at that sparkling radiance, the radiance of the supernal radiances, the radiance that emerges from the supernal point, and will shine and sparkle with the radiance of all the lights from all directions. (*Zohar Ḥadash, Tikkunim* 105c)[44]

The enlightened are distinguished in that they alone know how to look at the words of the Torah, not only in their revealed mode, but also in all contexts, extending to their root within the Godhead. In the words of this extraordinary homily, the mystics are those who contemplate "over the matter (or: word)" (*al davar*), meaning beyond the realm of speech—beyond the sefirah *Malkhut*, the "speculum that does not shine." The task of the *maskil* is to pass from an understanding of reality from within the state of consciousness known as the "speculum that does not shine" to a state of consciousness and seeing through the mystery of the "speculum that shines."

In this particular passage, the verse from Daniel describes the process of mystical attainment and apprehension: the mystic's perseverance in contemplating the source from which things derive brings him to attain and shine—not only with the radiance of the sky (*Tiferet*) that is above him, but rather, with the radiance that is beyond the sky, which shines and sparkles from within. There is particular beauty in the way this description of the process of abstract theosophical contemplation recalls the imaginative experience of gazing at the night sky—sometimes compared to a dark canvas, in which the stars appear as tiny holes through which shines a light, seemingly from above.

In the unique poetics of the Jewish mystical tradition, the radiance of the sky and the light of the stars are seen as the light of the Torah. In this connection, mention should be made of another image drawing on the theme of the night sky: Contemplation of the canvas of the Torah scroll and its letters as forms through which the divine light illumines and shines, flowing continuously throughout all existence, like the river issuing from Eden, from the most hidden point within the divine.

Awakeners and Arousers

An entire chapter of this book is devoted to the themes of awakening and arousal and thus I will discuss here only the essential meaning of these terms.[45] The Companions of the Zohar see themselves as awake in a world characterized by sleep. They are unique in that their consciousness, their minds, their souls, and their hearts are awake, while the rest of humanity is in a state of deep slumber. They are the "open-eyed" who see the foundation of existence, and by virtue of their being "full of eyes" they understand the secret dimension of the Torah.

The members of the circle are able to awaken and arouse themselves, to awaken and arouse others, and especially to awaken and arouse the words of Torah. They are aroused by the Torah (which they see as their beloved) and in turn cause her to be aroused and to impart her secrets to her lovers—a mutual erotic arousal of the learner and the Torah. In their act of arousal, the Companions know how to generate the ultimate arousal of reality. This awakening is a kind of cosmic law in which the upper world is aroused and pours forth its bounty in response to the arousal of the world below, the world of humanity. *It'aruta de-le'ila* (the arousal above) is dependent on the power of *it'aruta de-letata* (the arousal below), and this arousal represents one of the key aims and quests of the Companions.

"Those who turn darkness into light . . ."

In one of the utterances of the Zohar's heavenly herald, we learn some important characteristics of the zoharic mystic: "Who among you turns darkness into light, bitter into sweet before arriving here? Who among you awaits each day the light that shines when the King visits the doe and is glorified—declared King of all kings of the world? Whoever does not await this each day in that world has no portion here."[46] This passage is perhaps an ironic paraphrase of a verse in Isaiah: "Ah, those who call evil good, and good evil; who present darkness as light and light as darkness; who present bitter as sweet and sweet as bitter!" (5:20). In its biblical context, this verse describes a lack, an inability of discernment; whereas the Zohar, it seems, emphasizes that which comes after discernment—the ability to penetrate to the inner meaning of things, and the ability to bring about a transformation in the qualities of reality.

It is also possible that this passage refers to Maimonides' opening words of the second chapter of *Hilkhot De'ot* (Lore of Insight) in the *Mishneh Torah*:

> To those who are physically ill, the bitter tastes sweet and the sweet bitter. . . . [The verse from Isaiah follows, as well as a description of the morally ill.]
>
> What is the remedy for the morally ill? They should go to the wise, for they are the healers of souls. They will heal them by teaching them proper traits, until they return to the good path.

Whereas Maimonides advocates the golden mean so as to enable divine worship without unnecessary interruptions, the divine voice in the Zohar seeks, on the contrary, to summon those who are not moderate, but rather those who are able—through a supreme religious effort—to transform the evil, darkness, and bitterness of existence into goodness, light, and sweetness. The Zohar thus demands from the mystic a religious, mystical fervor in all its power.[47]

Those who turn darkness into light   The ability to transform the world's qualities is among the unique characteristics of the zoharic mystic. The mystic knows how to reveal the light amid the darkness and even how to transform the darkness itself into light. In the Zohar, light and darkness are fundamental symbols for good and evil, holiness and impurity. Sometimes, darkness and evil are understood as forces operative in reality that ought to be avoided, while in other places, the Zohar suggests that they must be confronted, their domain entered. In terms of their function in reality, darkness and evil are also the shadow image, the underside of light and good, and they are thus vital so as to enable a true understanding of the essence and meaning of things.

> Just as light benefits from darkness; for were it not for the darkness, the light would be unrecognized—and the world would gain no benefit from it. (Zohar 3:47b)

Sometimes the need for evil emerges through a most extreme definition of religious existence:

> There is no light except that which emerges from darkness. . . . and there is no worship of the blessed Holy One except that which comes from darkness, and there is no good except that which comes from evil. (Zohar 2:184a)[48]

In defining the mystic as one who can transform darkness into light, we encounter the radical idea whereby the mystic must not only be able to overcome and subdue evil, but rather be able to transform evil into good.[49]

Those who taste the bitter as sweet   This epithet can be understood in two distinct ways. According to the first reading, this term, drawn from the language of taste, is synonymous with the expression "those who turn darkness into light." The second reading understands the epithet as referring to those who taste the sweet *amid* the bitter. The mystic knows that an envelope of bitterness encases the divine sweetness, yet knows how to reach the sweet, divine essence hidden within the layers of the world's bitterness. The mystic then, is he who has internalized the verse "O taste and see that YHVH is good" (Psalms 34:9). While it is usual for the experience of worldly bitterness to lead a person to doubt God's goodness, the mystic is characterized not only by his knowledge of the existence of divine sweetness, but also by his ability to taste it amid the bitterness. In this sensuous description of the mystic as the one who tastes the divine, one hears an echo of the verse from the Song of Songs that describes the experience of longing and love: "I delight to sit in his shade, and his fruit is sweet to my mouth" (2:3).

Those who await each day the light that shines when the King visits the doe   This epithet gives expression to the trait of perseverance and boundless yearning so central to the Zohar.[50] The mystic is he who yearns and waits, without despairing, for those moments when the world will be saturated with the revelation of God and the influx of divine flow, when the King visits his beloved doe, Shekhinah, and couples with her. The mystic hopes for, and indeed acts so as to bring about, those moments of grace when the female and male aspects of divinity will unite and pour forth their plenty upon the world and upon the soul of the witness to this union. In the Zohar, the light of these moments of love is the light of dawn, prior to the world's inundation with the strong light of the sun. It is in this soft, dim light of dawn that the union occurs, before the inevitable separation of the day from the night.[51] The mystic who perseveres in devotional practice at the hours of dawn, when light is mingled with darkness, merits a higher state called the "white light" or the "speculum that shines."

> *O God, you are my God, I search for you* (ashaḥareka) (Psalms 63:2). . . . —I will array the light that illumines at dawn (shaḥar); for behold, the light that appears at dawn does not illumine until it is arrayed below.
>
> And whosoever arrays this dawn light, even though it is black (shaḥor), attains the illuminating white light; and this is the light of the speculum that shines, and such a person attains the world that is coming.

This is the mystery of *and those who seek me will find me* (*u-mshaharai yimtsa 'uneni*) (Proverbs 8:17).

U-mshaharai (*those who seek me*)—who array the black light of dawn.

Yimtsa 'uneni (*will find me*)—It is not written *yimtsa 'uni* (with one *nun*), but rather *yimtsa 'uneni* (with two *nuns*)—he merits two lights: the black light of dawn, and the illuminating white light.

And he attains the speculum that does not shine and the speculum that shines—that is why it is written *yimtsa 'uneni*. (Zohar 2:140a)[52]

This passage outlines the nature and process of the mystical path. The *maskil*, wise of heart, "arrays"* the black light of dawn,[53] and in so doing ascends to the state of consciousness known as the "speculum that does not shine"—the dimension of the sefirah *Malkhut*. Working within this dimension he attains and ascends to a higher level—the "speculum that shines," the symbol of the sefirah *Tiferet*.

The great task of *tikkun* and the belief that through adorning and arraying the black light, one will ultimately reach the white light, are among the key characteristics of the Companions.[54] This persistent optimism and the belief that ultimately good will win out are not optional traits for the mystic. Rather, they are among his chief obligations. The obligation to await each night the dawning of the new day is a profound symbol for hope in the coming of redemption, at both the national and personal-spiritual level. This great hope and yearning can also be heard in the words of Judah Halevi in his famous Ode to Zion:[55]

Happy is he who waits and lives to see
your light rising, your dawn breaking
forth over him!

---

* In the Zohar, to "array" light most often means to garb it so that it may be experienced without danger of over-exposure.

3

"Happy is this generation"

The Three Generations with Which the Zoharic Circle Identifies

As we have already seen, surrounding the figure of Rabbi Shim'on is the circle of mystics, the Companions; surrounding them is yet a broader circle still: the entire generation of Rabbi Shim'on bar Yoḥai. It is important to be familiar with the unique characteristics of this generation in order to understand the significance that the Zohar ascribes to it, as well as its place within the framework of historical and messianic consciousness.

The Companions understand the time in which they live as a special age (reckoning human history from the time of Adam until the coming of the Messiah), in which the thick clouds that usually cover the skies of consciousness have departed, the skies are opened, and the present generation merits—through the special light now discernable—visions of the living God. Matters that had been concealed throughout the ages are now suddenly revealed to Rabbi Shim'on's generation.

While the Zohar certainly understands its own generation as possessing a new consciousness, it does not, however, view its own age as inaugurating the Messianic Era, but rather as one chapter—unique, to be sure—heralding a breakthrough in human consciousness and thus paving the way for messianic times.[1] Just as this new consciousness arose and flourished, so it will cease and come to an end, to be followed by a period of darkness and closure, in which the light experienced by the current generation will be sealed and hidden away. According to the Zohar, the uniqueness of this generation lies precisely in the fact that there will be none like it until the generation of the Messiah.

This peculiar consciousness of the Zohar, which presents the fruit of its own labors as a teaching (*torah*) that is destined to be forgotten, recalls the first-century declaration of the sages of Yavneh, in their assembling to create the new Torah of the oral law, that their teaching (*torah*) too was destined to be forgotten.[2] The Companions of the Zohar live with the consciousness that of the mysteries revealed in their generation, only an essence—a jar containing the manna of Rabbi Shim'on's teachings—will remain.[3]

It is from this vantage point that the authors of the Zohar identify with a number of unique generations across the span of Jewish history—periods in which spiritual consciousness attained new heights:

1. The generation of Moses, the wilderness generation, *dor de'ah* (the generation of knowledge)—distinguished by their experience of the continuous presence of the divine.

2. The generation of King Solomon: the generation of place, center, and temple; a generation of perfection and wholeness, and of the revelation of mysteries in every word; a generation symbolized by the full moon.

3. The generation of the tanna Rabbi Shim'on bar Yoḥai, the generation responsible for the creation of the oral Torah.

The authors of the Zohar identify profoundly with the latter generation; they experience themselves as Jews of antiquity living in the Land of Israel, and they create from within that inspired horizon.[4]

The Wilderness Generation

The wilderness generation has been the subject of piercing criticism both in the Bible itself and in rabbinic thought; indeed, according to one view, the members of that generation have no portion in the World to Come.[5] This negative view is traced to their stubbornness despite having merited the divine presence in their midst, their endless complaints and their desire to return to Egypt, and above all, because of their identification with the spies who spoke slanderously about the land of Israel.

In the Zohar, on the other hand, we encounter an unbridled admiration for this generation,[6] especially apparent in the literary unit called *Rav Metivta* (Master of the Academy).[7] In this unit, the members of Rashbi's circle embark on a wondrous journey to the upper worlds, where they meet the wilderness generation and its leaders in their astral existence. The Companions observe them learning and praying in their celestial academies, performing various rituals in extraordinary celestial festivities. The author of this zoharic unit creatively drew upon and developed the rabbinic midrashim on those who perished in the wilderness,[8] interpreting the punishment decreed upon this generation after the incident of the spies—to die in the wilderness and not to enter the Land of Israel—as a ritual act whose purpose was to purge and purify. In a daring interpretation, the verses outlining the divine decree, "In this wilderness they will come to an end (*yittamu*), there they will die" (Numbers 14:35) and "In this wilderness shall your corpses fall" (ibid., 29), are interpreted as referring to the way in which the members of this generation merit the eternal life of the soul that follows the death of the body, and to their attaining perfection and completeness—the word *yittamu* being interpreted as signifying wholeness (*tam*).[9] Night after night, through the ritual act of digging a grave for themselves, entering within, and then emerging, their deficiencies fall away (*yipplu figreikhem*)—the noun *peger* being interpreted by this unit's composer as referring to deficiencies—thus leaving only their purified essence.[10] The Companions are amazed by the extraordinary things they see and learn in this unique, celestial reality, and their celestial guides explain to them the greatness of the wilderness generation.

> Do you see those mountains? They are all the Heads of the Academies of this people in the wilderness. And they merit now what they did not merit when they were alive. And every New Month, Shabbat, and festival, these Heads of the Academies assemble at the mountain of Aaron the Priest and are aroused by him. They enter his academy and are reinvigorated there with the purity of the holy dew that descends upon his head and with the anointing oil that

flows upon him, and with him they are all renewed with the rejuvenation beloved of the Holy King; so the place is called The Academy of Love. . . . all the righteous women of this generation also come to Miriam during those times and then they all ascend like pillars of smoke in this wilderness. . . . Happy is this generation more than all the generations of the world! . . . about this generation is written: *Happy are the people who have it so, happy the people whose God is YHVH!* (Psalms 144:15). (Zohar 3:163a)

The generation of giants,[11] the generation without land, which lived with the revealed presence of God and beheld Him eye to eye, is understood by the Zohar's composers to have no peer in the annals of Jewish history.[12] The wilderness generation has no physical inheritance in the world; its inheritance rather, is the divine itself. Indeed, the Rabbis already claimed that "what a maidservant saw at the Sea, not even Ezekiel the son of Buzi saw,"[13] and it is with this unusual ability to see the divine that the Zohar so strongly identifies.

At the end of their journey, the Companions are privy to a spectacular, sensory experience of celestial sights and sounds, in which they hear biblical verses recalling Israel's sojourn in the wilderness; like the wilderness generation, the Companions too are vouchsafed a vision of the divine glory.

When day broke, a voice was aroused as before and said, "O Nation mighty as a lion, whose men are like tigers, ascribe glory to your Master, as is written: *Therefore a fierce people must honor you!* (Isaiah 25:3)." . . .

[The Companions] turned their heads and saw the entire desert enveloped by clouds of glory, shining and sparkling with many colors. They said to one another, "Certainly the blessed Holy One wishes to be praised through the praises of the wilderness generation. For never has there been in the world a supernal generation like this one, nor will there be another until King Messiah comes. Certainly all that the blessed Holy One has shown us was only to inform us of their Master's love for them, to inform us that they have a good portion, and that they have a place in the World to Come; and that in the future, when the blessed Holy One raises the dead, these are destined to be revived first, as is written: *O let Your dead revive* (Isaiah 26:19)." (Zohar 3:168b)

The wilderness generation serves as a source of profound inspiration for the generation of the Zohar; indeed, the food of that generation, namely, manna, is the subject of frequent interpretation in the Zohar.[14] The Zohar understands the eating of manna as testament to the high, spiritual consciousness of the members of the wilderness generation, who merited eating "bread from heaven," divine sustenance that opened them to experiences of the divine. As opposed to the Bible, where the manna is understood as a test—to see whether the people can in fact live not by the work of their own hands, nor by gathering and storing, but rather by believing each day that God will provide the heavenly food (Deuteronomy 8:3)—in the Zohar, this kind of existence represents the Companions' greatest desire. According to the Zohar, the ingestion of manna signifies the ability to be sustained by "that which comes from YHVH" and not that which derives from material existence. Like the people of the wilderness generation, the members of Rashbi's circle also merit being nourished by the spiritual food of the heavens, and indeed from beyond the heavens—from the finest of the fine nourishment that trickles from the skull of *Atika Kadisha* (the Holy Ancient One), described as the crystal dew or the seed of *Atika*:

> Every single day, dew trickles down from the Holy Ancient One [*Atika Kadisha*] to the Impatient One [*Ze'eir Anpin*], and the Orchard of Apple Trees [Shekhinah] is blessed. Some of the dew flows to those below. . . . Israel ate of that food in the wilderness.
>
> Rabbi Shim'on said: Some people are nourished by it even now! Who are they? The Companions who engage Torah day and night. . . .
>
> The highest food of all is the food of the Companions, those who engage Torah. For they eat food of the spirit and soul-breath; they eat no food for the body at all. Rather from a high sphere, precious beyond all: Wisdom . . . from that sphere called the sweetness of God. . . . Why from this sphere? Because Torah derives from Wisdom on high, and those who engage Torah enter the source of her roots; so their food flows down from that high and holy sphere. . . . At that time, the holy dew trickles down from the concealed Ancient One and fills the head of the Impatient One, the sphere called Heaven. And from that dew of the supernal, holy light, the manna was drawn forth and would descend below. . . . all those sons of faith go out and gather, and praise the holy name for it; and that manna would emit all the fragrances of the Garden of Eden, through which it had passed when it descended below. . . . Then he is blessed to his core and contemplates and knows above and gazes at the supernal wisdom; and because of this they are called the generation of knowledge (*dor de'ah*). And these were the initiates of faith—and to them the Torah was given, to contemplate her and know her ways. (Zohar 2:61b)

The Companions see themselves as a group who out of great hunger—not for bread, but rather for the living presence of the divine—chose to turn their back on the earth and to surrender their fate to heaven. They do not toil to bring forth bread from the earth; rather, they gather the heavenly manna. This turning to spiritual nourishment is in itself an act of faith, an affirmation that such nourishment will indeed be found and will satiate the hungry.

In the Zohar's commentary to the portion *Vayeḥi* that discusses the death of the patriarch Jacob (and at the same time the death of Rabbi Shim'on), we encounter yet again a deep identification with the wilderness generation. In the story that tells of the Companions' experience of great loss after the death of their teacher, Rabbi Shim'on is described as "the millstones with which fine manna is ground." This appellation is connected with his special rank, namely, his association with the sefirah *Yesod* and to his being the earthly manifestation of this divine grade. In the Zohar the millstones are a symbol for the sefirot *Netsaḥ* and *Hod*; they symbolize the function of the testicles—where sperm is stored to be discharged at the appropriate time through the male sexual organ into the womb of the female. Rashbi is portrayed here in sexual terms as the male power that fertilizes the entire generation, and this fertilization is precisely the nourishment needed by his generation. The members of Rashbi's generation, like the members of the wilderness generation, merited every day to taste the divine manna— ground up for them by their leader—each according to his need and ability. Rashbi's greatness was such that in his generation, "The one with the least gathered ten *ḥomers*" (Numbers 11:32).[15] Expressed differently, the revealed divine flow was so abundant in this generation that even the simple experienced its bounty. Yet paralleling the magnitude of the divine flow accompanying Rabbi Shim'on's presence in the world is the overwhelming sense of drought and lack that accompanies his death.

> [Rabbi Yose said,] "Rabbi Abba raised his hands to his head and wept, and said, 'Rabbi Shim'on, the millstones with which fine manna is ground every day, and then gathered, as is written: *The one with the least gathered ten ḥomers* (Numbers 11:32)! Now millstones and manna have disappeared; nothing remains of them in the world except what is written: *Take one jar and put in it a full omer of manna and set it before YHVH for safekeeping* (Exodus 16:33)—it is

not written *revealed* but rather *for safekeeping*, for concealment. Now who can reveal secrets, and who will know them?" (Zohar 1:217a; Matt 2004–2007, vol. 3, pp. 308–9)

Of the manna, only a small amount (an *omer*ful) remains for a keepsake; and even this, it seems, will be lost to the world.[16]

The zoharic Companions identify deeply with the world of the wilderness generation on many different levels. Just as the religious consciousness of the wilderness generation was not, according to the Zohar, confined to a holy place—to a specific patch of earth (and therefore this generation does not enter the promised land)—so the Companions see themselves as attaining their religious experiences beyond the horizons of the Land of Israel. They look upon the members of the wilderness generation as partners, who like them experienced the eruption of a new religious consciousness.[17] Like them, they live with the consciousness that God is ever present among them, and that connection with Him is their spiritual patrimony. According to the Bible, the entire wilderness generation merited an unmediated experience of the presence of the divine; likewise the generation of Rabbi Shim'on bar Yoḥai is described as an age in which even the simple folk among the people, and even nature itself, are filled with divine wisdom. Above all, just as the wilderness generation, that "fierce people," merited the faithful shepherd Moses[18] as their leader, so the generation of the Zohar merits Rabbi Shim'on bar Yoḥai as its teacher and leader.

Rabbi Ḥiyya opened and said: *YHVH said to Moses, "You are soon to lie with your fathers"* (Deuteronomy 31:16).

Come and see: As long as Moses was present in the world, he would chastise Israel so that they would not be found guilty before the blessed Holy One. And since Moses was present among them, there will never be a generation like that one until the generation when King Messiah comes—when they will see the glory of God as they did, for they attained what no other generation has ever attained.

We have taught: A handmaiden at the sea saw what Ezekiel the prophet never saw.

If they attained so much—all the more so the women of Israel, their children, the men, the Sanhedrin, the princes! And all the more so the supernal, faithful prophet Moses, who is higher than them all!

And now, if these donkey drivers of the wilderness possess so much wisdom, all the more so the wise of this generation, and all the more so those who stand before Rabbi Shim'on and learn from him every day, and all the more so Rabbi Shim'on—who is supreme above all!

After Moses died, what is written? *The people will go astray* (Deuteronomy 31:16). Woe to the world when Rabbi Shim'on will depart! For the springs of wisdom will be sealed to the world, and a person will seek a word of wisdom and will not find anyone who can speak. And the whole world will err in Torah, for there will not be found among them anyone to be aroused in wisdom.

About this time is written: *If it is that the whole community of Israel has erred* (Leviticus 4:13)—and if they err in Torah and do not know her way about some matter, *since the matter is concealed from the congregation* (ibid.), for they cannot find anyone who knows how to reveal the profundity of Torah and her ways. Woe to those generations who are present then in the world!

Rabbi Yehudah said: The blessed Holy One is destined to reveal profound mysteries of Torah in the time of King Messiah, *For the land shall be filled with knowledge of YHVH as water covers the sea* (Isaiah 11:9), and it is written: *No longer will they need to teach one another and say to one another, "Know YHVH," for all of them, from the least of them to the greatest shall know me* (Jeremiah 31:33). Amen, may it be so![19] (Zohar 3:22b–23a)

In another part of the Zohar comparing the spiritual level of Moses with that of the patriarch Jacob, Moses' special rank is defined by virtue of his having actually ministered to Shekhinah in this world, while Jacob ministered to her in a symbolic fashion alone. While discussing the greatness of Moses, the Zohar points out that the members of the wilderness generation did not need to enter the Land of Israel because the whole matter of entering the Land was for the restoration of Shekhinah, whereas the members of this generation, because of Moses, merited a reality in which Shekhinah was already restored. Just as Moses did not enter the Land because he was of the grade *Tiferet* and not *Malkhut*, and thus did not need to undergo a constriction of this kind, so it was not the members of the wilderness generation who entered the Land, but rather their children, who were not of the same degree as their parents. Thus we read: "All those who entered the land resembled the originals [their parents], but did not experience an ascent as high. For there will never be, nor has there ever been, a generation like those originals, shown the splendid luster of their Lord face-to-face."[20]

In short, Moses is the ideal leader, and his generation is the most admired by the Zohar's composers. In describing their ancestors' greatness, the authors reveal their own deepest wish: to see "the splendid luster of their Lord face-to-face."

The Generation of King Solomon

Following rabbinic midrashim, the Zohar understands the generation of King Solomon as a generation of perfection. The Bible extensively describes the wisdom of King Solomon, his role as the builder of the Temple, as well as the majesty and wealth of his kingdom; and tradition attributes to him three biblical books—Song of Songs, Proverbs, and Ecclesiastes. Rabbinic literature is filled with aggadic accounts of his great wisdom,[21] and of his expertise in magic and occult sciences, and it is here that we also find the view that in King Solomon's generation the institution of kingship reached its pinnacle,[22] when a perfect king sat on the throne of God: "Solomon reigned over the upper and lower [realms], as is said: *Solomon sat on YHVH's throne* (1 Chronicles 29:23)."[23] In expressing the perfection of Solomon's kingdom, midrashic homilies described his age as one in which "the moon was perpetually full,"[24] without blemish or diminution, but rather always in a state of radiant perfection.

The Zohar is deeply interested in King Solomon, and repeatedly we encounter the statement that all of Solomon's words contain profound, concealed wisdom. For example: "[Rabbi Yitsḥak said:] 'We have contemplated the words of King Solomon and they appear to be obscure. But all those words spoken by Solomon are to be read with wisdom.'"[25]

Verses from Solomon's three books are interpreted in the Zohar more frequently than the other biblical books in the Writings or even in the Prophets. The obscure verses in Ecclesiastes are expounded on many occasions with the assumption that these words contain concealed secrets, and that the categorical statements uttered by Koheleth (the man speaking in

Ecclesiastes) are in fact questions—their answer to be found through mystical exegesis.

Verses from Proverbs are also the object of interpretation, if somewhat less frequently. However, there can be no doubt that of all the writings attributed to Solomon, the Song of Songs is by far the most significant for the zoharic circle. It constitutes foundational language for the Zohar's heroes. In their eyes, it occasionally attains a rank even beyond the Torah. In the Zohar, the Song of Songs is described not only as comprising the entire Torah but also as the completion of all being—past, present, and future.

> On that very day [the day of dedication of Solomon's Temple] this praise [Song of Songs] was revealed, and Solomon composed it with the holy-spirit. The praise of this song comprises the entire Torah—the Work of the Beginning, the mystery of the patriarchs, the exile of Egypt, and Israel's departure from Egypt and the Song at the Sea, the Ten Commandments and the standing at Mt. Sinai, and all the wanderings of Israel in the wilderness until they entered the Land and the Temple was built. It comprises the crowning of the holy, supernal name in love and joy, Israel's exile among the nations and their redemption, the resurrection of the dead until the day that is a Sabbath to YHVH; that which has been, that which is, and that which will be on the seventh day when there will be a Sabbath to YHVH: all is in the Song of Songs. (Zohar 2:144a)

It is difficult to imagine any greater praise for the Song of Songs than the above passage, clearly amplifying the famous saying of Rabbi Akiva, who claimed that "the whole world is not as worthy as it was on the day on which Song of Songs was given to Israel; for while all the writings in Scripture are holy, the Song of Songs is the holy of holies" and thus assured that book a place in the scriptural canon.[26] What the Torah and its verses were for the tannaitic and amoraic expounders, the verses of the Song of Songs are for the Zohar's heroes; this is their book of books, so to speak; and some of the most profound homilies in the Zohar are based on its verses.

The Zohar adopts the rabbinic image of the moon in its fullness and develops this idea in its own unique way. In the Zohar, the perfection of the moon designates not only the perfection of the earthly kingdom, but also the perfection of the sefirah *Malkhut*. According to the Zohar, Solomon—

the lover of a thousand women (1 Kings 11:3)—took upon himself the mythic task of acquiring a full understanding of the feminine.

More than anyone else in the world, Solomon possesses a deep knowledge of the attribute of *Malkhut*, whose characteristics include knowledge of good and evil, knowledge of the *Sitra Aḥra* (the Other Side), and the dynamics of disclosure and concealment. In other words, Solomon knows the sefirah *Malkhut* in all its luminous and holy aspects, as well as its dark and demonic side.[27] Thus we read the words of Rashbi: "Because King Solomon inherited the moon in fullness, he sought to inherit her in defect, so he strove for the knowledge of spirits and demons to inherit the moon in all her aspects. In the days of King Solomon the moon shone completely."[28]

Solomon's construction of the Temple is viewed by the Zohar as having enabled the moon to stand in its full stature, to be in intimate union with *Shlomo*, "the King who is peace (*shalom*)," namely, the combination of the sefirot *Tiferet* and *Yesod*. Typically, Solomon represents the sefirah *Yesod*, the divine grade that brings the connection between *Tiferet* and *Malkhut* to sexual perfection.[29] This coupling that transpired in the generation of Solomon created a near-perfect opening of the conduits of connection between the upper and lower worlds, as well as harmony between these worlds, all of which receives poetic expression in the Song of Songs.[30] For the kabbalists, the Song of Songs expresses the love and yearning between Shekhinah and the blessed Holy One, between the soul and the divine, between the lower worlds and the upper worlds. The mere fact of the revelation or writing of the Song of Songs in Solomon's time is in itself an expression of his greatness and that of his generation. In his generation, the powers latent in the letters of the Hebrew alphabet are revealed in actuality, and language itself reaches its greatest heights in terms of its ability to express the structure of reality.

> And so the world continued with the mysteries of the aleph-bet until Solomon arrived. When Solomon arrived, the letters stood in their place, and then it was written: *And Solomon's wisdom was great* (1 Kings 5:10), and the moon stood in its perfection. Then the Song of Songs was revealed to the world. And then he said: *I went down to the nut grove* (Song of Songs 6:11)— just like a nut, whose fruit is found only at the end, so it was with the world,

until the husks ceased and the world stood in its essence, and the moon in its perfection. (*Zohar Ḥadash*, Ruth, 83a)

In *Shekel ha-Kodesh*, Moses de León explains the extent of Solomon's wisdom in terms of the ability to attain a complete apprehension of the sefirah *Malkhut* and the perfection of her being. As we have already seen, this is the view of the Zohar, but presented here in a clear and complete formulation.

What does [Scripture] mean, *YHVH gave Solomon wisdom*? (1 Kings 5:26)....
Just as there is an upper wisdom, so He (may He be blessed) created a lesser wisdom, and the lower wisdom is called "the wisdom of Solomon." And with this [wisdom] Solomon knew all that he knew and attained all that he attained. . . . Certainly the wisdom of Solomon is called the tree of knowledge of good and evil; and King Solomon, even though he was wiser than all other people, wanted and intended to perfect the content of this level through the mystery of good and evil.[31]

Often in the Zohar, the discussion about King Solomon and his generation is presented in the context of a comparison with the generations of Moses and of David (and, as we shall see below, of Rabbi Shim'on bar Yoḥai). The two passages below describe the relationship between the tabernacle of Moses and the Temple of Solomon, and in so doing present an overview of the history of the Jewish people, told from the mythical-historical perspective of different states of union between the sefirah *Malkhut* and the sefirah *Tiferet*.

When the Temple was built below, and the palace was perfectly arrayed, then the Song of Songs was revealed, for Temple needed to be joined to Temple.
    When Moses was in the wilderness, because of the sins of Israel the union of Moses [with Shekhinah] was back-to-back, male and female joined as one. Then, *the house in its being built* (1 Kings 6:7), bit by bit. When Israel crossed over the Jordan and Moses died, the blessed Holy One sawed [separated] Her and arrayed Her in the tabernacle of Shiloh—until She was perfected in the Eternal House and coupled with King Solomon, and the worlds were [aligned] face-to-face. . . . then the Song of Songs was revealed. (*Zohar Ḥadash*, Song of Songs, *Midrash ha-Ne'elam* 62c–d)

Come and see: At first, Moses arrayed the tabernacle with the mystery of that supernal level in which he abided. Solomon arrayed the Temple with the mystery of that river that issues from Eden, which is the perfection of the house and the pleasure of the house. And the mystery of the tabernacle is the drawing near of love, through the level of the body, that level in which Moses abides; the drawing near of love and not pleasure. When Solomon arrived and arrayed that temple, it was arrayed in the mystery of the love of pleasure, and thus is written: *he will be a man of rest* [or: pleasure] (*menuḥah*) (1 Chronicles 22:9). (Zohar 2:242a)

The generation of Moses, its greatness and unique ability to apprehend supernal levels of divinity notwithstanding, was not advanced in its ability to effect union between the male and female aspects of the Godhead. In the wilderness, the union between these grades of the divine was through the love of the body alone, without the sexual and erotic perfection of total intercourse, and thus the description of this state is that of male and female joined back-to-back. Solomon is the one who brings Shekhinah to a state of perfection in the Temple, a perfection accompanied by sexual satisfaction and pleasure.[32]

In another passage, the difference between them is that whereas Moses is understood as having effected the union of Shekhinah with the lower world by virtue of his coupling with her, Solomon is portrayed as having brought about her union with her partner in the upper world, and—in building the Temple—as having enabled the drawing down of the supernal male and female together into the lower world.[33] Solomon thus united the upper and lower worlds. (Incidentally, the view of the Zohar here is the opposite of that found in the Babylonian Talmud, which celebrates the magnitude of the love and passion between Israel and God in the days of the tabernacle, as opposed to the cooling of relations between them in the days of Solomon's Temple.[34]) The generation of Solomon represents therefore a peak chapter in the "sacred history" of the relations between the male and female grades of divinity.

This myth describes a narrative arc in which *Malkhut* passes from her state of unfruitful union with the male, joined back-to-back, to her independent state after her separation from the male, to her development and growth in Shiloh, to her perfect union in Solomon's Temple, followed by her bitter divorce with the destruction of the sanctuary. The protagonist of the next great chapter in this myth is Rabbi Shim'on bar Yoḥai, who raises Shekhinah from the dust and restores her through his coupling with her.

Out of its fondness for comparisons, and in particular out of its desire to demonstrate the superiority of Rabbi Shim'on and his generation, the Zohar elsewhere points out that despite the perfection of Solomon's generation, the revelation of mysteries in his age was esoteric and restricted to sages alone, and even then was confused. In contrast, the generation in which Rashbi abides is one whose divine destiny is the flowing and luminescent disclosure of mysteries of Torah.

> King Solomon perceived and saw that even in that generation which was more perfect than all the other generations, it was not the wish of the supreme King that wisdom should be revealed through him to such an extent. The Torah that had been sealed from the very beginning was disclosed—he had opened doors; and even though he opened [them], they still remained closed except to those sages who were worthy, and even they stammered in them and did not know how to open their mouths with them.
>
> And this generation in which Rabbi Shim'on bar Yoḥai abides, it is the desire of the blessed Holy One, for the sake of Rabbi Shim'on, that the sealed things should be revealed by him. But I am astounded by the sages of this generation, how they can forfeit even one single moment of standing before Rabbi Shim'on to study Torah while Rabbi Shim'on is still alive in the world. Nevertheless in this generation, wisdom will not be forgotten from the world. Alas for the generation when he departs and the sages diminish, and wisdom will be forgotten from the world! (Zohar 2:149a; transl. after the Heb. transl. by Tishby and Goldstein)

The Zohar also criticizes King Solomon for the incompleteness of his relationship with the female grade of divinity. In a few places, the Zohar praises Solomon's father, King David, for knowing, appreciating, and pining for Shekhinah also in her state as a cistern, empty and longing to be filled, and in laboring for her perfection through love and praise. Solomon inherited a full moon from his father and sinned in seeing this fullness as representing the permanent state of affairs—and thus not concerning himself with the strengthening and nurturing dimension of Shekhinah in the world.[35]

> "David strove all his days to fashion fullness for Her, playing and singing below. When David departed from the world, he left Her in fullness, and King Solomon obtained Her in fullness, for the moon had emerged from poverty and entered richness.... Therefore, Solomon did not need to play like David—just to utter a song that is passion of richness, encompassing all praises of the world, praise of the *Matronita* sitting upon the throne facing the King....

"Solomon erred in this—seeing the moon approaching the sun; right hand embracing, left hand beneath its head. As they neared one another, he said, 'Look! They approach as one. What is the right doing here? For the right is intended only to draw near. Since they are already near one another, why is it needed?' Immediately, *silver was not considered [as anything] in the days of Solomon* (1 Kings 10:21).

"The blessed Holy One said to him, 'You have rejected the right! Upon your life, you will have need of *ḥesed*, kindness, and will not find it!' Immediately, the sun turned from facing the moon, and the moon began to darken. . . ." (Zohar 1:249b–250a; Matt 2004–2007, vol. 3, p. 537)

Solomon desired only the power and perfection of Shekhinah in her state of completeness—as a flowing well and as the moon in its fullness. Solomon's sin lay in his inability to understand the mystery of poverty, and the mystery of the feminine as that which is filled and emptied continuously.

In positioning Rashbi amid the succession of those who attained knowledge of the divine mysteries, the Zohar claims that the generation of Rabbi Shim'on bar Yoḥai merits receiving mysteries of the same level of profundity as those revealed in the days of King Solomon.

The Companions wept and said: Alas, master! When you depart from the world, who will reveal concealed, profound mysteries like these—not heard since the days of King Solomon until now? Happy is the generation who hears these things, and happy is the generation in which you abide! Woe to the generation that will be orphaned of you! (Zohar 3:236a)

In fact, the Zohar even positions Rabbi Shim'on and his generation above that of the biblical king:

We have taught: Solomon inherited the moon in all her aspects, and because of this he ruled over all in wisdom. Whereas Rabbi Shim'on bar Yoḥai ruled with wisdom over the whole world; all those who ascended to his levels, only did so to be perfected with him. (Zohar 3:61a)

The Generation of Rabbi Shim'on bar Yoḥai

The generation with which the composers of the Zohar identify more than any other generation is of course the generation of the sage Shim'on bar Yoḥai, and it is this identification that bestows upon the entire composition its literary dress, backdrop, language, and setting. The decision of the Zohar's composers to house their story in a tannaitic (or tannaitic-like) form is testament to their admiration for the generation of the Mishnah's composers, and to the creative force of those who fashioned the oral Torah. Their desire to dress in tannaitic garb is an expression of the renaissance wish of the Zohar's composers to revive in their own day the creative power of the tannaitic period—and to dare, like them, to produce a new oral Torah that would revive religious experience among the Jewish people.[36]

As a pseudepigraphic composition, the Zohar presents itself as authentically located in the tannaitic period, and thus we of course do not find an explicit comparison between the Zohar's composers and the figures they imitate. The generation of Rabbi Shim'on is the most admired of all the generations; yet sometimes it is difficult to determine whether the Zohar is speaking about the historical tannaim, or whether—in writing about this generation—the Zohar's authors are in fact speaking about themselves and their own generation.

Nevertheless, in examining the language that the Zohar employs to speak about this generation, we can distinguish a tension between the extreme admiration for this generation on the one hand, and its portrayal as standing on the brink of the disappearance of knowledge of the divine on the other—a generation that precisely because of its precarious situation needs a Rabbi Shim'on.[37] The overall impression, however, is that the scales are tipped in favor of this generation. It is presented as a fleeting moment within a span of generations of inferior divine consciousness, both in relation to those that came before and those that will come after. While the opening of the *Idra Rabba* does indeed describe a world in which the mystics—the "field's reapers"—are few, it should be remembered that the ascendant and elect ones (*benei ha-aliyah*) are always few in number; we should thus be wary of inferring a harsh characterization of the members of this generation. Furthermore, the Zohar's complaints are usually directed at *benei ha-olam* (the people of the world) and not *benei ha-dor* (members of the generation).[38] The Zohar gives testament to moments of exaltation of the soul in which the entire world and the current generation seem to shine with the wisdom of divine mysteries. We also read of more sober moments, in which, upon contemplating the reality of their generation and their lack of success in influencing this reality, the Companions are filled with bitter frustration. This complexity bespeaks an emotionally dynamic circle that cannot be reduced to a caricature.

In exploring the connection between pseudepigraphic identity and self-image, the Zohar's composers have decided to compare not only Rashbi's generation with other generations, and the Companions with the world at large, but also to compare the residents of the Land of Israel, among whom Rabbi Shim'on resides, with the sages of Babylonia. In an extension of the Israel-Babylonia rivalries found in rabbinic literature, the Zohar views the Babylonians as being unable to fully comprehend and teach the mysteries of the secret Torah. While they are guardians of the secret Torah, they stammer when presenting its mysteries.[39]

To whom could these remarks be directed? Who is this "Diaspora group" that neither breathes the air of the Land of Israel nor knows its mysteries? Is this perhaps another mystical group, contemporary with, yet more conservative than, the zoharic circle? Are the members of this group, as Boaz Huss has suggested, the circle of the students of Rabbi Moses Naḥmanides (also known as Ramban), who lived in Catalonia?[40] Whatever the case, the impression is that the "Babylonians" do not recognize the greatness of Rav Yeiva or Rav Hamnuna Sava, who are present among them. If these figures are in fact parallels to the figure of Rabbi Shim'on, then the veiled criticism (more subtle than that found in the *Ra'aya Meheimna*) is that the Babylonians do not recognize the greatness of the master of the generation, Rabbi Shim'on bar Yoḥai.

One of the most surprising aspects of the way in which Rashbi's generation is portrayed in the Zohar is the fact that we find no mention whatsoever of other great sages, aside from Rabbi Shim'on, with whom he and his circle converse and argue. The tannaitic context familiar to us from the Mishnah, in which many sages converse with one another and establish houses of study, does not exist at all in the zoharic narrative; it is as though all the known figures from the world of the sages have been removed from the landscape, with only Rabbi Shim'on bar Yoḥai remaining as the holy luminary and as the solitary pillar sustaining the world.[41]

The generation of Rabbi Shim'on is a generation of disclosure. The presence of the teacher within this generation opens the dimension of divine mysteries that had previously been sealed, and renders it flowing.

> Rabbi Ḥizkiyah said, "I know something—I am afraid to reveal it. In events of the world, wisdom is discovered."
> Rabbi Abba came and knocked him, saying: "Utter your word! Arm yourself with your weapon! In the days of Rabbi Shim'on, words are revealed!" (Zohar 1:226a; Matt 2004–2007, vol. 3, p. 360)

Rashbi himself attests to the greatness of his generation:

> Rabbi Shim'on cried and said: Now I know for sure that the High Holy Spirit is vibrating within you. Happy is this generation! A generation like this will not arise until King Messiah appears! Torah has been restored to her antiquity/ancientry![42] (Zohar 2:147a; Matt 1983, p. 131)

What is the meaning of the statement that the Torah is returning to her antiquity? It is possible that this is a paraphrase of the talmudic statement "restoring the crown to its ancient glory," used to describe the members of the Great Assembly* in their effort to find new ways to interpret all the attributes of the divine.[43]

The Torah "restored to her antiquity" also hints at the special exegesis of the Zohar that seeks to expose the Torah's deepest dimensions and to give expression to the Torah of the Holy Ancient One (*Atika Kadisha*)—the divinity in its primal, concealed aspect, abundantly merciful and undifferentiated. The exemplar is the Idra Rabba: in this special gathering, Rashbi and his disciples seek to realign the connection between the world, consciousness, and Torah, in their dualistic aspects, with their undifferentiated source in the world of the Holy Ancient One. The purpose of this attuning is to rectify the blemished world, characterized by an excess of judgment (*din*) and harshness, through a renewed connection with the source of the ancient, divine flow, out of which reality and being first emerged.[44]

---

* Here the Great Assembly, mentioned in Mishnah *Avot* 1:1, refers to a historical-mythical past generation of Jewish spiritual leaders coming after the prophets and before the sages. It is to be distinguished from the event in the Zohar known as the Idra Rabba (Great Assembly).

In this context, and with its characteristic sense of paradox, the Zohar understands "the Torah returning to her antiquity" as deriving precisely from the Companions' ability to innovate words of Torah and to renew the ability to experience the Torah as a living presence, just as when it was originally given. Returning the Torah to her antiquity is not a simple restorative act; there is no turning back the wheel of time here, but rather a renaissance act of connecting the new to the ancient. The pseudepigraphic garb of the composition itself brings us back, in a sophisticated manner, to ancient times, to the world of the tannaim. This return to antiquity is perhaps also connected to the expression "new-ancient words," a uniquely reflexive term that the Companions employ to describe their enterprise to find new meanings through the ancient words of Torah, and the ancient layers of divinity through their innovations.[45]

The tannaitic (or pseudo-tannaitic) world of the Zohar is viewed as a reality in which divine wisdom radiates out from the center—Rabbi Shim'on bar Yoḥai—in all directions. This divine wisdom is found in nature, in the mountains, under trees, among little children, donkey-drivers, and a range of eccentric, wondrous figures. This enormous explosion of divine wisdom flows from the power of Rabbi Shim'on's light and benefits the whole world. Thus Rabbi Abba declares: "Even children in the generation of Rabbi Shim'on are worthy of wisdom! Happy are you, Rabbi Shim'on! Woe to the generation from whom you depart!"[46] And similarly Rabbi Ḥiyya exclaims: "In the days of Rabbi Shim'on, even the birds of the sky murmur wisdom! Behold, his words are known above and below!"[47]

As we shall now see, "the generation in which Rashbi abides" is a generation "inscribed above and below." Its idealized description, as a generation fearing sin and full of righteous people, is counterposed with the less generous way in which the Zohar describes the rest of the world. It is possible that the word "generation" designates the community immediately surrounding the Companions. And perhaps this generation's being "inscribed above and below" represents a development of the image of the "fearers of YHVH" who are inscribed before God in the "Book of Remembrance" mentioned in the biblical book of Malachi.[48] This is, therefore, the appropriate generation for Rabbi Shim'on, and he is the appropriate leader for this generation.

> Come and see: The people of the world do not have permission to utter concealed things or to interpret them, except for the holy luminary Rabbi Shim'on. For behold, the blessed Holy One consented through him, since his generation is inscribed above and below. Therefore matters are said explicitly by him. There will not be another generation like this one in which he abides, until King Messiah comes! (Zohar 3:159a)

Rabbi Shim'on's disclosure of mysteries is the fruit not of his own free will, but rather of divine consent that allows him and his cohorts to be a generation of revelation rather than concealment. Those who do not have this agreement from above are prohibited from participating in the disclosure of concealed matters.

Ensuing generations surely had to reckon with the obstacle set up by the Zohar, in its having chosen to prohibit the disclosure of mysteries following the master's death. It is difficult not to see in the words just quoted one of the reasons why the composition underwent a process of sanctification, arousing forms of interpretation saturated with awe, while its call to innovate Torah went relatively unheeded.[49]

PART II

"WHILE YOU WALK ON THE WAY, WHEN YOU LIE DOWN, AND WHEN YOU RISE"

On the Companions' Way of Life

The focus of the following four chapters is the life of the zoharic circle and its main modes of activity—in which, and through which, mystical experience transpires.

The mysticism of the Zohar is a *mysticism of the group* (Chapter 4); that is to say, the mystical life of the circle takes place through a special encounter among human beings and not through the seclusion of the individual. The circle lives its life amid a multidimensional reality, whose spiritual-imaginary-soul aspects are stronger than its realistic aspects.

This reality of the zoharic world serves as a live platform for mystical occurrence, which transpires through a unique exegetical activity that takes place in two key arenas: the Companions' journeys while *walking on the way* (Chapter 5), and the *nocturnal delight*—the special engagement with Torah, undertaken in a group with other companions from midnight till dawn (Chapter 6). These ways of life are in fact practices that function to promote the spiritual-mystical aims of the circle. The last chapter in this part (Chapter 7) will explore the appearance of wondrous characters, and the journeys of the Companions in the upper worlds.

4

Mysticism of the Group

In the Zohar, the world of religious experience, of human contact with the world of divinity, transpires amid the many stories of Rabbi Shim'on and his circle. The literary or narrative layer of the Zohar, which mainly deals with matters spoken by the protagonists to one another, is a central vehicle for imparting the ways in which the composition as a whole treats mystical experience.

The Zohar is not a diary or journal of the life of a mystic, nor is it a monologue or manual; it is rather a kind of mystical epic. In this unique epic, the protagonists' journey transpires not only along the paths and roads of an imaginary Land of Israel, but mainly also among the different registers of biblical verses. The protagonists' homeland, and the territory in which they operate, is the Torah—the object of the Companions' love and desire. The Torah is the main manifestation of the divine presence in the world and sometimes is even identified with divinity itself. The interpretation of Torah then, in all its myriad forms, is in fact a journey along the paths of insight and experience generated by these different dimensions of interpretation.[1]

Mystical experience in the Zohar occurs, almost exclusively, in a context of more than one person. Further, it is the fruit of the unique encounter among a group of people united in their intensive search for the divine. To-gether they search among the deeper layers and meanings of biblical verses, the commandments, prayer, and the natural environs in which they live. The idea that the encounter between students of Torah brings about a spe-cial religious experience—namely, the indwelling of Shekhinah—is already found in the writings of the sages. So for example, in tractate *Avot* (3:6), we find that "when two people sit and occupy themselves with words of Torah, Shekhinah rests among them, as is said: *Then have those who revere YHVH been talking to one another. YHVH has heard and noted it, and a Book of Memory has been written at His behest concerning those who revere YHVH and esteem His name* (Malachi 3:16)." The Zohar extends this idea and develops a unique myth in which this "talking" among "those who revere YHVH" is actually the Com-panions' mystical engagement with the Torah. The words of Torah uttered by the mystic circle below ascend to the divine worlds, stand, and speak themselves before the blessed Holy One, who in turn delights in them.[2]

[Rabbi Shim'on] opened and said: *Then have those who revere YHVH been talking to one another. YHVH has heard and noted it, and a Book of Memory has been writ-ten at His behest concerning those who revere YHVH and esteem His name* (Malachi 3:16). This verse requires contemplation. *Have . . . been talking* (*nidberu*, lit. "were spoken")?—It should have said, "then they talked" (*dibberu*)! What is the mean-ing of *were spoken*? It means they were spoken above . . . since those holy words ascend above . . . and all of them speak themselves before the supreme King.

Who has seen the delight? Who has seen the praise when they ascend through all those firmaments, when those words ascend before the Holy King and He looks at them and is crowned with them, and they ascend and sit in His lap and He delights in them, and from there they ascend to His head and become a crown? About this the Torah has said: [*I will be with Him as a confidant,*] *A source of delight every day* (Proverbs 8:30). It is not written *I was*, but rather *I will be*, every time that supernal words ascend before Him.

Those who revere YHVH is written twice in the verse. *Those who revere YHVH*—above, *Those who revere YHVH*—below. Those who revere YHVH stand below and those words stand in their image above. . . . Afterward they are written in a Book of Memory before Him, to stand and abide before Him always. *Esteem His name*—who are the ones who esteem His name? This is as we have already established: All those who esteem words of Torah so as to attain their Master in the mystery of the holy name—so as to attain knowledge of Him, so that the wisdom of His name should abide in their heart—as is written: *esteem His name*, this is the mystery of the holy name. (Zohar 2:217a)

The Companions recite and create words of Torah; and these words in turn assume an active quality, adorning and beautifying Shekhinah, and even arouse the masculine dimension within divinity. The members of the mystical circle, the initiates of the palace (*benei ha-heikhal*), the partners of Shekhinah, are the very handiwork of the blessed Holy One, and the sky is the living book of memory that proclaims and records their words. The sky—the stars, the constellations, and all the luminaries—is the parchment of the divine scroll and the entire world of divinity is brimming with praise for the Companions' words.

> "So *The sky proclaims the work of His hands* (Psalms 19:2)—the Companions who join this Bride, masters of Her covenant, Her partners.
>
> "*Proclaims*—inscribing every single one.
>
> "Who is *the sky*? The sky embracing sun, moon, stars, and constellations— the Book of Memory. He *proclaims* and inscribes them, recording them as initiates of the palace, constantly fulfilling their desires.
>
> "*Day to day pours forth speech* (Psalms 19:3)—a holy day of those supernal days of the King. They praise the Companions and repeat the word each one told his companion. *Day to day expresses* that *speech* and praises it.
>
> "*Night to night* (ibid.)—every rung ruling the night extols to one another each Companion's *knowledge*, ecstatically becoming their companions and lovers." (Zohar 1:8b; Matt 2004–2007, vol. 1, pp. 57–58, reformatted in part)

Sometimes, the most powerful religious experience in the Zohar is the patrimony of a small group alone, comprising only two or three partici- pants. In the Zohar's more climactic moments, however, such experience can be collective, involving a larger group,[3] and sometimes it comprises even the entire mystic circle, as in the great gatherings of the *Idra Rabba* and the *Idra Zuta*. If we compare this phenomenon of group mysticism with testimonies of mystical experience that are mainly the product of solitary striving, we find that this dialogical encounter generates a different kind of mystical experience.[4]

The very existence of the other—present as witness or participant—as well as the existence of the teacher Rabbi Shim'on (even if not always physically present) establishes an experiential world acutely aware of the need for expression, articulation, and interpretation. In some instances, it is simply the narrative frame that prompts this articulation; if one of the protagonists has experienced something of note, a colleague invariably asks him to recount it.

In terms of the experiential range, such group mysticism functions in two ways. On the one hand, the framework of the circle of mystics encourages experiential intensity and enables the group to encompass and contain exceptional experiences, and even to bestow upon them meaning. On the other hand, such mysticism is moderate by its very nature, arising from the social requirement to mediate and describe the experience, and to bestow upon it a more expansive meaning than the solitary, idiosyncratic experience of the individual.

Human contact with the divine, then, is not the fruit of the soul's seclusion with its divine source, but rather the product of the resonances and echoes among human beings speaking with one another. The spoken word among companions, the response, the conversation of Torah, and its explication, are all the ladder for the soul's exaltation and for the possibility of touching the divine world. The connections between people—between a man and a woman, a sage and his colleague, or a person and a stranger chanced upon "on the way" who together open words of Torah—are of mystical value in the Zohar. Their joining in love on earth is a kind of healing (*tikkun*), which in turn generates healing and mending in the upper worlds.

The presence of the other person is not an obstacle to mystical life, but rather a necessary precondition for it. As we have seen in the Zohar passages just cited, it is not thought or sound alone, but rather the spoken word uttered among companions, and connected by them to the female aspect of the divine, the sefirah *Malkhut*, that brings about harmony in the divine world.[5]

"While you walk on the way"

The Locus of Mystical Experience

Most of the Zohar's stories take place outside, in nature: while walking on roads and paths, or sitting—in the inner recesses of caves, among the shade of rocks, beside springs, and beneath the pleasant shade of trees. When the narrative moves to human habitations, these are mainly anonymous houses in forsaken places, simple inns, and only occasionally the house of a Companion or Rabbi Shim'on himself.[1]

Zoharic stories frequently open with the structure, "Rabbi Ḥiyya and Rabbi Yose (or any other members of Rashbi's circle) were walking on the way." In the Zohar, people are always on the move, journeying from one place to another—and it is in this situation that we encounter the protagonists of the zoharic world. Sometimes, such journeying has a destination—to reach Tiberias or the Tower of Tyre—while other times, no destination or purpose is stated. The Companions walk "on the way," and whatever that way has in store for them constitutes the story or teaching of the wandering mystics.

Two central literary forms follow the opening sentence about the wandering Companions. According to one type, one of the Companions opens with a suggestion to innovate words of Torah while walking on the way, in which case the plot of the narrative is generated by the dynamics of the interpretation of verses. According to the second type, a surprise awaits the Companions on their journey—suddenly the Companions see a snake, a stranger approaches, night descends and with it the fear of darkness, to name but a few of the twists and turns characteristic of the zoharic story—and it is this surprise event that generates the plot as well as the kinds of expositions expounded in reaction to what has just transpired.

In both generative formats, the objective "reality" of the journey and the "reality" of the exposition of verses are connected. External reality is attuned to the reality of the expositions and indeed responds to them. The converse is also the case—the verses expounded by the Companions indicate an associative and intuitive attention to the divine hints and clues scattered in the seemingly external events.

On many occasions, the verses expounded on the way and the events of the way are ingeniously intertwined within the general context of the Torah portion being interpreted. For example, in the Zohar's commentary to the Torah portion *Shemini*, we read about two of the Companions walking on the way who encounter a child traveling with jugs of wine. Associatively, the Companions begin expounding a range of matters connected with wine, which leads them ultimately to interpret the passage in *Shemini* that prohibits the priests who are serving in the sanctuary from drinking wine.[2]

The interplay and intermingling between Torah and "the way" are in themselves a critique of the limits of ordinary human consciousness—which fails to sense the connections among all levels of reality. This literary structure is nevertheless imbued with optimism, raising the possibility of expanding the borders of consciousness to encompass all at once the multiple dimensions of being.

We are not dealing here with a relationship between a "true" ("objective" or "hard") reality in which the Zohar's narratives transpire, and an "imagined" ("subjective" or "soft") reality emerging from the interpretation of the Torah's verses. The dimensions of ordinary human existence, and of the divine and the demonic, as well as the dimensions that flow from the creative power of the homily, are all dimensions of reality—and are all experienced in the Zohar. The Zohar does not privilege physical, "objective" reality over these other realities; indeed, in many cases it seems to favor the subtler reality of one's inner being and yearning for the divine. For the Zohar, then, the reality of the verses of the Torah is no less "true" than that which befalls the Companions on their journeys.

The Torah of the Zohar appears mainly as a Torah that transpires while "walking on the way": in fact, not one of the composition's stories takes place in a house of study (*beit midrash*) or synagogue (*beit knesset*). The world of the Mishnah, in which the Zohar implants its stories, is indeed replete with accounts of journeys, yet alongside them are stories set in the *beit midrash*, the central institution and innovation of the tannaitic world. Yet the *beit midrash*, the "dynamic front" of tannaitic culture, is absent from the Zohar. When we do encounter the institution of the yeshiva, it appears as a celestial institution rather than an earthly one, the zoharic yeshiva (*Metivta*) being a place visited by the soul garbed in its astral form, where it is able to meet various figures from different periods in Jewish mythological history.[3]

In addition to the locus of the zoharic story, the characters who bear its most profound divine wisdom also express the Zohar's revolutionary perspective regarding the location of divine wisdom in its composers' generation. Excluding Rabbi Shim'on and the Companions, the characters who offer the most memorable expositions are unmistakably marginal in terms of the hierarchy of authority as developed by the Rabbis or the medieval Jewish communities of Spain. In the generation of Rabbi Shim'on, knowledge is found on the lips of babes, unidentified old men, and donkey-drivers. These and other marginal types encountered by the Companions on their travels are often revealed in the course of the narrative to be miraculous beings.[4] Even nature itself—animal, vegetable, and mineral—is brimming with hints of the divine.[5]

In the narratives found in the Zohar's main corpus, we almost never hear words of Torah from the mouths of authoritative rabbinic personages of Rabbi Shim'on's generation as familiar to us from classical rabbinic literature. The exceptions are Rabbi Pinḥas ben Ya'ir, portrayed in the Zohar as Rabbi Shim'on's father-in-law, and Rabbi Yose ben Shim'on ben Lakunia, variously depicted as Rabbi El'azar's father-in-law and brother-in-law.[6]

Other known tannaim are, for all intents and purposes, nonexistent in the Zohar's main corpus; they are never cited, and there are no dialogues or dealings with them as in the Mishnah and Talmuds.

Also absent from the Zohar are political authorities, be they from antiquity (such as the *nasi*, "patriarch") or the Middle Ages. Even the Companions themselves, the disciples of Rabbi Shim'on, are portrayed in ironic fashion: on the one hand, they are named and bear the title "Rabbi," and they view themselves as sages and perhaps even as mystics. On the other hand, the stories repeatedly imply their inferiority vis-à-vis the anonymous, wondrous characters they meet on their journeys, in that it is from the latter that we hear the more complex, profound innovations in Torah.

The Zohar's ironic relationship with the world of the sages and the Companions is subtle, complex, multivalent, and humorous—and indeed there is an element of play and the carnivalesque in the Zohar's representations.[7] This is not the case, however, in the *Ra'aya Meheimna*, where we find no ambivalence toward the world of halakhic study: there it is depicted with flagrant sarcasm.[8] Even so, alongside the Zohar's efforts to dissolve external authority, it bestows total and divine authority on Rabbi Shim'on. Furthermore, the absence of formal institutions of study does not imply the loss of learning. On the contrary, the stories of the Zohar are filled with learning, study, analysis, and contemplation of Torah, prayer, and the commandments—only the intentions underlying the relationship with these forms of Jewish culture have changed.

But what is the meaning of the authors' radical choices to locate their stories "on the way," and to divorce themselves from formal institutions of study? Yitshak Baer has raised the possibility that the values of the new spiritual world of the Zohar, and in particular its later strata (especially the *Ra'aya Meheimna*), perhaps reflect the authors' critique of the established world of Torah study in Spain in the latter half of the thirteenth century, a world they experienced as devoid of the divine spirit. Baer also suggests that the milieu of the Zohar's authors was heavily influenced by that of Franciscan monks.[9]

Perhaps the journey motif was also inspired by pictures and stories of medieval knights and chivalry, or wandering troubadours. To these conjectures, we must add the possible influence of various Muslim groups of the Iberian Peninsula, for whom wandering and roaming were central aspects of their religious experience.

Israel Ta-Shma has extensively researched the historical reality in which the Zohar was written and has sharply criticized the way that Baer characterized the intellectual and religious climate in which the Zohar was produced. In Ta-Shma's opinion, the members of the zoharic circle located their Torah study "on the way" and in the wee hours of the night out of their desire to highlight the distinctive spiritual emphases of their group, and not out of protest against the culture of the *beit midrash* of their day. According to Ta-Shma, the members of the zoharic circle were fully at home in this culture, adopted its innovative spirit, and even received from it the impetus for their own innovations.[10]

We can also appeal to more abstract historical-sociological understandings of intellectual processes by postulating that the absence of the *beit midrash* in the Zohar lies in the distinction, first posited by Moshe Idel, between primary and secondary elites. If it is indeed true that the circle that produced the Zohar belonged to the secondary elite of Jewish Spain, namely, a circle of scholars outside the primary circle of spiritual and communal leadership, then the decision not to mention any central or authoritative figures hints at this group's anarchistic character. The members of this group, it seems, did not seek to ground themselves in the legitimacy of the central communal authorities of their day, and their flight to "the way" expresses their decision to position their world rather differently.[11]

A different explanation for the Zohar's omission of prominent features of the world of Rabbi Shim'on's generation—the *beit midrash* as well as well-known sages and leaders—emerges through a literary rather than an historical analysis. In adopting this special literary structure, the Zohar creates a nuanced tension between the familiar and the foreign. The Zohar sets its characters in late antiquity, in the time of the tannaim and against the familiar landscape of the Land of Israel, yet it alters the tannaitic depictions. This absence of expected features engenders in the reader's mind a vague dissonance. If the dissolution of familiarity is indeed a conscious literary conceit, it is a particularly fitting strategy for the Zohar, which seeks to undermine the reader's normative and habitual view of reality.

Another solution comes from considering the driving force that underwrites the entire zoharic enterprise, and more specifically from reflecting on the zoharic conception of divinity. According to the Zohar, both human and divine wisdom have left their abode in the *beit midrash* and are now wandering. The Companions' departure from the formal institutions of the Jewish community thus imitates the condition of divinity in the world.

After the destruction of the Temple, the blessed Holy One (the male aspect of the divine) departed to the uppermost heavens, and only Shekhinah (feminine divinity) remains in the world. The destruction of the Temple is understood by the Zohar as signifying the dissolution of the family—the divorce of the royal, holy couple[12]—the consequence of which is that the blessed Holy One has withdrawn his direct involvement from the world, leaving only Shekhinah as the sole worldly presence of holiness, compassion, and providence for the Jewish people.

In this myth, the Children of Israel are identified as children coming from a house in which anger, sin, jealousy, and volatile relationships have brought about its destruction. Furthermore, the face of female divinity has also now changed, and she no longer resides in the shade of her lover, the blessed Holy One, the sefirah *Tiferet*. She wanders and roams without a fixed abode, lonely, longing for her partner. She is dependent on her children, the people of Israel, for her very being in the world. Shekhinah no longer has a physical home in the world; she is no longer Matronita residing in a glorious palace, or even for that matter in the *beit midrash* or the *beit knesset* (synagogue) that were also her abodes, seemingly because the word of God is no longer present in them.[13] From now on, Shekhinah's abode is to be human beings themselves, who through their worship and service transform themselves into sanctuaries in which Shekhinah can dwell.[14] Shekhinah roams the paths and roads of the world, and it is there among the people who wander like her that she finds a place to reside.[15] Now Shekhinah's sanctuary and chariot consist of "the way" and of people's hearts.

Within this harsh myth there are, nevertheless, moments of grace, of reconciliation, and of harmonious union between the sacred couple. Even so, they are never again husband and wife, or mother and father living in partnership in their home, the Temple. The "place" has been destroyed, and while the abode of Shekhinah is now the entire world, she is without the stability and influence she once enjoyed in the mythical past.[16]

The Companions of the Zohar roam along paths and roads, and it is there that they find the ever-moving, homeless, living, present divine word. In "walking along the way," the Companions actualize their deep identification with their mother and their beloved, Shekhinah, who like them is found there. The Companions experience their encounters with one another on the way as an encounter with Shekhinah. Their meetings with Rabbi Shim'on on the way marks a double indwelling of Shekhinah, insofar as Rashbi himself is Her earthly manifestation and is described as the "mouth of Shekhinah."[17] The Zohar's decision to focus on the reality of "the way"—its events, its surprises, its ever-changing sense of time through morning, evening, night, and dawn—expresses the desire to experience over and over the surprising encounters with Shekhinah, now resident there.

While the view of the Companions as the ones who give aid and support to Shekhinah in their going out to meet her on the way, and as the ones in whose hands her redemption lies, is present in the Zohar itself, later generations of kabbalists and Zohar commentators have offered stronger expressions of this same idea. Such formulations are found, for example, in Rabbi Shim'on Ibn Lavi's commentary on the Zohar, *Ketem Paz*, as well as in Rabbi Moses Cordovero's extensive writings on the Zohar. Indeed, the departure to roads and paths in order to be with Shekhinah was understood by the kabbalistic community of Safed in the sixteenth century as a model to be imitated. Among his voluminous works, Moses Cordovero has left a short treatise by the name of *Sefer Gerushin* (Book of Wanderings, lit. Book of Expulsions), describing his journeys with his teacher, Rabbi Shlomo Alkabetz, in the environs of Safed.[18] These trips were a mystical practice inspired by the stories of "the way" found in the Zohar. The two rabbis would roam and wander along paths and roads, waiting for verses to come associatively to their minds, from which they would create surprising expositions. Roaming byways and wandering among nature was also practiced by the circle of Rabbi Isaac Luria and his students, as was the custom of going out to greet Shekhinah in the *Kabbalat Shabbat* ceremony innovated by these same Safed kabbalists.

Moses Cordovero emphasized the purpose of the journey in the Zohar as helping and supporting the exiled Shekhinah:

> We should first of all understand the matter of the wanderings of these sages, like Rabbi Shim'on and his Companions, in that most of their words were uttered on the road. There is no doubt that this was not to be occupied with matters of the world. Rather, this was done with utmost intention that all their discourse would be on the way, for since the Temple was destroyed, Shekhinah has been exiled from the sanctuary of the King of the World, and no longer has union with Him, and wanders and roams from place to place. . . . and they said there: It is fitting for the servant to be like the master, and He decreed that the houses of the righteous should be destroyed. . . . It is true that the righteous, the masters of the Kabbalah, have the strength to be wanderers. . . . therefore the masters of Kabbalah, Rashbi and his Companions, who studied the wisdom of Kabbalah, would wander from place to place and divorced themselves from their homes, to be a chariot for *Malkhut* in the secret of Her exile. And by virtue of this wandering and exile, they attained Her; and She would dwell upon them.[19]

We might also explain the Companions' choice to take Torah on the road, so to speak, as representing a way of life—a poetics of the religious, interpretive, and exegetical way of the Zohar. The departure on a journey, along with a search for the novelties characteristic of a journey's fluidity and indeterminacy, is, in a way, a motto for the zoharic enterprise. The journey is then the symbol for the search for the new-ancient word of Torah. It represents the great quest to find forms of study capable of *opening new paths in the Torah*, as well as of opening its students' hearts to a new, surprise encounter between the Torah and life, so as to discover how divinity resides in them both.

At the end of one such story, which appears in the Zohar's commentary to the Torah portion *Vayakhel*, the Companions return to their teacher Rabbi Shim'on and recount all that befell them on the way, the expositions they expounded as well as the aspects of divinity they experienced. Rabbi Shim'on then states in subtle midrashic language the meaning and significance of the "Torah of the way." He expounds this passage: "The path of the righteous is like radiant sunlight, ever brightening until noon. The way of the wicked is all darkness" (Proverbs 4:18–19). He opens by noting that the passage requires further contemplation. In a virtuoso interpretation, Rabbi Shim'on expounds it as a manifesto for the entire zoharic circle.

> *The path of the righteous*—what is the difference between "path" and "way"?
>
> They have already clarified the matter; but a path is that which has just now been opened and revealed, and was made in that place a path, where no feet have trodden before.
>
> *Way (derekh)*, as it is written, *as one who treads (dorekh) in the winepress* (Isaiah 63:1), where the feet of all who wish tread.
>
> That is why where the righteous walk is called *path (orah)*, since they were the first to open that place. And even when others, the people of the world, walk in that place, now that the righteous walk there it becomes a new place, for now that place is new as though never trod upon by any before, because the righteous invigorate that place through the sublime words in which the blessed Holy One delights.
>
> And what's more, Shekhinah goes in that place, which was not the case before. And that is why it is called *the path (orah) of the righteous*, because the sublime, holy guest (*oreah*) visits there.
>
> *Way (derekh)*—is open to all, and all who wish tread (*dorekh*) there, even the wicked.
>
> *Way (derekh)*—this is the secret of *who made a road (derekh) through the sea* (Isaiah 43:16). Since the other, forbidden side has trodden there and rules to defile the sanctuary, therefore the righteous alone stand and rule over that place called Path. As we have clarified, a way is open to all, to this side and that side.
>
> And you sublime, holy ones have entertained a holy, supernal guest; and sublime, supernal words were arranged before the Ancient of Days. Happy is your portion! (Zohar 2:215a)

While the simple meaning of the passage is built on the opposition between the righteous (and light) and the wicked (and darkness), Rabbi Shim'on constructs his homily precisely through the dramatic opposition between *orah* (path) and *derekh* (way), which in the Bible appear as synonyms. Rabbi Shim'on interprets the word *orah* as the opening of a new path, an exegetical avenue in Torah unrevealed until now; and the word *derekh* as signifying those interpretations that have already become "the king's highway," well paved and well traveled—and thus also open to the forces of evil, to bandits and thieves, and to the various calamities awaiting interpretations that have already been accepted and fixed.

The singularity of the Companions' exegetical endeavor lies in their knowing how to open paths in those places where no people have trodden, namely, to innovate and disclose that which has never been said before, and at the same time, in their ability to transform well-worn thoroughfares, trodden by many, into renewed paths, experienced anew through the force of their innovations. The yearning for innovation and renewal is the sign of the zoharic circle, a yearning saturated with explicit eroticism.

Infused by the spirit of his own exposition, Rabbi Shim'on creates a new path of his own, in his surprising interpretation of how the word *oraḥ* (path) is connected with *oreaḥ* (guest). The path of the righteous, both the Companion's journeys as well as their innovative exegesis, causes Shekhinah to visit them as their honored, beloved guest.

The Torah conceived "on the way" thus serves the broader spiritual objectives of the Companions. The journey and the search for its surprises constitute an essential praxis in the Zohar's deep quest to awaken and arouse the people of the world, and to ensure that a surprising new Torah will be found on their lips. The homilies that the Zohar's protagonists seek to create on the way are such that their form and content cannot be pre-planned. They are not constrained by rational, normative, or linear thought whose place is indoors, seated in the *beit midrash*; rather, they are nourished by the spirit of freedom of the journey and the outdoors.

The "Torah of the way" has the power to bring both the speaker and those listening to his words into contact with the divine world and to cause the indwelling of Shekhinah in the world. The Companions must leave the *beit midrash* and roam with open eyes, Torah in their hearts, the willingness to be surprised in their souls, and the desire for an encounter with the divine. The Torah born of "the way" is of a different order, and for us the readers, it seems that never before have we encountered anything like it.

6

"In the wee hours of the night"

The Nocturnal Delight

Introduction to the Nocturnal Delight

As already noted, in the zoharic world we encounter the Companions in two main situations: while walking on the way, and during their special engagement with Torah from midnight till morning.[1] While mystical experience in the Zohar can occur at any hour of day, the most auspicious time for such experience is the night-watch from midnight till dawn. The mystics who rise at midnight to study Torah with their companions merit that their souls participate, at the same time, in another dimension called the Lower Garden of Eden, where they enjoy an intimate encounter with the divine.

This nightly activity of the zoharic circle—the awakening at midnight and the special engagement with Torah until the first light of day—is the most unique and distinctive practice of all the Companions' spiritual endeavors.[2] According to their own testimony, this ritual takes place every weekday night, whether in their private homes, in the hostels and inns they frequent on their many travels, or in the caves in which they seek shelter when night falls while walking on the way. Only on Sabbath Eve, rather than arising to study Torah, do the mystics awaken for sexual relations with their wives, with the special intention of unifying the sefirot and drawing down the divine flow into their sexual union and into the offspring produced through that union.

This special wakefulness from midnight till dawn is understood by the Zohar as a ritual praxis requiring certain techniques of preparation, as well as an understanding of its phases, in particular the climax at its end. The distinctiveness of this praxis lies in the fact that a participant's consciousness is able to experience simultaneously two different dimensions of reality. The first is the experience of studying Torah, which occurs down below on earth, awake and in the body; and the second is the experience of delight in the Lower Garden of Eden, experienced by the soul on a spiritual plane and in a spiritual garb. These hours from midnight until dawn are viewed by the Zohar as a special and auspicious time, and it is around them that the Zohar weaves a great myth repeated many times throughout the composition—the myth of the nocturnal delight (*sha'ashua*) of the blessed Holy One with the souls of the righteous in the Lower Garden of Eden.

The Zohar's nocturnal myth rests upon and develops the Talmud's famous statement about the different watches of the night. In tractate *Berakhot* 3a, we find the following well-known passage:

> Rabbi Eli'ezer says: There are three watches in the night; and in each and every one the blessed Holy One sits and roars like a lion, as is said: *YHVH roars from on high, / He makes His voice heard from His holy dwelling, / He roars aloud over His abode* (Jeremiah 25:30). The sign is: At the first watch, the donkeys bray; at the second, dogs bark; at the third, the child sucks at its mother's breast, and the woman converses / has intercourse with her husband . . .
>
> Rabbi Yitshak the son of Shemu'el said in the name of Rav: There are three watches in the night; and in each and every one the blessed Holy One sits and roars like a lion and says: "Woe to the children on account of whose sins I destroyed My house, burned down My sanctuary, and exiled them among the nations!"

Both Rabbi Eli'ezer and Rav present us with a highly mythical image intertwined with a realistic description of the different watches of the night. Night is the blessed Holy One's time of mourning, having lost His kingdom on earth. The blessed Holy One's mourning, however, is not confined to the immediate aftermath of the destruction of the Temple. The destruction, rather, has radically changed the history of the Jewish people, and even the figure of God Himself. The exiled deity—who in His wrath destroyed His house, killed His children, and exiled the survivors—is unable to be consoled, experiencing anew every night the pain of His and His people's fate.

The second part of the passage describes the sounds that characterize the different phases of the night, all of which are portrayed as expressions of the roaring divine voice: the donkeys bray; the dogs bark; and finally, in the dawn watch, the loving, tender image of a child sucking at its mother's breast and the woman conversing with her husband. Interestingly, the voices of the night, which are not portrayed here in demonic terms, and which realistically describe the natural course of the world, are employed as symbols of God's roaring over the loss of His abode.

In the continuation of the passage in tractate *Berakhot*, King David is presented as the "hero" of these hours between midnight and dawn. Rabbinic legends describe David as rising at midnight to the sound of the north wind playing his harp: he would praise and thank God in prayer and poetry until—with the onset of dawn—he would be called to focus on his kingly duties and the affairs of state.[3]

The Zohar's authors transformed the details of this aggadah into a mythic-cosmic drama. According to this myth, nighttime—every night—is the period during which transpires a divine drama, the protagonists of which are the world of divinity and the world of human beings. The first half of the night, from sunset until midnight, is considered by the Zohar a dangerous time, in which judgment and darkness govern the world. This is the time of God's great mourning over the destruction of His house and the ruin of His children.[4] During this half of the night, when it is proper to sleep, the souls of human beings ascend and traverse through different celestial realms and experience all manner of adventures. The souls of the righteous, unhindered by the forces of judgment, rise to the Lower Garden of Eden where they gaze upon God and bathe in the bliss emanating from the divine.

At midnight, the north wind is aroused, at which point all awakens: human beings awaken to study Torah on earth,[5] the blessed Holy One awakens to enter the Garden of Eden, the Garden of Eden awakens and begins to utter song, and the souls in the garden begin to praise and sing to God. Every night at midnight, the blessed Holy One—the male aspect of divinity, represented in the sefirotic structure by the sefirah *Tiferet*—enters the Lower Garden of Eden and delights in the souls of those engaged in His worship and His Torah.

The awakening at midnight and the poetic-mystical engagement with Torah throughout the night are the fruit of the authors' deep identification with the figure of King David, especially as represented in rabbinic legend, and as developed by the Zohar as a mystical, ecstatic figure with a female soul, identified with the sefirah *Malkhut*.[6]

> "All his days, King David would engage in the worship of the blessed Holy One, rising at midnight, praising and offering thanks in hymns of praise, to array his site in the kingdom above. For when a north wind aroused at midnight, he knew that at the same moment the blessed Holy One aroused in the Garden of Eden to delight with the righteous. So he rose at that moment and invigorated himself with songs and praise until morning arose. For we have established that when the blessed Holy One appears in the Garden of Eden, He and all the righteous in the garden together listen to his voice, as is written: *Companions listen for your voice; let me hear!* (Song of Songs 8:13). Moreover, a thread of love is drawn upon him by day. . . . Moreover, those words of Torah that he utters all ascend to be adorned before the blessed Holy One." (Zohar 1:178b; Matt 2004–2007, vol. 3, pp. 80–81, reformatted)

For the Zohar's authors, David is the archetypal mystic, a model for imitation, and the way to follow in his path is to know the mysteries of midnight and dawn.

Upon entering the Garden of Eden at midnight, the blessed Holy One gathers unto Himself the souls of the righteous abiding there, inhales their aroma, and kisses them; and He, together with all the inhabitants of the garden, awaits the words of Torah that ascend from the nocturnal scholars below.[7] The Lower Garden of Eden and the souls of the righteous are associated with the feminine and female aspect of the world, and God's entry into His garden has clear erotic overtones. The garden represents Shekhinah, and the souls of the righteous represent the Assembly of Israel—identified with Shekhinah, the partner of the blessed Holy One. The engagement with Torah on the earthly plane generates an erotic, arousing quality.

On the mythic-divine plane, these words of praise and love produce *mayin nukbin* (female waters), the fluids of passion and longing of the feminine aspect of the divine (Shekhinah, or the sefirah *Malkhut*).[8] Mythically, symbolically, and theurgically speaking, the nocturnal study of the mystics below beautifies and adorns Shekhinah, the bride, making her desirable to her lover, the blessed Holy One. In the soft, dim light of dawn, when the image of the goddess-bride has been arrayed in all her beauty, the climax of the nocturnal drama occurs. The male and female aspects of divinity join together, the moment of encounter akin to a wedding every dawn. The two then enjoy complete union—*zivvug* (coupling)—full of love and eros, drawing down blessings into all reality. After the *zivvug* and the commingling of the male and the female, the painful yet necessary moment of separation follows. The beloved separates from her lover and ascends with the rising light of morning.[9] The Zohar's treatment of *tikkun leil Shavuot* offers the most spectacular and complete model of this praxis.[10]

Arenas of the Nocturnal Delight

The nocturnal delight transpires simultaneously in two different arenas: the earthly arena of the gathering of the Companions at midnight, and the divine arena of the Lower Garden of Eden. The Lower Garden of Eden is portrayed as a realm from which it is possible to attain knowledge of, and even gaze upon, the divine.

According to the Zohar, God first placed Adam in the Garden of Eden to attain knowledge of the divine glory, such knowledge constituting the main purpose of human existence.[11] Following the exile from the Garden and the loss of the idyllic existence as portrayed in Genesis 2-3, God formed the souls of the righteous from the splendor of the supernal glory, in order to delight in them. From here on, it was to be the souls alone that would gain knowledge of and see the divine.

The Companions' nocturnal activities serve then to heal the breach of the exile from the Garden, for their praxis gives man the opportunity, while still alive, to connect with divine knowledge and to return to the divine garden from which he came. The Zohar relates that God created the Leviathan (interpreted as the sefirah *Yesod*) as a plaything with whom to sport; in the same way, I would suggest, the souls of the righteous (the fruit of the union of the sefirot *Yesod* and *Malkhut*) were also created for God's delight.[12] The souls are the handiwork of the deity, they are His, and He craves their intimacy.[13]

The idea that the delight is first and foremost that of the blessed Holy One, and that the pleasure experienced by the human participants in the drama is consequent on the divine pleasure, emerges clearly in a story appearing in the Torah portion *Terumah* that interprets a verse from Song of Songs: "King Solomon made him a palanquin of wood from Lebanon" (3:9). As Rabbi Shim'on explains, the palanquin symbolizes the sefirah *Malkhut* and the Lower Garden of Eden: "This palanquin and all those souls of the righteous exist so that the blessed Holy One will delight in them."[14]

The nocturnal delight is not a random experience; it is, rather, part of the cosmic order and is dependent on human awareness and intention. The Companions are the ones who know the laws and arrangements of the Garden of Eden. In their earthly study, they hold the map to this celestial world, as well as the techniques to act in this world of after-midnight delight. As Rashbi explains: "The Companions have been aroused about the laws of the Garden of Eden, as it is in the supernal mystery. . . . and no eye has sway [in the Garden of Eden], except for the souls of the righteous, for they are engraved above and below, so as to contemplate from there the secret of their Master with pleasure on high."[15] The souls of the faithful are thus capable of gazing at, and delighting in, the divine even while their bodies, which remain in this world, continue to function as normal. The Zohar explains this extraordinary ability as deriving from the fact that the mystic's astral image is inscribed both "above and below."

Here, then, lies a partial explanation for the Companions' ability to engage in Torah study after midnight in this world and simultaneously to participate in the celestial delight in the Garden of Eden. The Zohar describes a separation of the soul's parts, such that the mystic is able to remain alive and

awake, while at the same time to partake in the divine delight. The mystic—
or more precisely, his body and the parts of his soul that remain active on
earth below—is aware of aspects of the soul's celestial experience above.

This is a unique praxis, as the mystic is neither asleep nor in a meditative
state with eyes closed, so as to enhance his visionary and imaginative facul-
ties. The practitioner who remains awake during these hours does not do so
in seclusion, but rather he usually enjoys the company of one or more companions. The awakened mystics praise the blessed Holy One and engage in
Torah; they speak with one another and create *ḥiddushei Torah* (innovations
in Torah) from one another's words.

The capacity to remain both active and alert and at the same time to
maintain a contemplative consciousness that participates in the upper world
is distinctive. It differs, for example, from praxes whose focus is *devekut*,
cleaving to God while in a waking state, as outlined by Maimonides, for
whom attachment to the active intellect is dependent on the quieting of
external, earthly activities.[16] It differs also from contemplative practices demanding total concentration on God, as found in a variety of techniques
derived from the verse "I have placed YHVH before me always" (Psalms
16:8),[17] and from similar Sufi practices,[18] insofar as the Companions' interpersonal attention in the two arenas of activity remains heightened. The simultaneous yet differential participation of different levels of consciousness,
however, resembles various shamanic practices.[19]

The nocturnal delight is the focal point of the zoharic companions' activities, and the Zohar is replete with descriptions of this celestial drama and
its significance. Nevertheless, many questions remain regarding the character and nature of this activity. One central question is the status of the
dimension of reality known as the Lower Garden of Eden for the Zohar's
protagonists. The impression given is that Companions are privy to the laws
of the Garden of Eden and relate to it as real—the divine orchard—and
that they understand both its varied phases and aspects, as well as how to act
upon entry into this divine dimension. Interestingly, the Companions' individual existences or the individual integrity of their souls are preserved and
they are able to identify one another in the Garden of Eden, where they are

garbed in their astral forms.[20] At the same time, however, we cannot help
but gain the impression that the Lower Garden of Eden is a kind of "virtual
reality" whose laws are not entirely fixed and that continues to develop and
unfold with the Companions' experience.

Participants in the Delight

The nocturnal delight is an active, reciprocal experience for all the participants. The blessed Holy One delights in the souls of the righteous, and
at the same time human beings on earth delight in the Torah and thereby
delight God.[21]

The delight in the Garden of Eden is with both the souls of living and
the dead together.

> Rabbi Yitshak said, "So every single night souls of the righteous ascend, and
> at the moment of midnight the blessed Holy One comes to the Garden
> of Eden to delight with them." With whom? Rabbi Yose said: "With all of
> them, both those whose abode is in that world and those dwelling in their
> abode in this world. With all of them the blessed Holy One delights at mid-
> night." (Zohar 1:82b; Matt 2004–2007, vol. 2, p. 25, reformatted)

In another story that takes place on the banks of the Sea of Ginnosar,
the Companions expound the meaning of "the King's palanquin," namely,
the Lower Garden of Eden; in the course of their expositions, they reflect
on the difference between the delight of the soul already separated from its
body in this world and the delight of living souls.

> The souls above that have no body in this world imbibe from the light that
> flows from the pure balsam, and they delight in that supernal delight. The
> souls that have a body in this world ascend and imbibe from the light of
> that palanquin; and they descend. And they give and they take: they give
> of the fragrance of the good deeds they perform in this world, and they
> take from the fragrance found in the garden. . . . and all are found in the
> same garden, these ones delight above and these ones delight below. (Zo-
> har 2:127b)

In preparation for the nocturnal delight, the souls of the dead are arrayed
with a supernal light, in which they then delight with God. The delight with
the souls of the people of this world, however, transpires through the blessed

Holy One's yearning-filled attentiveness to the voice of praise and of Torah that ascends from the Companions below, and the drawing forth of His love and mercy upon them from above.

The participation of the souls of the living with the souls of the dead and with Shekhinah and with the blessed Holy One is presented as a real and clear possibility in the world of the Garden of Eden. Nevertheless, a question remains regarding the precise nature of this participation. The language employed by the Zohar to describe the relationship between the soul and the various divine figures in the Garden sometimes seems to suggest partnership or collaboration, as in the example of the maidens' taking part in decorating the bride, where the participation is born of identification. The Zohar, however, also describes a more essential partnership or cooperation, in which the theurgic dimension is paramount. In this case, aspects of the Companions' nocturnal activities below are transformed into active forces influencing the divine world above, while at the same time, the events of the Garden of Eden become active forces experienced by the Companions below, forces that continue to act upon them even with the onset of day.

Rituals of Preparation

In all of the Zohar's many accounts of the nocturnal delight, we find that a number of Companions (at least two of them) take part in this nightly praxis in order to ensure the presence of Shekhinah among them. The Companions assemble so as to join as one, and their joining brings about their union with Shekhinah, the necessary condition for the nocturnal delight—"now we have union with Shekhinah."[22] The centrality of fellowship is, as we have noted, of prime importance for the zoharic world; and in constructing religious experience and religious activity, the Zohar emphasizes cooperation, communication, and contact among loving companions, who in turn together love the Torah.

The nocturnal delight is preceded by a number of preparatory rituals. The first is the ritual washing of the hands upon arising at midnight, portrayed in the Zohar as a custom of the "ancient ḥasidim (pietists)"—

an epithet sometimes employed by the Zohar when describing kabbalistic innovations.[23]

> Rabbi El'azar speaking "This is what the ancient *hasidim* used to do: In front of them was a receptacle of water, and when they awoke at night they would wash their hands, rise, and study Torah—and offer a blessing over the crowing of the rooster. For the moment that the rooster crows is precisely midnight, when the blessed Holy One appears with the righteous in the Garden of Eden." (Zohar 1:10b; Matt 2004–2007, vol. 1, pp. 69–70)

Another preparatory ritual is the recitation of select biblical verses prefaced by special *kavvanot* (intentions) in order to arouse appropriate states of mind and soul. One verse recited in this context—"A river flows from Eden to water the garden"—functions, as we will see in detail,[24] as a verse of arousal throughout the composition. In the context of the kabbalists' nocturnal activities, it illustrates the way that they employ biblical verses as suggestive agents to awaken mystical consciousness. Such verses evoke the connection between the river and the garden, the divine and the human, the masculine and the feminine, as well as the wondrous and mysterious power of the divine. This preparatory ritual, it should be noted, is a mystical praxis in its own right and functions as a preparation for other ritual activities as well.

> And we have learned: Whoever arises at night, when the blessed Holy One enters the garden to delight in the righteous, must say this verse with desire of the heart, and attune his desire to it: *O YHVH, You are my Elohim, I will extol You, I will praise Your name, for you have done wonderful things, even counsels of old, in faithfulness and truth* (Isaiah 25:1). Afterward he shall say: *I praise You for I am awesomely, wondrously made, Your work is wonderful, I know it very well* (Psalms 139:14); and after that, *A river flows from Eden to water the garden* (Genesis 2:10).
>   And this is the praise of the ancient *hasidim* when they arose at midnight, and they would arrange their praises and engage Torah. (*Zohar Hadash, Balak*, 53b)[25]

Yet another technique practiced by the Companions in preparation for the nocturnal delight is the ceremonial raising of the hands (*nesi'at kapayim*). While it is possible that this was an established custom among the Companions in all their prayers, in the context of the psalms interpreted here and their connection to the kabbalists' nocturnal activities, it seems clear that raising the hands is connected to the ritual hand washing, and that it constitutes a symbolic-mystical act akin to the standard "raising of the hands" during the priestly blessing. *Nesi'at kapayim* involves directing one's intentions to the "sanctuary" (*kodesh*), from which divine abundance flows and pours forth to human beings.[26]

> *Now bless YHVH all you servants of YHVH [who stand nightly in the house of YHVH]* (Psalms 134:1) . . . this is the praise of all the sons of faith. And who are the sons of faith? They are the ones who engage Torah and know how to unify the holy name as is fitting. And the praise of those sons of faith, the ones who awaken at midnight with Torah . . . *who stand nightly in the house of YHVH*—these are called *servants of YHVH*, these are worthy to bless the King and their blessing is [indeed] a blessing, as is written: *Lift your hands toward the sanctuary and bless YHVH* (Psalms 134:2). You are worthy that the Holy King should be blessed by you, and the blessing uttered by you is a real blessing.
>
> *Lift your hands toward the sanctuary.* What is the sanctuary? The supernal place from which issues the fountain of the deep stream, as is written: *A river flows from Eden to water the garden.* And Eden is called supernal sanctuary, hence: *Lift your hands toward the sanctuary.*
>
> And of the man who does so and merits this, what do they proclaim about him? *May YHVH bless you from Zion* (Psalms 134:3). (Zohar 3:12b–13a)[27]

The Order of the Night in the Upper and Lower Worlds

The Zohar's accounts of the nocturnal drama are characterized by a simultaneous description of the events of the upper world and the events of the lower world. Crowning, mingling, and saturation are key concepts in these descriptions. The nocturnal praxis brings the dynamic flow of the divine plenty to a potent climax. This is accomplished, as we have already noted, through the Companions' words of Torah, which function as the quality that binds the Companions with Shekhinah. This binding, the union of the human being with Shekhinah through the words of Torah, causes Her to exude lower waters, waters of desire, which in turn arouse the blessed Holy One to unite in sexual intercourse with His Shekhinah.

Indeed, this continuum of desire and yearning that wells forth, flowing fluids of plenty, stands at the heart of the entire nocturnal delight.

> Rabbi Shim'on said, "When the blessed Holy One adorns Himself in His crowns, He crowns Himself above and below. Above, from the site deepest of all; below, with what? With the souls of the righteous. Then vitality is lavished above and below, embracing the site of the sanctuary on all sides. The cistern is filled, the ocean consummated, providing for all. . . . Desire of the female toward the male arouses only when a spirit enters her and she gushes water toward upper, masculine waters. Similarly Assembly of Israel arouses desire toward the blessed Holy One only by the spirit of the righteous entering Her. Then waters flow from within Her toward waters of the male, all becoming one desire, one cluster, one nexus. Rapture, total rapture! An amble ambled by the blessed Holy One with the souls of the righteous."
> (Zohar 1:60a–b; Matt 2004–2007, vol. 1, pp. 345–47)

The interdependence of the upper and lower worlds is presented here with great clarity. The mystic knows that without first uniting with the female divine dimension, without implanting a spirit within Shekhinah, arousal cannot occur. Indeed the source of the generation of that new spirit lies in joining with the female, and the divine flow has no way of reaching the world without the coupling (*zivvug*) between the human being and Shekhinah.[28]

The result of the union between the human being and Shekhinah—the arousal of Shekhinah and thus of the blessed Holy One in response to the presence of His aroused Shekhinah—is the generation of "one desire," the precondition for the nocturnal delight. During the delight, God gathers unto Himself the souls of the righteous, kisses them, and inhales their fragrant aroma; and this erotic-tender description is applied by the Zohar to the words of Torah that ascend before Him as well.[29]

The following passage, one of the most detailed accounts of the nocturnal delight found in the Zohar, highlights the interconnection between the events transpiring in the upper world and those transpiring below. The souls of human beings, together with their words of Torah—the fruit of their thoughts and emotions—are transformed into a gift bestowed by the Assembly of Israel to the blessed Holy One. They function as an aphrodisiac

arousing the union between God and His Shekhinah. The delight is characterized by the arousal of the entire reality of the Lower Garden of Eden—
with light, song, joy, and play preceding the dawn union.

> Rabbi Abba said, "Now is certainly the time for the blessed Holy One's
> desire; and many times we have been aroused by this, that at midnight the
> blessed Holy One enters among the righteous in the Garden of Eden and
> delights in them. Happy is he who engages in Torah at this time!"
>   Rabbi El'azar said, "How does the blessed Holy One delight in the righ-
> teous in the Garden of Eden? At midnight the blessed Holy One is aroused
> with love from the left [side] toward the Assembly of Israel. . . . and the
> Assembly of Israel has no gift with which to draw near to the king, nor
> any important, excellent [offering] like the spirits of the righteous that the
> blessed Holy One sees crowned with many good deeds and many merits
> attained that day. And the blessed Holy One is more pleased with them than
> with all the sweet savor of the sacrifices and offerings. Then a light shines
> and all the trees of the Garden of Eden utter song and the righteous are
> crowned there with the delights of the world that is coming. When a person
> arises at that hour to engage Torah, he partakes with the righteous in the
> garden." (Zohar 2:173b)

The union with Shekhinah in the celestial arena is described in mythic
terms: the queen seated in her sanctuary, with the souls of the righteous
portrayed as her maidens or palace intimates. In the earthly arena, the union
with Shekhinah is described through the experience of the assembling of
those Companions who unite to praise God and thereby achieve the indwelling of Her presence. God's delight in the soul is expressed via a rare
idiom in the Zohar: *tiyyul*, an amble or stroll.[30] The blessed Holy One ambles among the souls of the righteous.

In both biblical and midrashic contexts, the world *tiyyul* is associated
with effortless, pleasant strolling, in some cases with no end in mind, and
many times the locus of such ambling is among gardens and orchards.[31]
The connection between ambling, God, the Garden of Eden, and souls
perhaps derives from the passage in Genesis 3:8 that recounts the sound
of God moving about in the garden at the breezy time of day.[32] The great
midrashic leap, however, linking all the above elements, is found in the *Sifra*,
where the joint ambling of God and the righteous in the Garden of Eden is

understood as flowing from the shared essence of the human being and the divine—such a shared essence being crucial for understanding the nocturnal delight in the Zohar:

> *I will be ever-present in your midst* (Leviticus 26:12)—A parable: This may be likened to a king who went out ambling into the orchard with his tenant. The tenant attempted to hide, and the king said to the tenant: Why do you hide from me? I am just like you.
>
> So too the blessed Holy One said to the righteous: Why should you be frightened of Me?
>
> In the future the blessed Holy One will amble with the righteous in the Garden of Eden. The righteous will see Him and be frightened, but He will say to them: I am just like you.[33]

In the Zohar, God's ambling among the souls is associated with pleasure, joy, and delight, and it has strong erotic overtones.[34] While the Zohar contains only a few brief references to the divine ambling, Rabbi Moses Cordovero elaborates on this theme in his book *Shi'ur Komah*, suggesting that ambling is connected with the movement of pleasure, and that it serves as a synonym for delight:

> Our sages of blessed memory explained "I will amble among you in the Garden of Eden," and they transformed the meaning somewhat and said that a person can be called *mithalekh* (one who is moving about/roaming) even when the "movement" is not that of going from place to place, but rather the ambling (*tiyyul*) is transferred from the domain of walking to that of pleasure. . . . And Rabbi Shim'on explained the matter of the ambling, and said that Shekhinah uniting in supernal union is called "delight" and is called "ambling"; and that since She attains union by means of the deeds of the righteous, She is described as ambling among them, and the righteous also delight in this union . . . for they take pleasure, delight, and amble just like this sefirah *Tiferet* delights in its union with *Malkhut*, on account of the additional light emanated upon them together, and thus "I will amble among you in the Garden of Eden."[35]

Cordovero describes here a connection with the divine, which, while not quite "union," is nevertheless characterized by the pleasurable spreading of the divine throughout the soul. Rabbi Ḥayyim ben Atar offers a similar account in his commentary on the Torah, in his interpretation of "If you follow (*telekhu*) my laws" (Leviticus 26:3): "The kabbalists have said that this ambling (*tiyyul*) is a degree of delight beyond which there is no higher. Happy is the one who attains this! . . . through engaging Torah you will go (*telekhu*)—this is the walking concealed from all living beings, namely, the ambling. By means of the Torah you will amble in concealed places."[36]

In our discussion of the myth of the nocturnal delight in the Zohar, it is important to note that the weekday nocturnal delight differs from that of the Sabbath. Every night during the days of the week, the blessed Holy One enters the Garden of Eden to delight in the souls of the righteous, while on the Sabbath these souls ascend from the Lower Garden of Eden to the Upper Garden, where other holy souls in turn descend to adorn the holy nation. Such is the celestial drama in the upper realms.

The "earthly arena" too is witness to a unique midnight delight on the Sabbath. During the first part of the night, when the wise are asleep, their weekday soul, together with and under the direction of their additional Sabbath soul, ascends to gaze upon the divine glory. At midnight, the souls return to their abode in the body, at which point the wise awaken, as is their practice, to engage in sexual relations with their wives.[37]

This sexual act is, according to the Zohar, especially joyful and pleasurable on account of the additional Sabbath soul. During the Sabbath, the similarity between the lower and upper worlds intensifies. In contrast to the other nights of the week (when the pleasure enjoyed by the upper worlds is the fruit of the praise and Torah study of the male companions below), on the Sabbath this celestial pleasure is caused by the sexual intercourse of men and women in this world. The Companions who join together on weeknights create a symbolic union with one another and with Shekhinah. The union between a man and woman, on the other hand, is an actual bodily union—as well as a symbol for the "real" union between *Tiferet* and *Malkhut*, insofar as it is the human sexual act, termed by the Zohar *it'aruta be-ḥedva de-shimusha* (the arousal through the joy of sexual intercourse),[38] which brings pleasure to the Garden and its inhabitants. The female waters that are produced every day through the kabbalists' arousal of Shekhinah are produced on the Sabbath through the act of physical sexual union accompanied by appropriate *kavvanot*.

The act of Torah study and the joining together of the Companions into *ḥibura ḥada* (a single bond) assumes here a pronounced erotic significance. We must ask whether Torah study is a sublimation of sexual desire, or conversely, whether the ultimate or "truest" eros is between man and God through the Torah, of which the sexual act between man and woman is merely a symbol or echo.[39]

During the week, the paths of the majority of humanity and the paths of the Companions diverge in their opting for different means of *devekut* (cleaving): the people of the world opt for sexual union, while the Companions choose the path of Torah. Nevertheless, the Companions' sexual union with their wives on the Sabbath night is considered by the Zohar the most praiseworthy way of cleaving to God, insofar as their sexual act is directed to the divine union itself.

> Human sexual intercourse is fixed for certain times so as to direct one's will to cleaving to the blessed Holy One. They have already taught: At midnight the blessed Holy One enters the Garden of Eden to delight in the righteous, and the Assembly of Israel praises the blessed Holy One; and this is an auspicious time to cleave to Him. The Companions who engage Torah associate themselves with Her, the Assembly of Israel, to praise the Holy King and engage Torah. But for the rest of humanity it is an auspicious time to sanctify themselves with the sanctity of the blessed Holy One and to direct their will to cleaving to Him. As for the Companions who engage Torah, their intercourse [with their wives] takes place at the time of another intercourse—and this is from Sabbath to Sabbath. (Zohar 3:49b)

The Experience of Delight

Both for God and for the souls of the dead and the living, the experience of the nocturnal delight is one of pleasure and satisfaction. The pleasure is at once sensual and erotic and also quintessentially Jewish,[40] insofar as it derives from God's listening to the words of Torah uttered by the mystics below. In the Lower Garden of Eden, the contemplation of the Torah (a fundamental religious injunction) and speech itself (so central in the world of the Jewish mystic) are transformed into pleasurable and pleasuring activities.

Yet God's pleasure is in fact a form of consolation, for as we have already seen, during the course of the night, God sits in mourning and lamentation and castigates Himself for destroying His house, divorcing from His partner, and exiling His children among the nations.[41]

> A voice arouses in the middle of the firmament and loudly calls out and says: *Remember, O YHVH, against the Edomites the day of Jerusalem's fall; how they cried, "Strip her, strip her to her very foundations!"* (Psalms 137:7). Then [is the time] of His panic and trembling. . . . and since there is no joy and delight for the blessed Holy One aside from the hour when the righteous stand there, therefore He swears and says: *If I forget you, O Jerusalem, let my right hand wither, let my tongue stick to my palate if I cease to think of you, if I do not keep Jerusalem in memory even at my happiest hour* (Psalms 137:5). Wherever there is joy for the blessed Holy One, this voice goes forth and calls out. Then, it soars forth from there, splits firmaments, and roars mighty roars—until all the legions of heaven are panic-struck. . . . Then a wind blows and strikes the leaves of the mighty tree, and all its branches strike one another, and a voice arouses from within the trunk of the tree. . . . When this voice is aroused, Old Man Abraham hears and awakens at the auspicious time of the King, and he is consoled with Him. At that time, a spirit from the south side is aroused and all desire, joy, and healing are aroused in the world. (Zohar 3:303a; *Tosafot* 10)

The mourning, the delight, and the consolation—the key elements of the nocturnal drama—appear in varying orders in different places in the Zohar; in the account cited above, the mourning is subsequent to the delight and pleasure in the upper world.

Seen from a mythological perspective, the nocturnal delight is the way in which humanity comforts God. The zoharic myth is highly attuned to the continual recurrence of periods of mourning, separation, and bereavement, as well as times of harmony, unification, and love. The Zohar is profoundly aware that while there may be no end to the mourning of the great loss of both divine and human harmony, nevertheless this mourning does not color the entirety of being. The destruction of the Temple, described by the Zohar as the destruction of the divine coupling and as the divorce between God and His Shekhinah, is ever present in the Zohar's consciousness. At the same time, however, the Zohar insists on the possibility of moments of love and unification between the lover and his beloved. The hope and the belief in the possibility of intimacy and love are strengthened when the great father hears the voice of his children, whom he has lashed and punished with exile. In this familial myth, it is the words of the children that provide solace and comfort—and that create the possibility of the return and reunion of the mother and father.

Humankind's words of Torah constitute the most beloved praise of the blessed Holy One—theirs is the voice He desires and indeed, during the nocturnal delight all the voices and sounds of the Garden of Eden fall silent when the voice of man begins to be heard.[42] God's delight is His arousal to the love of His world and His creatures, an awakening brimming with consolation and comfort in that there is hope after all, that there are Jews in His world, that the study of Torah continues, that there are reciprocal relations of love between Himself and humanity, and that His Shekhinah may be raised from the dust at any moment. His response is a love-filled game with the words of man, their souls, and His Shekhinah.

The Companions' experience of the nocturnal delight on earth is portrayed mainly as one of irrigation. The Zohar describes the mystical experience of human contact with the divine as the pleasure of being watered by the river that issues from Eden, from the depths of divinity, which flows into the Garden of Eden and onto man. This experience is distinguished by the simultaneous participation of the souls in the garden above and humanity on earth below.

> Happy are Israel above all the nations, for the blessed Holy One gave them a holy Torah and bequeathed them holy souls from a holy place, so as to fulfill His commandments and delight in the Torah! For whoever delights in Torah fears nothing, as is written: *Were not your teaching my delight I would have perished in my affliction* (Psalms 119:92). What is *my delight*? Torah. For the Torah is called a delight, as is written: *a source of delight every day* (Proverbs 8:30). And this is as we have learned: The blessed Holy One comes to delight in the righteous in the Garden of Eden. What does it mean "to delight"? To rejoice in them. As we have learned: Happy are the righteous, of whom is written: *then you will delight in YHVH* (Isaiah 58:14), to delight in the saturation of the stream, as is written: *He will satisfy your thirst with sparkling flashes* (Isaiah 58:11)! The blessed Holy One delights in them, as it were, from that same saturation of the stream in which the righteous take pleasure, and on account of this He comes to delight with the righteous. (Zohar 3:67b)

The following passage provides a clear account of the mystical experience that transpires at the climax of the nocturnal delight. This is an experience of the World to Come (sometimes translated as "world that is coming"), namely, the world of the river that issues from the depths of Eden, and that—upon reaching humanity—bathes and saturates it. It should be stressed here though, that the Companions' nocturnal activities serve also a quintessential theurgic-mystical end. Their activities comprise both the quest to act upon the world of divinity as well as the desire for unmediated contact with the divine.

> Rabbi Ḥizkiyah said: "Certainly whoever engages in this [namely, Torah at this time] shares constantly in the world that is coming."
>
> Rabbi Yose asked: "What do you mean 'constantly'?"
>
> He replied: "So we have learned: Every midnight, when the blessed Holy One arouses in the Garden of Eden, all the plants of the Garden are watered profusely by the stream called Stream of Antiquity, Stream of Delights, never ceasing. If one rises and engages in Torah, then that stream gushes upon his head, as it were, saturating him among those plants of the Garden of Eden."
>
> Rabbi Yose said: "Since all those righteous in the Garden listen to him, he shares in the saturation of that stream; in consequence, he shares constantly in the world that is coming." (Zohar 1:92a–b; Matt 2004–2007, vol. 2, p. 81)[43]

The mystic who engages Torah at midnight thus experiences himself as part of the garden—the saturation and watering of which are the very purpose of the flow of the divine river that issues from Eden. The river is the world that comes and flows continuously into reality from within the hidden inner recesses of divinity, and all the Companions' nocturnal activities are directed to the dimension of being in which it is possible to experience something of that river.

Any reading of the Zohar's nocturnal delight highlights the centrality of eros, sexuality, and sensuality in this myth. Zoharic eros is ever present in all arenas of human experience, with no dichotomous separation between the sensual and the spiritual, body and speech, matter and spirit, or emotion and intellect, as both bearers of eros and its objects. Eros informs all, and just as a new word of Torah generates erotic, sensual pleasure, so the experience of contemplating a physical rose, for example, brings pleasure whose eros might be intellectual or religious.

As activity and as experience, the nocturnal delight involves both the masculine and feminine. From the perspective of the masculine, the delight is a form of pleasure, and regardless of whether the source of this pleasure is the word of Torah issuing from the lips of man below or is caused by the divine itself, such pleasure is connected with the divine grade of *Yesod*. This grade is an expression of masculine sexuality in all its forms, from the most mythic as the divine phallus, to more subtle forms as in the joyful production of *ḥiddushei Torah* (innovative interpretations of Torah).[44] The delight is play or a game of love—God gathers and raises the souls of the righteous, inhales their fragrance, kisses them, and is adorned by them—prior to the union of *Tiferet* and *Malkhut*. The delight of the righteous in the Torah and in Shekhinah is also an erotic and sexual activity. Their words of song and praise, together with their arousal of the spirit, are in fact the courtship or foreplay preceding intercourse.

From the perspective of the feminine, the delight involves the pleasuring of Shekhinah with the souls of human beings, Her earthly lovers, as well as Her beautification and fulfillment through the love they bestow upon Her. Her greatest delight, however, is surely with Her lover, the blessed Holy One, who is filled with erotic yearning and jealousy on account of the pleasure She enjoys with the souls of the righteous. Shekhinah thus enjoys a "double delight"—that which comes from the world below through human beings, and that which comes from above, from the arousal of the blessed Holy One who comes to delight in Her.[45] The Zohar emphasizes the dependence of all delights—be they spiritual or physical, divine or human—on the quality of the sefirah *Yesod*, or in the language of the Zohar, "the righteous one" (*Tsaddik*).

> And this Lower Garden is the portion of this point [*Malkhut*] to delight in the souls of the righteous on earth; and She thus enjoys from all sides, above and below. Above with the righteous one and below with the fruit of the righteous one. And there is no delight either above or below except through the righteous one. (Zohar 2:211b)

The Zohar is totally unapologetic about the deep connection between religious experience and both sexuality and eros. Eros is foundational in the Companions' life, the generative force of the entire composition, and is as Yehuda Liebes has said, "the radiance of the Book of Radiance."[46]

But what remains of the nocturnal experience during the day? The sages of the Talmud taught that "whoever engages in Torah at night, the blessed Holy One emanates a thread of grace upon him by day."[47] In the Zohar, this thread of grace is transformed into a luminescent quality and is the sign or imprint of the upper worlds that remains with the soul upon its return from the nocturnal delight. The thread of grace is the residual radiance of the joyous harmony of the union between the King and Matronita in which the Companions participated, and it stays with them throughout the entire day and even protects them from the forces of judgment.[48] During the day, the thread of grace of the nocturnal delight becomes an agent of blessing for the mystic and indeed for all reality.

It should be stressed that the midnight awakening to engage Torah is not presented in the Zohar as a mere suggestion—to be adopted or not as the practitioner sees fit—but rather constitutes the most essential and characteristic religious-mystical activity of the zoharic Companions. The mystical-poetic and social engagement with Torah from midnight till dawn is what defines the Companionship and structures its way of life. Consequently, the awakening at midnight is a key component in the Zohar's many narratives. In some of these stories, while on the road, the protagonists find themselves at a stranger's house or at an inn, and we hear them wondering how they will awaken for their nightly study. In many cases, the first expositions they expound upon arising take as their subject matter midnight, the nocturnal delight, and the celestial attunement to the voice of humanity below.[49] Such stories are the primary means for imparting the custom of arising at midnight,[50] as well as for illustrating the kind of expositions that bring such intense pleasure and satisfaction to both the human and divine worlds.

Central as this praxis is, the Zohar is not blind to reality and repeatedly laments the fact that the nocturnal delight, along with the pleasure, blessings, and protection associated with this ritual activity, has not become the patrimony of all; in the words of the Zohar, "no one is aroused, except the truly virtuous, who rise and arouse themselves with Torah."[51] The people of the world choose to close their eyes, ears, and heart to the divine drama—a drama that, as we have seen, lies at the heart of the kabbalists' quest. The entire nocturnal delight is then the patrimony of a small group, "the truly virtuous," "the sons of faith," who are of course the Companions themselves.

The Companions' self-perception as the "holy initiates (or: sons) of God"—that is, as sparks of souls from the heavenly academies scattered among the living in this world—derives from their despairing of the rest of humanity (who do not choose to awaken to participate in the divine drama).[52] Theirs is a sectarian and elitist consciousness, and the Companions' disappointment in the world only strengthens their sense of fraternity as the ones capable, by virtue of their coming together, of accomplishing anything, insofar as they are the ones who engage in Torah and who are united with a single heart and a single desire. While the rest of the world slumbers and fails to rise and arouse, "*we* [the Companions] stand *here* to be aroused by the words of Torah!"[53] The Companions' view of themselves recalls the self-perception of medieval knightly orders and monastic groups, and even Gnostic sects from late antiquity.

The Companions' nocturnal engagement in Torah is no ordinary learning event; it is rather a devotional practice filled with the song and praise of Torah, and with a focus on the Torah's secrets rather than her simple meaning (*peshat*). The Zohar, which is highly attuned to the significance of the different times of the day and the inherent power and dangers associated with them, views the statutory morning prayer (*Shaḥarit*) as a "meditation" with God during a time of grace, the statutory afternoon prayer (*Minḥah*) as a "moaning" during a time of judgment, while the hours after midnight are the auspicious time for poetry, song, and praise. That night should be a time especially designated for song and poetry is derived by the Zohar from the oft-repeated verse, "By day YHVH directs His grace; at night His song is with me" (Psalms 42:9).[54] (In the following chapters we will explore the special forms of study and interpretation employed by the Companions at different times.)

Perhaps the most extraordinary aspect of this entire ritual is the kabbalists' recognition and awareness of the auspiciousness of different times of the day, month, and year, and their preparedness to respond to and participate in the varied chapters of the ongoing and unfolding divine story. The cycle of each day and the commandments associated with it are, as we have seen, witness to a grand drama: the drawing near, union, separation, mourning, and sorrow of the divine powers—a drama that drives reality and that determines the content of the smaller episodes in the divine drama, namely, the life of human beings.

The theurgic effort—to be there, to participate, to influence and be influenced—is what drives this mythic drama. The hours of grace, joy, and harmony are the small hours of the night, the hours when the world is illuminated by the silvery, multihued light of the moon and stars. For the protagonists of the Zohar, the climax of the last watch of the night is the brief, enchanting moment of dawn, when the dark light of night and soft light of morning intermingle just before sunrise. The Zohar thus offers an interesting (and perhaps harsh) comment about the domain of the day, where everything is illuminated by the strong light of the sun, the time when God the King, the male, reigns supreme—a time of law, certainty, and stability.

In this world of day, the mystic-poet finds no place for the deepest expressions and yearnings of his soul. He is, rather, a man of the night, a son of the Kingdom of Shekhinah, full of secrets, shadows, and imagination. The engagement with Torah after midnight and the endeavor to participate, day in and day out, in the nocturnal delight in the Garden of Eden lie at the core of the mystic's service and worship; and it is this spiritual task that determines his way of life and his soul's orientation.

In order to more fully understand the world of mystical experience in the Zohar, we need to appreciate the significance of the Companions' diligence in arising every night at midnight and, in the words of the Zohar, "awaiting each day the light that shines when the King visits the doe and is glorified and is declared King of all kings of the world." Mystical life is dependent on this praxis, and to belong to the Companionship one must fulfill this physically and spiritually demanding responsibility, for "whoever does not await this each day in that world has no portion here!"[55]

We conclude this chapter with one of the Zohar's most beautiful accounts of the nocturnal delight both on earth below and in the Garden of Eden above. In this account, which precedes the description of the confusion, panic, and consolation we saw earlier, various components of the delight combine to produce a complete picture.

The homily opens with a description of the recitation of verses of arousal, among them "a river flows from Eden to water the garden" (Genesis 2:10), which comprises the essence of the "mystery of faith," in order to generate the appropriate state of mind and intention for the encounter that awaits.

The order of the nocturnal delight is then described: below on earth, the awakening followed by the arrangement of praises and Torah study; above in the upper world, the bathing of the souls in the dew of the resurrection; their arrayal in supernal light; their encounters with the messiah, Elijah the prophet, and the forefathers; and their Torah study in the celestial academy. The male and female souls, together with their newly created words of Torah, gather before God, who delights both in them and in their words of Torah, inhaling their fragrant aroma.

The account concludes with the experience of revelation, when the souls behold the divine bliss (no'am YHVH). The experience of gazing upon God—upon the divine bliss—fills the souls with light and saturates them with joy, and bestows fruitful blessings on the world.

> . . . the two that are one, the river and the garden.
>
> The river that issues from Eden and the garden that is watered by it—here is the entire concealed mystery of faith. And we have learned: Whoever arises at night, at the time when the blessed Holy One enters the garden with the righteous, must say this verse [a river flows from Eden] with desire of the heart, and must attune his mind to it; and afterward he shall say, I praise You for I am awesomely, wondrously made; Your work is wonderful, I know it very well (Psalms 139:14).
>
> And this is the praise of the ancient ḥasidim when they arose at midnight and would arrange their praises and learn Torah. . . . When the blessed Holy One enters at midnight, all stand fittingly arrayed [as well as] all their engagements in innovations in Torah in which they engaged that day. The

blessed Holy One's yearning is for those righteous who innovate words in [Torah], and He delights in them and in those words. Afterward, all are arrayed, male and female; and the blessed Holy One—after He inhales [their fragrance] and delights in them and in all those words, their secrets of wisdom—is revealed upon them and they behold that delight of YHVH [*no'am YHVH*]. Then, all rejoice with great joy until their splendor and light illuminates forth. And from the splendor and light of their joy fruits are made for this world. (Zohar 3:303a; *Tosafot* 10)[56]

Wondrous Characters and Journeys
in the Upper Worlds

In discussing the Companions' major arenas and modes through which mystical experience transpires, we need to mention two special types of experience: the Companions' encounters with wondrous characters on the way, and their collective journey into the upper worlds as recounted in the literary unit *Rav Metivta* (Master of the Academy).

The Appearance of Wondrous Characters

In many of the Zohar's narratives, a new insight, or a surprising revelation of the dimension of the secret, enters the story and the Companions' consciousness through the appearance of a wondrous character who does not belong to the circle of Rabbi Shim'on's disciples.[1] We meet these surprising characters at crossroads, in caves, in fields, by the seashore, or while they are goading donkeys on the way. Typically, these wondrous beings appear as marginal figures in terms of both their social and intellectual standing—for example, as young children, as donkey-drivers, as old men, or as hermits in the desert—and generally we are not told their names.

These wondrous figures play an important role in the Zohar's deep wish to awaken and arouse its readers. If we simplify the zoharic narratives in which these characters appear to their barest and most essential structure, we find a narrative arc in which the ordinary understanding of reality is undermined. This undermining is a critical step on the path to a more expansive, altered conception of reality. The wondrous character enters a scene that already features one or more of Rashbi's disciples. The Companions' first reaction is one of derision,[2] an attitude that expresses the stasis of their understanding of normative, social reality. It is as though the Companions are saying: "We are sages, the elect disciples of Rabbi Shim'on; and you, who are you, anyway? What can you possibly offer us? Certainly you have nothing to teach us in matters of Torah!" It is at this point that the narrative unfolds and the plot is overturned.

The seasoned Zohar reader already expects this narrative twist, knowing that the initial scorn directed at the mysterious character is a sign that things are about to change. And thus, in the context of the all-too-normative expositions by the Companions in the story, we find the surprising intervention of the donkey-driver, the old man, or the young child, who offers extremely profound Torah interpretations—to which the Companions' own expositions pale in comparison. The ironic space of the story has opened, and the Companions suddenly understand that reality is far more complex than they had previously thought.

What transpires is nothing less than a carnivalesque inversion, insofar as the sages are revealed as fools, and the donkey-drivers or young children are revealed as superlative sages and hidden masters of the esoteric Torah. And just like the carnival, the purpose of the undermining here is not to annihilate the existing social order—to claim that the sages have no knowledge whatsoever, and that only the donkey-drivers and children are of worth. (Such a venomous, radical tone may perhaps be discerned in parts of *Tikkunei ha-Zohar* and *Ra'aya Meheimna*.) These stories, rather, manage in a subtle and nuanced way to expand consciousness and broaden its boundaries. Generally, at the end of these stories the Companions kiss the wondrous figure who has just disclosed mysterious secrets of Torah. They acknowledge his greatness. Thus is the world of these wondrous, marginal characters brought into the world of the Companions.

Moreover, in most cases it turns out that the donkey-driver was no ordinary donkey-driver and the young child no ordinary child, but that each one of them in fact has a distinguished lineage in the chain of mystical masters. Just as the Companions' consciousness is expanded as they stand in awe of the wondrous being whom they have encountered, something similar happens in the experience of the reader: reality is not as it seemed at first.

Who are these wondrous characters? From reading the many stories in the Zohar in which such miraculous beings appear, the possibility emerges that they are in fact the shadow image or alter ego of Rabbi Shim'on himself. In these stories, Rashbi is nowhere to be found; the Zohar contains not a single encounter or dialogue between Rabbi Shim'on and these wondrous beings.[3] Significantly, in many instances, after the enigmatic encounter with such a character, the disciples go to Rabbi Shim'on to have him explain and interpret for them the meaning of the mysterious figure's words. And indeed, Rashbi explains to his students both the identity of the wondrous character as well as the significance of the Companions' encounter with him.

In a most delightful and playful manner, the wondrous characters often refer to Rabbi Shim'on himself, and Rashbi then completes the game—and the plot—by taking up the challenge that they posed to the Companions in his absence. A prime example of this is found at the end of a story from the Introduction to the Zohar. At the end of their encounter with a wondrous old donkey-driver, two Companions are excited and amazed; their emotional and psychological state displays all the signs of zoharic mystical experience: "Rabbi El'azar and Rabbi Abba fell before him. Meanwhile they did not see him. They rose, looking in every direction, but could not see him. They sat down and wept, and could not speak to one another."[4] The Companions' encounter with a being whom they understand to be a divine figure heralding from another world (namely, the apparition of the late Rav Hamnuna Sava) brings about a change in their consciousness seen in their response: they fall on their faces, weep, and (for a certain time) lose their ability to speak.

On the continuation of their journey, and arising from the recognition that they merited a face-to-face encounter with a divine figure, they attain an additional experience of heightened consciousness: at nightfall they hear the song of the trees in the hills. This change in consciousness is not restricted to the Companions alone, for even their donkeys refuse to walk on and leave the sacred site of that revelation.[5]

When the Companions reach Rabbi Shim'on, even before they are able to tell him of all that has befallen them, Rashbi, the all-knowing hero of the Zohar, tells them that they have most certainly arrived from a journey filled with "heavenly miracles and signs," for he saw in his dream Benayahu son of Yehoyada (the biblical hero of Rav Hamnuna's exposition) sending them two crowns by the hand of a certain old man. When the Companions recount the details of their encounter to Rabbi Shim'on, he weeps, raises his hands above his head, and exclaims: "What a privilege that you saw Rav Hamnuna Sava, radiance of Torah, face-to-face! I was not so privileged."[6] In Rashbi's words here, we can discern a veiled and subtle sense of humor at work, for after all it is Rabbi Shim'on himself who is called "the face of Shekhinah" and "Shekhinah."[7] From that day on, we are told, Rabbi Shim'on called Rabbi El'azar and Rabbi Abba by the name *Peni'el* (the face of God, as in Genesis 32:31), for they had seen God face-to-face.

Another particularly amusing example is found in the story *Sava de-Mishpatim* (The Old Man of [the Torah portion] *Mishpatim*) where an old man propounds a riddle to Rabbi Shim'on's disciples. He asks them to solve it upon meeting their teacher: "Companions, when you go to that rock upon which the world rests, tell him to remember the day of snow when beans were sown of fifty-two hues, and we cited this verse; and he will tell you.... When you remind him of this sign, he will complete [the matter]."[8] It is clear that the "rock upon which the world rests" alludes to Rabbi Shim'on.[9]

When the disciples indeed meet their teacher and tell him the details of the encounter, Rashbi responds in an ironic and humorous way. He is delighted and amazed—and wonders how it is that his students, who attained all this, when they met a heavenly lion, a powerful hero, were unable to identify him immediately. "I am amazed," adds Rabbi Shim'on, "that you escaped his punishment!"[10]

What we have here, then, is a game of roles, as the authors play with Rashbi's character. In the persona of Rabbi Shim'on bar Yoḥai, he appears as the hero of the composition, "the central pillar," "the lamp of the world," "the holy luminary," the great teacher, etc.; as such, he appears as a persona whose words bear authority ex cathedra. On the other hand, when Rashbi appears in the guise of a wondrous character, he represents a different order of knowledge, expanding the possibilities for learning the divine wisdom; Rashbi now is neither alone nor the single and solitary pillar. This represents a democratization of Rabbi Shim'on's wisdom, or of the divine wisdom: circulating in the margins of society are unknown characters brimming with divine wisdom akin to that of Rashbi.

The sparkling of profound divine wisdom in these characters, or among the birds of the sky and the animals of the mountains, does not, it should be stressed, generate tension or competition with the wisdom of Rabbi Shim'on; rather, it broadens the significance of the zoharic concept "a generation in which Rabbi Shim'on abides." We have already seen how this concept signifies the Zohar's protagonists' understanding of their own time as an era and generation of divine illumination, whose chief representative is Rabbi Shim'on bar Yoḥai.[11] Significantly, Rashbi glorifies and praises these wondrous characters each time he hears of their adventures.

We have here a subtle and sophisticated sense of humor vis-à-vis the character of the work's hero. At the same time, although this is not explicit in the Zohar, it may be that these characters are supposed to be construed as sparks or souls derived from the soul of Rabbi Shim'on—and that they exist in every generation. Rabbi Isaac Luria, whose thought affords a more central place to reincarnation of the soul and its different parts than the Zohar does, understood these characters in precisely this way.[12]

Collective Journeys in the Upper Worlds

In the literary unit called *Rav Metivta* (Master of the Academy), which appears in the Zohar's printed editions in its commentary to the Torah portion *Shelaḥ Lekha*, we are witness to a unique phenomenon in the life of Rabbi Shim'on's circle. The entire circle attains a mystical, ecstatic experience, as they pass from studying Torah below on earth to a new dimension of being in the heavenly land of life—the Garden of Eden of the wilderness generation. During this journey, which the Companions experience in their bodies and not only in their souls, their awareness that they are earthly tourists in the celestial world is preserved throughout.

The setting of this event, after intensive Torah study in which the Companions expound the mystical meaning of the wilderness generation and its unique fate, allows us to assume that the Companions' leap to a higher dimension of being is the fruit of their mystical exposition. On the other hand, since the leap itself is not documented, it may be that we are dealing with an editorial arrangement; namely, the editors decided to insert a separate literary unit because of the homiletic and thematic context of the biblical story of the spies and those who died in the wilderness. What is important for our purposes, however, is that the Companions narrate their unique mystical experience and contrast their celestial visit with their ordinary earthly domain.

As noted above, the moment of the leap is not recorded; and the manuscript editor of the printed Zohar attests that in all the copies he had before him, the beginning of this unit is missing. The absence of the story's opening can lead to a fascinating detective-like search throughout the Zohar's many pages, for it might be assumed that there once was an opening to this story that has, unfortunately, been misplaced, garbled, or lost. Yet it is also possible that the dramatic gap (that juxtaposes speaking about the dead of the wilderness generation with an actual visit to their celestial abode) is intentional—as if the very moment of the ascent itself cannot be documented. It seems to me that the fragmentary opening that has made its way into our hands is the precious description of a change in the order of being or in the protagonists' consciousness.

> . . . with one another what they were unable to say previously.
>
> They departed from that opening and sat down in the garden beneath the trees.
>
> They said to one another, "Since we are here and have seen all this, if we die here, we will certainly enter the world that is coming!"

They sat down, slumber descended upon them, and they fell asleep. In the meantime, the official came and roused them.

He said to them: Arise, go to the orchard outside! (Zohar 3:161b)

We can assume that the beginning of the sentence was something like: "And they were able to speak with one another . . . " The entry into the new state of the reality of the celestial garden is characterized, first and foremost, by a new ability to utter what had previously been unutterable. This is a most remarkable expansion of the definition of the enlightened mystic (*maskil*), defined, as we have seen, as one who "contemplates by himself, from himself, words that other human beings cannot mouth." Here the experience enables the expansion of the boundaries of verbal communication.[13]

This first experience also expresses the erotic moment of the removal of the veils interposing between lovers—such removal enabling a face-to-face encounter, in which what was previously concealed is now openly revealed. Similarly, in the old man's parable of the maiden in the palace, here is how he describes the intimate moment when the beloved removes her veils: "She reveals herself face to face and tells him all her hidden secrets, all the hidden ways, since primordial days secreted in her heart."[14]

To return to *Rav Metivta*, we observe that the Companions describe the intensity of their experience, the expansion of vision, and the awareness that they are in a different plane of reality. They testify that they are prepared to die; and the palpable sense of proximity to the "world that is coming" and the slumber beneath the trees are expressions of the shock at the moment of entry to mystical experience.[15] The official who awakens them tells them to enter the orchard (*pardes*), clearly alluding to the mystical journey into the divine orchard in the talmudic story "the four who entered paradise."[16] With an enhanced sensory capacity, the Companions are able to fly from place to place, to gaze upon flying souls, to inhale the aroma of roses and apples in passage from state to state, to contemplate a celestial figure that changes shape from an eagle to a man, to join with figures from the wilderness generation, and to learn their Torah from them—all amid the dissolution of the laws of ordinary time—and to behold a collective, mystical ritual of burial and re-birth, whose purpose is purification and preparation for immortality.[17]

These examples, along with many others in this story, are the expression of an exceptional mystical experience in the Zohar. The experience relayed here, like its precedents in the *Heikhalot* literature, is of a journey into the divine world, for the duration of which the Companions maintain their earthly identity—even if at one point they remark that they have forgotten what it is like to be human.

In many parts of this journey, the role of the Companions is that of viewer. The experience is not merely an emotional, psychological, or sensory impression; rather it has a content, a body of knowledge that must be learned, although without the dimension of fear and terror found in the *Heikhalot* literature. The participants experience a process in which they pass from the margins of the celestial reality they are visiting to its very heart.[18] However, as already noted, this description is one of a kind; and in the majority of the Zohar's narratives, the character of mystical experience is quite different.

PART III

THE ZOHARIC QUEST

Methods of Generating Mystical Experience

So far we have met the Companions and their characteristic way of life. In this part, we penetrate to the core of the composition and acquaint ourselves with the deep quest of the zoharic world through an understanding of the forces that motivate its heroes. What is the purpose of their religious service? What do they seek on their journeys, in their nocturnal awakening, and in the intense life of the circle centered around the teacher? Focusing on these questions also illuminates the world of the composition's authors.

This part explores, in turn, three aspects connected to the very heart of the existence of the zoharic circle and the quests that motivate its members:

The mystery and its homilies—The Companions seek to reach, through special modes of interpreting biblical verses, the dynamic layer of reality, which in the Zohar is called "the mystery" (or "the secret"). In this layer, human beings can participate (in different ways) in the dynamic life of divinity, and they can even influence it. This dimension of reality is mainly hidden from the eye, the heart, and the intellect; yet according to the Zohar, the world abides by virtue of "the mystery." Chapter 8 examines the meanings of this crucial zoharic concept and the ways to attain this dynamic dimension of reality. Chapter 9 explores Zoharic hermeneutics, that is, the way in which the protagonists of the Zohar read meaning into the verses of Torah, and the way that they use both classical and innovative forms of midrash to bring about and enhance mystical consciousness.

Awakening (Chapter 10)—The language of arousal is central to the Zohar. It comprises many aspects of the fundamental quest to arouse in human consciousness a more expansive, enhanced, and stimulated state than that which exists in ordinary states of wakefulness. The purpose of such awakening is to enable the fuller realization of humanity's existence and destiny as having been created in the divine image. The desired awakening relates to all dimensions of the human being; and the erotic, intellectual, sensorial, and emotional aspects of this awakening, as well as those pertaining to consciousness, are intertwined.

Verses of awakening and arousal—In the Zohar's language of experience, the verse "A river flows from Eden to water the garden . . ." (Genesis 2:10) functions as a concentrated expression, or kind of code, comprising the dynamic structure of reality in all its different dimensions. Chapter 11 explores the extraordinary array of this verse's symbolic meanings, and the ways it is employed as the central verse of awakening.

Concealed and Revealed

The Dimension of Mystery

Whether we encounter the Companions while walking on the way or in their nightly study vigil, we find that the distinguishing feature in all their activities is their interpretation of biblical verses. The Companions expound the Torah in a way that enables them to access its secret dimension, to reveal the divine dimensions found within its verses, and to be transformed by them. Indeed, the mystical experience in the Zohar is dependent on the possibility of entering the dimension of the secret.

In the rich language through which the world of the Zohar defines itself, the centrality of the concept "secret" or "mystery" is readily apparent. The Zohar repeatedly states the idea that in every single word of the Torah, the Prophets, and the Writings, divine mysteries lie concealed. As Rabbi Shim'on teaches: "And you do not find a single word in the Torah or even a tiny letter in the Torah that does not hint at the supernal wisdom and contain heaps and heaps of mysteries of the supernal wisdom."[1]

But what is "the secret" in the Zohar, and what is "the mystery" hidden in the words of the Torah? It is important to state at the outset that "the secret" in the zoharic world is not a body of knowledge forever sealed and concealed on account of its sanctity or because of the inherent danger associated with it. The dimension of the secret is also not by nature unattainable. As opposed to other medieval conceptions of esotericism, the secret in the Zohar designates the dynamic layer within reality—the dimension that in fact constitutes the foundational quality of the world; in the words of the Zohar: "The world endures only by virtue of the secret."[2]

The divine medium through which it is possible to enter the divine realm of the secret is Torah—that is, the Hebrew Bible. In a wonderful homily appearing in the Zohar's commentary to the Torah portion *Shelah Lekha*, Rabbi Shim'on instructs his disciples about entry into the world of the secret through his interpretation of the story of the journey of the spies in the Land of Israel. In this homily, the Land of Israel of the biblical account is transformed into a symbol for the divine lands of the secret, which are revealed through a special familiarity with the words of the Torah. Rabbi Shim'on explains that in order to appropriately enter the worlds awaiting those who know the secrets of Torah, one must first of all "spy them out," that is, clarify matters concerning them. Torah is the map to the lands of the secret as well as a divine land in and of itself. The secret is a total world and dimension in which one must know in advance how to act.

> The blessed Holy One praises the Torah and says: Walk in My ways, engage in My service, and behold I will grant you entry to good worlds, to supernal worlds.
>
> Human beings do not know, do not believe, and do not consider!
>
> The blessed Holy One says: Go, spy out that good world, the supernal world of yearning.
>
> They say: How are we to spy it out and know all this?
>
> What is written: *Go up there into the Negev* (Numbers 13:17)—engage Torah and you will see that [the land] stands before you, and from her you will know that [world]. (Zohar 3:159b)

It is true that sometimes in the Zohar "the secret" refers to a closed, esoteric body of knowledge; the Zohar speaks of the secrets of cosmogony, physiognomy, the secrets of the structure of the soul and its destiny after death, the secrets of the other side, the world of evil, and the secrets of the structure of divinity and its emergence from its infinite hidden recesses to active, attainable divine being. In these contexts, the word "secret" connotes specific content. Typically, however, for the Zohar "the secret" refers to a dynamic, unfolding dimension of being that is intricately connected with, and arising from, the narrative or exegetical context. As noted by Rabbi Joseph Gikatilla, one of the key personalities associated with the Zohar's composition, the secrets of Torah are "concealed secrets revealed to the eye."[3] The secret is found within the revealed verses of the Torah and is neither uniform nor univalent.[4]

The Zohar thus removes the veil of esotericism that characterized the major currents of medieval Jewish thought, both in philosophy and in Kabbalah. Concealment and exclusivity are no longer self-evident strategies in the chain of transmission of secrets. The Zohar transforms the meaning of the concept "secret" and creates new paths to understand the appropriate means for the transmission of secrets as well as the ways in which they are created. Indeed this removal of the veil of secrecy greatly impressed later Zohar commentators, as attested by the words of the eighteenth-century kabbalist Ḥayyim Joseph David Azulai:

> Even though all the Torah is comprised of names of the blessed Holy One, the Torah cloaked herself in stories; and when a person reads and understands the stories, he contemplates the simple level of *peshat*. But the Zohar contains the secrets themselves, explicitly. . . .
>
> It is true that the study of the Zohar is greater [for the rectification of the soul than the study of Mishnah, Talmud, and Scripture], because Scripture, Mishnah, and Talmud are extensively cloaked and the secret is not recognizable in them. This is not the case with the Zohar, which speaks explicitly of the secrets of Torah.[5]

In order to understand how it is possible to enter the dimension of the secret as defined by the Zohar, we must first understand how the Zohar's protagonists read the Torah. What is their conception of the essence of the canonical text they interpret?[6] Extending upon the outlook of the sages of the Talmud as well as the *Heikhalot* literature, the Zohar views the Torah as a divine, dynamic, and feminine entity. Rabbinic midrashim created new understandings of the Torah, not only as the blueprint for all creation inscribed on the arm of the blessed Holy One, but also as an entity with a quintessentially female persona. The sages described the Torah as resting in the lap of the blessed Holy One, and as playing before Him hundreds of generations prior to the world's creation.[7] It was Rabbi Akiva who bequeathed to all Jewish mystics who succeeded him the belief that every word, letter, and coronet of the Torah contains countless mysteries and secrets.[8]

The eroticization of the Torah is also the fruit of rabbinic thought. The Rabbis described the Torah as a subject, or perhaps more accurately, as an erotic object: "Just as the gazelle's womb is narrow and she is pleasurable for her husband every time just like the first time, so too the words of Torah are pleasurable to those who study them every time just like the first time."[9] The eros of Torah study is described here as the pleasure of exegetical penetration, virginal intercourse, in reaching new layers of meaning.

To this rabbinic view, the kabbalists added their own new conception, centered on the mutuality of this erotic relationship. While for the Rabbis the Torah, or the gazelle, is an erotic object, for the mystics she is revealed as an active subject.[10] In the Zohar, the Torah is not understood merely as a text or as a thing, but as the living presence of divinity, engaging in mutual relations with the person studying her. Furthermore, in zoharic consciousness the Torah is analogized to a beloved engaging in dynamic relations of active, reciprocal courtship with her lovers.

This conception of the Torah is presented in its full splendor in the zoharic literary unit called *Sava de-Mishpatim*. In this story, an old man teaches two young and arrogant members of Rashbi's circle the great lesson of understanding the act of Torah study as an erotic pursuit. In fact, the old man's words signify the initiation of the young disciples as lovers of Torah.

Amid the esoteric interpretation of the Torah portion *Mishpatim*, whose secret meaning is the story of the human soul, the old man tells the disciples a parable of a beautiful maiden in a palace.[11] The parable presents the web of relations between the student and the Torah as a dynamic, romantic, and erotic love story between a lover and a beloved. The arousal and awakening to the Torah is likened to the perpetual courting of the beloved by the lover—the constant hovering about the gates of her palace, the ever-increasing yearning to read her signs, the desire to behold her face, to discover her, and with her to reach the climax of the love act: totally disclosed, no secrets withheld.

In this web of relations, the beloved is also active. She sends out signs of seduction to her lover, arouses his passion for her through playful games, and exposes alluring secrets; she is thirsty for love and to be loved. The beloved undresses gradually and seductively before her lover, out of her desire to disclose at the appropriate moment the mysteries secreted within her since primordial times. The community of Torah lovers is therefore a community of lovers each in love with the one beloved, who engages in a personal and unique relationship with each and every one of her lovers. Owing to the importance and beauty of this parable, we cite here the text in full:

A parable: To what can this be compared?

To a beloved maiden, beautiful in form and appearance and hidden deep within her palace. She has one lover, unknown to anyone; he is hidden too.

Out of his love for her, this lover passes by her gate constantly, lifting his eyes to every side.

She knows that her lover is hovering about her gate constantly.

What does she do?

She opens a little window in her hidden palace and reveals her face to her lover, then swiftly withdraws, concealing herself.

No one near the lover sees or reflects, only the lover, and his heart and his soul and everything within him flow out to her.

And he knows that out of love for him she revealed herself for that one moment to awaken love in him.

So it is with a word of Torah: She reveals herself to no one but her lover. Torah knows that he who is wise of heart hovers about her gate every day.

What does she do? She reveals her face to him from the palace and beckons him with a hint, then swiftly withdraws to her hiding place.

No one who is there knows or reflects; he alone does, and his heart and his soul and everything within him flow out to her.

That is why Torah reveals and conceals herself. With love she approaches her lover to arouse love with him.

Come and see! This is the way of Torah: At first, when she begins to reveal herself to a human she beckons him with a hint. If he knows, good; if not, she sends him a message, calling him a fool. Torah says to her messenger: Tell that fool to come closer, so I can talk with him! as it is written: *Who is the fool without a heart? Have him turn in here!* (Proverbs 9:4).

He approaches. She begins to speak with him from behind a curtain she
has drawn, words he can follow, until he reflects a little at a time. This is
derasha.

Then she converses with him through a veil, words riddled with allegory.
This is *haggadah.*

Once he has grown accustomed to her, she reveals herself face to face and
tells him all her hidden secrets, all the hidden ways, since primordial days
secreted in her heart.

Now he is a perfect human being, husband of Torah, master of the house.
All her secrets she has revealed to him, withholding nothing, concealing
nothing.

She says to him: Do you see that word, that hint with which I beckoned
you at first? So many secrets there! This one and that one!

Now he sees that nothing should be added to those words and nothing
taken away. Now the *peshat* of the verse, just like it is! Not even a single letter
should be added or deleted.

Human beings must become aware! They must pursue Torah to become
her lovers! (Zohar 2:99a–b, *Sava de-Mishpatim*; Matt 1983, pp. 123–25)

During the old man's lesson to the disciples, the ground rules of the zoharic
world are generously laid bare before the reader. The unique reflexive game
of entering and exiting the exegetical world, as well as the simultaneous
account of the eros and religious experience of Torah study, are spelled out
here more than in any other zoharic story.

Nevertheless, the paradigm presented in *Sava de-Mishpatim* is not unique
to this literary unit but rather informs exegesis throughout the composition. The hermeneutical premise of the Zohar, namely, that the relationship
between the student and the text is not that of a subject and an object but
rather of two subjects—and an erotic one at that—opens up many avenues
regarding what constitutes awakening to the Torah and its study, as well as
the nature of the student's activity when engaged in interpreting and innovating Torah.

In the Zohar, the student of Torah does not turn to the text merely to
describe or interpret. Rather, he brings to the biblical text a set of carefully
considered strategies designed to cause the divine qualities hidden within
the Torah—namely, her secrets and mysteries—to awaken and be revealed
to his eyes and heart.[12] The act of reading and interpreting the Torah is

understood by the Companions as a means to heighten their consciousness and their senses—in particular, their sense of sight—directed at the body of their beloved, the Torah. The protagonists of the Zohar perceive themselves as "full of eyes" in their quest to see more and more of the Torah, to behold her in all possible ways. The purpose of this enhancement of the Companions' visionary capacity is the melting away of the veiling layers of the text, to render them transparent in order to see, with a more intensified and diverse vision, the body of the Torah, which is, as we have seen, an erotic secret.[13]

Understanding the religious work of the Companions as the enhancement of vision also explains the way in which the active contemplation of the Torah transforms the Torah from being unseen, abandoned, and transparent into an entity that is seen, beloved, and radiant.[14] Every contact with the Torah, each gaze cast upon her words, is performed with the deliberate intentions of a lover; in the eyes of such a lover, every part of the beloved's body is full of beauty and arouses interest. It is true that some parts of the beloved's body may seem more important than others,[15] yet each limb—be it a story, a verse, or a word in the Torah—calls for the lover's attention. In the world of the Zohar, then, study and interpretation are quintessentially erotic activities. The art of zoharic exegesis is erotic. The knowledge, wisdom, and experience that emerge from the zoharic homily are also erotic in nature.[16]

While there are no bounds to the Companions' love for the Torah, her greatest lover is of course Rabbi Shim'on bar Yoḥai. The literary unit *Rav Metivta* (Master of the Academy), which describes the collective journey of Rabbi Shim'on and his circle into the celestial worlds of the wilderness generation, contains a hymn of praise and love uttered by Rashbi to the Torah. This hymn, one of the poetic high points of the zoharic corpus, is not uttered directly to the Companions. This is, rather, a special occasion in which the heroes of the Zohar—and with them we the readers—are privy to the intimate revelation of Rashbi's unending love and yearning for the Torah as the mother and source of light and divine bounty in the world. In addressing the Torah as his beloved, Rashbi also reveals his distress as the great master over the limits of his ability to contain the abundance of the Torah, and of his capacity to impart and reveal this bounty to his students.

> Rabbi Shim'on cried and wept.
>
> He opened and said: *A loving doe, a graceful mountain goat. Let her breasts satisfy you at all times, be infatuated with love of her always* (Proverbs 5:19).
>
> Torah, Torah, light of all worlds!
>
> How many oceans and streams, springs, and fountains spread forth from you in all directions!
>
> All is from you, on you depend the upper and lower [realms], a supernal light issues from you.
>
> Torah, Torah, what can I say to you?
>
> You are a loving doe and a graceful mountain goat.
>
> Above and below are your lovers.
>
> Who will merit to suckle from you as is fitting?
>
> Torah, Torah, delight of your Master,
>
> Who is able to reveal and utter your secrets and mysteries?!
>
> He cried and placed his head between his knees and kissed the earth.
>
> (Zohar 3:166b)

The Zohar explicitly compares the religious practice of the kabbalists with lovemaking. In the Zohar's commentary to the Torah portion *Terumah*, a collection of homilies explores the relationship between the kabbalists' activities during weekdays and their activities on the Sabbath. The mystical-theurgic purpose of their service is to connect with the divine world and effect union within that world, as well as between the divine world and our world, in order to draw down blessings to all the dimensions of reality. During the days of the week, the kabbalists work to this end through assembling at midnight and studying Torah until dawn in love and companionship.

On Sabbath eve, as we saw in Chapter 6, this same end is accomplished through the physical act of lovemaking between the kabbalists and their wives. The act of lovemaking penetrates the very depths of the divine world and arouses the union of the blessed Holy One with His Shekhinah. The pleasure that infuses all the worlds on the Sabbath derives from the simultaneous union of the blessed Holy One with His Shekhinah and the union of all men and women engaged in the physical act of lovemaking on earth.

The sexual relations between a man and woman performed with appropriate mystical intentions have a profound impact on the divine world because of the similarity between the human act of lovemaking and the mythical activity of union within the divine world.

The isomorphism in the structure of the various worlds reaches its apex here, insofar as now there are no speeches or interpretations about union, but rather actual embodiment. We find here a preference for the physical, concrete act of lovemaking over the sublimation and abstraction that characterize the exegetical activity of the kabbalists every other night of the week.

The erotic essence of the Companions' endeavors is highlighted by the zoharic concept *mayin nukbin* (female waters). The kabbalists' nightly engagement with the Torah, as well as their lovemaking with their wives on Sabbath eve, serve the theurgic function of generating female waters. These female waters are the fluids of passion of the divine female, Shekhinah. The arousal and intensification of these fluids arouses the passion of the lover, the divine male, toward his beloved, and from this arousal emerges the union of the male and female within divinity.

The human being is thus a key partner in the generation of these female waters and assists in the grand enterprise of bringing about the divine union.[17] From the foregoing, we can infer that the act of Torah study, and especially the familiarization with her secrets, is a quintessentially erotic endeavor, which—above and beyond the immediate pleasure and meaning it bestows upon the student—is directed to cosmic and theurgic *tikkun*. In the Zohar, the secret and eros are inseparable, and they serve the grand purpose of the rectification of all reality.

Who Needs Mysteries Anyway?

The assumption that blessings reside especially in those things concealed from the eye is found already in the writings of the sages,[18] yet in the Zohar this privileging of the hidden receives new meaning. The dialectic of disclosure and concealment mirrors the relationship between the source of the divine bounty (concealed and plentiful) and the way that the divine is revealed in the world (dualistic, contracted, and brimming with judgment).

The revealed lies exposed to the harsh and penetrating gaze of the attribute of judgment, which is not the case with the concealed.

> "I have learned a secret: The blessed Holy One—concealed and revealed. 'Revealed'—Lower Court of Justice. 'Concealed'—site from which all blessings flow. So blessings settle upon everything kept concealed, whereas everything revealed is occupied by that site of the Court, it being a site revealed. All within supernal mystery, corresponding above." (Zohar 1:64b; Matt 2004–2007, vol. 1, p. 377)

As we have already noted, context is a crucial element in understanding the world of mysteries. The disclosure of secrets is viewed favorably only when the measure of disclosure is appropriate, the one revealing is deserving, the receivers of the secret are found worthy, and above all, when the cosmic time is suitable. In these circumstances, the revelation of mysteries bestows vitality and life upon the world. Conversely, the disclosure of secrets to one who is not worthy (who is not of "faithful spirit," as the Zohar puts it), by one who is not deserving, and at an inappropriate time creates a dangerous reality.[19]

The Zohar views the world as enduring only by virtue of the secret; this perspective transforms the question of disclosure and concealment into a meta-theme running through the entire work.[20] In the dramatic opening to the *Idra Rabba*, Rabbi Shim'on cries and says, "Woe if I reveal! Woe if I do not reveal!"—his words here being a motto for this central motif in the Zohar. The entire question of the disclosure of secrets is discussed through an erotic prism—appropriate disclosure engenders a holy and fruitful union, while inappropriate disclosure is viewed as tantamount to the sin of *gilui arayot* (prohibited sexual relations and exposure of the genitals).

At the symbolic-mystical level, the concealment of secrets and their disclosure to the appropriate person at the appropriate time are an expression of the initiate's identification with the most erotic aspect of the sefirah *Yesod*. The erotic power of this divine attribute, symbolized by the male genital organ, lies in guarding the divine flow, refraining from wasting this flow in vain, and joyfully transferring this bounty to the one(s) worthy to receive, namely, the sefirah *Malkhut* in the divine world, as well as the righteous and mystical initiates of this world. In the human realm, this power is expressed through guarding the Covenant, refraining from wastefully "spilling seed," and the joyful actualization of sexuality through intercourse with one's lawful partner.

For the mystics of the Zohar, such identification with the sefirah *Yesod* in relation to the secret is one of the mainstays of religious life. The task of the mystic is to know when to guard the secret and refrain from premature disclosure, as well as to determine the appropriate timing—cosmically and in light of the alignment of the divine powers—to disclose and indeed innovate secrets to those worthy of their reception. An outstanding example of this is found in the opening to the *Idra Rabba* mentioned above, where we find Rabbi Shim'on vacillating and agonizing over whether to disclose mysteries. Only after the disciples' assurances that they are indeed worthy, and only after having sworn a vow establishing a circle capable of receiving and containing the secret, does Rashbi begin to reveal mysteries.[21]

> Rabbi Shim'on sat down. He cried and said: Woe if I reveal! Woe if I do not reveal!
>
> The Companions were silent.
>
> Rabbi Abba rose and said to him: If it pleases the Master to reveal, it is written: *The secret of YHVH is for those who fear Him* (Psalms 25:14), and behold these Companions are God-fearing. . . .
>
> Rabbi Shim'on opened and said: *He that walks about as a talebearer reveals secrets, but he that has a faithful spirit conceals the matter* (Proverbs 11:13).
>
> *Walks about as a talebearer*—this verse is difficult. It should have said "The man that is a talebearer." What is the significance of *walks about*? It means the man who is unsettled in his mind and is not stable keeps whatever he hears moving about inside him, like bran in water, until he casts it out. Why is this? Because he does not have a stable spirit. But of the man of stable spirit, it is written: *But he that has a faithful spirit conceals the matter*.
>
> *A faithful spirit*—a stable spirit, as in *I will fasten him as a peg in a stable place* (Isaiah 22:23). The matter depends on the spirit [alt. secret]. It is written: *Do not allow your mouth to cause your flesh to sin* (Ecclesiastes 5:5), and the world endures only by virtue of the secret. And if in mundane matters of the world there is a need for secrecy, how much more so in the secrets and mysteries of the Ancient of Days, which have not been transmitted even to the supernal angels! (Zohar 3:127b–128a, *Idra Rabba*)

We have just seen the forms of expression and behavior of the zoharic kabbalist in relation to the secret emerging from his male persona. Yet alongside this persona the zoharic kabbalist also speaks and acts in his female persona; in so doing his attitude toward the secret is quite different.

According to the erotic meta-myth of the Zohar, the task of the mystical exegete in his female persona is to identify with the attributes of King David—the symbol of feminine divinity—and thus to encompass and be filled with the divine light he experiences in interpreting verses of Torah. The exegete, now filled with light, needs to find a way to communicate this light (*lesapper*—the root here implies sapphire, book, story, and sexual union) so that it will shine through him to the companions listening to his voice and on to all reality.

This process is highlighted by the Zohar's interpretation of the verse "at daybreak I shall prepare for You, and I wait (*atsappeh*)" (Psalms 5:4), the latter word interpreted here mystically as meaning to coat and cloak. In interpreting *atsappeh* in this way, the exegete (in this case, Rabbi El'azar) reveals the story of the sefirah *Malkhut* in relation to the sefirot above her, as well as the essence of the mystic's endeavor in his guise as King David. Rabbi El'azar presents his words as a profound mystery, "a word of truth coming from afar." In terms of sefirot, this verse tells of how *Malkhut*, at the moment of union, envelops and encompasses within herself the strong light of *Yesod*, called here "the morning of Joseph." Thus she enables reality to be safely nourished by, and exposed to, the force of the light of *Yesod*.

In the human realm, it is the psalmist David in his feminine persona who knows how to encompass this light that cannot be fully revealed. King David, and with him the mystics of the Zohar in their feminine persona, possess unique poetic and erotic qualities that enable them to encompass the divine light, just as the female genital organ encompasses that of the male. They are the ones who know how to contain the powerful divine light they experience as well as to coat it—to give it a covering, a garment, to express it in language—and in this way enable the divine light to be experienced in the world.

> Hear my voice, O YHVH, at daybreak; at daybreak I shall prepare for You, and I wait (atsappeh) (Psalms 5:4).

I wait—what does this mean? Surely all the people of the world hope and wait for the goodness of the blessed Holy One, even the animals of the field. Wherein then is David to be praised more than all the people of the world?

Indeed, I have inquired concerning this matter, and such have they told me; and it is a word of truth coming from afar.

The primordial light that the blessed Holy One created shone so brightly that the worlds could not endure. What did the blessed Holy One do? He made a light for His light, to be cloaked this one in that one. And so with all the remaining lights, until all the worlds stood firm and were able to endure.

And therefore the levels spread forth and the lights cloaked, and these are the ones called supernal wings, until they reached this "morning of Joseph.'" And He [*Yesod*] took all the upper lights, and since all the upper lights depend on Him, His light flared forth from the end of the world to the end of the upper world, so the worlds below could not endure.

David came and arrayed a light, a canopy for this "morning of Joseph," so that it could be covered, to sustain the worlds below, and about this is written: *at daybreak I shall prepare for You, and I cover* (*atsappeh*), as is written: *He gilded* (*va-yitsappeihu*) *it with pure gold* (Exodus 37:2). And since this light is from David and is dependent on him, He said that he [David] will be a canopy for this morning." (Zohar 3:204b)

The Zohar variously and repeatedly portrays the dynamic and rich character of the female's yearning to be filled by the male, be it in the erotic experience of a woman, or, as in our case, Shekhinah's desire to receive the flow from above, and in the experience of the kabbalists themselves while in a feminine state.

Drawing on the French feminist tradition, Elliot Wolfson has emphasized the way in which Jewish male mystics have related to the feminine and femininity as void and emptiness, pure passivity with no essence and being of its own, save for its encompassing the masculine. His comments and insights in this matter are important and interesting, and there can be no doubt that such attitudes can indeed be found in the Zohar.

Nevertheless, to my mind, the Zohar's understanding of the feminine and femininity is much more complex, diverse, and nuanced. Alongside the Zohar's portrayal of the feminine as absence and lack, or as part of the masculine, we find also numerous passages describing the feminine as an autonomous, independent quality with which the masculine seeks to unite.

For example, the zoharic homily just cited portrays the feminine (as well as poetry and mysticism) as the mystery of the quality that veils that which cannot be fully exposed—and thus, in fact, as the quality that enables the safe disclosure of the concealed. The language, values, and tone of this homily describe the feminine through a multivalent, active myth that celebrates David's (namely, the feminine's) desire to joyfully envelop—"to cover with pure gold"—the masculine, in order to enable the masculine to be safely revealed through her. The feminine then is an expression of the two senses of the word *atsappeh*: on the one hand, yearning, expectation, and the desire to be filled; and on the other hand, the active capacity to cover and envelop the divine light within her.

In contrast to Wolfson, I repeatedly discern in the Zohar's pages the positive, erotic, and reciprocal drama of the feminine's yearning to joyfully fill her living, spacious, and desiring womb with all the variegated qualities that flow into her. I do not find here lack and absence, ruthless penetration, negation, and submersion in the masculine, but rather—on the contrary—a total language of feminine erotics, which surprisingly was formulated so poetically and with such nuance by men.[22]

Seen from this vantage, the task of the speaker is to encompass the divine light found within and beyond the words of the Torah, and to do so in such a manner that this light takes on the garments, the golden covering, which will enable it to be revealed to the world in a fruitful way without the perils of overexposure. As a dynamic, reciprocal process between the student and the Torah or between a master and his disciples, the disclosure of secrets is compared, as we have seen, to the delicate and complex act of lovemaking between a lover and his beloved.

As such, this is a game of seduction, concealing as much as revealing. The process is incremental, the lovers contemplating whether to expose more and more layers, culminating in great joy at the moment of mutual disclosure. In the context of this erotic metaphor, it is no surprise then that the secret is not fixed and known at the outset, but rather is revealed in all its great variety with every act of reading the Torah's words.

The Companions' complex relationship with the world of mysteries and their disclosure calls to mind the famous talmudic legend about King David and his yearning to build the Temple. According to the legend, David excavates the foundations of the sanctuary, reaches the primordial depths that lie sealed with a bundle of earth or a shard of pottery, and is warned on pain of death not to remove the seal. With no regard to the consequences, and with the lure of touching the primordial deep—the font of being—so strong, David removes the cover. The great abyss then rises up and threatens to inundate the entire world. In the end, it is only David's Songs of Ascent that restore the appropriate balance between the watery chaos below and the world of order lying above.[23] The lack of disclosure of the secret leaves the world dry and without vitality, while excessive disclosure endangers its very existence. Just like David, who through song and poetry found the balance between the primordial deep and the world, the Companions too must identify the appropriate measure, delicate and fruitful, between disclosure and concealment.[24]

The Never-ending Story

Not every form of Torah study prompts the waters of yearning to pour forth from the Torah and Shekhinah. The stories of the Zohar teach that it is only in learning the secret layer of the Torah, in uncovering her mysteries, that these forces are aroused. It should be stressed that we are not speaking here about secrets of *kabbalah* (reception) in the sense of a closed body of knowledge transmitted by authoritative teachers and received by the Companions, but rather about secrets that in many cases are the creation of the Companions themselves.[25] The dimension of the secret is exposed and created through their interpretations and *hiddushei torah* (innovations in Torah) that tell the story hiding beneath the *peshat* (simple meaning) of the text.

Concealed within the Torah lies what we may term "the Great Story," the story of the world of the divine flow in its passage from infinite oneness to the finite world of separation, and the subtle upward return of all that is divine in reality, up the river of emanation, back to its source in the divine Eden. The Great Story is a never-ending, dynamic story, within which lies the great erotic drama of intimacy and separation, attraction and rejection, jealousy and longing between the masculine and feminine powers in the world of divinity, as well as in all the worlds created in the divine image.

The zoharic homily is distinguished by its ability to tell this story of "the great chain of being," sometimes called *Raza de-Mehemenuta* (Secret of Faith), in countless ways and through hundreds of verses. In many places we find that under the surface of the Bible's verses lies a story whose major components are known in advance. For example, the Zohar's interpretations of "Hear, O Israel, YHVH is our *Elohim*, YHVH is one" (Deuteronomy 6:4), "The heavens declare the glory of God (*El*)" (Psalms 19:2), or "The sun rises and the sun sets and glides back to where it rises" (Ecclesiastes 1:5) all tell of the dynamic relations between the masculine and feminine within the Godhead, the world, and humanity. This story represents the verse's secret, uncovered through a game of hide-and-seek between the reader and the text, a game of seduction between the student and Torah.

Rabbi Shim'on Ibn Lavi, the author of the Zohar commentary *Ketem Paz*, drew attention to the fact that Zohar does indeed repeatedly expound what he terms *derekh ha-yiḥud* (the way of unification). Ibn Lavi's fascination with the composition derives from his understanding that the power of the Zohar lies not in its having innovated a particular message or teaching—for after all, "the story of the world of unification" is already well known to the reader in terms of its fundamental structure and detail—but rather from its experiential force. As Boaz Huss has demonstrated, Ibn Lavi established that "desire and great yearning" are necessary conditions for a "successful" reading of the Zohar; and that one who would instead employ an intellectual or allegorical reading strategy will struggle to understand why these structures are so frequently repeated. According to Ibn Lavi, Zohar study is experiential and seeks to connect the reader again and again to the experience of the totality of the world of the Godhead:

> He who reads [the Zohar] metaphorically without desire and great yearning will say: What is the purpose in repeating these matters about the way of unification in each passage, for we have already heard them many times in the Torah portion *Bereshit* and in all the portions that come after, and what have we gained in interpreting the Torah in this fashion?!

And you, my son, shall answer: Why should a person eat bread, wine, and meat today, has he not already eaten them yesterday and the day before? Why should he eat them again? Behold, the Torah has prepared her table, prepared her meat, poured her wine, and proclaims: *Come eat my food and drink the wine that I have mixed* (Proverbs 9:5); and she says: *and you shall meditate on it day and night* (Joshua 1:8). For in meditating on the Torah, one contemplates and thinks about the Exalted One constantly, and He never departs from his heart; for all the Torah is the names of the blessed Holy One, and from the combination of her letters the name of God, may He be exalted, is known; for He is all, and in Him is all, and all is found in Him, and there is nothing aside from Him (may He be exalted and blessed). And therefore, He is inscribed and alluded to in all the stories of the Torah so as to make known that he was there, and among them dwells God, as at Sinai in holiness.[26]

The Great Story, then, is not so much repeated as experienced anew through the act of yearning-filled learning. What is surprising, however, is that many of the verses from which the Companions extract their Great Story seem to lack even the tiniest hint or allusion to the grand drama that they manage to find within them. Desiring to find ways to connect with and influence the divine world, and certain that the Torah and her interpretation are the means to this end, the protagonists of the Zohar succeed in drawing forth this spectacularly dynamic world from the words of the Torah.[27] The Great Story lies concealed in the hidden depths of the Torah's words and stories, awaiting the kabbalist's kiss in order to emerge from hiding and be disclosed to the world.

The disclosure of the secret is not a public act of exposure; such exposure would surely destroy the delicate eros and tarnish and cheapen its essence. The disclosure of the secret in the Zohar is likened to the intimate disclosure between lovers; and as such, the Zohar stresses that the revelation of mysteries and secrets is intended only for the Torah's lovers, for whom it is intended and through whom it can bear fruit.

"But now (Aval hashta)": The Portal into Mystery

The Zohar employs a unique literary structure for signifying the passage from various modes of interpretation to the exegetical mode whose focus is the revelation of mysteries. As readers, we begin our journey with the biblical verse itself and ascend to the degree of *midrash*—a degree usually designated by the Zohar as a teaching already "clarified or established by the Companions" (*ukmuha ḥevraya*), be they the Companions of Rabbi Shim'on or the broader circle of biblical exegetes across the generations, whose waters the Companions imbibe.

Following this first-order *drash* in the ever-deepening chain of interpretation, we often find the assessment "they have spoken well" (*shapir ka'amru*). The speaker appreciates and values that which has just been said, as a fine and appropriate reading of the biblical text. The term "they have spoken well" signifies then the interpretive efforts of generations past.

Yet after the *ukmuha ḥevraya* or the *shapir ka'amru* comes the word "but" (*aval*), opening a portal to an exposition in which the reader is suddenly transported to a different world. This word signifies to the circle of listeners within the composition, as well as to the reader, that the expositions of biblical verses expounded till this point do not pertain to the secret inner core of the verses; these will come in the homily that follows. The word "but" encodes the desire to ascend yet another degree, to illuminate that which remains concealed in the shadow of the verse, and especially to tell once again the never-ending story of the world of the Godhead, whose protagonists embrace and separate, yearn and recoil, ascend and descend in continuous movement, as well as of the soul's desire to connect with and be delighted by this world, to affect rectification and thus receive the flow of divine blessings.

In disclosing the secret dimension of biblical verses, therefore, the Zohar does not present the divine drama just as it had been received in esoteric traditions from preceding generations, but rather as it emerges and is created in contemplating a particular verse in the never-to-be-repeated time and narrative context in which the Companions find themselves.

The word "but" appears in a number of characteristic formulas: *aval raza de-mila* (but the secret of the word/matter is); *aval be-raza de-ḥokhmata* (but according to the secret of wisdom); *aval be-Matnita di-lan* (but in our Mishnah);[28] *aval be-oraḥ kshot* (but according to the way of truth); and *aval raza de-kra* (but the secret of the verse is).[29] Following these "buts," the Zohar begins to reveal the mystery relevant to the verse. The secrets revealed usually refer to kabbalistic truths about the structure of reality derived through applying various hermeneutic tools to the words of the verse.

To my mind, the most interesting "but" formula in the Zohar is the *aval hashta*,[30] meaning "but now." This is a particularly zoharic "but." It is as though the text is saying: "Interesting interpretations of the verse that we are discussing have been offered, *but* in the particular, singular, and unique situation in which we *now* find ourselves (in the story or in the homily), we must seek another meaning—another secret—which cannot be revealed without an awareness of the singularity of this occasion. This is the Torah of the specific moment, and those aspects of Torah revealed in this moment are unique."

A beautiful example of this kind of transition into the dimension of the secret is found in the account of *tikkun leil Shavuot*, the ritual of arraying Shekhinah on the eve of the festival of Shavuot. Rabbi Shim'on opens with the verse "The heavens declare the glory of God . . ." (*Ha-shamayim mesapperim kevod El . . .* ; Psalms 19:2), about which he says "*kra da ha ukmuha lei*" (this verse has already been clarified). This is immediately followed by a "but": "*But at this time*, when the bride is aroused so that she may enter the bridal canopy on the morrow," which launches Rabbi Shim'on to expound the singular interpretation of the verse in the context of her preparations for her wedding ceremony. Rashbi here explicitly expresses the consciousness of innovation so central to the Zohar: it is improper to reiterate previous interpretations of the verse, insofar as this unique context calls on the the expounder to find new paths of correspondence between the verse and the occasion.

All the "buts" in the Zohar point to the dimension of the secret, the disclosure and refining of which are among the most central of tasks for the member of the zoharic circle. While it is true that the use of the word "but" suggests that the dimension of the secret is about to be revealed, implying the disclosure of something new and unique, the syntactical valence of the term is one of joining rather than negation. As such, when a member of the zoharic circle offers a new interpretation of the words of the Torah, he does not annul that which already exists, but rather adds to existing interpretations and thereby demonstrates the infinity of Torah.

The Ideal State of Disclosure: Between the Concealed and the Revealed

The Zohar's attitude toward secrets and their disclosure is complex and multilayered.[31] Even so, analysis of both Rashbi's and the Companions' homilies, as well as their responses to them, allows us to sketch the ideal relationship between disclosure and concealment. The world of the Zohar (or, in the language of the Zohar, "the generation in which Rashbi abides") is positioned between two poles vis-à-vis the world of mysteries. The first pole is that of total concealment, characterized by a lack of awareness of the very existence of the dimension of the secret, or the deliberate dismissal of this dimension. According to the Zohar, the majority of the world abides in this state. The second pole is that of total disclosure. This condition lacks the complexity, depth, and multidimensionality; it is a totally exposed state, devoid of any sense of mystery and concealment.

The ideal attitude to the world of mysteries lies poised between these two poles, and it is this attitude that the Companions establish through their interpretations. The unique flavor of the zoharic homily is found precisely in the subtle game of disclosure and concealment, the tension between them, as well as the Companions' awareness of this tension.

A story that appears in the Introduction to the Zohar (*Hakdamat ha-Zohar*) contains some important references to themes of innovation and disclosure. The story discusses the nature and status of speech and innovation in Torah and the role of speech in creating reality. The story also describes the unique and blessed reality generated by innovations in Torah and innovations in wisdom, namely, the revelation of secrets that up until the moment of their disclosure did not yet exist.

> Rabbi Shim'on opened, ". . . and every word innovated in Torah by one engaged in Torah fashions one heaven. . . . that word ascends and presents herself before the blessed Holy One, who lifts that word, kisses her, and . . . that secret word of wisdom, innovated here . . . is transformed into a heaven. So each and every word of wisdom is transformed into a heaven. . . . He calls them *new heavens*. . . . As for all other innovated words of Torah, they stand

before the blessed Holy One, then ascend and are transformed into *earths of the living*. (Zohar 1:4b; Matt 2004–2007, vol. 1, pp. 25–26)

Immediately following this passage, the Zohar describes the converse, undesirable situation—the improper disclosure of secrets by one innovating Torah without being well versed in the ways of the secret:

"One who is unaccustomed to the mysteries of Torah and innovates words he does not fully understand—when that word ascends . . . [he] transmogrifies her into a distorted heaven called *chaos*." (1:5a; ibid., p. 28)

Out of the acute awareness of the responsibility and great danger associated with innovation and disclosure, Rabbi Shim'on concludes his words to his disciples with a note of caution:

Rabbi Shim'on said to the Companions, "I beg of you not to utter a word of Torah that you do not know and have not heard properly from a lofty tree." (1:5a; ibid., p. 29)

In light of the potency of speech, the disclosure of secrets must be a considered and conscious act, anchored in a tradition which guarantees that the secret will not be lethal and will not engender a distorted reality. It is perhaps because of the potential danger that the Zohar both seeks to arouse the people of the world to open their mouths and let words of Torah shine forth, and at the same time restricts that call to the generation of Rabbi Shim'on, a generation that sees itself as disclosing and creating only by virtue of the force of Rashbi's presence. Thus this anonymous teaching: "In the days of Rabbi Shim'on, a person would say to his companion, 'Open your mouth, may your words shine forth!' (BT *Berakhot* 22a); and after Rabbi Shim'on's death they would say, '*Do not let your mouth cause your flesh to sin*' (Ecclesiastes 5:5)."[32]

The open state of disclosure and enlightenment is a special grace enjoyed by the world while Rabbi Shim'on is alive. However, it is temporary. The Companions of the Zohar experience their own time as a period of grace—in which the clouds that usually enshroud the radiance of the sky have temporarily passed, and for a brief moment it is possible to behold the brilliant light of the heavens. This clarity, however, is destined to be short-lived, the skies of consciousness fated to be covered once again with clouds of darkness.

> Come and see: Later generations are destined to arise when the Torah will be forgotten among them, and the wise of heart will assemble in their places and there will be none to close and open. Woe to that generation!
>
> From here on, there will not be a generation like this one until King Messiah comes and knowledge will be aroused in the world, as is written: *for all of them, from the least of them to the greatest, shall know Me* (Jeremiah 31:34). (Zohar 3:58a)

Even in the generation of Rabbi Shim'on, the disclosure of secrets does not imply that the mysteries of Torah lie exposed without the interposition of garments. Disclosure, rather, implies instruction in the ways of illuminating the world through interpretations of Torah by revealing mysteries *ke-de-ka ye'ot*, "fittingly," that is, as appropriate. The appropriate disclosure of secrets and innovations in Torah is the product of the combination of daring on the one hand, and the acceptance of the authority of the teacher and his teaching on the other. Innovations transpire within a traditional framework: they flow from a novel reading of the canonical text, and usually they are subject to the judgment and illuminating comments of the master teacher, Rabbi Shim'on bar Yoḥai.

The *Idra Rabba* describes what is without doubt the climactic and central moment in the Zohar, particularly with regard to the revelation of mysteries as a constitutive and restorative act within the world of divinity. The Companions who participate in this assembly, all of whom are students of Rabbi Shim'on, are required in turn, at their teacher's behest, to stand and to dare to innovate secrets pertaining to the mystery of the Godhead, so as to be transformed from mere disciples to pillars upon whom the world might endure: "Every single one shall say a new word of Torah."[33] Yet prior to the homilies themselves, the *Idra* begins with a special and extensive discussion about the disclosure and concealment of mysteries.[34] In the opening of the *Idra Rabba*, Rabbi Shim'on calls to the Companions in pathos-laden and exalted tones to assemble for an emergency gathering in which "they must act for the sake of YHVH." He calls upon them "to enthrone and acknowledge the King, who has the power of life and death," namely, God, but in this case also the tongue—that is, the power of language—so as to be able to utter reality-founding mysteries. Rabbi Shim'on weeps and expresses his ambivalence about whether to reveal or conceal those mysteries. Just prior to the entry to the Idra—an event characterized by the disclosure of the most profound mysteries of the Godhead—he expounds the verse "Cursed be the one who makes a carved or molten image, the works of the hands of an artisan, and sets it up in secret" (Deuteronomy 27:15):

> It has been told: Rabbi Shim'on said to the Companions: How long will we sit on a one-legged stand? It is written, *Time to act for YHVH! They have violated Your Torah!* (Psalms 119:126). . . . Assemble, Companions at the threshing house, wearing coats of mail, with swords and spears in your hands! Arm yourselves with your array: Design, Wisdom, Intellect, Knowledge, and Vision, the power of Hands and Feet. Enthrone and acknowledge the King who has power of life and death, that words of truth may be ordained, words followed by high holy ones, happy to hear them and know them!
>
> Rabbi Shim'on sat down. He cried and said: Woe if I reveal! Woe if I do not reveal!
>
> The Companions were silent.
>
> Rabbi Abba rose and said to him: If it pleases the Master to reveal, it is written, *The secret of YHVH is for those who fear Him* (Psalms 25:14), and these Companions are God-fearing. . . .
>
> Giving hands to Rabbi Shim'on, raising fingers above, they entered the field and amidst the trees sat down.
>
> Rabbi Shim'on rose and prayed his prayer. He sat down among them, and said: Let everyone place his hands on my breast.
>
> They placed their hands, and he took them.
>
> He opened and said: *Cursed be the one who makes a carved or molten image . . . and sets it up in secret!* (Deuteronomy 27:15).
>
> They all responded "Amen." (Zohar 3:127b; Matt 1983, pp. 163–64)

Many Zohar commentators have seen in this verse a warning against corporealizing and anthropomorphizing the divine. This is a surprising interpretation given the Zohar's rampant and unapologetic anthropomorphisms.

Yehuda Liebes has interpreted this warning as Rabbi Shim'on adjuring his disciples to disclose only those words that they have received through his inspiration and presence, thereby implying that mysteries not connected to Rabbi Shim'on's teaching are false and artificial, like a carved or molten image.[35] I would add that the meaning of the warning here is that he who reveals mysteries and innovates Torah without being connected to the tradition of mysteries—to antiquity (*atikut*)—is reckoned as though he has made a carved or molten image *ex nihilo*, an entity with no root in the world of divinity. The innovation of mysteries requires originality, in the sense both of creating that which emerges and flows from the origin, as well as something novel.

Furthermore, the sin referred to here is clearly not the transgression of the second commandment, the representation of the divine in a carved or molten image, for had that been the case the text could easily have cited a verse from the Ten Commandments.[36] The sense here, then, is a warning to the participants of the Idra not to solidify and freeze God's dynamic faces, not to render them into a fixed divinity devoid of the dynamic divine mystery. To do so is to perform an act of mystical idolatry, like worshipping the golden calf about whom the Israelites said, "These are your gods, O Israel!" (Exodus 32:4).

In a similar vein, the Companions here are warned not to expound in such a way as to privilege concealment over disclosure—disclosure being the order of the day in the Idra. He who "sets it up in secret," namely, he who conceals mysteries for himself at a time when it is precisely disclosure that is required is, according to our text, accursed. (Many of the warnings in that passage of communal curses, from which our verse is taken, pertain to matters performed in hiding and therefore subject not to legal punishment but rather to divine curse.) This reading is also borne out through the words of the verse itself, which is not cited in full by the Zohar: "Cursed be the one who makes a carved or molten image, abhorred by YHVH, the work of the hands of an artisan, and sets it up in secret!"

Perhaps, too, the phrase "the work of the hands of an artisan (*ḥarash*)" alludes to silencing (for the like-sounding verb *ḥeresh* means "to be silent"); and perhaps also these words need to be understood in their zoharic context as referring to sorcerers (*ḥarashim*)—namely, to those who use the power of divine mysteries for their own benefit rather than as a theurgic act whose focus is the restoration of divinity and the world. Finally, the choice of this verse from the Torah portion *Ki Tavo* (which concludes the terms of Israel's covenant with God by reciting a litany of blessings and curses) also bestows something of the grandeur of the liturgical contract confirmed by the nation on the dramatic opening of the Idra.

Total Concealment of Mystery

A world unaware of the existence of the secret is, according to the Zohar, a world asleep. Indeed, the Companions view the majority of people around them as living in a state of deep slumber: the secret is nonexistent, for there is no awareness of the hidden dimension of being. In this state, the dimension of the secret does not enliven reality; the river of divine plenty that flows from Eden does not pour forth to water the garden of reality, for the secrets that create the possibility of this flow lie blocked.

The Zohar sees in this state of slumber a harsh denial of the hidden powers of humanity to arouse reality, and a lack of attentiveness to the awakening power of the Torah. Thus the character known as "the old man of *Mishpatim*" remarked: "How the people of the world are confused in their minds and do not look to the true path of the Torah! The Torah calls out to them every day, murmuring lovingly, but they do not want to turn their heads."[37] As we will see below, the Zohar does not spare these slumbering masses harsh words of rebuke; it abounds in dire warnings about the bitter end that awaits them as punishment for failing to fulfill their destiny as human beings created in the divine image.[38]

In addition to the condition of apathy toward the existence of the secret, the Zohar also speaks of another situation, in which people recognize the existence of the dimension of the secret yet are afraid to disclose it. We learn about this condition through Rashbi's comparisons of his circle, residing in the Land of Israel, with sages with whom he comes into contact from Babylonia. The Companions from the Land of Israel celebrate the opportunity for the abundance of disclosure and creativity, while the Companions from Babylonia fail to heed Rabbi Shim'on's invitation. Instead of creating and disclosing mysteries, they conceal his words in an iron seal, missing the opportunity to reveal, due to their treatment of Rabbi Shim'on's teachings as esoteric. "Babylonia" is therefore a symbol for undue concealment. As discussed in Chapter 3, the "Companions from Babylonia" may allude to the disciples of the Ramban (Rabbi Moses Naḥmanides, who lived in Catalonia) and his school.[39] That is, the epithet *Bnei Bavel* (Babylonians) perhaps alludes to a group of sages for whom the awareness of the Land of Israel is not as central to their self-perception as it is to the zoharic circle.[40] Whatever the case may be, it is important to stress that the Zohar's attitude toward the *Bnei Bavel* is not one of total denigration; they are, after all, termed "Companions"—and not, for example, fools, evildoers, or sectarians. In forgiving and ironic fashion, Rabbi Shim'on permits their concealing behavior owing to the fact that they are residents of the Diaspora. Nevertheless, his frustration at their fear to assume a more open stance regarding the disclosure of secrets is readily discernable, a fact made all the more apparent as his rebuke appears following a collection of mysteries disclosed by his disciples.

> Rabbi Shim'on said, "When I am among those Companions of Babylonia, they gather around me and learn subjects openly, and then insert them beneath an impregnable seal of iron, shut tight on all sides.
>
> "How often have I described to them the pathways of the garden of the Holy King and the supernal pathways!
>
> "How often have I taught them all those rungs of the righteous in that world!
>
> "They are all afraid to utter words, but rather toil in study stammeringly.
>
> "So they are called stammerers, like one who stammers with his mouth."
> (Zohar 1:224b–225a; Matt 2004–2007, vol. 3, p. 352, reformatted)[41]

Rabbi Shim'on views the study of "the pathways of the garden of the Holy King" and "the supernal pathways," most likely referring to the mysteries of Shekhinah and the blessed Holy One (*Tiferet*), as the appropriate means for the disclosure of secrets. The frightened "Babylonian" consciousness precludes the Babylonians from innovating in these mysteries and employing them creatively. Unlike the "mighty ones of the Land of Israel," they are unable to recognize the ways of the garden of the King so as to create new mysteries through them, and pave new paths with them. The Babylonians know only to conserve the secret, to cherish and guard the mysteries of divinity in a treasure chest sealed with an iron lock.

The Babylonians, then, reflect the traditional concept of *kabbalah* as a closed body of secrets received and transmitted from one generation of initiates to another, whereas Rabbi Shim'on's mystical circle of the Land of Israel belongs to the innovative and creative mystical tradition. In the following section, we will see yet another zoharic story in which Babylonia appears as the land of concealment.

Disclosure without Concealment: A World without Mystery

While a world of concealment without disclosure is a world in slumber, a world of disclosure without concealment is equally unbalanced, lacking not only the vital tension between the seen and unseen but also the depth created through multidimensionality.

A unique story appearing in the Zohar's commentary to the Torah portion *Lekh Lekha*, the story of *Kfar Tarsha* (Clod Village), explores aspects of the interplay between revelation and concealment. In this story, Rabbi Abba of Rashbi's circle and his son Ya'akov, arrive at a village called Tarsha. Its anonymous members, whom Rabbi Abba first takes to be commoners, are revealed in the course of their nocturnal Torah study to be masters of mystical lore.

Rabbi Abba and Ya'akov are invited by their host to stay an extra day, in order to participate in the celebration of his son's circumcision. In the course of the night, the host's friends assemble and each expounds in praise of the *brit milah*. The villagers' nocturnal expositions, each exploring different aspects of the rite of circumcision, gather momentum and reach an ecstatic climax in the morning. Overawed, Rabbi Abba asks the people why mystical masters such as themselves should dwell in such a remote village, to which they reply that it is only in such a place that the Torah can settle in their hearts. They further add that they are living there to rectify some past sin.

The children of the village prophesy that the circumcision will be accompanied by a revelatory event; and indeed, during the circumcision, the people of Kfar Tarsha enjoy a collective mystical experience. Fire descends from the heavens and they all experience a revelation paralleling the giving of the Torah on Mt. Sinai; Rabbi Abba's face shines, and the participants lose all sense of the passage of time.

When Rabbi Abba returns to Rabbi Shim'on and the other Companions, he recounts the events to Rabbi El'azar, Rabbi Shim'on's son, yet he is afraid to tell Rabbi Shim'on himself what he has seen.

Later, in the presence of Rabbi Shim'on, who is expounding matters associated with Abraham and the covenant of circumcision, Rabbi Abba asks permission to tell his teacher about the sublime matters he had heard during his stay at Kfar Tarsha. Rabbi Shim'on assents and Rabbi Abba explains that he fears that the Tarshans will be punished on his account. Rabbi Shim'on reassures him, so Rabbi Abba narrates all the details of his visit to the village. In a surprising response, Rabbi Shim'on castigates Rabbi Abba: "All those sublime words were concealed within you—and you didn't convey them?!" Rabbi Shim'on punishes Rabbi Abba for not revealing these events to the Companions, by decreeing that "for the next thirty days, whatever you study you will forget."

Even more surprisingly, Rabbi Shim'on decrees that the people of Kfar Tarsha should be "exiled to Babylonia among the Companions."[42] Rabbi Shim'on explains to Rabbi Abba, now downcast and feeling guilty, that the people of Kfar Tarsha have been exiled because of him, but that the decreed exile is not a punishment; rather, there is a lesson that the villagers need to learn from the Babylonians. Since the people of Kfar Tarsha do not know how to conceal secrets and mysteries, and because supernal matters are so openly revealed by them, they need to be among the Companions in Babylonia so as to learn the ways of concealment. Rabbi Shim'on concludes the story with the declaration: "For words are revealed only among us [the Companions], since the blessed Holy One has authorized us to reveal them!"

The story of Kfar Tarsha is a literary and exegetical masterpiece. For our purposes, it is important merely to understand the nature of Kfar Tarsha's reality and the meaning of Rabbi Shim'on's harsh stance toward it. Kfar

Tarsha is a settlement of people living in a reality in which the experience of the Garden of Eden and of Mt. Sinai is available with exceptional immediacy. The entire village displays unmediated contact with divine revelation. The villagers do not seek Torah in the established centers of learning; rather, they live in an ideal reality, in which the forces of judgment are absent.

During the first half of the night, the watches of judgment, the men of the village sleep, and, like the Companions, they arise at midnight and engage in the mystical study of Torah until dawn. In the morning, "fragrances of fields and glistening rivers enlighten them with Torah that is embedded in their hearts"; as the villagers themselves say, "whoever departs from here is like one who departs from eternal life."[43]

If we compare this statement to the regnant view among Rashbi's circle, we find an important difference: the Companions relate to Rabbi Shim'on as the pillar upon which the world stands and as the Tree of Life, whereas here the place is decisive. Owing to its special attributes and the character of the learning done there, Kfar Tarsha serves as an alternative to the presence of Rabbi Shim'on in bestowing eternal life.

In a moment of clarity, Rabbi Abba blesses the villagers and describes them as "ordained princes, shield-bearing warriors of that land called Land of the Living, whose princes feast on manna of holy dew."[44] He celebrates their great cleaving to God untainted by the forces of judgment: "But you, truly virtuous, holy ones of the Most High, sons of the Holy King, do not suck from this side but rather from that holy site above. Of you is written: *You, cleaving to YHVH your God, are alive every one of you today!* (Deuteronomy 4:4)" (1:95b; Matt 2004–2007, vol. 2, p. 107).

The villagers of Kfar Tarsha (who remain unnamed throughout the story) live among fields, rivers, and trees. Their village is a kind of Garden of Eden, in the middle of which stands the Tree of Life to which they hold fast and cleave. This Tree of Life is of course the Torah, and in the sefirotic register it signifies the sefirah *Tiferet*. Expressed differently, Kfar Tarsha's God is the explicit name itself, the tetragrammaton. Rabbi Abba, the most senior of Rashbi's disciples, is enchanted by the Tarshans and stands awestruck by the enigma of this village. He is overwhelmed by the fact that people residing in an unknown place, standing outside the chain of tradition, and without the authoritative instruction of a teacher, should know how to live within the secret dimension of the Torah.

Like Rabbi Abba, we as readers may be surprised and disappointed, at first reading, with the story's end. The reader who visits Kfar Tarsha through Rabbi Abba's eyes cannot but fall in love with the village and its villagers. Why then is Rabbi Abba punished for not revealing the story? Why is his punishment that he is destined to forget his Torah? And above all, why does Rabbi Shim'on decree upon the people of Tarsha that they be exiled to Babylonia?

The reader's expectation here, as in many other zoharic stories, is that Rabbi Shim'on will extol the virtues of the villagers as the truly righteous who cleave to the Tree of Life, and that the story will end with an account of the enigmatic connection between Rabbi Shim'on and the village, whose members all seem "zoharic," or perhaps even hyper-zoharic.[45] Here, however, Rashbi does not supply the happy ending, and the story and its curious end remain open to interpretation.

The most extreme reading views the end of the story as testimony to the existence of opposition to Rabbi Shim'on's circle. For here, in Tarsha, at the end of the world, in an unknown place, resides a leaderless, teacherless mystical group engaging the secrets of Torah, causing fire and cloud to descend from the heavens, a group whose entire being is of the order of the revelation at Mt. Sinai. One of the participants at the circumcision feast expounds the verse "Happy are you, O land, whose king is a free man" (Ecclesiastes 10:17) about the village. The "land" is of course Kfar Tarsha, and the "king" is the blessed Holy One, rather than a king of flesh and blood. Well-versed readers of the Zohar will recall that elsewhere this same verse is applied to Rabbi Shim'on himself.[46]

According to this reading, Tarsha represents an alternative model to the zoharic circle. The Companions of the Zohar experience themselves as *bnei aliyah* (the ascendant and elect ones), a minority within a minority, who owing to their election by Rabbi Shim'on as the ones capable of entering and exiting the orchard of the King are deemed worthy of the revelation of secrets. Kfar Tarsha, on the other hand, declares that "all YHVH's people are prophets,"[47] and, even more striking, that the verse so frequently expounded by the Companions—"All your people are righteous and will inherit the land forever" (Isaiah 60:21)—is an actual rather than potential reality. The villagers of Tarsha bypass the zoharic circle and reach the Tree of Life faster and with greater ease.

It is here that Rabbi Shim'on establishes a boundary—the right to disclose secrets is reserved for his circle alone, and such revelation can be undertaken only with divine consent. Rabbi Shim'on's decree is therefore understandable as an attempt to safeguard his circle's exclusive status.

In reading the story this way, it is important to clarify the Zohar's authors' motivations in including such a subversive and oppositional account. It is possible that the story presents a model of a less hierarchical mystical group, only to ultimately side with the great teacher and against a democratization of the disclosure of mysteries. Such a decision, however, leaves the reader feeling uneasy, with a bitter—or at the very least, unsatisfying—taste.[48]

Another reading is that the story of Tarsha is an *ars poetica*, a mythical account of the Zohar's authors' own sources of knowledge. That is, the composers of the Zohar draw upon two sources of nourishment: the first—the traditions in which Rabbi Shim'on figures as the hero—signifies authoritative traditions, which in one way or another found their way to that medieval mystical group. The second source—represented by the story of Kfar Tarsha—is esoteric and anonymous. This source of nourishment flows from the illuminated reality of Kfar Tarsha, from the unmediated and immediate contact with the Tree of Life and the Torah.

A third and more moderate reading views the story in light of the Zohar's own internal grammar, which evinces a deep ambivalence surrounding the disclosure and concealment of secrets. As we have already seen, the disclosure of secrets parallels the sexual act; exposure, giving, and fertilization are among the central elements in this process. The discloser of a secret is masculine and phallic, and he is identified with the sefirah *Yesod*. The receiver of a secret is like the fertilized female, who receives and gestates that which had been disclosed.

In his role as great teacher, Rabbi Shim'on represents the sefirah *Yesod*. He guards the Covenant (*brit/Yesod*), meaning that he decides when to store the divine flow and when to bestow it upon the worthy—and thereby fertilize reality with the bounty hidden within the secrets of divinity.[49] According to the Zohar, it is precisely the tension between concealment and revelation that establishes and orders reality. Too much concealment, and reality loses its fluidity; while excess disclosure threatens the durability of being. Thus, in the mind of the Zohar's authors, neither of these states can properly be considered erotic. Appropriate eroticism, then, lies in the pleasurable balance between the two. According to this reading, Rabbi Shim'on's critique of the reality represented by Kfar Tarsha is clear: those villagers have not yet discovered the meaning of concealment.[50]

9

Zoharic Midrash

The main praxis through which spiritual-mystical experience transpires in the Zohar is, as we have seen, in the coming together of two or more of the Companions to engage in the interpretation of the Bible's verses, mainly while walking on the way during the day or while sitting and studying together after midnight.[1] As the interpretations progress, the participants generate a religious-emotional energy that intensifies until it engenders a mystical experience in one or more of the Companions.

This is an experiential-mystical praxis, insofar as the collective creation of the homily (midrash)—which since the rabbinic period has served as a central cultural-religious language—is transformed into an activity invested with both divine and human purposes of great significance: theurgic purposes directed to the divine world and its rectification; the intention of causing the indwelling of Shekhinah within human reality; and the creation of mystical experience among the gathered participants. Seen in this light, we have an intensification of an existing cultural model for new and daring aims. If in rabbinic-era texts we find, for example, Ben Azzai explaining the appearance of the fire that surrounds him as a phenomenon accompanying his exegesis,[2] then the zoharic Companions engage in midrash with the intent to experience the river of divine plenty, to feel the divine fire of Mt. Sinai, and to effect *tikkun* (repair) in divinity and in the world. The zoharic homily has its own unique characteristics; in exploring its contours, we will be better able to appreciate the power of zoharic midrash as a transformative activity.

Hermeneutical Dynamics

When the Zohar's protagonists assemble to penetrate the depths of the Bible's verses and to expose within them a chapter of the grand divine story and to reveal its secrets, they do so without these words losing their original simple meaning. This is the secret of the zoharic homily's power. The steps on which we stood at the start of the homiletical journey—moving from the simple reading of the verse to the rabbinic interpretation, and from there to the kabbalistic secret—remain in place also at the end of the journey. For the zoharic kabbalists, the interpretation of Torah is "level upon level, concealed and revealed": each concealed level that is revealed exposes yet another concealed level above or within itself, and so on to infinity.[3]

The zoharic reading of the biblical text is not truly allegorical. An allegorical reading of Scripture assumes that the verse signifies another specific, univocal reality, which constitutes the "true" content of the verse, while the verse itself merely points to this reality. Such a reading sometimes leaves the source text entirely devoid of its primary meaning; as the Rabbis might say, "it never existed, it is all a parable."[4]

The Zohar, in contrast, views the source text as a symbol. In essence, it is dynamic, multivocal, and connected with that which symbolizes, namely, the different dimensions of the world of divinity that are constantly in motion. The power of the symbol lies in its ability to direct the expounder and the reader to the multiplicity of meanings hidden within itself.[5]

Moreover, zoharic language invites its readers to embark on a journey within the words, to a reality characterized by continuous movement. We readers are invited not merely as passive contemplators, but rather as necessary partners in the journey of decoding. It is only through our own endeavors that we are able to align ourselves with the interpreting circle within the composition, and to become active contemplators—or perhaps even to heed the call to enter the circle of expounders and experience something of their experience. As Rabbi Moses Cordovero (the kabbalist and zoharic commentator of the sixteenth century) said: "Those who engage in the sweet Kabbalah, like the secrets expounded in the Zohar, should enter within them and thus add to them, like them, for room has been granted to us."[6]

The Zohar loves reflexivity and so usually, at each stage in the homiletical journey, we hear the voice of one of the Companions, the heroes of the composition, or even Rabbi Shim'on himself, offering a reflexive evaluation on the path already traversed. Within the world of the zoharic homily, the Companions expend great effort in attuning themselves to the process of exposing the world of mystery, and the creative use of this world. They do so in order to generate union between the human and the divine, as well as between the masculine and feminine within divinity. This act of reading and expounding is, therefore, a continuous search for a chapter of the grand divine story hidden within the interpreted text.

Let us compare the zoharic homily with the classical rabbinic interpretive mode known as the *petiḥta*. In the successful *petiḥta*, the element that arouses admiration is the artistic and complex manner in which the speaker strings the words of the "distant verse" (taken from the Prophets or the Writings, and cited at the beginning of his exposition) with the verse from the Torah portion that he is expounding. The art of rabbinic midrash reaches its pinnacle when the intersection of the distant and close verses is surprising and bears a new idea or message. The motive of the speaker and the manner in which he finds a way to express his new idea are the yardstick for evaluating the rabbinic homily.[7]

While the zoharic homily does indeed make broad use of rabbinic tools of interpretation, we readers find ourselves before a dynamic, complex, and often erotic divine story, which emerges and bursts forth from the Bible's words—which (on the surface at least) seem innocent of the meaning found within them. At its peak, the zoharic homily evokes in us a sense of wonder or mystical awakening, even preventing us from seeing the verse's earlier meaning, at least temporarily.[8] In terms of the details of the mythic and mystical narrative, the divine story that emerges is not new. Yet the way in which it is carved from the verse, as from a treasure-mine, and the way in which it is constructed arouse deep wonder.

An array of hermeneutical tools serves this endeavor of drawing forth from the Bible's verses a chapter of the infinite, dynamic story of the world of divinity and humanity. Moshe Idel has defined a number of these exegetical tools. First and foremost among them is the interpretive method that he describes as the "dynamization of verses": the kabbalistic expounder transforms simple, syntactical verses into a dynamic drama of the divine world.[9] So, for example, "Lift your eyes on high and see who created these" (Isaiah 40:26) means, in the biblical context, look up to the sky to contemplate the wonder of creation. In the Zohar, the words are interpreted as describing the ongoing process of the emanation of the name of God, *Elohim*, through the emanation from the sefirah *Binah*, represented by the word "who" (*mi*), through the seven sefirot beneath her, represented by the word "these" (*eleh*), to produce the name *Elohim*, made up of *mi* and *eleh*.[10] Another example is the Zohar's interpretation of "*Elohim*, You are my God, I search for You" (Psalms 63:2), where the Zohar finds within the words *Elohim*, "my God," and "You" references to different rungs that make up the world of divinity, as well as the manner in which the human being is connected to it.[11]

Idel also defines a particular kind of homily as "telescopic"—that is, it focuses on a verse or a story as through a telescope that captures the general structure of things while deliberately ignoring their details.[12] The Zohar's midrash on the Book of Ruth, for example, can be seen in this way as a "hyper-extensive" reading of the text. According to this reading, the story of Ruth and its heroes—from Elimelech to David—describes the process of the emanation of the divine worlds from their subtle source (unable to be materialized in differentiated reality, and symbolized by the name Elimelech) to the sefirah *Malkhut* and the reality of the everyday world (symbolized by the birth of David).[13]

Idel describes other homilies as "microscopic"; these ignore the word's context in the verse and, to borrow a term from photography, "zoom in" on an isolated word or letter, through which some kind of supernal secret is then exposed. The array of homilies on the tetragrammaton as describing all the divine worlds, for example, is of this kind. Similarly, in the Zohar's homily on the word *yimtsau'neni* (will find me) in "And those who seek Me will find Me" (Proverbs 8:17), the odd duplication of the letter *nun* is interpreted as indicating two divine worlds, the world of the "black" light of the sefirah *Malkhut* and the world of the "illuminating" light of the sefirah *Tiferet*. The latter is promised only to those who lovingly labor in the mystical service of *Malkhut* at dawn.[14]

I would like to suggest here yet another exegetical device employed by the Zohar that is absolutely central to the composition. It is the emotional attitude of the speaker himself. This attitude is at once an exegetical tool, a precondition for the act of interpretation, and a precondition for the experience that the exegesis seeks to awaken.[15] This hermeneutical tool involves the softening of conventional consciousness (the self-evident, or the consciousness of common sense). In order to create a broader, more expansive experiential and exegetical field, which will enable the concealed qualities of the biblical text to be exposed, the zoharic expounders forgo the confines of common sense and the conventional reading, so as to create space for other meanings. So, for example, in the Zohar's homily on "The heavens declare (*mesapperim*) the glory of God" (Psalms 19:2), the word *mesapperim* is interpreted not according to its simple meaning, namely, as connected to the word *sippur* (story), but rather to the more unlikely referent *sappir* (sapphire). The verse thereby exposes the way in which the divine masculine ("the heavens") illuminates and irradiates his partner, the feminine aspect of the divine ("the glory of God").

A more acute example is found in the homily on "Hear my voice, O YHVH, at daybreak; at daybreak I prepare for You, and I wait (*atsappeh*)" (Psalms 5:4),[16] in which the word *atsappeh*, as we have seen, is interpreted not in the usual sense of expectation or hope, but in the sense of covering and enveloping, derived from the word for coating or plating (*tsippui*). In opting for the less obvious and more distant sense of the word, the Zohar reveals the mythic story of the way in which the feminine sefirah *Malkhut*, and its correlate in the mystic's soul, receive into themselves, as in sexual intercourse, the strong divine light (signified by the word "daybreak") that they then envelop so as to enable this light to be exposed in the world in a safe and beneficent way.[17]

Another particularly beautiful example is found in the Zohar's homily on "I declare that Your name is good (*tov*) in the presence of (*neged*) Your faithful ones" (Psalms 52:11). The Hebrew preposition *neged* is interpreted not in its ordinary sense ("in the presence of" or "opposite") but rather in terms of the like-sounding Aramaic verb (*nagad*) for flowing and pouring. The verse is thus transformed into a dynamic image of the flow of the divine plenty from *Atika Kadisha* (Holy Ancient One) through the male sefirah *Yesod* (signified in the verse by *tov*) into the feminine, the sefirah *Malkhut* (signified by "faithful ones").[18]

This exegetical device of shifting the meaning of a word from its conventional sense to a more distant or special sense was already one of the foundational hermeneutical tools of the classic rabbinic homily. When the Rabbis produced midrashim of the *al tikrei* ("do not read it that way, but rather this way") kind, they gave themselves permission to stray far indeed from the word's simple meaning. So, for example, in the well-known midrash on "inscribed (*ḥarut*) upon the tablets" (Exodus 32:16), they read *ḥarut* (inscribed) as *ḥerut* (freedom), thereby claiming a connection between receiving the "yoke of heaven" and becoming free. The freedom to play with language is one of the hallmarks of midrash in general. The expounder's motivation—to draw forth an ideological message, a poetic image, or an emotional response—is what determines the choice of the surprising sense of the expounded word.

What distinguishes the rabbinic homily (and even the mystical homily, like those of Rabbi Akiva) from the zoharic homily is the motivation. In the homilies cited above on the words *mesapperim* and *atsappeh*, the semantic shift reveals the motivation that underwrites many zoharic homilies: the eroticization of the verse.[19] The kabbalist's loving gaze frequently exposes the erotic aspects of the textual reality. In order to enable the erotic secret to surface in the words and verses of the Bible, the Companions encourage the softening of conventional consciousness, the consciousness of the text's simple meaning (*peshat*). This softening of consciousness or of logical thought is in itself an erotic act. The special state of consciousness that characterizes the Companions' homilies from midnight till dawn, or while walking on the way, reveals aspects of the text that could not be seen in the strong light of day, or construed via the legalistic logic of the *beit midrash*.[20]

Understanding the exegetical enterprise of the Zohar as an erotic activity sheds new light on the interpretive endeavor to innovate Torah and words of wisdom. As in a state of erotic arousal, every time the lover casts his gaze on the body of his beloved, he discovers something new, curious, and arousing. From an erotic perspective, therefore, it would be remiss of the kabbalist to repeat what he has said. Amid his desire to unite with the body of the Torah, the speaker must find a way to express this love differently, with a new or surprising focus.

Describing the Companions of the Zohar as "kabbalists" (*mekubbalim*, receivers) is thus most problematic, insofar as their enterprise is the total antithesis of *kabbalah* in the sense of receiving, preserving, and transmitting an esoteric body of knowledge.[21] As an "arouser and awakener of Torah," the member of the zoharic circle cannot merely repeat what he has received; rather, he must innovate and create. The meaning of the esotericism of the secret has changed here, for the story of the unfolding of the divine is already well known. The secret now is *the special way in which this story is revealed.*

Another central tool for imparting secrets is the very structure of the zoharic story. From rabbinic midrashic and aggadic literature we are familiar with the literary form in which different opinions about biblical verses appear as collected statements by the sages from different periods, or as disagreements in the *beit midrash*. The Zohar created a new literary form—the zoharic story itself—in order to trace the exposure of the various layers of meaning of the Bible's verses from simple (*peshat*) to secret.

Many stories in the Zohar begin with an expression of wonder and surprise regarding the meaning of a particular verse. Often the interpretations presented at the beginning are familiar from rabbinic midrash, or at least are similar in style. Generally, the narrative unfolds such that a new figure—typically someone marginal in the world of the rabbis, or sometimes Rabbi Shim'on—appears bearing a new and more profound interpretation of the verse.

The narrative structure itself functions as a tool in the endeavor to penetrate into ever-deepening layers of meaning. Contact with the secret layer of the verse usually results in some dramatic emotional response by the story's protagonists. They cry, laugh, kiss the bearer of the mystical word, and view their exposure to the deep meaning of the Torah's words as their greatest privilege.[22] In some instances, the revealing of the secret generates a miraculous response in the surrounding environs: fire descends from heaven, or the room is filled with fragrances from the Garden of Eden. These intensified responses serve as signs or confirmation that something important has indeed been revealed. They are directed, of course, also to us readers, to sharpen our attention so as to share the Companions' emotional state. The zoharic story is therefore a central tool, facilitating entry into an order of reality that is capable of receiving the secret. We shall elaborate on this further, below.[23]

We turn now to the key characteristics and processes of the zoharic homily. Generally, one of the Companions begins by reciting and then expounding a verse. This opening homily can have different structures. Sometimes it is of the classic *petiḥta* kind, interweaving a verse from the Prophets or the Writings with a verse from the Torah, which in many cases turns out to be connected to the broader subject or Torah portion that the Companions are explicating. At other times, the opening is an expression of wonder or surprise at a particular word or topic in the biblical verse or story. In many cases, the opening is a repetition or paraphrase of a well-known rabbinic midrash.[24]

In some instances, the opening homily establishes the mystical standard for the homilies to follow, especially when the opening speaker is Rabbi Shim'on.[25] When one of the Companions finishes his homily, another one continues with an additional interpretation, and so on. In the stories that document particularly powerful experiences, a common topic or theme usually connects the various homilies and, as in Plato's *Symposium*, serves as their frame. Here are some examples:

- In the story of Kfar Tarsha, a group assembles at night on the eve of the newborn's circumcision, and each participant refers in his exposition to the theme of circumcision.[26]

- In the story found in the Zohar's commentary to the Torah portion *Vayakhel*, which discusses the ways in which a man can transform himself into a sanctuary for Shekhinah, and of the gift (*terumah*) that must be elevated (*leharim*) spiritually in order to establish his sanctuary, each Companion's homily refers to the verse "bring Me gifts" (Exodus 25:2).[27]

- In a story in the commentary to *Aharei Mot*, whose point of departure is the spiritual drought plaguing the world, each of the Companions assembled around the table of Pinḥas ben Yair offers an exposition whose focus is the union of the masculine and the feminine in order to draw down the divine bounty or spiritual rain into the world. Moreover, each Companion innovates words of praise for their divine teacher, Rabbi Shim'on.[28]

- On the eve of the festival of Shavuot, all of the homilies address the adorning of the bride, in order to escort her to the wedding canopy in all her beauty.[29]

- In the *Idra Rabba*—describing the great assembly of the entire mystic circle—behind each homily is the intention to explicate the exalted, ancient face of *Atika Kadisha*, in order to heal and sweeten *Ze'eir Anpin* (the face of differentiated and dynamic divinity operative in reality and suffering from an excess of Judgment).[30]

As in any ritual or praxis, the zoharic homily has clear guidelines:

(a) *Commitment to innovation.* The Zohar encourages and celebrates the capacity to innovate, from which it does not fear or recoil. The composition as a whole is concerned with the innovation of "ancient-new" words of Torah, words that renew and invigorate the Torah and divinity in the world of humanity. Homilies must contain innovation and cannot merely be repetitions of words already said either by the Rabbis or in the Zohar itself.

(b) *Commitment to the topic.*   If a subject has already been determined for the expositions, each speaker is obligated to address it in his homily.

(c) *Attention to the internal dynamic of the session.*   The speaker must have paid close attention to the homilies recited by his companions. He must have been totally present in the collective experience, so as to transmit the emotional-mystical energy that has accumulated in the preceding homilies and even amplify it.

On rare occasions, the guidelines become even more demanding. (In so doing, they recall poetic forms with well-defined structures.) The most dramatic homiletic challenge is in the *Idra Rabba.* During that assembly, the Companions must abide by stringent rules in offering their mystical homily before the group. Each participant must arise in turn and expound on one of God's facial features. Further, he must interweave this homily with another homily about God's attributes appearing in the verse "Who is a God like You . . ." (Micah 7:18). Through these means alone, he must innovate and instantiate the facial feature assigned to him in order to perfect—together with the other Companions—the totality of the divine countenance.[31]

Once a theme has been determined, the zoharic story continues and records the various homilies expounded on this theme in the course of the narrative. The artistry of zoharic midrash lies in the way that the Companions refer to and integrate the subject within the preset guidelines, and their beading together of allusions to Jewish literature—the Torah, the Prophets, the Writings, the teachings of the sages, as well as kabbalistic and esoteric lore—within their new and innovative exposition.[32]

The inspiration for this structure of "beaded midrash," designed to generate ecstatic experience, derives from the tannaitic description of Ben Azzai: he would sit and bead the words of the Torah to each other, and the Torah to the Prophets, and the Prophets to the Writings, with fire burning all around him.[33] The zoharic homily draws generously from all stores of inherited and written wisdom. It interweaves these diverse statements through its own unique design, to produce something totally new.

The Zohar describes the homily using the poetic image of the jewel (*tikkun*), the beaded adornments and finery decorating and beautifying Shekhinah's body.[34] The zoharic homily is the fruit of virtuosity and improvisation with given materials, a unique Jewish artistic form—with no parallel in any prior Jewish literature. The exposition produced and recited within the circle is supposed to create a new, original jewel for Shekhinah's invisible jewelry box.[35] This conception of the homily emphasizes its theurgic function: the purpose of the exposition is not merely to impart some piece of knowledge or even to implant the Torah in one's heart, but also to affect *tikkun,* to adorn and beautify the female divinity, in order to bring about a union of love between her and the male aspect of the divine.

Sometimes between the expositions there is a pause, and the text returns to the narrative frame. Generally, the purpose of such pauses is to remind readers about the story's broader perspective and to enable us to sense where the story stands in terms of its narrative development. In many instances, the pause gives the protagonists a chance to express their views, and especially their emotions, about the homily just now innovated in the world, as well as to hint at the direction of the exposition to come.

Analysis of the succession of expositions within the mystic circle reveals a tendency to increased daring and intensity from one homily to the next. The conditions that enable this amplification include the power of shared intention, the collective (and protective) nature of the gathering, and the periodic encouragement of the teacher, positioned as the axis around which the narrative unfolds. This is perhaps the main springboard from the world of experiential exposition to the world of mystical experience, for it is often after a succession of ever-intensifying interpretations that the mystical leap occurs.

A prime example is found in a story in the Zohar's commentary to the Torah portion *Aḥarei Mot,* in which after a series of expositions, one participant suddenly attests that the union of the male and female (for the sake of drawing down the divine bounty into the world) is no longer merely what they are speaking about, but is actually happening. The speaker begins to speak in the present tense, describing the experience of the descent of the divine flow upon the Companions during the gathering itself:

> And now, behold, the Holy Luminary crowns himself with the crowns of this level, and he and the Companions offer up praises from below to above, and She is crowned with these praises.
>
> Now, blessings must be brought down to all the Companions from above to below through this holy level. . . .
>
> And now, behold, the blessed Holy One gushes forth upon you blessings from the source of the stream. (Zohar 3:62a)[36]

Similarly in the *Idra Rabba*, Rabbi Shim'on attests: "For we are sitting in supernal holiness, the supernal fire surrounds us."[37]

The interpreting Companions thus can undergo a mystical leap, from a state of consciousness in which they expound a particular matter, to one in which they participate in the matter that they have just been expounding. They move from one state, in which their words create a picture, to another, in which they walk through the gate of their words into the dimension of reality they have just drawn, a dimension that they experience in a most dynamic way.

In terms of the erotic structure, the mystical leap is similar to the transition from foreplay to the moment of intercourse. Indeed, the language of eros is appropriate here, insofar as the purpose of many of the Zohar's homilies is, to use a later formulation, "for the sake of the unification of the blessed Holy One and His Shekhinah." The moment of transition—the expansion of consciousness, the passage from walking to flight, the moment of contact with the new and the departure from the ordinary and the known—is most dramatic and sensational. In the story *Rav Metivta* (Master of the Academy), as we have seen, the Companions testify to the power and force of this moment with their acknowledgment that, having touched this moment, they are now ready to die: "Since we are here and have seen all this, if we die now, we will certainly enter the world that is coming!"[38] Without the right tools, or the intention to return to life, it is indeed possible to die in this moment, as the story in the *Idra Rabba* attests, of the three Companions whose souls depart in a moment of ecstasy.[39]

In other stories, we encounter a zoharic hero explicating an experiential homily while at the same time reflecting on his own interpretive enterprise and experience. So, for example, in the story *Sava de-Mishpatim* (The Old Man of *Mishpatim*), an old man explicates in the presence of two of the Companions and repeatedly inserts into his homilies reflexive comments, vacillations, and personal accounts about his journeys in the wonderland of the homily.

The most dramatic story in this connection, about a speaker imparting in "real time" his mystical experience, is surely the *Idra Zuta*, which narrates the occasion of Rabbi Shim'on's departure from the world. Rashbi's words in this pinnacle moment are at once mystical homilies recited for his students as well as descriptions of the divine realities in which he is taking part. His personal experience is transformed into a body of mystical knowledge for the assembled Companions as well as for the reader. Rabbi Shim'on's exposition comprises secrets about the modes of operation of *Arikh Anpin*, *Ze'eir Anpin*, and the figure of female divinity (*Nukva*) in the divine worlds. On this occasion, his speech serves three functions: transmission of knowledge; self-rectification/redemption (*tikkun*); and the active, theurgic restoration (*tikkun*) of those very matters about which he speaks.

The end of the story is in fact an extraordinarily daring illustration of a double state of consciousness—Rabbi Shim'on enters an ecstatic state in which he experiences himself as the High Priest entering the Holy of Holies, a state that in essence constitutes union with Shekhinah, while at the same time he describes and explains, as a teacher to his disciples, the experience he is undergoing. The essence of this state is the simultaneous ability to be both within the experience and, at the same time, to maintain a reflexive stance toward it. Furthermore, Rabbi Shim'on instructs his most senior disciple, Rabbi Abba, to write down all that transpires. Expressed differently, this is a mystical experience transformed into an oral Torah, and then again into a written Torah. At the end of the story, as Rabbi Shim'on is completing his homily, his soul departs in a moment that interlaces the religious and erotic ecstasy of penetration into the inner recesses of the divine being of Shekhinah.[40]

To conclude our exploration of zoharic collective midrash and its central characteristics, we return to one of Rabbi Shim'on's homilies that we have already encountered in our discussion of the Companions' practice of walking on the way.[41] The essence of the Zohar's secret world lies in its unique mode of reading, and the way in which its hermeneutical endeavor enables the words and letters of the biblical text to reveal their hidden contents. Rabbi Shim'on expounds "The path of the righteous is like radiant sunlight, ever brightening until noon" (Proverbs 4:18; transl. NJPS) as defining the special way in which the mystics create paths in the Torah and in divinity. The uniqueness of the "path of the righteous" lies in innovation, in opening new paths alongside the paved and well-trodden ways of interpretation, through illuminating a verse with a meaning as yet unconsidered. Innovation also implies the ability to traverse well-known ways, and the capacity to renew or innovate them as never before. The innovation of the path of the righteous gives special prominence to the teaching of the moment—the Torah of the present. The innovation transpires "now," in the present, while walking and talking.

> *The path of the righteous*—what is the difference between "path" and "way"?
>
> They have already clarified the matter; but a path is that which has just now been opened and revealed, and was made in that place a path, where no feet have trodden before.
>
> *Way* (*derekh*), as it is written, *as one who treads* (*dorekh*) *in the winepress* (Isaiah 63:1), where the feet of all who wish tread.
>
> That is why where the righteous walk is called *path* (*orah*), since they were the first to open that place. And even when others, the people of the world, walk in that place, now that the righteous walk there it becomes a new place, for now that place is new as though never trod upon by any before, because the righteous invigorate that place through the sublime words in which the blessed Holy One delights. (Zohar 2:215a)[42]

A Jazz Interlude

An artistic form from which it is possible to learn a great deal about the artistry of the zoharic homily is the jazz jam session. In a jam session, a number of musicians take part, each with a different instrument, and the session is constructed out of the musical tension and play generated by the diverse instruments and musicians.

The musicians begin together with a melodic theme familiar to all, and for the first few minutes all play this known tune. Afterward, one of the musicians strikes out on a musical solo, which is an improvisation related to the theme and its harmonic structure. This improvisation can be moderate (a variation on the theme) or it can be free and bold (departing dramatically from the theme). All the other instrumentalists accompany and support the soloist's musical journey.

When that soloist completes the improvisation, the group returns for a few moments to play the theme with which they began, until another musician embarks on an improvisation.

Jazz virtuosos will frequently integrate into their own improvisation elements from the turn of the previous musician. All the participants are familiar with the rules of the game, and every jam session entails a new journey of improvisations. In many cases, the personal musical journey of a particular musician reaches a crescendo of beauty, surprise, and complexity, arousing admiration among the other participants. Some of the greatest improvisations have become jazz classics.[43]

Similarly in the art of zoharic midrash: All the companions are familiar with the "theme" of the verse, all must embark on a solo to create a new and innovative homily. The homily must artistically connect with the theme, and each expounder must return to it. Each homily employs conceptual elements that arose in the previous homilies.

Both of these artistic forms require the total presence and profound mutual attunement of the participants. Yet above all else, what is required is something less tangible: neither the musician nor the instrument nor even the melody, but rather the tension and play among the players, the eros of the improvisation. The more virtuosic the participants in the jam session—or in the circle of expositions—the more wonderful and surprising their improvisations will be.

"If you wake and rouse love"

Language of Awakening and Arousal

The reader of the Zohar discovers, among its many treasures, an array of motifs reappearing in different guises. The theme of sleep, wakefulness, and the call to arouse is one such motif. It occupies a central place in the Zohar. This motif establishes a rich, thematic, mystical structure whose imprint is embedded throughout the zoharic corpus.

In different places in the Zohar, the reader encounters dramatic, pathos-filled passages that call upon the people of the world to awaken from their slumber, to open the eyes of their soul, to see the true path of Torah, and to actualize their destiny in the world. These calls are voiced mainly by three speakers: a hero of the composition, usually Rabbi Shim'on; a heavenly herald;[1] or the Torah itself. Often their voices intertwine one with another. Each of these voices activates, in its own way, the composition's addressees—both the Zohar's protagonists and its readers. These dramatic passages are filled with gloomy descriptions of the state of consciousness of the majority of humanity (namely, self-imposed slumber), and of the bitter consequences of this lowly state. They also describe the good that awaits those who awaken—and by extension, the world—in rectifying this situation.

The Zohar develops a unique language of awakening and arousal derived from its different understandings of the root '-v-r (עור): as awakening from sleep, as a clarification of an idea (as in the contemporary Hebrew use of a note or comment—*he'arah*—to a text[2]), and as an emotional amplification or sensual-erotic intensification. This language establishes a comprehensive, mystical worldview in which the different kinds of arousal function in a dynamic and integrated way. This integration spans the awakening of human consciousness to its essence and destiny, the erotic arousal toward the Torah, and the awakening of thought engendering the clarification and understanding of the Torah's words.

These different awakenings, whose locus is the human being, together generate an additional awakening—the mystical-erotic-theurgic awakening of the finite, human world toward the divine world. This awakening, termed by the Zohar *it'aruta de-letata* (awakening below), in turn awakens the different sefirot in the world of divinity, their subsequent union prompting the descent of the divine flow and blessing—to the kabbalists in particular, and to the lower world in general. In the language of the Zohar, this second awakening is termed *it'aruta de-le'ila* (awakening above).

This chapter examines the Zohar's language of arousal as a dynamic structure in its mystical enterprise.[3] We look at the meaning of such language within the composition and the circle of mystics, its importance in understanding the worldview of the Zohar's authors, and the way it fulfills a performative function activating the reader.

Analysis of the language of arousal is crucial for understanding the Zohar's view of the reality of human consciousness, and the relationship between such reality and the latent potential of humanity. Through this language, we will learn not only about the self-image of the zoharic Companions as awakeners, but we will also understand the foundational ideas in the mystical-intellectual world of the Zohar's authors, who are present throughout as the "implied author."[4]

Moreover, analysis of this language is instructive in appreciating the Zohar's self-perception as a composition whose ultimate *telos* is the awakening of humanity, insofar as the many voices of awakening are the voices of the Zohar's composers, and the voice that calls out to humanity is in fact the voice of the Zohar's authors directed to its readers. Indeed, in the relationship between the Zohar and its readers, this language of arousal serves a performative function; it seeks to bring about an experiential change in the readers' consciousness.

Human Beings, Torah, and the Study of Torah

In order to understand the impulse, the daring, and the presumption of the Zohar's heroes in their quest to awaken humanity, it is important to recall certain interpretive premises that inform the entire corpus. We must keep in mind the Zohar's conceptions of humanity and its destiny in the world; the nature of the Torah; and the character of the relationship between the student and the Torah.

Humanity, created in the image of God, is understood as the crown of Creation. By virtue of their possessing a soul, a spark of divinity, human beings share something essential with the divine. The structure of the human body and the structure of the human soul are described in the Zohar as paralleling the structure of the sefirot (the active face of the divine in the world as well those aspects of divinity open to human comprehension and experience).[5] The human being has been given a body, eyes, ears, heart, mind, and—above all else—a soul with which to comprehend the divine.[6] The importance of the connection between this exalted conception of humanity and arousal is expressed in numerous passages in the Zohar.

Rabbi Shim'on opened: "*I roused one from the north and he comes . . .* (Isaiah 41:25).

"Come and see how foolish people are! For they neither know nor reflect upon the ways of the blessed Holy One! They are all asleep, unawakened, slumber in their sockets.

"Come and see: The blessed Holy One formed the human being corresponding to the pattern above, all according to wisdom...When the whole body is arrayed in its limbs fittingly, the blessed Holy One joins with it, inserting a holy soul—to teach the human how to walk in ways of Torah and observe His commandments, so that he will perfect himself. As long as the holy soul is within him, a person should expand the image of the supernal King in the world. This mystery is that the flowing, gushing river never ceases; therefore a human should never cease his river and source in this world, so that he grasp it in the world that is coming. (Zohar 1:186b; Matt 2004–2007, vol. 3, pp. 136–37, reformatted)[7]

The great teacher, Rabbi Shim'on bar Yoḥai, complains here that despite God's extraordinary design in creating humans as beings capable of following the ways of the Torah—of being perfected and fulfilling their destiny in expanding the likeness of the divine in the world[8]—they choose instead to fall into a slumber of consciousness. This turning away from humanity's true destiny is understood here as sleep and stupidity, and the misapprehension of the purpose of human existence is presented as opposed to the divine plan. In this homily, the river that flows forth from Eden is the river of souls that flows into the world, and the destiny of humanity is to actualize the dynamism of the divine river in one's life in this world. The entry of the river into the garden of reality depends upon humans' capacity and readiness to improve themselves through performing the commandments and producing offspring,[9] as well as through becoming a vehicle for the river of the divine flow.

In employing such symbols as multiplying the likeness of the king in the world and guarding the flow of the divine river, this description of humanity's *telos* also highlights their theurgic task. Human beings are not merely a specific representation of the divine in a finite, material world. Rather, they are responsible for the actualization of divinity in the world so as to ensure the harmonious flow of the divine bounty, both within itself and from itself into the world.

> Come and see: The blessed Holy One created man with the mystery of wisdom and made him with great skill; and He breathed into his nostrils the breath (*neshamah*) of life, so that he might know and contemplate the mysteries of wisdom—to know his Maker's glory, as is said: *Every one that is called by My name, I have created him for My glory. I have formed him, indeed I have made him* (Isaiah 43:7).
>
> *I have created him for My glory*—precisely!
>
> The mystery is: *I have created him for My glory.* We have learned that this glory below, the mystery of the holy throne, is not restored in the world above except through the restoration of the world's inhabitants. . . . this disposition is placed in man so that he shall be on the earth like the upper

glory. . . . In this fashion, He created man upon the earth, who is like a model of that upper glory, to restore this glory and complete it on all sides. (Zohar 2:155a)

The restoration of the holy throne above is dependent on the restoration of humanity below. The soul was created both on the pattern of the divine world and from its essence, in order to enable the flow of the divine glory through human agency from below, and the flow of the divine bounty onto the human being from above. Humanity has been granted the tools to actualize its purpose, and insofar as this potential lies planted within, human beings have the responsibility to undergo *tikkun* and to fulfill their destiny. Were it not for the uniqueness of humanity among God's creatures, they would be unable to awaken, and there would be no meaning in the quest to awaken from slumber.

The Torah, the hidden jewel of the blessed Holy One, is understood in the Zohar as the divine force cloaked in letters, words, and stories.[10] The Torah is the dimension that mediates between the soul of the human being and the divine. It is through loving the Torah, engaging and studying her words, that human beings clarify the path on which they ought to walk in order to fulfill the purpose of their existence.

> The Torah who created them [the angels] and created all the worlds and for whose sake they all exist. . . . In descending to this world, if she did not put on the garments of this world, the world could not endure. So this story of Torah is the garment of Torah. . . . But the essence of the garment is the body; the essence of the body is the soul. So it is with Torah. . . . The wise ones, servants of the King on high, . . . look only at the soul, root of all, real Torah! (Zohar 3:152a; Matt 1995, p. 135–36)

The Torah is the object of the Companions' desire and their engagement with her—through interpreting and expounding her, and through removing her garments to reveal her secrets—is in fact the central preoccupation of the mystical circle.[11] Seen from this vantage point, the Zohar's literary or "epic" layer[12] stands alone among the known epic traditions: The "land" or the space in which the protagonists' adventures transpire, more than being the imagined Land of Israel, is rather the Torah—and her stories, her verses, and her letters' crowns and coronets.[13]

Voices of Awakening and Arousal

As noted above, calls to awakening are voiced by three speakers—Rabbi Shim'on bar Yoḥai, the heavenly herald, and the Torah—with each voice activating its addressee in a different way. We will now explore the meaning of "sleep" and "wakefulness" as they are presented through the medium of these three voices. This will enable us to analyze the function of these voices in generating experiential change among the Zohar's readers.

"RABBI SHIM'ON OPENED": THE VOICE OF RASHBI

Rabbi Shim'on bar Yoḥai is the central hero in the Zohar, the omniscient teacher; and in his calls to awaken, he addresses his disciples with a tone of castigation. These words of rebuke, however, are not directed to the Companions—for they define themselves as awakened ones and awakeners—but rather to the sleeping masses of humanity. In fact, Rashbi's words of rebuke actually strengthen the Companions' identity, encouraging them to continue on their path. In the following passage, we find a high concentration of the essential components of the Zohar's language of awakening.

> Rabbi Shim'on opened and said: *All the streams flow into the sea, yet the sea is never full* (Ecclesiastes 1:7).
>
> Rabbi Shim'on said: I am astounded by the people of the world, for they have neither eyes to see nor a heart to pay attention, and they do not know and do not attune their hearts to look to the will of their creator. How do they slumber and not awaken from their sleep before that day arrives—when darkness and the shadow of death will cover them and the Master of Accounts will demand a reckoning from them!
>
> A herald calls out to them every day, and their souls reprove them every day and night.
>
> The Torah raises her voice in every direction and proclaims, saying: *"How long will you simple ones love simplicity?"* (Proverbs 1:22); *"Let the simple enter here!"* To those without a heart she says, *"Come eat my food and drink the wine that I have mixed!"* (Proverbs 9:4–5).[14]
>
> But there is no one who inclines his ear and no one who awakens his heart! (Zohar 3:57b–58a)

The stylistic inspiration for Rabbi Shim'on's dramatic address here, as in his other calls to the people of the world, is to be found in the writings of the Sages. For example, in the talmudic tractate *Ḥagigah*, Rabbi Yose says: "Woe to the creatures who see yet do not know what they see, who stand yet do not know upon what they stand!"[15] Implied in Rashbi's words is the distinction between the members of his mystical circle and the "people of the world," a distinction that in fact defines the Companions and their destiny in a polemical fashion against the rest of the Jewish world. The Companions of the Zohar, be they a literary fiction or a reflection of a historical reality, define here the world in which they operate: a world of walking sleepers, of sealed and impervious hearts, and of forgetting the divine.

From these statements we also learn about the self-perception and self-image of the Zohar's authors, or more precisely, the "implied authors" present as the composition's general voice: they are already awake; and like Rashbi, with whom they identify, they set themselves the task of awakening humanity. Furthermore, from the description of the state of the world in the previous homily, we can also discern something of the way the mystics from the generation of the Zohar viewed the Jewish community of Spain at the end of the thirteenth century, or at the very least, the way they viewed their ideological opponents. All the components of a homily of this kind serve the composition's goal of rousing its readers. Such passages call out to them, inviting them to abandon the sleeping masses of humanity and to join the awakened ones.[16]

In referring to the people of the world as having "neither eyes to see nor a heart to pay attention," Rashbi uses the sarcastic language employed by the Bible in speaking about idolatry: "They have eyes but cannot see, they have ears but cannot hear. . . . those who fashion them shall be like them."[17] Human beings have been granted the gift of eyes, heart, and soul, but these precious gifts have been encased in the forgetfulness of sleep. The bitter lot of humanity is the consequence of their not assuming their true destiny and nature. Only the awakening of the eyes and the heart to the existence of the soul, which God planted within the human being, can enable the actualization of humanity's destiny in the world.

Amid his call to awakening, Rashbi invokes two additional voices of awakening that call out to the sleeping masses: the heavenly herald and the Torah. As the hero of the composition, Rabbi Shim'on encompasses in his call the other voices of arousal and awakening that appear throughout the Zohar.

"AN EVER-TURNING VOICE TRAVERSES THE WORLD": THE VOICE OF THE HEAVENLY HERALD

When the call to awaken originates in man, and in particular with Rabbi Shim'on, the style is, as we have seen, one of dramatic prose. In contrast, the voice that calls out from heaven is full of pathos and has the rhythm of poetry or a hymn.

Passages of awakening of this second kind appear in disparate places throughout the Zohar, in many cases at the beginning of a homily but sometimes at its end. The unique literary layers called (in printed editions of the Zohar) *Tosefta* and *Matnitin* are especially characterized by these calls, whose explicit purpose is to awaken the listener to a new consciousness.[18] The passages in which the heavenly voice appears share conceptual, literary, stylistic, and linguistic features that bestow upon them their special character: heightened, ornate, and terse language; short, pathos-laden sentences; dramatic repetition; and frightening, threatening rhetoric. These passages are, in part, modeled on rabbinic precedent, as in Rabbi Yehoshu'a ben Levi's statement: "Every day a heavenly voice goes forth from Mount Horeb proclaiming and saying: Woe to humanity for their disdain of the Torah!"[19]

Another source of inspiration for these passages is perhaps to be found in Maimonides' description of the sound of the shofar as encoding a rhetoric of rebuke:

> Even though the sounding of the shofar on Rosh Hashanah is a scriptural decree, it contains an allusion. It is as if [the shofar's call] is saying: Wake up, you sleepy ones, from your sleep; and you who slumber, arise! Inspect your deeds, repent, remember your Creator, you who forget the truth in the vanities of time and throughout the entire year devote your energies to vanity and emptiness that will not benefit or save![20]

The awakening from sleep is the fundamental metaphor for the awakening of the soul (or, as we might say today, the awakening of consciousness[21]) to its hidden potential, to the work it must perform, and to the pleasure that lies in store upon fulfilling its purpose. Thus Rabbi Yose explains: "Every day a herald goes forth and calls out: 'People of the world, awaken your heart before the holy king! Awaken to be careful of your sins! Awaken the holy soul that He placed in you from the supernal, holy place!'"[22]

The "herald" is a divine voice whose task is to awaken the eyes, heart, mind, and soul from their sleep. This slumber of the heart and soul about which the Zohar speaks is the opposite of the ideal state of the mystic, one of whose most important models is the beloved in the Song of Songs. In the Jewish literary tradition preceding the Zohar, this beloved is the Assembly of Israel or the soul.[23] In the Song of Songs, the beloved is "asleep" while her heart is "awake" (5:2); like her, the human soul needs to be awake to receive its beloved, the holy king, the blessed Holy One. In other words, ideally, even when a person is asleep, the soul is in a state of wakefulness. As opposed to the beloved, who signifies the correct state of the human being, the Zohar claims that the people of the world are *awake* while their hearts are *asleep*. In awakening from their slumber, human beings accede to the unique gift that God has bestowed upon them.

MISHNAH:
The will of the deed, the knots of faith!
A voice, the voice of voices awakened from above and below.
Open-eyed we were.
A wheel rolled from above to numerous sides,
A melodious sound awakened:
Awaken sleepy, slumbering ones, with sleep in their sockets
Who do not know and do not look and do not see!
Impervious ears, heavy heart, they sleep and do not know.
The Torah stands before them, yet they pay no heed, and do not know upon
    what they gaze; they see yet do not see.
The Torah sends forth voices: Look foolish ones, open your eyes and you will
    know!
Yet there is none who pays heed, and there is none who inclines his ear!
For how long shall you remain in the darkness of your desire?
Look to know, and the enlightening light will be revealed to you!

Zohar 1:161b

The above passage is characteristic of the *Matnitin*—the hymn-like, dramatic, enigmatic style as well as the short, piercing, decisive sentences. Following the unfathomable opening line, we encounter a description of the scene in which these mysterious words are proclaimed to the world. This is a dramatic event, calling on all the senses, perhaps akin to the revelation at Mt. Sinai or to prophetic experience.

At first, the heavenly voice is heard, the "voice of voices" is awakened above and descends to the world. Then those who experience this voice are described—the mystics, the open-eyed ones. (The expression "open-eyed" is one of the Zohar's central epithets for the sages of truth, the mystics, those awakened souls whose eyes are open to the experience.) They see a wheel rolling above them to numerous directions, and perhaps it is through this rolling that the melodious sound is awakened and heard. The heavenly voice proclaims stern words of rebuke to the people of the world. This is a voice of awakening, of castigation and warning, without any attempt to mask or soften the ideological platform placed before the reader. This is a direct, programmatic call to the reader with ecstatic overtones.

The programmatic aspects, as well as the panoply of prophetic images encoded in the heavenly voice, are expressed in the following passages.

The essence [lit. body] of the Mishnah:
We were drawing near.
We heard an ever-turning voice revolving from above to below, traversing throughout the world.
A voice smashing mountains, breaking mighty rocks,
Great stormy winds ascending.
Our ears were open.
[The voice] said on its travels:
The end of ends!
Silent sleepers, sleep is in their sockets, they stand in their place. . . .
They all do not feel and do not know that a book is open, and with a name it shall be written. . . .
Woe to them, woe to their lives, woe to their feelings [or: souls]! About them is written:
May they be erased from the book of life (Psalms 69:29).

Zohar 1:121a

The heavenly voice is cited here by the mystics, "the ones with open eyes, heart, and ears"; ironically, it is only those already awake who merit to hear this awesome, cosmic voice, while the people of the world, the voice's ultimate addressees, remain in their slumber. In other words, the people of the world and we readers are likely to encounter this great voice only through the mediation of the Zohar's protagonists, who have already experienced it and have transmitted what we readers are able to hear. In terms of the composition's impact upon the reader, this structure of transmission serves both to glorify the group of "hearers" as well as a call inviting the reader to become one of them.

> The voice returned:
> "O high, hidden, concealed ones, open-eyed, roaming the entire world, gaze and see!
> "O low, sleeping ones, close-eyed, awake!
> "Who among you turns darkness into light, bitter into sweet before arriving here?
> "Who among you awaits each day the light that shines when the King visits the doe and is glorified—declared King of all kings of the world?
> "Whoever does not await this each day in that world has no portion here."
>
> Zohar 1:4a; Matt 2004–2007, vol. 1, pp. 21–22, reformatted

In these two passages,[24] the voice of calling contrasts the evil awaiting those who choose to remain asleep with the divine good in store for those who awaken. The punishment of the sleepers is that they will be erased from the book of life. This heavenly voice is most unforgiving toward the sleeping masses of the world. We can even discern here frustration in the majority's choice not to follow the mystics' path.

In opposition to the sleeping masses and their punishment, the heavenly voice defines he who is worthy to enter the world above, "to gaze upon the beauty of YHVH and to frequent His Temple" (Psalms 27:4). Indeed, we can find here an important collation of the characteristics of the ideal mystic according to the Zohar.[25]

The following passage is also illustrative of the call type that begins with enigmatic, unfathomable utterances, full of pathos, followed by a description of the heightened sensorial state of consciousness of those undergoing the experience, and culminating with the frightening voice that reproaches the sleeping masses of the world.

> TOSEFTA   Incredible clusters! Impregnable castles! Quaestors of quaestory! Those of open eyes, open ears!
>
> A voice—voice of voices—descends from above, pulverizing mountains and boulders:
>
> "Who are those who see without seeing, ears blocked, eyes shut? Neither seeing, nor hearing, nor knowing through contemplation the one encompassed by two within them, cast away by them."
>
> Zohar 1:62a; Matt 2004–2007, vol. 1, pp. 358–59, reformatted

The voice of the heavenly herald differs from the voice of the teacher insofar as the latter is a known figure who addresses a defined and familiar audience, namely, his students. It is true that sometimes, in order to be able to hear the voice of the heavenly herald, one must already be in a heightened state of consciousness—open-eyed, open-eared, and open-hearted—and thus it is necessary for the mystics to be the bearers of the herald's message. Nevertheless, the heavenly voice is a voice for the entire world, a mighty cosmic voice, "smashing mountains," devoid of human tones, arousing terror. The heavenly voice rarely contains interpretations of verses, but rather it is characterized by a special rhetoric of concise, enigmatic sentences, overflowing with castigation and divine judgment.

"THE TORAH CALLS OUT EVERY DAY IN LOVE": THE VOICE OF THE TORAH

As opposed to the voice of Rashbi and the voice of the heavenly herald, the voice of the Torah is feminine. Her voice is seductive and enticing; and in contradistinction to the castigating quality of the other voices of awakening, the voice of the Torah displays an emotional desire to be seen, considered, and loved. As we have seen, the Torah is portrayed as an active entity in the world, who every day calls out to the human being in love.

> Come and see! This is the way of the Torah: At first, when she begins to reveal herself to a human, she beckons him with a hint. If he knows, good; if not, she sends him a message, calling him a fool. Torah says to her messenger: "Tell that fool to come closer, so I can talk with him!" as it is written: *Who is the fool without a heart? Have him turn in here!* (Proverbs 9:4).

He approaches. She begins to speak with him from behind a curtain she has drawn, words he can follow, until he reflects a little at a time. . . .

Once he has grown accustomed to her, she reveals herself face to face and tells him all her hidden secrets, all the hidden ways, since primordial days secreted in her heart. (Zohar 2:99a, *Sava de-Mishpatim*; Matt 1983, p. 124–25)

Generally, human beings stand before the Torah as fools or simpletons rather than as evildoers, and the Torah's call to them is a call of courtship. It encourages them to leave behind the rank of fools and to gradually become "masters of Torah," to become worthy of knowing her secrets. The voice of the Torah is an ever-present voice in the world, never ceasing to hope that there will be those who will open their ears and hearts to heed her call. Thus Rabbi Yose teaches: "The Torah reproves him every day, and a forceful voice calls out: *Who is the fool without a heart? Have him turn in here!* (Proverbs 9:4)."[26]

In most of the passages in which the Torah's voice appears, she calls out to humanity via that same verse. Typically accompanying her inviting call is another voice, sometimes that of the expounder and sometimes that of the heavenly herald, which bemoans (with sober pessimism) the tragic fact that despite her efforts, the people of the world do not awaken from their slumber.[27]

Those who remain asleep are destined to pay a heavy price for their slumber—for their disdain of the Torah, the central agent of awakening placed in the world by God, left abandoned and forgotten.[28] In turning their backs on the Torah, the people of the world stand diametrically opposed to Rabbi Shim'on and his disciples and their vigilant attention to the many nuances of the Torah's voice. Indeed, the Companions' entire enterprise is the interpretation of Torah and the contemplation of her secrets; and as we have already seen, one of the Zohar's foci is the endeavor to grant its readers a taste of the extraordinary love for the Torah displayed by the composition's composers, and in so doing to engender in the reader the appropriate relationship with her.

The three voices of calling are similar to one another in their demand to rouse, and in their cautioning against the bitter consequences of the soul's sleep. They differ, however, in terms of the character of the call, the nuance of their message, and even in terms of the audience addressed. In their direct calls to the people of the world, these voices represent one of the clearest expressions of the all-encompassing desire of the composition to awaken the reader. As a literary stratagem, their variety expands the audience of potential listeners, in that each voice strikes a chord with different readers.

Awakening and Erotic Arousal

Sleep and wakefulness are part of the Zohar's deep language and are crucial components in its worldview. Accordingly, the motif of awakening appears many times, with two primary meanings: awakening from sleep, and erotic arousal.

Awakening from sleep   As we have just seen, the focus of awakening in the Zohar is that of the human being, like Jacob's awakening from his dream to the awe-filled recognition of God's presence in the world.[29] The state of consciousness of ordinary wakefulness is understood by the Zohar as sleep; the people of the world are awake, yet sleep is in their eyes. It is this slumber of consciousness that prevents them from seeing reality as it truly is, from understanding their true place in the order of things, and from awakening to a new apprehension of being.

One can discern here resonances of ancient Gnostic motifs that view the world and human consciousness as dwelling under a blanket of sleep, creating the illusion of tranquillity but in reality causing the "son of light" to forget his true origin and purpose. A prime example of this motif can be found in the "Hymn of the Pearl," a Gnostic work most likely dating to the second half of the second century, which allegorically narrates the story of the destiny of the soul—from its origin in the world of light, to its descent and slumber in this world of darkness and evil, and on to its eventual awakening to its divine destiny:

> [they] mixed me [drink] with their cunning and gave me to taste of their meat; and I forgot that I was a king's son and served their king. I forgot the Pearl for which my parents had sent me. Through the heaviness of their nourishment I sank into deep slumber. . . .

And they wrote a letter to me and each of the great ones signed it with his name.

From thy father the King of Kings and from thy mother, mistress of the East, and from thy brother, our next in rank, unto our son in Egypt, greeting. *Awake and rise up out of thy sleep*, and perceive the words of our letter. Remember that thou art a king's son: behold whom thou hast served in bondage. . . .

At its voice and sound I awoke and arose from my sleep, took it up, kissed it, broke its seal and read. Just as was written on my heart were the words of my letter to read. I remembered that I was the son of kings and that my freeborn soul desired its own kind.[30]

According to the Gnostic view, sleep is a metaphor for our state of existence in the world, and the response to the herald, to the calling voice, is the awakening that enables salvation.[31] Sleep is understood here as a conspiracy of the forces of darkness, the forces of this world, as deployed against the daughter of light, the soul.

In the Zohar, by contrast, sleep is described not as a conspiracy but rather as a weakness on humanity's part. Moreover, sleep does not ensue as a consequence of material existence, for the Zohar sees in the human bodily form a reflection of the divine being and a holy divine plan. And unlike the Gnostic texts, the Zohar speaks of ever-present forces of awakening, the forces of good. The continuing slumber of the soul is thus the result of the imperviousness of the heart and ears to the voices that call out.

As in the Gnostic texts, the Zohar also speaks of the awakened as few in number, "the reapers of the field are few";[32] but as opposed to the Gnostic position, which sees in the division between the sons of light and the sons of perdition a fateful distinction with tones of predestination, the Zohar claims that within every human being resides the ability to awaken. It is because of this that the Zohar is so stern in its rebuke of both the Jews and the other people of the world in their failing to respond to the call to awaken, and why it so bitterly laments their preference for sleep.[33] Awakening brings an end to the slumber of consciousness and enables the soul's opening of its eyes to its essence.

Erotic Arousal   The second sense of awakening and arousal designates the intensification and amplification of human sensory perception and consciousness. Having awakened from sleep, with eyes now open, arousal refers to the lover's intensity, persistence, and indefatigable force in relation to the objects of his love—the Torah and God. The kabbalist's engagement with the Torah is full of passion and desire; it flows from his yearning to rejoice in revealing her secrets, and in so doing, to experience the presence of the divine in the myriad ways that it is revealed through her.

Erotic arousal characterizes the spirit of the entire zoharic corpus. This is the arousal of vitality, the flow of life and of pleasure,[34] an awakening out of love. It comprises a playful and novel combination of "awakening" as rousing from sleep and "awakening" as an enhancement of alertness, sensuality, and erotic sensibility. The Zohar's authors' use of the different inflections of the verbal root '-v-r (עור) is especially attuned to the language of the Song of Songs. The oath with which the beloved adjures the maidens of Jerusalem occurs three times: "Do not wake or rouse love until it pleases!"[35] We find in these verses a nuanced distinction between "awakening" and "arousal." Amid the web of relations between the lover and the beloved are many elusive transitions from sleep to waking, from dreams to fantasy; and it is these transitions that are characteristic of being in love and the erotic experience. The erotic force of arousal in the verse "Under the apple tree I aroused you" (Song of Songs 8:5) is also abundantly clear.

The Song of Songs' language of love, as well as Rabbi Akiva's interpretation of the Song as describing the nature of the connection between God and the Assembly of Israel,[36] is deeply embedded in the consciousness of the Zohar's authors. It constitutes the paradigm for the relationships between God and the Jewish people, between God and the soul, and among aspects of the divinity itself. The entirety of reality is erotic; and in order to recognize this reality and to operate within it, the mystic must possess an amplified sensorial, emotional, and intellectual alertness.[37]

As we have seen, the relationship between the student and Torah in the Zohar is characterized by the dynamic relations between a lover and his beloved. According to their own self-perception, the Companions do not "interpret" verses. Rather, they are aroused toward them—and in turn they arouse those verses[38]—and they are thus termed those who "arouse themselves with Torah":

> A herald proclaims potently: 'You are addressed, holy ones of the Most High, those among you whose ears have been penetrated by spirit to listen, whose eyes are open to see, heart receptive to know!'
> ". . . but no one is aroused, except the truly virtuous who rise and arouse themselves with Torah." (Zohar 1:77a–b; Matt 2004–2007, vol. 2, pp. 3–4)

The Torah too has many ways to arouse her lover, the student of Scripture.

> So it is with a word of Torah:
> She reveals herself to no one but her lover. Torah knows that he who is wise of heart hovers about her gate every day.
> What does she do? She reveals her face to him from the palace and beckons him with a hint, then swiftly withdraws to her hiding place.
> No one who is there knows or reflects; he alone does, and his heart and his soul and everything within him flows out to her.
> That is why Torah reveals and conceals herself. With love she approaches her lover to arouse love with him. (Zohar 2:99a, *Sava de-Mishpatim*; Matt 1983, p. 124)

The expression "the Companions have been aroused" (*it'aru ḥevraya*) is repeated hundreds of times throughout the Zohar. Indeed this is the most frequently cited expression to describe their activity: they are aroused by the verses of the Torah, they arouse in them hidden layers of meaning. They even intertwine, embrace, or unite with them. For in addition to the root *'-v-r* (עור), the Zohar adds the similar root *'-r-h* (ערה; stimulate; pour forth; mix) to its understanding of "awakening," both in the sense of pouring spirit into a receptacle, as in "Till a spirit from on high is poured out (*ya'areh*) on us" (Isaiah 32:15; transl. NJPS), and in the erotic sense of intertwining and copulation, as in the talmudic interpretation of *ke-ma'ar ish ve-loyot* (1 Kings 7:36) as "a man intertwined with his wife";[39] and in the language of the Zohar, *it'aru da be-da* (they fused with one another).[40]

The transformation of the human being into a *maskil* (an enlightened one), that is, into a kabbalist, is described in the Zohar as a process of sensorial enhancement and intensification. This is an arousal directed above, to the divine, expressed through the senses. According to Rashbi, it can be expressed through the sense of smell (which is spiritual and elusive as well as erotic): "*See, My servant shall be enlightened (yaskil)* (Isaiah 52:13)—mystery of faith. *See, he shall be attentive (yaskil)*, for an arousal is aroused above, like one who inhales the scent and is aroused to investigate [or: contemplate] (*le-istakkala*)."[41]

The "truly virtuous" are those who awaken from their slumber of consciousness; and their labor is the falling-in-love with, and courting of, the Torah. The arousal of the Torah is in fact the intensification of the contemplation of its details, amplifying these details to mythic and cosmic proportions. Under the gaze of the Zohar's protagonists, the Torah shimmers, grows, and expands. Just as in an intensified erotic state, there is no part of the body of their beloved (the Torah) that does not evoke their interest, curiosity, and wonder.

The kabbalists experience their arousal of the Torah as a rectification of her situation in the world.[42] The lack of attention paid to the Torah and the absence of those who contemplate her secrets in love brings about a diminution of her dimensions. Or expressed more drastically: since the Torah is not seen, she does not exist. This description of the Torah emerges from the famous riddle of the wondrous old man at the beginning of the story "The Old Man of *Mishpatim*":

> Who is the beautiful maiden who has no eyes and a body concealed and revealed, she comes out in the morning and is hidden all day, she adorns herself with adornments that are not? (Zohar 2:95a, *Sava de-Mishpatim*; Matt 1983, p. 121)

The Torah is seen and sees only by virtue of her lovers' loving gaze. The contemplation and arousal of Torah restores her to her appropriate state in the world. These reflections on the arousal and contemplation of the Torah as well as lovemaking with the Torah parallel, as we shall see below, the Zohar's comments on the restoration of Shekhinah.

Of the circle of kabbalists associated with the composition of the Zohar, the language of awakening and arousal is the hallmark of the writings of Rabbi Moses de León. The verb '-*v-r* (עור; awaken, arouse) appears again and again throughout his writings with the same meanings and inflections

THE ZOHARIC QUEST   222

found in the Zohar. At the beginning of his essay *Mishkan ha-Edut*, de León writes explicitly about the slumber of humanity, and about the necessity to write in order to awaken them to the truth:

> I looked at the ways of the people of the world and saw how in all that concerns these [theological] matters, they are enmeshed in foreign ideas and false, strange notions. One generation passes away and another generation comes, but the errors and falsehoods abide forever. And no one sees and no one hears and no one awakens, for they are all asleep, for a deep sleep from God has fallen upon them, such that they do not question and do not read and do not search out. And when I saw all this I was forced to write and conceal and study so as to reveal [the matter] to every wise man (*maskil*).[43]

De León sees himself here as writing and concealing (!) in order to awaken the sleeping masses of humanity. Further, in the poem that opens *Sefer ha-Rimmon*, he writes: "After God aroused my spirit and my mind, the author said: The spirit of YHVH has spoken within me, and guided me saying: How is it you sleep in the thoughts of your desire? Arise and call to your God and establish the thoughts of your heart. For YHVH your God is in your midst."[44] The language of arousal serves therefore as a litmus test for identifying his writings, and it attests to his deep involvement in the Zohar's composition.[45]

"Arousal below and arousal above"

Beyond the specific purpose of the kabbalists' endeavor (namely, to awaken themselves or to arouse themselves with Torah) lies the ultimate objective: to arouse the feminine dimension of the divine so that the masculine dimension of this reality will in turn be aroused toward her. The arousal of both of these aspects reaches its climax with their union, and the ensuing pleasure of this union prompts the flow of divine plenty into the world.

The spiritual task of the arousal of the upper world by the human world below is called by the Zohar *it'aruta de-letata*, the awakening below, with the arousal of the upper worlds designated by the term *it'aruta de-le'ila*, the awakening above. These partnered concepts engender an erotic myth in which humanity, the feminine divinity, and the masculine divinity are all active participants.

The relationship between the masculine grade of the divine and its corresponding feminine aspect—or in terms of the sefirot, between *Tiferet* and *Malkhut*—is complex, the harmony between them being broken most of the time. The harsh face of reality, as it is presented to us, is a reflection of the lack of harmony between the divine lovers in the world of divinity. In the reciprocal, interdependent relations between the divine world and the human world, the lack of harmony between the masculine and feminine aspects of the divine is understood as a consequence of human sin.

However, just as human beings are the source of the rupture, they are also the ones capable of effecting rectification (*tikkun*) and mending. Human beings, and in particular the righteous and those who know the mysteries of divinity, have been given the capacity to influence the rectification of the relationship between the masculine and feminine aspects of divinity. The performance of good deeds and the observance of the commandments, as well as all religious activity performed with the special and conscious intention of uniting the divine male and female—or in the words of the kabbalists, "unifying the blessed Holy One and His Shekhinah"—engender the possibility for union within the world of divinity. The religious-spiritual work of the kabbalists is focused on strengthening, rectifying, mending, and supporting Shekhinah (the sefirah *Malkhut*, the divine beloved).[46]

While it is true that the kabbalists are not the Shekhinah's "primary partners," the nature and quality of their focus on her is quintessentially erotic. The spiritual work of the kabbalists and their total devotion to Shekhinah are transformed in this mythic scheme into a quality that arouses and stimulates her.[47] Shekhinah is filled with yearning that causes her to pour forth "female waters," the fluids of her desire. The yearning and desire of Shekhinah causes her lover, the divine male, to become aroused and be filled with love, mercy, and desire for his beloved, whom until now he had rejected. The masculine aspect of Divinity is aroused toward his beloved, and their union restores harmony to the divine and human world. This harmony, however, is temporary, perhaps the inevitable consequence of the erotic and sexual language in which this harmony is embedded. The "awakening below," then, designates both the erotic arousal of the human male toward the feminine divine reality above him, and the arousal of the feminine aspect of divinity toward her male lover.

Seen from a more structural and abstract vantage, the movement of arousal in this myth is always from the lower level upward, in order to receive the bounty from a higher level. This is the grand myth of the Zohar; and the centrality of erotic arousal is readily apparent here, insofar as the actions of human beings constitute an intervention in a mythical-erotic system that cannot function without their arousal.

In one of the Zohar's more extraordinary descriptions of this myth, we encounter the rejected beloved, who out of great suffering because of her separation from her lover, has been transformed into a tiny black point, an invisible entity. The task of the kabbalists is to rectify and beautify Shekhinah so that her lover will desire her, and thus they act to arouse her. The kabbalists arouse Shekhinah through their roars, which express their desire and yearning to experience her presence, and their roars also arouse the emotions and desire of the blessed Holy One. The intimacy and contact between the lover and his beloved, as well as the embraces and kisses, arouse her and slowly restore her living presence and regal stature.

What is unique in this myth is the quintessential theurgic task of human beings, in their endeavors to establish a harmonious reality in the world of divinity. Human beings are simultaneously Shekhinah's children and her erotic arousers toward her lover, the divine male, their father. In their spiritual labors, the kabbalists also fulfill a messianic function, as the ones who prepare the ground and hasten the possibility of the redemption through the face-to-face union of the divine male and female.

> I am black and beautiful, O daughters of Jerusalem. . . . Do not look upon me because I am dark (Song of Songs 1:5–6). . . . When she [Shekhinah] [feels] great love for her beloved, because of the impulse of love that she cannot endure, she makes herself extremely small until nothing can be seen of her but the tiniest point. What is this [point]? [The letter] yud. Then she is concealed from all her hosts and her camps; and she says I am black because there is no white at all inside this letter, as there is with the other letters. This is the meaning of I am black, namely, I have no room to bring you under my wings. . . . Therefore, Do not look upon me. You will not see me at all because I am a tiny point.

What do the powerful warriors, all her hosts, do? They roar like mighty lions, as is said: *The young lions roar after their prey* (Psalms 104:21). And because of these loud and mighty roars that the powerful warriors roar like lions, the beloved hears in the realms above and knows that his love is as deeply in love as he, so that her image and beauty are not seen at all.

And then, because of the loud and mighty roars of her powerful warriors, her adored beloved leaves his palace with many gifts, with perfumes and spices, and comes to her—and finds her black and tiny, with no image or beauty at all. He draws near to her, embraces her, and kisses her, until she is gradually aroused by the perfumes and spices and the joy of having her beloved by her side; and she is restored to her image and her beauty, [the letter] *hei* as at the beginning. And this is what the mighty warriors have done for her. . . . And of this is written: *The mighty in strength who fulfill His word* (Psalms 103:20). *Fulfill His word* indeed, for they repair this word [Shekhinah] and restore her to her original form. (Zohar 3:191a)

It is the erotic arousal of the beloved, generated by the kabbalists, and the ensuing arousal of the lover toward her that instantiates her anew. The love directed toward her, both from the human side and from her divine partner, causes her to be present and existent in the fullness of her beauty and vitality.

According to this zoharic myth, the feminine is not present without the arousal of yearning and desire directed toward her. The female upon whom no eyes gaze—Shekhinah or the Torah—is precisely that "beautiful maiden who has no eyes"; and it is only in gazing upon her that her sight is restored.[48] The "awakening below" in order to bring about the "awakening above" is a cosmic law in the Zohar, with only a few dramatic exceptions.[49] In addition to the numerous and diverse restatements of this myth, the Zohar also presents this central dynamic in abstraction, expressed by Rabbi El'azar as a cosmic law of causality: "I see that arousal above transpires only with arousal below, for arousal above depends on desire below."[50]

Pekiḥu de-'Eina: *Eyes Wide Open*

The various voices that call upon the people of the world to awaken from their slumber have been analyzed here as a kind of activist manifesto. Alongside them, the Zohar also employs an array of more subtle stratagems, whose purpose is to turn to the reader and invite him to alter and perfect his consciousness, so as to be able to experience dimensions of divinity ordinarily hidden from view.

In all of these diverse forms of calling, the existence of an addressee external to the text is beyond doubt. In other words, the voices of calling, as well as the other forms of address, not only attest to Rashbi's and the Companions' self-perception as awakeners, but also give expression to the Zohar's author, whose most fundamental aim and quest is the desire to awaken its readers. The awakening that the Zohar so passionately seeks is neither moral nor political nor aesthetic; it is rather the awakening of consciousness. It is human consciousness (or the human soul) that is in need of a pleasant fragrance in order to awaken, so as to comprehend reality as it truly is, saturated with the divine.

The images that describe the different aspects of awakening in the Zohar—the awakening to the awareness of dimensions beyond those perceived by ordinary consciousness, the arousing engagement with the Torah and with Shekhinah, and the arousal to the interpretation of verses of Torah—are intertwined with one another. And all of these are connected to the ancient myth that simultaneously encompasses awakening, knowledge, and eros—the story of the Garden of Eden: "Then the eyes of both of them were opened and they perceived that they were naked" (Genesis 3:7; transl. NJPS). The opening of the eyes in the Torah's account of the Garden of Eden is both the awakening to knowledge and the awakening to sexuality, with these two aspects intertwined and interdependent.

Indeed, the principal endeavors of the Companions—the multilayered exegetical worlds that they create—all present the inseparability of knowledge and eros.[51] The mystic of the Zohar is he who is destined "to be opened in Torah and to open [his] eyes to her."[52] To have one's eyes "open to Torah" signifies the capacity to perceive and express the experience of the encounter with the Torah's different levels.

Awakening, which receives its ultimate expression through becoming "open-eyed," is a central symbol for the experiential dimension in zoharic mysticism.[53] Mystics are termed by the Zohar as "open-eyed" and "full of eyes,"[54] an epithet focused on the mystic's ability to activate different forms of seeing and perceiving the world, as well as multiple ways of reading the sacred text. One's eyes must be stripped bare of the mask that veils them—or in the language of the Zohar, of the sleep that conceals them—in order to behold the wonders found underneath the garments of the *peshat* (simple meaning), as Scripture itself attests: "Unveil my eyes so I can see wonders out of Your Torah" (Psalms 119:18).

In the Zohar's commentary to the Torah portion *Mishpatim*, in the introduction to the parable of the maiden in the palace, the Zohar reveals something of the secret relationship between the written word of the Torah and the eye that is opened toward her:

> The blessed Holy One enters all the concealed matters that He has made in the holy Torah and everything is found in the Torah.
>
> The Torah reveals that concealed matter, and immediately it is cloaked in another garment and is concealed there and not revealed.
>
> Even though the matter is concealed in its garment, the wise, who are full of eyes, see it from within its garment. Just as that matter is revealed, before it enters into a garment, they cast open-eyed-ness upon it, and even though it is immediately concealed it is not removed from their eyes. (Zohar 2:98b)

The task of the kabbalist, "full of eyes," is therefore to cast their "open-eyedness" on the words of the Torah. In line with medieval scientific understandings, "seeing" is understood here not as reception or taking in, but rather as an active operation; and the multiple eyes signify the multiple ways of reading the Torah, as well as the amplification of the light cast upon her, thus bringing about the revelation of that which had previously remained concealed.

The epithet "full of eyes" is also an erotic image describing intensified and total arousal and contemplation;[55] the lover becomes "full of eyes" so as to see his beloved. The experience of disclosure and concealment experienced by the one studying Torah is understood by the mystics of the Zohar less as a change in the way that they apprehend the Torah, than as an action originating with the Torah itself. The Torah reveals her words and immediately cloaks herself in a garment, both as a gesture of seduction and as a necessary operation, so as to be able to be revealed in the finite world as an enlivening force.

It is into this small space between disclosure and concealment that the wise, full of eyes, cast their open-eyed-ness—their heightened, ever-alert consciousness, which does not allow anything to escape its gaze. The descriptions of what they saw with their mind's eye surely account for the enchanting power of the Zohar on its readers across the generations.

"A river flows from Eden"

Verses of Awakening and Arousal

In the Zohar's unique language of arousal, specific biblical verses frequently appear, sometimes within a readily apparent context, and sometimes without being required at all for the development of the homily in which they are found. Analysis of the way in which these verses are employed in zoharic homilies reveals that they have a function beyond the immediate needs of the specific midrash in which they are embedded, or the zoharic story in which they are inserted.

In general, the function of these verses is to signal to readers the transition to a new level of reading and interpreting the Bible's verses, and to arouse them to a state of mystical consciousness. In light of this special function, and because these verses encode a complex signal for the reader, I term them "code verses." Sometimes this signaling is explicit, while at other times it is extremely condensed, discernable only by the "ideal reader"—one who is familiar with the whole composition and able to discern its various structures.

"A river flows from Eden to water the garden": A Code Verse

The biblical verse most frequently cited by the Zohar's protagonists is "A river flows from Eden to water the garden" (Genesis 2:10). It appears dozens of times in full, and hundreds of times in shorthand versions. The Zohar also employs other verses, or fragments of verses, in parallel and in combination with our verse from Genesis, and often for the same purpose:

- "A river of fire streams forth and issues from before Him" (Daniel 7:10)
- "You shall be like a watered garden, like a spring whose waters do not fail" (Isaiah 58:11; transl. NJPS)
- "You let them drink at Your Edenic stream" (Psalms 36:9)

The verse from Genesis is interpreted in a variety of ways, yet we always find an experiential core. In the Zohar, this river symbolizes the continual flow of the divine plenty within itself, and from itself into different worlds. The movement of this flow is also present in those dimensions of reality constructed in the image of divinity: the structure of the universe, the erotic and sexual dynamics between man and woman, and the processes of human consciousness. The reflection of this flow in different planes of reality serves a performative function that endeavors to evoke in the consciousness of the Zohar's heroes the reality of the river's flow, and in so doing, in the consciousness of the reader.

The Zohar's authors are particularly interested in this verse, as well as in the parallel verse from the book of Daniel because all their verbs are constructed in the present tense.[1] In other words, the divine flow represented in these verses is not a phenomenon confined to the past, of which only verbal traces remain. The river, rather, issues continuously into reality; its flow from Eden to the garden never ceases. The river is, then, a dynamic, eternal dimension continuously bringing life to all existence.

It is the existence of the river in the present that enables the zoharic protagonists to seek to connect with it. The Zohar tells of these endeavors and describes experiences of human contact with the divine river flowing from Eden. This encounter is described as being watered and saturated by the divine river, an experience of plenty and pleasure, flowing down on the mystic, bringing blessings to his surroundings.

As a code verse, "A river flows from Eden to water the garden" signals a transition between different hermeneutical registers: a shift from reading biblical verses as referring either to external reality or to values, beliefs, and opinions, to an experiential reading that reveals through its words the river of divine plenty. It is a sign to remind the reader of the interpretive motivation informing the entire Zohar. It is as though the verse calls out: "Look, we are now in the reality of the Zohar; we are seeking the divine flow that exists beyond and within ordinary reality!" The repetition of this verse prompts the ideal Zohar reader to return to its fundamental motivation, and to develop his ability to look at the Torah (and indeed at all reality) in the manner of the Zohar's heroes, in order to touch the dimension called "a river flows from Eden."

As we shall see below, the endeavor to connect with the river of divine plenty is intimately connected with the kabbalists' wish "to shine like the radiance of the sky." Given the self-consciousness of the Zohar, the function of this verse from Genesis is so internalized that sometimes it appears in shorthand or by allusion only, as if the heroes of the composition already know what the river is and why it is being mentioned.[2]

Each part of the verse is interpreted. Sometimes the focus is on Eden as the source—the place or quality from which the river emerges. At other times the emphasis is on the river itself and its continuous connection with its source, and the dynamic, multifaceted qualities that flow within it. In still other cases, the focus is on the verse's end: the garden, whose watering represents the ultimate end of the river's flow.

"A river flows from Eden" in Prior Exegesis

Midrash Genesis Rabbah attempts to explain the difference between Eden and the garden, and the relationship between them, in order to reconcile the verse "YHVH Elohim planted a garden *in* Eden" (Genesis 2:8) with our verse "A river flows *from* Eden to water the garden," as well as with other appearances of "garden" and "Eden" in the books of Isaiah and Ezekiel.[3] Surprisingly, this verse does not appear in the early medieval mystical work *Bahir*, which often focuses on matters pertaining to the creation and emanation of all reality. Nor is it expounded in a manner approximating its zoharic interpretation in the writings of early kabbalists: Rabbi Isaac the Blind, the commentaries of Rabbi Ezra and Rabbi Azriel of Gerona on *Ma'aseh Bere-ishit*, and Rabbi Moses Naḥmanides' commentary on the Torah.

In the *Commentary on the Thirteen Attributes* by the Provençal kabbalist Rabbi Asher ben David, one of the students of Rabbi Isaac the Blind, we do, however, find an interpretation of this verse describing the dynamic structure of the flow of the divine plenty among the divine attributes. In this work, Rabbi Asher quotes—"according to the Kabbalah," as he puts it—the interpretation of this verse as it will appear again and again, in Aramaic paraphrase, in the Zohar:[4]

> According to the Kabbalah . . . [this is] the spring that comes from *Ein Sof*, which spreads out from the source without any separation, and without ever ceasing—not for a day, an hour or even a single moment; and this is what Scripture said: *A river issues from Eden to water the garden* (Genesis 2:10). And the meaning of "A river" (Heb. *nahar*) is from the word for light (Aram. *nehora*): that is, the inner light, which continuously comes from Eden. Therefore it says "issues" and does not say "issued," because it does not cease and is spreading all the time among the attributes. That is why it is called the "world that is coming." "To water the garden"—and this means to pour forth the influx of His light, His glory, and His blessing among all those attributes.

In another manuscript we read:

> That is why it is called the "world that is coming," that is to say, that it comes continuously without ceasing, to water the garden; and this means to bestow His light, glory, and blessing among all the aforementioned attributes so as to do His will through them. And therefore one must not separate the *mevorakh* (that which is blessed), namely, the tree, from the *mevarekh* (the one who bestows blessings), namely, the root and the place from which it [the tree] is blessed.[5]

Already here we find four elements that will play an important role in the Zohar's understanding of our verse:

· the reading of "river" (Heb. *nahar*) as connected to "light" (Aram. *nehora*),[6] and understanding this "light" as the inner light that comes from Eden;

· emphasis on the significance of the verb ("issues" or "flows") appearing in the present tense;

- the expression "that comes without ever ceasing" or "because it does not cease" as a description of the perpetuity of the expansion of the divine flow; and
- reading the word "come" in the expression "World to Come" as signifying the present continuous, "the world . . . that . . . comes continuously without ceasing."

The Zohar's interpretations of this verse are suffused with the language of this tradition of interpretation as quoted by Asher ben David. The uniqueness of the Zohar, however, lies in the new *function* ascribed to the verse, namely, its role in awakening the mystic and/or the reader to mystical consciousness. The Zohar thus sees this verse as describing not only the quality of the divine flow from *Ein Sof* to the divine attributes, but also the dynamic structure structure that lies at the core of all reality.

Components of the Code: Nouns and Verbs

Eden   The noun Eden is interpreted by the Zohar as referring to the source of the constantly emerging, differentiated, divine plenty. The ability to know or return to Eden is of course paradoxical, as is the yearning to return to any source. The movement of the river is from Eden toward the garden; indeed, this is the direction of the flow of divine reality. While the intention of the mystic is to connect with this downward flow, he seeks also to pursue its source, through connecting to the subtle movement of the return of all being to its source. In different places in the Zohar, it seems that this source cannot be apprehended discursively: Eden is of the domain of questions and cannot be expressed in words.

Yet as we shall see, even if Eden cannot be apprehended, it can nevertheless be experienced.[7] Eden is the very beginning of the impulse of expansion of the concealed divinity within itself. Seen in this light, Eden is the beginning of all being.[8] In the sefirotic structure, Eden symbolizes either *Keter* (crown), *Ḥokhmah* (the supernal father), or *Binah* (the supernal mother) in her continuous union with *Ḥokhmah*.[9] (This union renders *Binah* the mother of all reality insofar as it is from her that all the other sefirot are born and sustained.)

River (nahar)   On the divine plane, the river represents the divine plenty that flows outward from within the concealed aspect of the Godhead. This flow is the beginning of differentiated reality. This conception of the river draws on the Neoplatonic image of the divine substance that flows beyond its banks and thereby establishes the possibility for the creation of extra-divine reality. The river is thus the dynamic face of the divine, the perpetual movement from within the Godhead outward to all reality.

On the human plane, the river is the divine flow that waters the human consciousness that is prepared for its reception, namely, the consciousness of the *maskilim*, the kabbalists. The river of divine plenty is revealed to them via their intensified reflections on the Torah's verses, the reasons for the commandments, and the hidden laws of nature. The Companions' special process for reading the Torah creates the possibility of recognizing the river, and recognition of its reality enables them to experience its flow. The Zohar employs our verse in describing mystical experience as the pleasurable watering by this river.

On the sefirotic plane, the river is sometimes a symbol for the unceasing flow of the divine plenty emerging from the perpetual union of the sefirah *Hokhmah* with the sefirah *Binah*. Sometimes the source of the river is *Binah*,[10] with the river itself symbolizing *Tiferet* and the sefirot around him; and sometimes the river is a symbol for the sefirah *Yesod* when joined with *Malkhut*.[11] Generally, the river is dynamic. As we shall see below, it is also phallic—with the "watering" of the garden as its most essential purpose.[12]

Garden   On the divine plane, the garden is the feminine aspect of the God-head that receives into herself the male and female aspects of the divine above her. In terms of the sefirot, the garden is the tenth one (*Malkhut*, Matronita, Shekhinah, the partner of the blessed Holy One), nourished by the river of the masculine sefirot above her. The watering of the garden is, then, the erotic union between this grade with the male grades of the divine.

The sefirah *Malkhut*, symbolized by the garden, represents two essential qualities: The first is the gathering and containment of the flow of the sefirotic river above her—a passive quality—whereby the garden is the great ocean into which flow all the streams, namely, the river. The second quality of *Malkhut* is the active leadership and nourishment of her denizens, namely, the worlds outside the world of emanation. The garden is then the worldly reality that exists by virtue of the divine plenty that flows into and waters it.

The garden is also human consciousness, and its watering symbolizes distinctive mystical states when the divine flow waters and saturates this consciousness. In this state, consciousness receives the qualities of *Malkhut* and is transformed into a receptacle worthy of containing the divine qualities that flow into it.

The garden is also a woman. Already in the Bible, in the Song of Songs, the lover describes his beloved as a garden: "A garden locked is my sister, my bride" (Song of Songs 4:12). The lover describes the body of his beloved, the object of his desire, as a garden of delights into which he enters: "I have come into my garden, my sister, my bride. I have gathered my myrrh and my spices, I have eaten my honey and honeycomb, drunk my wine and my milk" (5:1). Also in Midrash *Pirkei de-Rabbi Eli'ezer*, so beloved by the Zohar's authors and frequently cited by them, we find the garden interpreted as a woman: "*That is in the midst of the garden* (Genesis 3:3) . . . This is merely a euphemism. . . . *In the midst of the garden* refers to that which is in the middle of the woman, for *garden* means here merely 'woman,' who is compared to a garden, as is said: *A garden locked is my sister, my bride* (Song of Songs 4:12)." In the Zohar, too, the garden symbolizes a woman (and the river, the man who unites with her in intercourse), as Rabbi Yose explains: "The tree of which we have spoken was watered, flourished and rejoiced, as is said: *A river issues* [flows] *from Eden to water the garden* (Genesis 2:10). *The garden*—this is woman, the *river* entering Her, watering Her, and all was one."[13]

The Verbs Yatsa *(Flow, Issue)* and Shakah *(Water)*

Even more than the nouns, the authors of the Zohar are interested in the verbs of our verse and what they have to teach about the relationship between the nouns.[14] The use of this verse as a code in the Zohar is connected to its peculiar dynamism, established by its verbs "issue, flow" and "water." These verbs, which appear in the present continuous form, describe unceasing movement.

Our verse as a whole is interpreted as describing a range of processes:

- The "river that flows from Eden to water the garden" symbolizes the movement of the entirety of divine reality. (Indeed, the deepest wish of the kabbalist is to be exposed to this river, to be influenced by its plenty, and to be watered by and immersed in it.)
- Our verse describes the essence of the complex dynamic of the divine consciousness within itself, the expansion of this consciousness from within itself, and the creation of realities outside of itself as well as their nourishment.
- Our verse is elsewhere interpreted as describing the processes of human consciousness, constructed in the image of the divine.
- Our verse also contains symbols of the masculine and the feminine; it describes the eros active in the world in its various modes.
- On the physiological plane, our verse describes the journey of the sperm from the brain to the male reproductive organ and into the woman's womb.

In all these different planes of interpretation, we find that same quality flowing continuously from its source to the place of gathering, which by virtue of the flow is given life.

In the Zohar's interpretations of this verse, we find simultaneous reflections on divine and human consciousness, on divine and human eros, as well as on human physiological processes. This simultaneity flows from the paradigmatic and reciprocal relations between the different structures of reality as they are conceptualized in zoharic thought. As such, these interpretations, as is the custom of the Zohar, are neither unequivocal nor univocal; they are filled, rather, with echoes and resonances. The symbols, far from being fixed and stable, are dynamic and contextual. In the special poetics of the Zohar, the verse is able to display a wide array of meanings.[15] In *Shekel ha-Kodesh*, Rabbi Moses de León provides a poetic and conceptual summary of the profound meaning of our verse: "Behold, the river never ceases, and it is all, for it is all."[16]

The river that flows forth from Eden and waters the garden describes the ideal reality of the free, unencumbered flow from Eden to the garden. Yet sometimes the Zohar's authors reflect on less ideal circumstances, more frequent in our reality, in which the river does not reach the garden, but rather is gathered into itself. In these circumstances, the garden is not watered; and the divine, earthly, and human realities are described as eros-less, parched, dry, and deficient.

Citations of the Code Verse

The Zohar establishes a special connection between "A river flows from Eden to water the garden" and "The enlightened will shine like the radiance of the sky; and those who lead many to righteousness, like the stars forever and ever" (Daniel 12:3; transl. Matt). The Zohar's commentary to Exodus begins with a dramatic interpretation of that book's first verse, drawing on both of these biblical verses so central to the Zohar. The verse from Daniel is, as we saw in Chapter 2, the motto of the composition; it encapsulates the deepest desire of the kabbalists to "shine like the radiance of the sky and . . . the stars forever and ever," and in itself is a zoharic code verse.[17] The river that issues from Eden is not essential to this homily, insofar as "the radiance of the sky" can be interpreted without the help of the verse from the story of the Garden of Eden. However, according to this interpretation, "the radiance of the sky" is in fact the river that flows from Eden, sparkling as a stream of light. This streaming light is that which radiates from the kabbalists.

> *These are the names of the sons of Israel who came to Egypt with Jacob, each man with his household they came* (Exodus 1:1).
>
> *The enlightened will shine like the radiance of the sky (zohar ha-rakia); and those who lead many to righteousness, like the stars forever and ever* (Daniel 12:3).
>
> *The enlightened*—those who contemplate the mystery of wisdom.
>
> *Will shine*—shining and sparkling with luster of supernal Wisdom.
>
> *Like the radiance (zohar)*—shining (nehiru) and sparkling of the river (nahara) *issuing from Eden.* This is the concealed mystery called the expanse (ha-rakia)— in which exist stars, constellations, sun and moon, and all those lamps of light. (Zohar 2:2a; Matt 2004–2007, vol. 4, p. 1, adapted)[18]

The verse "A river flows from Eden" is not cited here in full, no doubt because the author of this homily assumes that the reader is already familiar with it and its meanings in the Zohar, and in this instance the function of this verse is to draw connections between the words radiance, light, and river. The radiance, so important to the work that bears this name, is in fact the streaming of the river that flows from Eden.

The significance of this appearance of the verse is that it defines a level of reading attuned to the awe-filled experience of gazing at the night sky. This experience is wonderfully expressed in biblical poetry, in particular in Psalm 19, which describes the perfection and beauty of creation, the handiwork of God, who can be known through contemplating the heavens. The heroes of the Zohar view the night sky as a book in which they themselves are inscribed. They are the ones who shine like the radiance of the sky and the stars described in the verse "the enlightened will shine like the radiance of the sky." They view the entire sky as a kind of river (perhaps because of the ever-changing position of the stars); and within this sky they identify a river of light (*nahar di-nur*), the Milky Way, a river that flows from the depths of the sky and pours forth its plenty on the world. Thus Rabbi Abba explains: "Who is the expanse illuminating Earth? You must admit, this is the river flowing forth from Eden, as is written: *A river issues* [flows] *from Eden to water the garden* (Genesis 2:10)."[19]

In the Zohar's commentary to the Torah portion *Terumah*, we find a story about Rav Hamnuna Sava that describes a special practice for drawing down a supernal spirit for use by the sages at the start of the Sabbath. In this story, we read of the teaching that Rav Hamnuna Sava would say after emerging from the river in preparation for Sabbath, when he would sit and gaze at the joyous sight of the ministering angels ascending and descending.

Rav Hamnuna describes the elevation of reality on the Sabbath and the drawing down of the divine flow into the world through his interpretation of Psalm 19, which opens with the words "The heavens declare the glory of God, the sky proclaims (*magid*) His handiwork" (transl. NJPS). The word *magid* is expounded by the Zohar to mean "flowing forth," as in the Aramaic *nagid*.[20] He describes the heavens as a river—full of love and yearning—flowing and streaming down into the world with the onset of the Sabbath. Here, the experience of gazing at the sky and the experience of the divine spirit that descends into reality are wonderfully connected:

> The heavens declare the glory of God, the sky proclaims His handiwork (Psalms 19:2).
>
> The sky proclaims—what does it proclaim? It flows forth and streams below from the Head of the King, full from all sides.
>
> The sky—that sky which is the fountain of the well. And this is the river that issues from Eden, and it flows and streams downward and brings forth the supernal dew that shines and sparkles from all sides; and this sky draws it downward in a current of love and desires to pour potions of delight at the entrance of the Sabbath. (Zohar 2:136b)

"A river flows from Eden" and Mystical Experience

We turn now to some homilies exemplifying the uses of this verse, in our endeavor to explore the motivation for mystical experience in the Zohar and the ways to attain such experience. While it is true that these homilies are found in different parts of the Zohar, there is nevertheless a conceptual coherence to them. According to the order in which I present them here, these homilies focus on the river that issues from Eden as a description of the dynamic structure of reality; the desire of the kabbalist to become the garden that receives the river of divine plenty; the meta-assumptions that enable the actualization of this desire; the appropriate time for experiencing this reality; the various practices designed to call forth the presence of the river's flow; and finally, the experience of the flowing river itself.

THE RIVER AS DESCRIPTION OF THE DYNAMIC STATE OF REALITY

First and foremost, the river that flows forth from Eden describes the fundamental movement that establishes all reality. The verse describes the process of the expansion of divine wisdom—its emergence from its own silent depths in order to create dynamic, differentiated reality.

The expansion of the divine plenty is described as a flow of a concealed secretion from the head of *Arikh Anpin*, the aspect of undifferentiated divinity, to the head of *Ze'eir Anpin*, symbolizing differentiated divinity and

comprising diverse attributes and modes of operation. This river that enters
Ze'eir Anpin continues and waters its entire body. In this description, Eden is
the concealed aspect of divinity from which the river emerges, and the river
symbolizes the more differentiated and dynamic divine reality, namely, *Ze'eir
Anpin*. This is the dynamic meta-structure that the Zohar's authors discover
in this verse. Such descriptions of the divine expansion are characteristic of
the language of the *Idra Rabba* and *Idra Zuta*, in which we find an intensive
engagement with the structure and movement of divinity.

> A membrane is spread over the brain that is the concealed wisdom. . . . silent
> and tranquil in its place like good wine upon its lees . . . this membrane
> ceases at *Ze'eir Anpin*, and thus His brain expands and goes out along thirty-
> two paths, as is written: *A river flows from Eden*. (Zohar 3:128b, *Idra Rabba*)

> This *Ḥokhmah* was engraved and brought forth a river that issues and streams
> to water the garden. It entered the head of *Ze'eir Anpin* and became a brain;
> and from there it flows forth and streams through the whole body and waters
> all those plants, as is written: *A river flows from Eden to water the garden*. . . . This
> *Ḥokhmah* is called Eden . . . and from this Eden we have beginning, for it was
> not so with *Atika*, which has no beginning or end. . . . this *Ḥokhmah* is the
> beginning of all, and from Her expand thirty-two paths. (Zohar 3:289b–290a,
> *Idra Zuta*)

THE RIVER AS QUEST

The Zohar's interpretation of Psalm 42—"Like a hind craving (*ta'arog*) for
watercourses, so my soul craves You . . ."—explicitly describes the ultimate
desire of the soul—and its counterpart, the Assembly of Israel—for God.
In this psalm, the hind symbolizes the soul, paralleling the garden in our
verse from Genesis, which symbolizes also the yearning female. The Zohar
chooses to describe the dynamism of the encounter with God as the irrigation of the mystic by the river issuing from Eden.

In this instance, the river is a code for the sefirah *Yesod* (*Tsaddik*), and this
experience of yearning for the divine saturation is described using erotic
imagery. Separation is characterized as thirst; according to the Zohar's reading of this psalm, the craving (*er'ga*) ascends to the "beds (*'arugot*) of spices"
(Song of Songs 6:2) to be saturated and filled with the divine flow. The

latter is described as the descent of semen from the brain along the spinal column into the testicles and finally into the male genitalia in preparation for intercourse.

> It has been taught: *Like a hind craving for watercourses* (Psalm 42:2)—this is the Assembly of Israel.
>
> *Craving for watercourses*—indeed, to be watered with potions from the fountains of the stream through the Righteous One (*tsaddik*).
>
> *Craving (ta'arog)*—as it is written: to the *beds ('arugot) of spices* (Song of Songs 6:2).
>
> *So my soul craves You, O Elohim*—to be watered by you in this world and in the world that is coming.
>
> What are the fountains of the stream? One is above, of which is written: *A river flows from Eden to water the garden*, and from there it issues and flows forth and waters the garden, and all these streams issue from it and flow and gather in the two fountains called *Netsah* and *Hod*; and these are called *watercourses*, at that level of the Righteous One from which they gush and flow, watering the garden. (Zohar 3:68a)

In considering the mystical resonances of the verse "A river flows from Eden," the verse mentioned earlier from Isaiah, "You shall be like a watered garden, like a spring whose waters do not fail" (58:11), is particularly significant. This verse describes the light, divine plenty, and pleasure awaiting the person who fulfills the will of God—namely, to defend the weak, to increase justice, and to eradicate evil from the world. Such action on the part of the human being brings about connection with the divine, the bursting forth of the human being's inner light, as well as his becoming a "watered garden" and "spring whose waters do not fail." Indeed that entire chapter from Isaiah has a mystical feel, the light and watering described there serving as expressions for the perfect human state; and the Zohar frequently employs the language of that chapter in its descriptions of the mystical state.[21] (The Rabbis already sensed the connection between Isaiah's words and our verse from the Garden of Eden story. In Leviticus Rabbah we find: "*You shall be like a watered garden*—this is the garden. *Like a spring whose waters do not fail*—this is Eden."[22]) Redemption is therefore the combination of Garden and Eden—the state of the Garden of Eden.

The watered garden, continuously saturated by the river, frequently appears in the Zohar's descriptions of the future perfection of humankind after the resurrection of the dead. In these passages, the perfection of the body and the soul is described as a shining and radiant unity. The human being—both body and soul—is described with a double image, as a garden continuously watered by the river that flows from Eden, and as a spring whose waters do not fail.

> The light of the soul will be intensified within the resplendent speculum, to shine with the body fittingly in full vitality. "So it is written, *You will be like a watered garden* (Isaiah 58:11). What does this mean? Its supernal waters never cease for all eternity; this garden, watered by them, is saturated constantly.
>
> "*Like a spring*—that flowing, gushing river whose waters never cease."
> (Zohar 1:141a–b; Matt 2004–2007, vol. 2, p. 284, reformatted)

THE RIVER THAT COMES CONTINUOUSLY

The question now arises—what is it that enables human beings to fulfill their wish to experience the divine river? The Zohar uses the verse "a river flows from Eden" to illustrate the continuous presence of the divine flow from (and within) divinity into the world. It is the fact that this reality always exists, in the present, that enables the human quest to experience this river. As we shall see, the righteous, namely, the mystics, are the ones who are able to attain that experience.

The following homily offers a daring interpretation of the rabbinic expression "the World to Come." In this passage, this expression is not understood in its usual sense as referring to the world that comes *after* or *beyond* this world in time or space, but rather as the world that never ceases from coming; it comes continuously into this world. It is in fact the river that continuously emerges from Eden to water the garden of the world.[23] Thus we read: "That river flowing forth is called the world that is coming—coming constantly and never ceasing. This is delight of the righteous, to attain this world that is coming, constantly watering the garden and never ceasing."[24] Likewise, Rabbi Shim'on elsewhere expounds: "It is written: *A river issues from Eden to water the garden.* . . . Of this is written *like a spring whose waters do not fail* (Isaiah 58:11). Therefore it is written: [*A river*] *issues* (Genesis 2:10)—*issues* unceasingly."[25]

In the Zohar, this perpetual coming has an erotic connotation, in that it is the fruit of the perpetual union of the sefirah *Ḥokhmah* with the sefirah *Binah*. The perpetual plenty that emerges from this union is that which arouses the eros and the vitality of all the dimensions of reality into which it flows.

THE APPROPRIATE TIME TO EXPERIENCE THE RIVER

In this world, the way to attain the experience of saturation by the divine river is through Torah study at night.[26] Nocturnal Torah study is conceptualized as song.[27] The verse "By day YHVH will command His love, and in the night His song shall be with me" (Psalms 42:9) describes the different qualities of engagement of Torah during the day and during the night. Torah study of this kind at night renders one worthy of the experience of saturation.

The following passage describes the delight of the blessed Holy One in the souls of the righteous after midnight. (Our verse from Genesis is not quoted in this passage, although it is alluded to via the similar verse "You let them drink at Your Edenic stream [or: stream of delights]" [Psalms 36:9].) The experience described here is particularly intense: he who studies at night experiences the divine flow as a flood gushing down upon his head.[28]

> Rabbi Ḥizkiyah replied, "So we have learned: Every midnight, when the blessed Holy One arouses in the Garden of Eden, all the plants of the Garden are watered profusely by the stream called Stream of Antiquity, Stream of Delights, never ceasing. If one rises and engages in Torah, then that stream, gushes upon his head, as it were, saturating him among those plants of the Garden of Eden."
>
> Rabbi Yose said, "Since all those righteous in the Garden listen to him, he shares in the saturation of that stream; in consequence, he shares constantly in the world that is coming." (Zohar 1:92b; Matt 2004–2007, vol. 2, p. 81)

HOW TO BE EXPOSED TO THE RIVER

The river and its source represent the telos of the worshipper's intentions. In the special soul-state of night, after midnight,[29] while plying Torah and engaging in prayer, the human being is granted the opportunity to join the ever-flowing river and to participate in the theurgic act of blessing the divine and drawing down the river's plenty from its source above.

> Whoever merits to arise at midnight to engage Torah, the blessed Holy One listens to him, as we have established. . . . and all the supernal camps and all the sons of praise who utter praise to their Master all fall silent for the praise of those who engage Torah [below], and they proclaim and say: *Now bless YHVH, all you servants of YHVH [who stand nightly in the house of YHVH]!* (Psalms 134:1)—you bless YHVH, you praise the Holy King, you crown the King! . . .
>
> *Who stand nightly in the house of YHVH*—these are called servants of YHVH, these are worthy to bless the King; and their blessing is [indeed] a blessing, as is written:
>
> *Lift your hands toward the sanctuary [kodesh] and bless YHVH* . . . —What is the sanctuary? The supernal place from which flows the fountain of the deep stream, as is written: *A river flows from Eden to water the garden.* And Eden is called supernal sanctuary, hence: *Lift up your hands toward the sanctuary.*
>
> And of the person who does so and merits this, what do they proclaim about him?
>
> *May YHVH bless you from Zion* (Psalms 128:5)—You bless the blessed Holy One from the place called "supernal sanctuary," and He shall bless you from the place called "Zion," so that you and Matronita shall be blessed as one. Just as your union was as one for the praise of the King, so from that place where the Assembly of Israel is blessed, from that place blessings shall be prepared for you. (Zohar 3:13a)

The Zohar here interprets Psalm 134 as describing a mystical theurgic practice. By virtue of a special form of Torah study, those who engage Torah at night actualize the coupling of the human being on earth with Shekhinah. In this theurgic act, they raise their hands and their intentions to "the sanctuary," namely, to Eden, the source of the river bearing the divine flow. When they bless this supernal aspect of the Godhead, their blessing brings about the descent of the divine flow to the worshipping individual below: "May YHVH bless you from Zion."

The status of the biblical text here is not merely that of a story from the past, in this case from the period of King David describing those who stood in Jerusalem's shrine at night. The Zohar, rather, employs this psalm as an active call *in the present* to mystics and to its readers (mystics in potential), to those standing in the spiritual House of YHVH that is the Torah, "*you* bless YHVH, *you* praise the Holy King, *you* crown the King!"

Those who learn Torah and recite blessings at night experience union with the sefirah *Malkhut*; while in this union they cultivate special intentions (*kavvanot*) in their prayers, reaching to the depths of Eden and to the emerging river that pours forth its plenty upon those engaged in study.[30]

THE EXPERIENCE OF THE EVER-PRESENT RIVER

In all the homilies cited so far, we have explored the nature of the river, the deep desire to be saturated by its flow, and the appropriate time and means to join with it. In a story appearing in the Zohar's commentary to the Torah portion *Aḥarei Mot*, we find a unique invocation of this verse at the precise moment of transition from the exposition of biblical verses to mystical experience itself, as experienced by the Companions.

Owing to the importance of this matter, I will first recount the story in its broader context: The world is dry and thirsty for rain. The Companions come to Rabbi Shim'on requesting that he act for the sake of the world. He sits down alongside them and explains that the absence of rain is an expression of the lack of harmonious relations between the masculine and the feminine aspects of divinity.

The Companions are seated around the dinner table in the house of Pinḥas ben Yair, Rabbi Shim'on's father-in-law, and each Companion is required to rise in turn and offer original interpretations of Torah.[31] They rise and expound, with each disciple connecting the end of his exposition with words of praise for their teacher, Rabbi Shim'on. Each exposition is more ecstatic than the last, and the praises lavished upon Rabbi Shim'on intensify with each new homily, culminating with his deification.[32]

Amid the series of expositions, Rabbi Abba begins his with a verse from the Song of Songs: "While the king was on his couch, my nard gave forth its fragrance" (1:12; transl. NJPS). It is his exposition that climaxes the story. He starts with two interpretations, both originating in rabbinic literature.[33] After these, he declares that the special occasion in which the Companions "now" (*hashta*)[34] find themselves necessitates that they exceed interpretations of this kind and penetrate to the level of interpretation he calls "the mystery of wisdom" (*raza de-ḥokhmata*).

Biblical verses can be interpreted in many different ways; it is the context that determines the character of interpretation appropriate for the moment. In the course of Rabbi Abba's exposition, a shift occurs—a leap—from mystical discourse to mystical experience. In the transition, he recites the verse "A river flows from Eden to water the garden" and interprets it as describing the erotic flow of the divine plenty at the time when preparation for intercourse within divinity is completed. Thus this verse now completes the verse "While the king was on his couch, my nard gave forth its fragrance," which opened the homily describing the quality of arousal of the moments preceding intercourse.

Rabbi Abba does not suffice with an exposition describing the descent of the divine flow into the lower worlds as a result of the intercourse between the King and Matronita, but rather he calls forth the descent of this divine flow upon himself and upon all the Companions. At this peak moment, Rabbi Abba hands over the continuation of the homily to Rabbi El'azar the son of Rabbi Shim'on, who describes in "real time" the Companions' experience. Rabbi El'azar closes the symposium and seals the experience with an interpretation of a verse appropriate to this end: "They returned the stone on the mouth of the well" (Genesis 29:3).

> Rabbi Abba opened and said: *While the king was on his couch, my nard gave forth its fragrance* (Song of Songs 1:12). The Companions have clarified this verse. When the blessed Holy One was present and ready at Mt. Sinai to give the Torah to Israel, *my nard gave forth its fragrance*—Israel gave forth a sweet fragrance that was to stand over them and protect them for all generations; and they said, *We will do and we will hear* (Exodus 24:7).
>
> Another interpretation: *While the king was on his couch*—While Moses was ascending to receive the Torah from the blessed Holy One and it was engraved on two tablets of stone, Israel abandoned that sweet fragrance which used to crown them, and they said to the calf, *These are your gods, O Israel* (Exodus 32:4).
>
> *Now*, this verse according to the mystery of wisdom.
>
> Come and see: It is written: *A river flows from Eden to water the garden* (Genesis 2:10).

This river spreads out toward its sides when Eden has intercourse with it in perfect union, through the path that is not known either above or below, as is written: *the path that no bird of prey knows* (Job 28:7), and they remain contented, for they do not separate one from the other.

Then fountains and streams go forth and crown the holy son with all those crowns. Then it is written: *the crown with which his mother has crowned him* (Song of Songs 3:11).

At that moment, the son comes into the inheritance of his father and mother and delights in that pleasure and luxury.

And we have taught: When the supernal King sits among the royal luxuries with his crowns, then it is written: *While the king was on his couch, my nard gave forth its fragrance*[35]—this is *Yesod*, which gives forth blessings so that the Holy King may have intercourse with Matronita through this level; and then blessings are given throughout all the worlds, and the upper and lower realms are blessed.

And *now*, behold the Holy Luminary [Rashbi] crowns himself with crowns of this level, and he and the Companions send up praises from below to above; and She is crowned with these praises!

Now blessings must be brought down to all the Companions from above to below through this holy level—and Rabbi El'azar his son shall speak of those sublime matters he learned from his father! (Zohar 3:61b–62a)

The verse from the Song of Songs is read as a visualization of the peak of erotic tension preceding intercourse. According to the special hermeneutics of the Zohar—namely, the reading strategy known as "the mystery of wisdom"—it becomes an image for the river of divine plenty in those moments prior to its watering the reality of the divine garden, the sefirah *Malkhut* (Matronita), as well as for the human garden, the consciousness of the kabbalists. The interpretation intensifies the occasion, and the intensity of the occasion illuminates and enables the interpretation.

In reflecting on the ecstatic nature of the homily and the Companions, Rabbi Abba identifies the teacher—Rabbi Shim'on bar Yoḥai—with the sefirah *Yesod*. Rashbi adorns himself with the crown of this level, and as he does so, we witness the incarnation of a divine attribute in a human being.

Appropriate to the verse that he is describing, Rabbi Abba's exposition is a quintessential reflection on the male aspect as manifest in the various levels of reality: to the sefirah *Yesod* that prepares the intercourse between the King and Matronita on the divine plane; to the male genital organ in the erotic relations between man and woman; and to the teacher, Rabbi Shim'on, in his relations with his students.

We turn now to the exposition that closes the gathering, which articulates the mystical experience and brings it to its conclusion:

Rabbi El'azar opened and said: *He looked—and behold, a well in the field, and there were three herds of sheep crouching near it, for from that well they used to give the herds to drink, and the stone on the mouth of the well was large. When all the flocks were gathered there, they used to roll the stone from the mouth of the well, give the sheep to drink and return the stone on the mouth of the well to its place* (Genesis 29:2–3).

These verses require contemplation, for they are of the mystery of wisdom, for so I learned from my father:

He looked—and behold, a well—What is this well? It is the one of which is written: *The well that the chieftains dug, which the nobles of the people started* (Numbers 21:18).

And there were three herds of sheep crouching near it—these are *Netsaḥ*, *Hod*, and *Yesod*, for they crouch near Her and stand upon Her; and from these the well is filled with blessings.

For from that well that they used to give the herds to drink—for behold, from this well the upper and lower realms are nourished, and all is blessed as one.

And the stone on the mouth of the well was large—this is harsh judgment that stands upon Her from the other side to suckle from Her.

When all the flocks were gathered there—these are the six crowns of the King that gather together and draw blessings from the head of the King and pour them into Her. And when they all unite as one to pour forth into Her, it is written: *They used to roll the stone from the mouth of the well*—they roll away that harsh judgment and remove it from Her.

Give the sheep to drink—they pour forth blessings in that well for the upper and lower realms.

Afterward, *they returned the stone on the mouth of the well to its place*—that judgment returned to its place, for it is needed to sweeten the world and to rectify the world.

And *now*, behold, the blessed Holy One pours forth upon you blessings from the fountain of the stream, and through you the entire generation is blessed. Happy is your portion in this world and in the world that is coming! About you is written: *And all your children shall be disciples of YHVH, and great shall be the happiness of your children* (Isaiah 54:13). (Zohar 3:62a)

Rabbi El'azar's exposition, which complements the exposition of Rabbi Abba, focuses on the female aspect of the different dimensions of reality, as they emerge from the verses about the well in the Torah portion *Vayetse*. The verses are interpreted here as symbolizing the way in which the sefirah *Malkhut* is blessed by means of the divine qualities that flow into Her, and the way in which She brings forth those blessings from Herself to the powers above and below Her "as one." The images from the biblical verses and the dynamic description of the filling of *Malkhut* join together and are transformed into a powerful visual image rendered in words in "real time" of the group's experience. The verses signify the reality of the divine world; at the same time they describe, in the language of the biblical story, the mystical experience of the group.

The Torah's ability to signify simultaneously the divine and the human points to a structural—or perhaps even ontological—essence shared between them. Indeed, it is this congruence that creates the very possibility of mystical activity. The Companions, like the well, are blessed from the fountain of the stream, and through them the entire generation is blessed. No longer merely a topic for exposition, the river is now present, flowing in the zoharic story itself and among the Companions.

The River of Human Creativity

The verse "a river flows from Eden to water the garden" is expounded again in one of the peak moments of the entire Zohar, namely, in the *Idra Zuta*, the occasion of Rabbi Shim'on's ecstatic departure from the world.[36] Rashbi convenes his disciples and explains to them the magnitude of the event. He discloses to his disciples the tension and ambivalence he experiences between his desire to reveal secrets before his death and his desire keep these secrets covered and concealed so as not to risk revealing them to one who is not worthy. After these reflections, and with a sense that his decision to reveal mysteries has been well received in the world above, Rabbi Abba records the following account:

> [Rabbi Abba said:] When the Holy Spark, the High Spark, finished this word he raised his hands and cried and laughed. He wanted to reveal one word.

He said: I have been troubled by this word all my days and now they are not giving me permission!

Summoning up his courage, he sat and moved his lips and bowed three times. No one could look at his place, certainly not at him!

He said: Mouth, mouth, you have attained so much! Your spring has not dried up! Your spring flows endlessly! For you we read:

A river flows from Eden to water the garden (Genesis 2:10), and it is written, *Like a spring whose waters do not fail* (Isaiah 58:11).

Now I avow: All the days I have been alive, I have yearned to see this day! Now my desire is crowned with success. This day itself is crowned! Now I want to reveal words in the presence of the blessed Holy One; all these words are adorning my head like a crown! (Zohar 3:291b, *Idra Zuta*; Matt 1983, p. 186)

This is perhaps the most dramatic and far-reaching appearance of this verse in the entire Zohar. Here the hero of the composition and its own deep structure are united. Throughout the entire zoharic epic, the river is ever present, interpreted over and over again in all its diverse significations. And here, in Rabbi Shim'on's final hours, the flowing river is present as the essence of his activity. In this context the verse describes creativity itself, as Rashbi himself attests to the unceasing creativity that he experienced all his days through the words of the verse. The source of creativity, Eden, generates an endless divine flow streaming from the mouth, with the garden here representing the students and the world. It should be noted that Rashbi speaks of his experience as an ongoing process, transpiring in the continuous present. The ecstatic experience—the crying, the laughter, the illumination, and the words that Rabbi Shim'on utters with his mouth—are illustrations of the way in which he experienced the divine river, which flowed and streamed within him all his life.[37]

The River: Conclusion

Having examined different exegetical images of the verse "a river flows from Eden," we will conclude with a passage from a homily that summarizes the verse's unique power of arousal. This homily presents the verse as generating mystical reality: it contains the concealed mystery of faith and therein lies its awesome power. One must recite this verse with special intention in order to actualize the transition from the consciousness of this world to the consciousness and experience of the world that is coming, namely, the world of the nocturnal delight of the blessed Holy One with the souls of the righteous.[38]

> Faithfulness and truth (Emunah omen) (Isaiah 25:1)—two that are one. One is the garden and one is the river. One flows from Eden and one is watered by it. Behold, here is the entire concealed mystery of faith.
>
> And we have learned: Whosoever arises at night, at the hour that the blessed Holy One enters the garden to delight in the righteous, must say this verse with desire of the heart, and attune his desire to it: O YHVH, You are my God, I will extol You, I will praise Your name, for you have done wonderful things, even counsels of old, in faithfulness and truth (Isaiah 25:1). Afterward he shall say: I praise You, for I am awesomely, wondrously made; Your work is wonderful; I know it very well (Psalms 139:14; transl. NJPS). And after that: A river flows from Eden to water the garden.
>
> And this is the praise of the ancient ḥasidim when they would arise at midnight, and afterward arrange their praises and engage Torah. (Zohar Ḥadash, Balak, 53b)[39]

The zoharic passages expounding the verse "A river flows from Eden to water the garden" create a rich tapestry of images, displaying the many dimensions that the authors of the Zohar discovered in this verse. Together these images attest to the unique way that the Zohar creates a living symbol. The appearance of this verse as a kind of refrain, and the way in which it is integrated into the zoharic text, highlight its function in arousing the reader's consciousness to experience the dynamism of reality in all its myriad forms.

This verse, it should be noted, is but one of the numerous code-verses found in the Zohar; and code-verses are but one of the many structures of awakening employed by the composition. Once aroused, the reader is invited and prepared to experience the flowing consciousness termed "the world that is coming," and it is perhaps this consciousness that is the true radiance of the Zohar.[40] In his book Shekel ha-Kodesh, Moses de León captures the essence of this experience in what could be read as an ode to the Zohar: "The World to Come is the world that is coming continuously, radiating radiance unceasingly."[41]

MYSTICAL EXPERIENCE

IN THE ZOHAR

Having acquainted ourselves with the heroes of the Zohar and their way of life, and having examined the deep desires and aims of the composition, we now turn to mystical experience as conveyed in the Zohar's unique language. Part IV focuses on numerous aspects of the experience:

- *Description of the experience*—Chapter 12 examines the different modes and images in which mystical experience in the Zohar is expressed, for example: light, water, cleaving, radiant face, and their contexts in Jewish culture and mystical traditions from around the world.

- Chapter 13 treats the *general qualities* that characterize mystical experience in the Zohar: a multifaceted experience; a dynamic, internal structure full of pleasure and delight; a softening of the boundaries between the human and the divine; and moderation and containment.

- *Mystical states of consciousness*—Chapter 14 brings the discussion to a climax, outlining the three main mystical states of consciousness that underlie the Zohar's mysticism.

- The book concludes with a discussion of the Zohar's diverse and complex views regarding the very *possibility of expressing in language* the personal experience of the encounter with the divine (Chapter 15), as well as the way in which the Zohar engages the question of the possibility, permission, and appropriate means of giving *written expression* to the world of mysteries (Chapter 16).

Descriptions of the Mystical Experience

The human experience of intimacy with the Holy is a secret one keeps deep within oneself, sharing only with God. Nevertheless, the translation of that experience into words allows us a glance into that hidden domain.

Such translation can be painstaking, expressed only with great difficulty, or it can resemble speech bursting its banks with great emotion. The speaker may sense that his words articulate his experience precisely, or that they are like a thick and heavy cloud, a mere impression of what he has undergone. The experience can be sensorial, emotional, and cognitive; whatever the case, what remains for us is the trace left behind through its translation into sentences, words, and letters. Language, then, both reveals and conceals; and in seeking to explore mystical experience in the Zohar, we have no recourse save these linguistic remnants.[1]

Testimony, reporting, and the recounting of the Companions' experiences are part of the world of Rabbi Shim'on's circle. A sensitive reading of the Zohar enables us to pay close attention to the unique and diverse idioms through which the Companions transmit their experiences. In his book *Shi'ur Komah*, Rabbi Moses Cordovero cautions us regarding the distinction between experience and verbal transmission, and between oral report and written testimony:

> And regarding the divine wisdom, I will reveal this secret: the mouth is unable to utter all that is fixed in the heart, and it should not enter the mind of anyone who reads books about the wisdom of Kabbalah [to think] that it is possible for a wise kabbalist to write all the things in a book as they are in the *maskil's* mind, for things are diminished from the heart to the mouth, and from the mouth to the book.[2]

We turn now to the central idioms in the Zohar's language of mystical experience. These include: light; water and saturation; delight and pleasure; cleaving, kissing, embracing and intercourse; an altered sense of time; smell; fire; and a radiant face. We will also indicate the contexts of these descriptive forms in Jewish literature across the ages, as well as in mystical literature from around the world.

Light

The experience of intimacy or contact with the divine is an experience infused with great "light." The language of light is without a doubt the most prevalent idiom in the Zohar for expressing mystical experience.[3] The Zohar's protagonists draw upon a deep reservoir of biblical, rabbinic, and kabbalistic descriptions of encounter with the divine as an experience of light:[4]

1. Foremost are the lights appearing in the Bible—the light at the beginning of creation, the prophets' experience of light, the light of the End of Days, and the description of wondrous light in Isaiah's prophecy where God appears as the "everlasting light" illuminating Israel at the end of time.

2. The Sages of the rabbinic period added the image of God as light,[5] and homilies about the light created on the first day[6]—the special light with which Adam was able to see "from one end of the world to the other," which was concealed (because of the wicked) for the righteous in the World to Come.[7]

3. To these were added the many hues, splendor, and radiance that fill the celestial realm in the *Heikhalot* literature; the illumination of *Sefer*

ha-Bahir;[8] the world of lights among the circles of the earliest kabbalists;[9] and that which appears in *Sha'ar ha-Kavvanah* in the *Iyyun* circle;[10] as well as manifestations of light as descriptions of the divine in the poetry of Spain.[11]

In the kabbalist's consciousness, the desire to experience the divine, as well as the very experience itself, is connected with the special appearance or presence of light; indeed, we find similar accounts in mystical testimonies from around the world.[12]

It is possible to distinguish among the kinds of light that the zoharic mystics seek to experience: the dark, black light of dawn, of Shekhinah; the light of the blessed Holy One (the sefirah *Tiferet*), of the King's countenance, also called the "speculum that shines" (*ispaklarya ha-me'irah*)—which both Moses and Rabbi Shim'on attained; and above and beyond, the white light of *Atika Kadisha* (the Holy Ancient One), "a white like which there is no whiteness in the world."[13] Every manifestation of these lights is accompanied also by the light unique to the composition—the radiance (*zohar*) itself.

This distinction among these three lights—the dark and blended light, the illuminating light, and the white light—parallels the structure of the divine world that appears in the *Idrot* passages: the divine world of *Nukba*, the feminine aspect of the divine; the configuration known as *Ze'eir Anpin* (Small Face); and *Arikh Anpin* (Long Face), the merciful countenance of *Atika Kadisha* (Holy Ancient One). (These elements parallel respectively also the sefirah *Malkhut*, the sefirah *Tiferet* or the six sefirot beneath *Binah*, and the sefirah *Keter*.) Sometimes the Zohar presents the entire process of emanation and the entire sefirotic world in terms of the illumination of different lights occupying diverse levels of concealment and illumination.

> "Then this radiance of unknown Thought strikes the radiance of the extended curtain, radiating with that which is unknown, unknowable, unrevealed. So this radiance of unknown Thought strikes the radiance of the curtain, and they radiate as one, forming nine palaces of palaces. . . . These fathom neither Will nor supernal Thought, grasping yet not grasping. In these abide all mysteries of faith, and all those lights from the mystery of the supernal Thought downward are called *Ein Sof*, Endless." (Zohar 1:65a; Matt 2004–2007, vol. 1, pp. 379–80)

In his book *Shekel ha-Kodesh*, Rabbi Moses de León writes of the structure of the divine world as a structure of lights. He suggests that the knowledge of how to contemplate these lights is the very secret transmitted to the kabbalists:

> For He (may He be blessed) made manifest the mystery of His being and emanated the radiance of the *ispaklarya* (speculum) that He drew forth from His light. And even so, the worlds could not endure Him, until He created light for His light and created worlds; and this light is called garment. . . . He gave the mystery of these matters to the wise who know religion and law, to gaze at and contemplate the supernal matters.[14]

Another personality connected with the zoharic circle, Rabbi Joseph ben Shalom Ashkenazi, views the kabbalists' attainment—what he terms the "seeing with the soul's eye"—as dependent on the presence of the divine light. This seeing of the soul, he writes, is dependent on a light that does not come from the physical luminaries (sun, moon, and stars) but rather from that divine light created on the first day, which activates the soul's latent visionary capacity:

> Just as the eye of a human being sees potentially but only will ever actually see when accompanied by the light of one of the physical luminaries, so the eyes of the soul will not actually see until the known light accompanies them. Understand this.[15]

> Know, my beloved, that just as this sun shines upon all flesh, so the sun and shield of *YHVH Elohim* is a light for the souls; and just as by virtue of this sun one of flesh and blood can discern among forms, so in the light of the sun and shield of *YHVH Elohim* the souls can discern every detail in every world of the ten sefirot.[16]

Basking in the Divine Light

The deep wish of the kabbalist is not merely to behold these lights, but through them to attain and experience the human potential of total vision "from one end of the world to the other," both in the sense of time and space;[17] this capability having been taken from humanity after the sin in the Garden of Eden and after the sin of the Golden Calf. According to the Zohar, *dor de'ah*, the wilderness generation, attained knowledge and vision through the highest specula, yet this seeing, which constitutes humanity's adornments and jewelry, was taken from them after their sin.[18] The kabbalist desires to attain a vision, purer and more refined than that of ordinary sensorial vision; and yet beyond his desire to come to know the light, he seeks to experience and internalize these divine lights—to become a radiant, luminescent body, drawing from the power of the light of God that flows upon him.[19]

The paradigmatic images of light radiating and flowing from a human being are of course those of Moses descending from the mountain after having been with God (Exodus 34:29) and the verses in Isaiah (58:8, 10, 11; and chapter 60) that describe the healing light that will issue from man: "Then shall your light burst forth like the dawn and your healing spring up quickly. . . . then shall your light shine in darkness and your gloom shall be like noonday." It is not difficult, especially when seeking the light in the manner of the kabbalists, to discern in these verses the deep structure of a light *hidden within* man, unable to be exposed in a world filled with injustice—like the light of the first day, which was later concealed on account of the wicked. It may be that God concealed the light within Himself, as in the verse in Daniel (2:22) "And the light dwells with Him," until such time when the world will be deserving that it once again shine. Rectification of the human world will, therefore, bring about the illumination of this light and enable the bursting forth of this divine light within humanity.

Yet another biblical image in which we find the human potential to shine emerges from the verse that lends the Zohar its name: "The enlightened will shine like the radiance (*zohar*) of the sky; and those who lead many to righteousness, like the stars forever and ever" (Daniel 12:3; transl. Matt). Furthermore, the mystics of the Zohar also have in mind the legends about the baby Moses who illuminated the house with light,[20] as well as the many stories about his radiant face.[21]

In his commentary on Exodus 34:29, Rabbi Abraham Ibn Ezra explicitly establishes the connection between the encounter with the divine and the condition of illumination: "*Moses was not aware* [*that the skin of his face was radiant*]—and the reason, *since he had spoken with Him*, because the glory appeared on his face and therefore it was radiant like the radiance of the sky."[22]

The idea that the righteous will be radiant in the World to Come is found in the classical midrashim, as in *Midrash Tehillim*: "*And well-being abound, till the moon is no more* (Psalms 72:7; transl. NJPS). Until when? Until the time when the moon ceases to be. Just as the sun and moon shine in this world, so too the righteous are destined to shine in the World to Come, as is said: *And nations shall walk by your light; kings, by your shining radiance* (Isaiah 60:3; transl. NJPS)."[23]

In the fourth chapter of Midrash *Pirkei de-Rabbi Eli'ezer*, the firmament (*raki'a*) of creation is identified with the expanse (*raki'a*) that appears in Ezekiel's vision: "Above the heads of the creatures was a form: an expanse, with an awe-inspiring gleam as of crystal" (Ezekiel 1:22; transl. NJPS). About the words "an awe-inspiring gleam as of crystal," the midrash says: "Like precious stones and pearls; it illuminates all the heavens like a lamp in a house, and like the sun shining with full force at noon, as is said: *the light dwells with Him* (Daniel 2:22). And so in the future will the righteous shine, as is said: *The enlightened will shine like the radiance of the sky* (ibid. 12:3)."

When Rabbi Joseph Gikatilla, a member of the zoharic circle, comes to describe the experience of contact with the profound secret of Torah, he describes it as contact with light that brings about the illumination of the one undergoing the experience: "How many rooms does the Torah have? Room after room . . . until reaching the place called mystery, which is the secret of *Keter*. . . . And this is the secret of *So that mysteries reveal light* (Job 28:11), that when a person reaches knowledge of the mystery, his eyes will shine with things hidden from him."[24]

For its part, the Zohar attributes to Enoch (Genesis 5:24) the unique quality of having had the divine light increase within him, until he was transformed into Metatron and gained entry into the celestial realm.[25] While different heroes in the Zohar attain the experience of illumination and merit having their faces radiate like Moses,[26] it is only Rabbi Shim'on who attains this mystical state and is able simultaneously to describe his experiences (that is, be both within mystical experience and aware of the experience).[27]

As we have already seen, Rabbi Shim'on is described in the Zohar by images filled with light. He is the lamp of the world, and in his hands he holds a pearl with which he illuminates the world; the light dwells with Rabbi Shim'on, and from him it goes forth and illuminates the entire world. As we learn from a mystic who is on the periphery of the Companions: "That light extends from heaven to earth, illuminating the entire world until the Ancient of Days comes and sits fittingly upon the throne."[28]

In *Shekel ha-Kodesh*, Rabbi Moses de León describes the totality of human religious service as directed to the goal of illumination by divine light:

> It is true that the essence of faith and the root of the holy intention in man's being in this world is to worship his creator and to rectify his soul to bask in the light of life. . . . the commandments and the good deeds are the oil to prepare the wick . . . so that the light shining above will shine upon him, so that he will shine before his creator; and this is as the master of secrets has said: *Let your clothes always be freshly washed, and your head never lacking oil* (Ecclesiastes 9:8), so that this light will shine upon him, as we have said. . . . for the essence of the commandments . . . is to prepare the soul . . . to draw down upon him the light of the abundance above.[29]

The souls that take part in the nocturnal delight and that gaze upon the delight and splendor of God, merit in turn to radiate joy-filled light and splendor. This pleasurable light is a fruitful light, an erotic agent that produces blessed fruits for the world:[30]

> And this is the praise of the ancient *ḥasidim* when they arose at midnight and would arrange their praises and learn Torah. . . . When the blessed Holy One enters at midnight . . . He delights in them and those words. Afterward, all are arrayed, male and female, and the blessed Holy One—after He inhales [their aroma] and delights in them and in all those words, their secrets of wisdom— is revealed upon them; and they behold that delight of YHVH. . . . Then all rejoice with great joy until their splendor and light shine forth. And from the emanation of the splendor and light of their joy, fruits are made for this world. (Zohar 3:303a, *Tosafot* 10)

Zohar *(Radiance)*

Radiance (*zohar*) is a central word in the vocabulary of light in the zoharic corpus, and it sparkles with a range of meanings throughout the composition.[31] The word is taken from the verse in Daniel that lent the composition its name:[32] "The enlightened will shine like the radiance of the sky; and those who lead many to righteousness, like the stars forever and ever" (12:3; transl. Matt). This radiance of the sky, like which the enlightened will shine, stands at the heart of the kabbalists' quest.

The beginning of the Zohar's commentary to the Torah portion *Bereshit* features a special and diverse collection of homilies on this verse. In one of those homilies, which we saw in Chapter 2, we found that the kabbalists' illumination with a radiating light is both the result of contemplation of divinity and a prerequisite for such contemplation; the kabbalists must radiate so as to be able to gaze upon and contemplate the world of divinity, and so rectify and support it. The "radiance of the sky" is the special light that constantly illuminates the kabbalists and that illumines Torah.[33] Let us explore this special homily once again:

> *The enlightened*—supernal pillars and sockets, contemplating in wisdom everything needed by that *pavilion* and its supports. . . .
>
> *Will shine (yazhiru)*—for unless they shine and radiate, they cannot contemplate that *pavilion*, looking out for all its needs.
>
> *Like the radiance (zohar) of the sky*—standing above *the enlightened* . . .
>
> *Radiance (zohar)*—illumining Torah.
>
> *Radiance (zohar)*—illumining the *heads* of that *living being*. Those *heads* are *the enlightened*, who constantly radiate and shine, contemplating that *sky*, the radiance flashing from there, radiance of Torah, sparkling constantly, never ceasing. (Zohar 1:16a; Matt 2004–2007, vol. 1, pp. 117–18, reformatted)

The openings to the Zohar's commentary to the Torah portions *Bereshit* and *Shemot* each dramatically employ a special use of the word *zohar*. As Yehuda Liebes has shown,[34] in both instances *zohar* appears as a kind of mantra that establishes the tone and rhythm of the reading, and it is not necessarily connected to the sentence it begins. In both instances, the word has a dramatic valence and functions as a refrain or code word. The author does not explain what the *zohar* is or where its source lies, and readers find themselves within a language that, even if not fully understood, nevertheless points to that *zohar* as an entity of great significance.

> Radiance (*zohar*)—Concealed of concealed struck its aura. . . .
>
> Radiance (*zohar*)—Sowing seed for its glory, like the seed of fine purple silk. . . .

Radiance (*zohar*)—Mystery! *In the beginning*, first of all. . . .
Radiance (*zohar*)—Concealed and treasured. . . .
Radiance (*zohar*)—Comprising all letters and colors. . . . (Zohar 1:15a–b;
Matt 2004–2007, vol. 1, pp. 109–13, adapted)

Radiance (*zohar*) of this expanse brilliantly illumines the garden. . . .
Radiance (*zohar*)! Fruit of the tree provides life to all. . . .
Radiance (*zohar*)! This tree rises above, above. (Zohar 2:2a; Matt 2004–2007,
vol. 4, p. 2, adapted)[35]

The word *zohar* appears in the context of each one of the lights found
in the composition's idiom of experience. We are told of the *zohar* that does
not shine and of the *zohar* that shines; of the *zohar* of the sky, the *zohar* of
Shekhinah, and numerous other *zohars* as well. As is the way of the Zohar,
these *zohars* cannot be apprehended or defined, but only experienced.

The secret of the four engraved names of the four radiances.

Each and every radiance (*zohar*) is comprised within its companion; and the
yearning of one is to enter the other, to be contained this one in that one. . . .
    One is called the radiance that is dark and not dark . . .
    The second radiance is the radiance that gathers within itself supernal,
concealed eyes; and this is the radiance that sparkles before the eyes, which
cannot gaze upon it. . . .
    The third radiance is the radiance that comprises three radiances. . . . this
is the one that "dashes to and fro" (Ezekiel 1:14). No one can hold fast to its
sparkling; this radiance is like the ball of the eye when closed. . . .
    The fourth radiance, *ehyeh*, "I am": this radiance is concealed, not seen at
all, for from this radiance the other radiances emerged. (*Zohar Ḥadash*,
Song of Songs, 61d–62a)

Of the varied uses of this word throughout the composition, one is
dominant. This *zohar* is the general name for the flow of sparkling colors
that erupts from the river of divine plenty, the power that creates and
sustains reality. This *zohar* is the "illumination of the sparks of the river
that flows from Eden."[36] It is the potentiality that bursts forth from the
divine river.

Recall that the river is also the radiant sky (*raki'a*) that appears in the
book of Daniel (like which "the enlightened will shine"). Thus this *zohar*
is also the totality of divine lights as reflected in the night sky—the screen

that conceals, reveals, and mediates that which lies above. It is with this radiance of the sky that the kabbalists so deeply identify in their quest to be creative and radiant. Parallel to the river that "flows from Eden to water the garden," this *zohar* lights up the garden: "*Zohar, Radiance*, of this expanse brilliantly illumines the garden"—the garden of reality and of human consciousness.[37]

The *zohar* is the overflow of the latent and eruptive potentialities from the divine phallus, from human consciousness, and from the male genital organ. The following passage describes the precious multihued radiance of the rainbow in the cloud, called "the sign of the Covenant," and interpreted by the Sages as the male genital organ. It connects these elements with Joseph, who merited the appellation "the Righteous One" (*Tsaddik*) on account of his having overcome sexual temptation (Genesis 39:7-12). Guarding the Covenant—vigilantly maintaining a sanctified and lawful sex life—leads one to radiate with the desired golden light.

> *His bow remained firm, the arms of his hands stayed agile (va-yaphozu)* (Genesis 49:24)—What is *va-yaphozu*? They sparkled most desirably of all. . . . They sparkled in supernal radiance when he kept the covenant, so he was called Joseph the Righteous. Therefore the rainbow is called "covenant," embracing one another. Luster of supernal glory, vision of all visions, vision resembling hidden vision, hidden colors, revealed colors. It is forbidden to gaze at the rainbow. (Zohar 1:71b; Matt 2004–2007, vol. 1, p. 422, adapted)

In the *Zohar Ḥadash* collection of homilies on "The enlightened will shine like the radiance of the sky," we find one in which the *zohar* appears as the gush (or burst) of the potent bounty that flows forth from the sefirah *Yesod*. This homily explains the form and significance of the biblical cantillation mark *pazer*, whose name means "to distribute or disseminate." (It is one of the longer and more intricate trope marks.) The trope is expounded in the context of "He gives freely (*pizzar*) to the poor, his beneficence (*tsidkato*) lasts forever" (Psalms 112:9), which in its simple sense describes the righteous householder and his deeds.[38] In our homily, this is the moment when the qualities of *Yesod* are revealed in the world. The revelation of the radiance is compared to the moment when Esther touches the tip of Ahasuerus' scepter.

The *pazer*, the potent flow of divinity, fills all the channels and transmits the flow to the "poor." It is through this phallic scepter, annointed with oil, that the enlightened are adorned, and through which they shine.

> *The enlightened will shine like the radiance (zohar) of the sky*—this is the sky in which are the sun, the moon, the planets, and the stars. . . . and your sign is: *He gives freely (pizzar) to the poor* (Psalms 112:9), for he [*Yesod*] transmits to all the lower [worlds]; for when the oil arises and increases, the oil of the light, "the great *pazer*," he [*Yesod*] arises . . . like this mark ‫פ‬ that is *pazer*. And this is your sign: *The King extended to Esther the golden scepter* (Esther 5:2). And we have taught: He extended it six cubits in her direction; from this *pazer* the channels are filled and are transmitted to the needy. And this is the scepter that is adorned in oil, and through this intonation of the oil they arise and are fittingly arrayed, and then *The enlightened will shine like the radiance (zohar) of the sky*. . . .
>
> *The enlightened will shine like the radiance of the sky*—who expand and illuminate below, when the scepter abides in the mystery of *pazer* and bestows and is lubricated with oil, and those two pillars [= thighs] are adorned with oil below, and the light is arrayed and they are aligned one with another. Then the enlighten will shine, for below is adorned with the adornment of male and female. (*Zohar Ḥadash, Tikkunim*, 105d)

The *zohar*, as we have seen, is also the fruit of the Tree of Life, and the enlightened are those who taste this life-bestowing radiance.

The central symbols for the *zohar* are, therefore, the river, the sky, and the Tree of Life, all of which form a single symbolic cluster whose key features are masculinity, bounty, royalty, sexuality, and fertility. In sefirotic language, the *zohar* is identified with *Tiferet*, yet even more so with *Yesod*. Dynamism and eroticism, as well as the tension between the illumination of the spark and its disappearance, between revelation and concealment, connect this *zohar* with the qualities of *Yesod*. The *zohar* is therefore the creative font of mystical experience.

The Light of Dawn

The most beloved light of the Zohar's authors is the dark light of dawn, the illuminating darkness in which the daily union between the King and Matronita transpires, and whose light the kabbalists hope for every day. Indeed, one of the criteria for membership in the zoharic circle is "He who

awaits each day the light that shines when the King visits the doe . . ."[39]
Whoever does not yearn daily for the light of dawn and the experience of
union cannot be counted among the Companions. Let us now examine the
homily that establishes the centrality of lights in the kabbalists' worship:

> Rabbi Abba opened the verse and said: *A psalm of David, when he was in the
> Wilderness of Judah* (Psalms 63:1; transl. NJPS). Why is this different from all
> the other praises, which do not recount where King David recited them? And
> why is it different here that it says *when he was in the Wilderness of Judah?* . . .
> To demonstrate David's praise to the entire world, that even though he was
> in distress and was being pursued, he endeavored to recite songs and praises
> to the blessed Holy One.
>
> And even though [David] spoke through the holy spirit, the holy spirit
> would not have dwelled upon him had he not endeavored to have her dwell
> upon him. And so it is in every place—the holy spirit above cannot descend
> until the human being arouses it from below:
>
> *O God, You are my God, I search for you (ashaḥareka)* (Psalms 63:2) . . . *asha-
> ḥareka, I search for you*—[the meaning] as it sounds is correct, but *ashaḥareka*—
> I will array the light that illumines at dawn (*shaḥar*); for behold, the light that
> appears at dawn does not illumine until it is arrayed below.
>
> And whosoever arrays this dawn light, even though it is black (*shaḥor*),
> attains the illuminating white light; and this is the light of the speculum that
> shines, and such a person attains the world that is coming.
>
> This is the mystery of the verse *and those who seek me will find me (u-mshaḥarai
> yimtsa'uneni)* (Proverbs 8:17).
>
> *U-mshaḥarai* (those who seek me)—who array the black light of dawn.
>
> *Yimtsa'uneni* (will find me)—It is not written *yimtsa'uni* (with one letter
> *nun*), but rather *yimtsa'uneni* (with two *nun's*)—he merits two lights: the black
> light of dawn, and the illuminating white light. And he attains the speculum
> that does not shine and the speculum that shines—that is why it is written
> *yimtsa'uneni*.
>
> And about this David said: *Ashaḥareka, I search for you*—I will array the
> black light of dawn, to shine upon it the illuminating white light. (Zohar
> 2:140a)

This passage requires a close reading, as it comprises many of the key components of the zoharic mystic's spiritual practice. This homily is embedded
in a long and wonderful story that recounts and illustrates the way in which
the Companions generate mystical experience. Rabbi Shim'on expounds
the never-ending quest of the sefirah *Malkhut*, whose appellation here is

tsedek (righteousness), to behold and unite with Her partner, the male aspect of divinity, termed here the "speculum that shines": "It is righteousness that constantly calls to the speculum that shines, it is never silent."[40] Rabbi Shim'on imports this paradigm (of continuous calling to the light from the divine world) into the world of the mystic: "And now the blessed Holy One has illuminated this path for us, and Rabbi El'azar my son, calls to the supernal light and does not cease."

Rabbi Abba's homily follows immediately and is built on the mystical foundation established in the preceding exposition, to call without ceasing, to find—even from a great distance—the connection to the illuminating light of the speculum that shines. His homily expounds Psalm 63, which opens with the verse "A psalm of David, when he was in the Wilderness of Judah." David is the mystic, and the wilderness symbolizes the existential situation of the kabbalist. The wilderness simultaneously incorporates two conditions: distance, and the space that engenders longing. The wilderness is therefore the absence that creates desire. David praises God even from a great distance, and it is from him that the mystic learns a great lesson: "And so it is in every place—the holy spirit above cannot descend until the human being arouses her from below."

The kabbalist's quest is therefore to draw down upon himself the holy spirit. This indwelling cannot transpire without the intentional and directed effort of the human being; he must "first prepare himself," that is, be aware of the purpose of the holy spirit's indwelling. King David, and all the mystics in his image, are the ones who array the black light of dawn, and he who is constant in his service of the dark light is assured of attaining the great light, the "speculum that shines."[41] Thus Rabbi Shim'on explains: "Come and see: The only arousal kindling this blue light, to be grasped by the white light, is Israel cleaving below."[42]

In the words of David in Psalm 57:9, the kabbalists "awake the dawn." Dawn is not merely another watch of the day; it is rather the great moment of coupling between the King and Matronita, for which the mystic has waited since his rising at midnight. The mystic's identification with Shekhinah and her dark light—the "speculum that does not shine"—makes him worthy of attaining, at the moment of union, the light that does shine, the light of the blessed Holy One, which illuminates within and from his beloved, Shekhinah. This is therefore their quest—to see the illuminating light and to be filled by it.[43]

The Speculum That Shines

The "speculum that shines" signifies a dimension of light that is bold, stable, and strong; the light of the countenance of the king, the vision of which is connected to the desire "to behold the king in his beauty" (Isaiah 33:17). According to Rabbi Yitsḥak, light therefore radiates from the face of the deity-king: "a King who is totally complete, his mind totally complete. What is the conduct of that king? His face always shines, for He is complete."[44]

This is the light that sustains reality, as in "With you is the source of life; by Your light do we see light" (Psalms 36:10). This is the light of the blessed Holy One, in which He cloaked Himself and created the world. This is the light that shines from the throne of the King and that bestows life to the world: "The light of the King's countenance is life" (Proverbs 16:15).

The special light of the King's countenance cannot be apprehended by the human being with ordinary vision; this is the light concealed from the eyes of all flesh and blood.[45] In rabbinic literature, we read that Moses—the perfect human being—was able to see through the "speculum that shines"; in the Zohar, Rabbi Shim'on is accorded the same status.[46] The lights of the "speculum that shines" are not experienced directly, but rather through their reflection in the "speculum that does not shine," or the visionary capacity called *Malkhut* (Shekhinah).

The mystic's hope is that the light of the King's countenance will indeed appear in the world, even if only in the future, as expressed by Rabbi Ḥiyya: "*By Your light do we see light* (Psalms 36:10)—This is the light that is surely stored and hidden away for the righteous in the future, as is written: *Elohim saw that the light was good* (Genesis 1:4). From this light Israel are destined to shine in the world that is coming."[47] That is to say, the divine light will be made present in the world through the people of Israel in another time.

Yet it is not the way of mystics to await this future era, but rather to at-

tempt to bring its qualities into their world right now. One way to accomplish this is through construing the technical term *olam ha-ba* (the World to
Come) as "the world that comes (continuously)," and the mystics' task as
connecting to its hidden presence.[48]

Another way is through engaging and plying Torah—and so drawing
down the thread-thin rays of divine light concealed within her, which are
then intertwined with the mystics' world.

> *Light is sown for the righteous* (Psalms 97:11) . . . [the light] is hidden and sown
> like a seed that gives birth to seeds and fruit. Thereby the world is sustained.
> Every single day, a ray of that light shines into the world and keeps every-
> thing alive, for with that ray the blessed Holy One feeds the world. And
> everywhere that Torah is studied at night, one thread-thin ray appears from
> that hidden light and flows down upon those absorbed in her. (Zohar 2:149a;
> Matt 1995, p. 90)[49]

The light of the King's countenance and the light of the "speculum that
shines" belong to a rich symbolic complex coalescing around the qualities
of the sefirah *Tiferet*. This is the light of the sun, the light of Torah, the King
seated on His throne, the truth, the light of day, the center, the heart, the
center bar running from end to end, the sky, the firmament, and the radiant
light like which the enlightened wish to shine. Generally speaking, this light
is associated with stability and majesty.

The zoharic mystic is described as "the one who contemplates by himself, from himself, words (or: things) that human beings cannot mouth"; and
what he understands "from himself" is precisely the hierarchical ordering of
divine lights, beginning with the highest, unseen light to the lowest light that
does not illuminate, the "speculum that does not shine." The concealed lights
are experienced by the mystic through their reflection in the light that does
not shine, either with eyes wide open or through employing a special praxis
(closing the eye and rolling the eyeball so as to behold the concealed lights
not revealed to the open eye). The enlightened, therefore, are the ones who
know how to contemplate the mystery of the seen and unseen lights.[50]

> [Rabbi Shim'on] replied, "Come and see: There are colors that are seen, and
> colors that are not seen. These are a supernal mystery of faith, yet human be-
> ings do not know or contemplate. . . .

"It is written: *The enlightened will shine like the radiance of the sky, and those who turn many to righteousness, like the stars for ever and ever* (Daniel 12:3). *The enlightened will shine.* Who are *the enlightened*? The wise one who contemplates, on his own, things that human beings cannot utter. . . .

"There are four lights. Three of them are concealed, and one revealed. A shining light. A light of radiance. . . . A light of purple. . . . A light that does not shine. . . .

"This is the mystery: close your eye and turn your eyeball, and those shining, glowing colors are revealed. Permission to see is granted only with eyes shut and concealed, for they are supernally concealed, standing above those colors that are seen and do not glow.

"Of this we read: 'Moses attained the speculum that shines,' which stands above the one that does not shine. The rest of the inhabitants of the world, that speculum that does not shine. . . .

"Mystery of the eye: concealed and revealed. Concealed, seeing the speculum that shines; revealed, seeing the speculum that does not shine." (Zohar 2:23a–b; Matt 2004–2007, vol. 4, pp. 79–81, adapted)[51]

In the following passage, part of which we have already seen in our discussion of the idiom of radiance, we find that the mysteries of the divine names are in fact the mysteries of the different hues of the divine lights; and that the higher, concealed lights are revealed only to the kabbalists' heart. It is through his identification with the lower light that the human being is exposed to the concealed lights above. The lower light is the beautiful dark light of Shekhinah, "*Adonai*," in which abides the never-ending desire to behold and join the lights above. The kabbalist who connects with Shekhinah becomes, like her, filled with that living desire to receive the bounty and flow of the concealed lights, which mainly lie beyond the boundaries of his conscious apprehension.

And this is the secret of secrets, the supernal chariot of the names: *Adonai, Tseva'ot, YHVH, Ehyeh.*

The secret of the four engraved names of the four radiances.

Each and every radiance (*zohar*) is comprised within its companion; and the yearning of one is to enter the other, to be contained this one in that one. . . .

One is called the radiance that is dark and not dark. . . . [When one] looks at it, it sparkles and glows with supernal light and beauty; and its light is gathered within itself, until another light strikes it. . . .

The second radiance is the radiance that gathers within itself supernal, concealed eyes; and this is the radiance that sparkles before the eyes that cannot gaze upon it. . . . and this one's desire is constantly to praise that first radiance. . . .

The third radiance is the radiance that comprises three radiances. . . . the forefathers attained this radiance, this is the one that "dashes to and fro" (Ezekiel 1:14); no one can hold fast to its sparkling. This radiance is like the ball of the eye when closed. . . .

The fourth radiance, *ehyeh*—this radiance is concealed, not seen at all, for from this radiance the other radiances emerged. . . . this radiance is not revealed at all but abides in the heart's understanding. For the heart knows and contemplates, even though it is not revealed at all, and this is because all those radiances emerge from it.

The desire of the lower radiance is to recite praises, to contemplate those radiances, to be comprised within them, to ascend and gaze upon that supernal beauty. And about this King David said: *One thing I ask of YHVH, only that do I seek, to dwell in the house of YHVH all the days of my life, to gaze upon the beauty of YHVH, to frequent His temple* (Psalms 27:4). (*Zohar Ḥadash*, Song of Songs, 61d–62b)

The quest to adorn the dark light of dawn with the white light is in fact a description, in the Zohar's language of lights, of the union of the masculine and feminine, which, as we have seen repeatedly, is the ultimate purpose of the mystic's religious worship. This is the union of the light of the "speculum that shines" with the "speculum that does not shine"; and the Zohar's protagonists, beyond their interest in the sefirot themselves or the lights as entities in their own right, are interested in the dynamic relationships among them.

Rabbi Shim'on opened and said: *But You, O YHVH, be not far off; my strength, hasten to my aid* (Psalms 22:20).

But You, O YHVH—All is one.

Be not far off—to depart from us, that the upper light depart from the lower.

For behold, when the upper light departs from the lower, then all the lights are darkened, and there is no light at all in the world. (Zohar 2:179b)

The White Light

The *maskil* wishes to attain both the dark light and the shining white light. The ascent of consciousness is described as a journey through a spectrum of colors, from the dark light up to the white light, the purest and most refined of all. Above and beyond all the colors and forms experienced by the mystic, the kabbalist seeks the whitest light of all, the light of *Atika Kadisha* (The Holy Ancient One), the light of the sefirah *Keter*.

> When a person gazes at the sky—from afar it seems blue,
> he draws nearer—it seems red,
> he draws nearer—it seems green,
> he draws nearer—it seems white like which there is no whiteness in the world!
>
> (Zohar 3:165b)

This white light is not the light that shines within human reality in the ordinary course of the world. This is the primal light; it lies at the very origin of reality. Within the Zohar's mythical-mystical reading of the story of the Exodus from Egypt, we find that the Israelites saw this great light, the light of *Atika Kadisha*, collectively on two occasions: on the banks of the sea, when the light of *Atika Kadisha* split and pierced reality ("then illuminated the illumination of all"); and at the giving of the Torah at Mt. Sinai.[52]

The further that one ascends among the divine grades, the whiter everything becomes. In the *Idrot* sections, the face of the most ancient, high, and exalted God (*Arikh Anpin*) is described as all white and crowned with white hair; He has white eyes (or one white eye) that are constantly open, and from which radiate a ceaseless stream of white light.[53] In the *Idra Rabba*, two faces of divinity are described and adorned: *Arikh Anpin* (the Long Face), *Atik Yomin* (the Ancient of Days; see Daniel 7:9), or the Patient One; and *Ze'eir Anpin* (the Small Face) or the Impatient One. The face of *Atik Yomin* is described so as to enhance its presence in the consciousness of the Idra's participants, and indeed in the consciousness of all reality. This is the face of complete and overflowing *ḥesed* (love).

The lower divine countenance, *Ze'eir Anpin*, is the representation of the divine intelligence spreading forth outside of itself; it is the expression of duality and differentiated reality. This face of divinity is characterized by the continuous oscillation and fluctuation between *ḥesed* and *din* (judgment), a fluctuation generally tending in favor of *din*. The *Idra* describes how this countenance is to be arrayed and rectified, and how the dimension of *hesed* can be strengthened: *Ze'eir Anpin* turns his head and eyes upward toward the white head, the ancient head of *Arikh Anpin*, and is thereby bathed in the whiteness of the *hesed*-filled light that overflows without ceasing from the eye of *Atik Yomin*.[54]

> . . . the eyes of the head [of *Ze'eir Anpin*] . . . the eye of *Atik Yomin* watches over them.
>
> And when the covers [eyelids] are raised, he looks like one who is arising from his sleep; and his eyes are opened and they see the open eye, and they bathe in the one whiteness of the good eye, as is written: *Bathed in milk* (Song of Songs 5:12).
>
> What is *in milk*? In the primal, supernal whiteness; and at that time, the gaze and guidance of love and mercy is found. (Zohar 3:136b, *Idra Rabba*)

This description, one of the dramatic peaks in the Zohar, is in fact a mythical account of the kabbalist's consciousness, endeavoring to ascend the varied grades of divine light so as to be illuminated by the white light of the face of *Atika*. The quality of this experience is represented in the Zohar through a particularly rich symbol—the solitary eye that ceaselessly radiates white light: "an eye that is white within white, and white that comprises all white."[55]

This image triggers associations of bounty connected with the human body: semen issuing from the male genital organ,[56] and milk flowing from the mother's breast. Indeed, in the *Idra* that appears in the Zohar for the Torah portion *Mishpatim*, we find that the whiteness that bathes the *din* (judgment) of *Ze'eir Anpin* is the whiteness of the ever sustaining milk of Mother *Binah*, poised here between *Atika Kadisha* and *Ze'eir Anpin*. The bounty that flows out of *Atika Kadisha* and the bounty that flows from *Binah* are called "the river that flows and does not cease."[57]

The white light is the most profound expression of divine *hesed*, the primal, undifferentiated divine quality that precedes all language or religion. The meaning of the desire to experience this light is, therefore, connected with the quest to ascend beyond differentiated reality, to touch the source from which all is created with the erotic intent of drawing this quality down into reality. The quest for the white light has another important aspect: the wish to be absorbed and subsumed within the divine—a kind of death wish, perhaps death by divine kiss—arising from the desire to attain the source of all.[58]

Water

Water, saturation, and the thirst-quenching drinking of water are central metaphors in the Zohar for mystical experience. They draw upon such imagery present in earlier Jewish literature. Already in the Psalms the yearning for intimacy with the divine is described in terms of thirst for water: "Like a hind craving for watercourses, so my soul craves You, O God" (Psalms 42:2). In the words of the prophet Jeremiah, God compares Himself to "the fount of living [that is, spring] water."[59] In the Bible's account of the end of days, the experience of total knowledge of God is conveyed through the image of the sea covering all the earth; and God's redemption is symbolized by the flow of "living" water from the Temple.[60] Rabbi Akiva likens God to the "*mikveh* of Israel," the reservoir of water that purifies man.[61] *Sefer ha-Bahir* is filled with images of the world as a garden, and of God's vitality and of life as water,[62] and the flow of divinity from its infinite depths into differentiated qualities is described as the flow of water.

Water, first and foremost, symbolizes divinity as abundance that flows and sustains all reality. The river that "issues from Eden to water the garden" is, as we have seen, a central expression in the Zohar for the flow of the divine bounty and its contact with humanity.[63] In the language of the Zohar, descriptions of divinity—and the descriptions of the experience of contact with divinity—regularly interchange images of light with those of water. Thus Rabbi Shim'on explains: "[*House of Jacob,*] *come let us walk in the light of YHVH* (Isaiah 2:5), as is written: *A river flows from Eden to water the garden* (Genesis 2:10). He planted this garden so as to delight there with the righteous who abide there."[64] This interchangeability might be explained because of the similar qualities of both as dynamic, flowing, expanding, and life-bestowing. These qualities are particularly fitting for the way in which the divine is present in the world, and for the nature of human contact with this presence. The interchange of water and light can also be explained by the linguistic affinity in Aramaic between *nahora* (light) and *nahara* (river). The expression "river of light" (*nahara di-nahora*) neatly illustrates this identity of the flowing of each.

In many of the Zohar's homilies, we find the presence of the divine bounty in the world described as water, and the kabbalist's desire to touch this bounty described as the yearning to be watered, or to be a vessel in which the fluids of bounty might be gathered. This system of experiential images presents the mystic's feminine face, for it stresses his receptive qualities. On the other hand, these images are also replete with descriptions of the yearning to transmit this flow of bounty to another vessel, namely, the world. This yearning to bestow and impart the bounty, to bless and fertilize reality, belong to the active dimensions of the kabbalist and his masculine guise.

> Come and see: The river that issues and flows waters all the garden . . . until it fills that place in the garden called *a well of living water* (Song of Songs 4:15); and from there the upper and lower [worlds] are nourished. . . . and he who merits to guard [the Covenant] merits being watered by that fountain of the stream [*variant reading:* in this world and] in the world that is coming—and it merits that the supernal well is filled to pour forth blessings from above to below. Happy is he in this world and in the world that is coming! And about this is written: *You will be like a watered garden, like a spring whose waters do not fail* (Isaiah 58:11). (Zohar 3:266a)

Another passage that expounds the same verse from Isaiah describes the experience of contact with the river of divine bounty, and the joy and satisfaction of contact with the ceaseless saturation of the desired divine fluid. The body and soul each encounter the divine, and the experience of the encounter is described both in terms of light and water. The garden, symbolizing the body or the soul, is watered and enjoys saturation. The Zohar connects the constantly flowing water with the erotic, overflowing bounty from the union of the masculine "source of the water" and the feminine "well of water," which together create the overflowing unity. This unity and the capacity to gaze upon (experience) its bounty are considered here as a supernal mystery of faith.

> ". . . the light of the soul will be intensified within the resplendent speculum, to shine with the body fittingly in full vitality. So it is written, *You will be like*

a watered garden (Isaiah 58:11). What does this mean? Its supernal waters never cease for all eternity; this garden (this body), watered by them, is saturated constantly. . . .

Come and see: a well of flowing water—This is a supernal mystery within the mystery of faith. . . . Whoever gazes at this well will gaze at the mystery of supernal faith. (Zohar 1:141a–b; Matt 2004–2007, vol. 2, p. 284)[65]

Just as the well that fills with bounty is a "mystery of faith," so the knowledge of "the river" is considered by the Zohar a secret of the wise.

A river flows from Eden to water the garden (Genesis 2:10). They have already clarified [this verse], but in this Garden of Eden below the river issues from Eden, indeed! And regarding this river that flows in the garden below, one should know its source and root. . . .

This Eden, supernal above all, the mystery of the world that is coming, knows the lower point [through] a certain righteous one [*Yesod*] from which a river flows that saturates it. And no one knows this but He of whom is written: *No eye has seen, O Elohim, but You* (Isaiah 64:3), for it grasps above and beyond, until *Ein Sof*.

And this river that flows from Eden below is a mystery of the wise, in the mystery of the verse *He will slake your thirst in parched places* (Isaiah 58:11). (Zohar 2:210b)

The Zohar describes the delight (*idun*) of the righteous as the pleasure associated with the kabbalist's experience of both contact with the divine river and with its source, Eden. In the following passage, which we saw already in the previous chapter, this experience of delight is described as one of filling and inspiration. Contact with the river transforms the kabbalist into a part of the divine flow, and in receiving the divine bounty he becomes a bestowing and generative source himself.

A river issues from Eden to water the garden (Genesis 2:10). . . . That river flowing forth is called the world that is coming—coming constantly and never ceasing. This is delight of the righteous, to attain this world that is coming, constantly watering the garden and never ceasing. (Zohar 3:290b, *Idra Zuta*)

The delight of the righteous is to merit the "world that is coming," described here as the flow of water emerging from Eden to water the garden of reality. Their desire is to attain the experience of being watered by the waters of the river of divine plenty.

According to the description here and in other passages, the river of bounty, whose source lies in the union of the sefirot *Ḥokhmah* and *Binah*, never ceases to flow. While it is true that the stream of divine water flows from its source continuously, sometimes, because of human misdeeds, this water does not always reach its destination in the world. Sin brings about a disconnection between earthly reality, which is under the sovereignty of the sefirah *Malkhut*, and the other divine qualities and worlds above her. This cutting off of *Malkhut* from the rest of the sefirot leads to a situation where the river is gathered in upon itself and does not reach humanity. The theurgic task of the mystic then is to unblock the divine conduits, to guarantee harmony in the world above, so as to bring about the unhindered flow of the divine abundance into the world below. Sometimes the absence of the presence of the divine river is not an ontological problem, but rather one of apprehension and attainment; in this case, the mystic redoubles his service to find a way to attain the river's saturating and ecstatic experience.

As we have already seen, this mystical experience of contact with the river can be attained by the participants in the central ritual of the zoharic circle, namely, the engagement with Torah from midnight till dawn. It is then that the experience that lies at the heart of the Companions' yearning, and which they describe as the stream of delights gushing upon their heads,[66] is likely to transpire.

The most daring zoharic homily presenting mystical experience in terms of irrigation appears in the homily on "Regarding this, let every faithful one (*ḥasid*) pray to You in a time when You may be found (*'et metso*), only that the rushing mighty waters not overtake him" (Psalms 32:6). According to the simple meaning of this verse, the rushing mighty waters signify trouble, tragedy, flooding, and death. The Zohar, however, transforms this flooding into the kabbalist's difficult-to-attain yet perennial object of desire.[67] "A time when You may be found" is the moment when reality merits being inundated with divine rivers of blessing. Every "faithful one" prays to connect with this unique time of favor, in order to merit the deep flowing waters of the divine bounty. According to this passage, it is clear that a person does not ordinarily attain the ecstatic experience of the "rushing mighty waters" from the depths of the divine river; he must pray to merit such an experience.

> Rabbi Yehudah used to recite: *Regarding this ('al zot), let every faithful one (ḥasid) pray to You in a time when You may be found ('et metso), only that the rushing mighty waters not overtake him* (Psalms 32:6).
> *Regarding this*—indeed.
> *In a time when You may be found ('et metso)*—we have established this, but *'et metso*—it is like that which is written: *Seek YHVH while He can be found [be-himmatso], call to Him while He is near* (Isaiah 55:6; transl. NJPS).
> Another word:
> *In a time when You may be found*—when the rivers flow and pour forth, and the fathers are satisfied and all are blessed.
> *Only that the rushing mighty waters*—what are the *rushing mighty waters*? These are the depths of the springs and rivers. Who will attain them, and who is worthy of drawing near and ascending there?! Therefore it is written: *only that the rushing mighty waters not overtake him*, for they are not worthy and are not able. (Zohar 3:79b)

The experience of watering has a strong erotic valence, as the fluid that descends upon the Companions is the fruit of the divine yearning, love, and intercourse between *Tiferet-Yesod* and *Malkhut*. The kabbalists who know how to penetrate into the divine plenty, and to open themselves up to this plenty, merit the flow of the divine bounty.

The further the bounty descends in the sefirotic structure, from the union of *Ḥokhmah* and *Binah* down below, the more specific the sexual imagery. The river of plenty enters *Yesod*, symbolized by the male genital organ, and from there (the "head of the righteous one"), the seed (the "blessings upon the head of the righteous one") streams into the female, from where the divine bounty spreads forth to all the worlds, including the righteous who stand prepared to join in these moments. The saturation, then, is also participation—indirect yet most intentional—in the climactic moments of ecstasy during divine intercourse.[68] So, for example, we find a zoharic homily in which inner-divine sexual processes and the sexual union between a man and woman are compared and indeed identified:

> Rabbi Yeisa the Younger was in the presence of Rabbi Shim'on. He asked him: "Regarding what is written, *Blessings upon the head of the righteous one*

(Proverbs 10:6), the verse should read, *upon the righteous one*. Why *upon the head of the righteous one?*

He replied, "*Head of the righteous one* is Holy Corona, as has been established.

"Further, *head of the righteous one* is Jacob, who receives blessings and channels them to Righteous One, from where they are flung in every direction, so all worlds are blessed.

"Further, *Blessings upon the head of the righteous one—head of the righteous one* is the name given to the site of head of Covenant, from which bubbling springs gush. Orifice of a flask, pouring wine, is a head. Similarly, *head of the righteous one*—that site flinging springs to female is called *head of the righteous one*. . . .

"Further, one who succeeds in guarding the sign of the holy covenant and enacts the commandments of Torah is called Righteous, so called from his head to his feet. When blessings flow into the world, they settle upon his head—from there subsisting in the world through holy, virtuous sons whom he engenders." . . .

"*I have been young (na'ar) and now I am old. So it is! . . . I have never seen a righteous man forsaken . . . . or his seed begging bread* (Psalms 37:25). What does this mean? When He flings and streams seed, He does not woo the female, since She abides with Him—never parting from Him, prepared for Him. For seed flows only when female is prepared, their mutual desire as one, in single cleaving, inseparable. So He doesn't have to woo Her." (Zohar 1:162a–b; Matt 2004–2007, vol. 2, pp. 404–6)[69]

Delight and Pleasure

In the Zohar, contact with the divine world is described as an experience of delight and pleasure. While it is true that these are not the only sensations in zoharic mystical experience, they are nevertheless far more present than sensations of dread, terror, and fear.

Delight ('oneg)   Whoever ascends among the sefirotic grades and gazes upon the divine attains the experience of delight. The terminology is taken from Isaiah 58:14, "Then you will delight [*tit'anag*] in YHVH; and I will set you astride the heights of the earth, and let you enjoy the heritage of your father Jacob." The book of Isaiah employs this term numerous times, describing the delight as consequent upon human social justice, namely, helping the weak and marginal members of society: the poor, the orphan, and the widow. Such action results also in one's light shining forth from within, and in God listening and responding to one's calls.

In the Zohar, Isaiah 58:14 appears dozens of times, sometimes quoted in full and other times in allusion and paraphrase, but always in the context of the outcome and reward of the kabbalist's labors, for his opening the upper worlds and uniting the separated grades of the divine. The word *az* (then) that begins the verse highlights the idea that the light and delight come as the result of the mystic's service—*then* comes the delight.[70]

In the Bible, delight is connected both with the experience of the divine and with the language of sensual and erotic love, as in "How fair you are, how pleasant! O Love, with all its rapture (*ta'anugim*)!" (Song of Songs 7:7).[71] The authors of the Zohar, who so seamlessly interweave religious and erotic experience, distilled this delight and rapture from the Bible's language and illuminated them with a new light.

In rabbinic literature, delight usually appears in the context of the Sabbath, whose name is Delight,[72] as well as in the context of the sure reward for the righteous in the future in the Garden of Eden, the locus of delight. Thus we read: "[The Assembly of Israel] said before the blessed Holy One: Master of the Universe, on account of the Torah that You gave me, which is called 'the source of life,' I am surely destined to delight in Your light in the future."[73]

In the minor tractates of the Talmud, "delight" appears in contexts associated with laughter and sex (areas addressed by the term *derekh erets*), thereby establishing its semantic field as spanning pleasure and sexuality.[74] In the Jerusalem Talmud, the word *ta'anug* is associated almost exclusively with the experience of anointing with oils and bathing; and it is interesting to note the mystical development of the experience of delight from these activities.[75]

The esoteric work *Sefer Yetsirah* affords a special and exalted place to "delight." In a statement pertaining both to the work's doctrine of language and to its conception of reality, we read: "Twenty-two elemental letters set in a wheel with 231 gates, turning forward and backward. And this is the sign: There is no good higher than delight (*'oneg*), and no evil lower than plague (*ne'ga*)."[76] We can assume that this assertion played a role in the

Zohar's choice of the term "delight" as an image for the highest experience of contact with the divine.

In *Sefer ha-Bahir*, we find the term *ta'anug* connected with mystical experience in the psalms of Habakkuk: "*O YHVH, I have learned of Your renown, I was awed* (Habakkuk 3:2)—About this, Habakkuk said: 'I knew that my prayer was accepted with delight and I also delighted; and when I delighted to a certain place and understood Your renown—I was awed.'"[77]

In *Sefer Ḥasidim* (§ 773), from the circle of the German pietists of the twelfth century, a passage clearly expresses the connection between joy, delight, and pleasure in the experience of mystical contact with the divine:

> When a person is praying and suddenly the joy of the love of God strikes his heart, [you should] know that God wishes to do His will, as is said: *How fair you are, how pleasant! O Love, with all its rapture [ta'anugim]!* (Song of Songs 7:7; transl. NJPS); and it is written: *Then you will delight [tit'anag] in YHVH* (Isaiah 58:14), and *Seek the favor [hit'anag] of YHVH and He will grant you the desires of your heart* (Psalms 37:4), and it is written: *When you seek the favor [tit'anag] of Shaddai, and lift up your face to God, you will pray to Him, and He will listen to you* (Job 22:26–27; transl. NJPS).
>
> If this joy strikes his heart at "Hear our voice" [in the statutory prayer known as the 'Amidah] or before he finishes "May the expressions of my mouth find favor," he should pray as follows:
>
> "May it be Your will that this love always be bound and planted in my heart and in the heart of all my seed," and he should not request anything save the love and desire of God.
>
> If the joy struck his heart at any other time of the day or night, while he is not praying, as long as his heart and soul are rejoicing in the blessed Holy One, he should not speak with anyone—until the joy departs his heart.
>
> As for the prophets—when their soul was bound in great love, their heart was with the blessed Holy One, it was as though they were not in this world, as is said: *What did that madman come to you for? He said to him, "You know the man and his ranting!"* (2 Kings 9:11; transl. NJPS).

Joy and delight are portrayed here as internal ecstatic experiences alone; and as long as the mystic has the divine joy in his heart, he is forbidden from speaking with anyone at all. He must, rather, abide within the experience and pray for the continual presence of divine love in his world. This experience, then, is clearly different from the experience of delight as described in the Zohar.

In Spanish kabbalistic literature preceding the Zohar, the authors frequently employed terms for "delight" and "joy" to describe their experiences.[78] Likewise, Rabbi Abraham Abulafia—a kabbalist connected to the circle of mystics who likely created the Zohar—affords "delight" an exalted status beyond that of comprehension, presenting it as the ultimate end of prophetic experience.[79]

The Zohar's interpretation of "Let your clothes always be white and your head never lack oil" (Ecclesiastes 9:8), focuses on the preconditions for ensuring that the "holy anointing oil" (the supernal divine flow) will pour upon a man's head in this world while it flows upon Shekhinah—"the supernal glory"—in the world of emanation. Anointment with the supernal oil is, in and of itself, a sign of mystical experience generating delight. Only he who fulfills the preconditions for the emergence of the internal divine light established by the book of Isaiah—that is, concern for the poor and feeding the hungry—can attain this experience of anointment with the divine oil:

> *Let your clothes always be white and your head never lack oil* (Ecclesiastes 9:8). Just as the holy anointing oil never ceases [to flow] upon the upper glory from the mystery of the world that is coming, so also with the person whose deeds are always white, that holy anointing oil will never cease [flowing] upon him.
>
> How does a man merit to delight in that supernal delight? At his table. Just as he delights the souls of the poor at his table, as is written: *and satisfy the afflicted soul* (Isaiah 58:10), and after it is written: *You will delight in YHVH,* etc., so too the blessed Holy One saturates him with all those delights of supernal holy anointing oil, which flows out continuously upon that upper glory. (Zohar 2:155a–b)[80]

Although this book focuses on passages from the main corpus of the Zohar, beauty compels me to include a text from *Ra'aya Meheimna*. It describes the delight from the human experience of contact with the infinite dynamism of the emergence of the divine bounty from Eden, and its flow through the river to water both the divine and human garden. In this text, the word *'oneg* (spelled ע-נ-ג) is expounded as an acronym of *'eden* (Eden), *nahar* (river), and *gan* (Garden).

> *And a river (ve-nahar) issues from Eden*—This is ו [*Tiferet*]—[that comes] *to water the garden.*

And a river—this is the central pillar. *Issues from Eden*—this is supernal Mother. *To water the garden*—this is lower Shekhinah.

At that time is said about Moses and Israel: *Then you will delight in YHVH* (Isaiah 58:14), the delight (*'oneg*) that is ע—*'eden*, נ—*nahar*, ג—*gan*; and the verse *Then Moses sang* (Exodus 15:1) will be fulfilled. (Zohar 1:26a)

Pleasure/Pleasantness (No'am)   In the Zohar's description of mystical experience, alongside the concept of "delight" we encounter the concept of "pleasure" or "pleasantness" (*no'am*). Like delight, *no'am* appears in the Bible both in the context of the divine and in the context of love and passion.

The Psalmist describes a quest with which the authors of the Zohar deeply identify: "One thing I ask of YHVH, only that do I seek: to live in the house of YHVH all the days of my life, to gaze upon the pleasantness (*no'am*) of YHVH, to frequent His temple" (Psalms 27:4). The pleasantness in this verse appears as a divine quality capable of being seen by the one seeking to fulfill the singular quest of connecting with God in His house. In another verse in Psalms (90:17), the *no'am* refers to the divine characteristic that the human being seeks to draw down upon himself: "May the favor/pleasantness (*no'am*) of YHVH our God be upon us." Rashi clarifies the meaning of the word *no'am* in this verse as referring to God's "presence (*shekhinato*) and consolation."

As a sense connected with love and desire, *no'am* appears in the Bible in such verses as "Saul and Jonathan, beloved and cherished (*ne'imim*)" (2 Samuel 1:23; transl. NJPS) and "How fair you are, how pleasant (*na'amt*)! O Love with all its rapture!" (Song of Songs 7:7). *No'am* is connected also with happiness, satisfaction, and the absence of strife, as in, "Her ways are pleasant ways, and all her paths, peaceful" (Proverbs 3:17; transl. NJPS) and "Pleasant words are like a honeycomb, sweet to the soul and a cure for the body" (Proverbs 16:24).[81]

In rabbinic literature, the word *no'am* is not employed extensively. It seems that its main use is connected with the description of personal experience, as we saw in the passage from *Sefer Ḥasidim*.

In the Zohar's description of mystical experience, *'oneg* and *no'am* sometimes appear as synonyms, and it is difficult to determine if we are dealing with experiences distinguished by their level of ecstasy or joyful tranquillity. The ways in which *'oneg* and *no'am* are used in Jewish literature preceding the Zohar greatly determine the way in which they are employed in the expression of zoharic mystical experience.

Ecstatic delight and serene, content pleasure both characterize many mystical testimonies in the world's religions. The descriptions of mystical experience recounted by William James in his book on religious experience, and by Jess Hollenback in his comprehensive study on mysticism, frequently employ the terms delight, pleasure, joy, and happiness,[82] even though neither author dedicated a chapter to those senses in their respective books. In Hinduism, especially in texts dealing with the perfection of the soul in order to arrive at the mystical state of union, the term *ananda* appears frequently—denoting a concept quite similar to the referent of the Zohar's *no'am*. This is a complete and satisfying joy or a sense of total happiness.[83]

According to the Zohar, the "pleasantness of YHVH" (*no'am YHVH*) originates above and beyond, within the depths of divinity; it is the liquid quality that trickles into the worlds worthy of its reception.

> *Her ways are ways of pleasantness and all her paths are peace* (Proverbs 3:17). . . . *Her ways are ways of pleasantness* corresponds to what is written, *Who makes a way through the sea* (Isaiah 43:16). For look, wherever in Torah one reads *way*, it is a way open to all, like a road open to every person. So, *her ways*—ways opened by the patriarchs, who dug in the great sea and entered her; those ways open up on every side, in every direction of the world.
>
> This *pleasantness* is the pleasure issuing from the world that is coming, and from the world that is coming all lamps radiate, lights scattering everywhere. That goodness and radiance of the world that is coming, absorbed by the patriarchs, is called *pleasantness*. (Zohar 1:197b; Matt 2004–2007, vol. 3, pp. 209–10, adapted)[84]

In the continuation of this homily, delivered by an anonymous and wondrous Jew who appears in the story, the *no'am* is expounded as a quality of the "world that is coming," whose presence in the world is dependent on a particular intentionality and preparation. The Sabbath is an auspicious time when the divine *ḥesed* (love) and *no'am* abide in the world; and therefore, at the Sabbath's end, when the worlds of *din* (judgment) are aroused once again, man must attune his awareness so as to draw down and receive the supernal pleasantness into this world.

> Alternatively, the world that is coming is called *pleasantness*, and as it arouses, all goodness and joy, all radiance and freedom of the world arouse. . . . When Sabbath departs . . . we should arouse and recite: *May the pleasantness of YHVH our God be upon us* (Psalms 90:17)—supernal pleasantness, joy of all! So, *Her ways are ways of pleasantness.* (Zohar, ibid.; Matt 2004–2007, vol. 3, p. 210, adapted)[85]

As an experience, the *no'am* is associated with many different senses. One of the Zohar's most interesting accounts of the *no'am* describes an experience akin to nourishment, satiety, and fullness, produced as a result of abiding in the presence of God. The Zohar describes this condition as the delight of the experience of eating manna, the divine bread that descends from the heavens. According to this homily, in the future manna will not be ingested by mouth, but rather the soul will be satiated through the very contemplation of the divine pleasantness. While it is true that this description pertains to the soul in the World to Come, the kabbalists of the Zohar, as discussed earlier, have knowledge of the "world that is coming" in this world; and as such, this condition of satiety properly pertains both to the quest and experience of the mystic.

> *By evening you shall know it was YHVH who brought you out from the land of Egypt; and in the morning you shall behold the Presence of YHVH* (Exodus 16:6). . . . Rabbi El'azar taught: The righteous are destined to eat of this manna in the world that is coming.
>
> And if you should ask: In the same manner [as the eating of the manna in the wilderness]?
>
> No! Rather, it shall be of a greater [quality], never before seen in the world.
>
> What is it? It is as we have clarified, as is written: *to gaze upon the pleasantness (no'am) of YHVH, to frequent His temple* (Psalms 27:4); and *No eye has seen, O Elohim, but You* (Isaiah 64:3). (Zohar 2:63a)

Those who experience this divine pleasantness (*no'am* YHVH) become radiant and fruitful.[86] In one of its most beautiful descriptions of the nocturnal delight and the resulting Edenic experience of the soul, the Zohar depicts vision of the divine pleasantness as a revelatory event. This revelation is preceded by the blessed Holy One's inhaling the souls' "fragrance," delighting in them, and pairing them with each other, male and female. The revelation of the divine pleasantness during the nocturnal delight attests to the heightened intimacy between the human being and God.

The vision of the divine pleasantness appears in the Zohar as the clear goal of the soul's quest, which upon beholding the supernal *no'am* is then filled with overflowing joy and light, from which "fruits are made for the world." The Zohar here employs the rabbinic idea that whoever engages in Torah at night, the blessed Holy One emanates a "thread of grace" upon him by day. The thread of grace becomes here an emanation of splendor, through which the male and female souls produce offspring.[87]

> And this is the praise of the ancient *ḥasidim* when they arose at midnight and would arrange their praises and engage Torah. . . . When the blessed Holy One enters at midnight . . . He delights in them and in those words. Afterward, all are arrayed, male and female, and the blessed Holy One— after He inhales [their aroma] and delights in them and in all those words, their secrets of wisdom—is revealed upon them, and they behold that pleasantness (*no'am*) of the YHVH. Then all rejoice with great joy, until their splendor and light radiates forth. And from the emanation of the splendor and light of their joy, fruits are made for the world. (Zohar 3:303a, Tosafot, § 10)

In the section known as *Sava de-Mishpatim*, the old man describes *no'am* as the experience of seeing the crown of King Solomon, which symbolizes the sefirah *Yesod*. This is the only place in the Zohar where the experience of *no'am* is connected with the vision of a particular sefirah.

> *Go forth, O Maidens of Zion, and gaze upon King Solomon, in the crown ('atarah) that his mother gave him on his wedding day, on his day of bliss* (Song of Songs 3:11)—but who can gaze upon King Solomon, the King to whom peace belongs? . . . Regarding what is written: *Go forth, O Maidens of Zion, and gaze upon King Solomon*, it [then] says *in the crown* and not *and the crown*, for whoever gazes upon that corona ('atarah) sees the pleasantness (*no'am*) of the King to whom peace belongs.
> *The crown that his mother gave him*—behold, we have taught: "He called her

daughter, he called her sister, and he called her mother" (Midrash Song of Songs Rabbah 3.2); and She is indeed all of these.

Whosoever contemplates and understands this, understands precious wisdom. (Zohar 2:100b)[88]

We can understand this most erotic of homilies in two ways. According to the first reading, the pleasantness is the experience that accompanies the vision of *Yesod* itself. It is connected here with seeing the divine phallus, or more precisely, seeing its corona ('*atarah*, which also means "crown"), understood to be the female aspect within *Yesod*.

According to the second and more likely reading, the human visionary capacity—including the eye of the imagination and the spirit—is limited and thus is able to contemplate and attain the sefirah *Malkhut* alone. *Malkhut*, the last of the divine powers, is the feminine quality of divinity; and she is the "crown," who is also the mother, the daughter, the sister, and the beloved. The pleasantness, then, is the quality of *Yesod* as seen within *Malkhut* when she is filled with the pleasantness of *Yesod* and *Tiferet*, that is to say, during intercourse.[89] The "Maidens of Zion," which serves here also as an epithet for the kabbalists, are able to go forth and gaze upon the pleasantness of King Solomon (*Yesod*) when it is brimming with the pleasantness of the higher sefirot. They do so "in the crown," namely, through or within the crown (*Malkhut*), which appears here as a containing or reflective vessel through which the pleasantness is experienced.

The pleasantness is described also as the divine quality that descended upon the Israelites at the giving of the Torah, and this special condition of the nation serves as a model for the revelatory experience sought by the Zohar's mystics. According to the Zohar, the light and splendor that illumined Moses' face (Exodus 34:29–30) derived from this divine pleasantness; and Moses' shining face represents the most perfect indwelling of the divine pleasantness in a human being.[90] The desire of the righteous is to see or behold the divine pleasantness, and to be filled with the supernal delight, both of which—according to the following passage—originate in the depths of divinity, in *Atika Kadisha* (The Holy Ancient One). Flowing forth from the world of *Atika Kadisha* are fine, subtle qualities, full of vitality, variously described by the Zohar as pleasantness, manna, and droplets of dew. This bounty fills the world of "heaven" (the sefirah *Tiferet*) and thus, through the mediation of *Tiferet*, the kabbalist experiences the qualities of the higher, unattainable sefirot. Expressed in zoharic language: it is through the divine pleasantness revealed in *Tiferet* (heaven) that the righteous merit to delight "over YHVH" (*le-hit'aneg 'al YHVH*), in the sense of "above YHVH," namely, an experience beyond that of *Tiferet*.[91]

> It has been taught: Rabbi Yitsḥak said: "It is written, *to gaze upon the pleasant-ness of YHVH, to contemplate in His temple* (Psalms 27:4). The desire of the righteous is to see this, and yet you say, *above YHVH* (Isaiah 58:14)!
>
> Rabbi Shim'on replied: "All is one, as implied by what is written, *pleasant-ness of YHVH*—proceeding from the Holy Ancient One to this heaven. The desire of the righteous is certainly so: above heaven. So it is written, *above YHVH*. Happy is the share of one who attains! Surely they are few!" (Zohar 1:219a; Matt 2004–2007, vol. 3, p. 324, adapted)

Sometimes *'oneg* and *no'am* are associated with the experience of being saturated by the flow of the divine river. In the following passage, *no'am* is identified with the divine plenty that flows in the river of the sefirot that issues from the Eden of *Hokhmah*. This *no'am* issuing from the sefirah YHVH can be withheld from the transgressing soul.[92]

> It is written: *that soul shall be cut off from before Me* (Leviticus 22:3). What does it mean: *from before Me?*
>
> This is the world that is coming, where all life abides.
>
> Another word: This is the supernal conduit, the river whose waters never cease. And it is all one. This is the river that carries the delicacies of the world that is coming. And from these supernal delicacies [that soul] will be cut off, from the site of the pleasantness of YHVH, and this is *from before Me*. (Zohar 2:170b)

The *no'am* trickles down from the depths of *Atika Kadisha* and extends into the world of *Tiferet* that, as we have already seen, functions as a kind of mediating dimension (through which the zoharic kabbalist experiences the unseen divinity). In the Zohar's commentary to the Torah portion *Va'ethanan*, a mystic experiences a vision of the upper worlds. In response to his companions' wonder as to how it is that he has seen that about which it is said, "No eye has seen, O YHVH, but You" (Isaiah 64:3), Rabbi Yose, the hero of the story, replies that although there are things that the eye cannot see, one can indeed gaze upon the pleasantness of YHVH.

> But the secret of the matter is in that which is written: *to gaze upon the pleasantness (no'am) of YHVH, to frequent His temple* (Psalms 27:4). And they have clarified this.
>
> *The pleasantness of YHVH*—that which comes from *Atika Kadisha*, and in which the blessed Holy One delights, for that pleasantness flows from *Atika*. (Zohar 3:267b)

In another passage, Rabbi Shim'on expounds the verse from Isaiah "then you will delight in YHVH" as a general description of the mystic's task, whose delight derives from his ability to experience divine dimensions beyond those of *Tiferet*, symbolized again by the tetragrammaton. The mystic delights "over YHVH," literally *al YHVH*, meaning "above and beyond *Tiferet*," beyond those dimensions capable of being expressed in language. The mystic's delight is that of the light, *no'am*, and *'oneg* that come from the undifferentiated divine world of *Keter*, known as *Atik Yomin*:

> Rabbi Hiyya opened, . . . "Happy is the share of one who dwells with the King in His house!"
>
> Rabbi Shim'on said, "Happy is the share of the righteous one who attains what is written: *Then you will delight upon (al) YHVH* (Isaiah 58:14). It is not written *with (im) YHVH*, but rather *above (al) YHVH*. What is *above YHVH*? A place from which above and below are drawn, and toward which they yearn, as is written: *From nothingness (Me-ayin) comes my help* (Psalms 121:1). And similarly: *He reached the Ancient of Days and was brought before Him* (Daniel 7:13). Desire and delight—to gaze upon that splendor of splendor whence issue and stream all those crowns." . . .
>
> Rabbi Abba said, . . . "As for the word spoken by Rabbi Shim'on, so it is, and all is one, as is written: *He reached the Ancient of Days* . . . (Daniel 7:13). All these words ascend to a single place."
>
> Rabbi Abba said to Rabbi Shim'on, "May my Master expound this verse entirely and how we establish it: *Then you will delight upon YHVH, and I will cause you to ride upon the heights of the earth, and feed you the inheritance of your father Jacob* (Isaiah 58:14)."
>
> He replied, "All has been said, for delight and bliss are *above (al) YHVH*, for it is written: *until the Ancient of Days* (Daniel 7:13). (Zohar 2:82b–83a; Matt 2004–2007, vol. 4, pp. 456–59, adapted)[93]

The Zohar's use of *'oneg* and *no'am* as basic vocabulary for mystical experience profoundly impacted upon the language of later Jewish mystics. A particularly beautiful example of influence can be found in the words of Rabbi Abraham Isaac HaKohen Kook:

> How great is my inner struggle,
> My heart is filled with an upward longing,
> I crave that the divine delight (*no'am*)
> Spread through my being,
> Not because I seek its delights (*'oneg*),
> But because this is as it should be.
> Because this is the true state of existence,
> Because this is the true content of life.
> And I am continually astir,
> I cry in my inwardness with a loud voice,
> Give me the light of God,
> The delight of the living God,
> The grandeur of visiting
> The palace of the eternal King . . .
> I am filled with anguish
> And hope for deliverance and for light . . .
> I will delight (*et'anag*) in the pleasantness (*no'am*) of the Lord,
> I shall discern the purity of the ideal will.[94]

Devekut *(Cleaving)*

In the Zohar's language of mystical experience, *devekut* (cleaving) denotes a special state of connection within diverse registers of reality: between the various parts of the divine world; between the people of Israel and the blessed Holy One; and between the human soul and the divine. It is this latter aspect that we explore here.

In the Zohar, the word *devekut* encodes a rich semantic field, starting with the appearances of the verbal root *d-v-k* in the Bible and spanning both Jewish philosophical and mystical literature preceding the writing of the Zohar.[95] In the Bible, *devekut* appears both in the context of the relations between a man and a woman, as well as a description of the ideal relations between the human being and God. In the creation account in Genesis, the paradigmatic relationship between a man and woman is described in the words, "Hence a man leaves his father and mother and cleaves to his wife, so that they become one flesh" (2:24). In cleaving to his wife, the man and the woman become a single entity, with the sexual act rendering them "one flesh." The book of Deuteronomy presents cleaving to God as a commandment: "You must revere your God YHVH: only Him shall you worship, to Him shall you cleave, and by His name shall you swear" (10:20), while portraying the covenant between Israel and God in a similar vein: "You, cleaving to YHVH your God, are alive every one of you today" (4:4; transl. Matt).

Following Neoplatonic thought, the Zohar views *devekut* as the form of the soul's connection with its divine origin. The unique erotic flavor that accompanies such *devekut* in the Zohar is the fruit of the authors' choice to adopt the language of love as the appropriate medium for describing the soul's relationship with God. It is, however, the rich store of experiences in the zoharic authors' consciousness, more than a particular philosophical conception, which shapes the composition's understanding of *devekut*. The central image for *devekut* in the Zohar is that of cleaving to "the body of the King," an image woven around the verse "You, cleaving to YHVH your God, are alive every one of you today," as well as the erotic image of lovemaking from the oft-repeated verse from the Song of Songs, "His left hand beneath my head, his right arm embracing me" (8:3).

The verse "You, cleaving to YHVH your God, are alive every one of you today" is cited dozens of times in the Zohar. It has the stature of a zoharic code verse. Thus its function, over and above its different meanings, is to awaken in the reader a mystical consciousness, whose focus, as we have seen, is contact with the dynamic world of divinity.[96] Like the verse from Isaiah (60:21) "Your people, all of them righteous, will inherit the land forever," this verse appears repeatedly, not only in the body of many homilies but also more prominently—at their beginning and end.[97] Its role is to awaken and remind readers of the good that awaits all who choose to walk in the path of the righteous. Those who "cleave to YHVH" are called "the truly alive," the ones who live the life of God, while in the zoharic context, "inheriting the land" signifies joining the land of life, the sefirah *Malkhut*. These verses serve a programmatic function, indicating the possibility— open to all—of reaching and cleaving to the divine worlds.

Everyone—which in this zoharic passage signifies all (circumcised) Jewish men—has the capacity of attaining the goal of inheriting the land and of meriting the life that comes from God, if only they actualize their righteousness and cleave to God. As in the code verse we examined in the previous chapter ("A river flows from Eden to water the garden"), in these two verses the zoharic authors focus on those words signifying present continuous action: everyone, forever, cleaving, alive, today. The possibilities latent in the mystical way are not only the patrimony of the past or latent in the future; they are possibilities for everyone, forever, here and now.

The verse "You, cleaving to YHVH, etc." addresses a great variety of forms of contact with the divine. Sometimes, *devekut* is interpreted as a cognitive activity, in which case the zoharic word *itdavkuta* means apprehension and understanding,[98] and in this context "alive" signifies the divine gift awaiting those who apprehend God.

Devekut is also interpreted as an expression of shared essence, as in the parent-child relations between God and the people (literally, children) of Israel. It is this *devekut* that enables Israel to be considered "the children of YHVH."[99]

According to the Zohar, the *devekut* or cleaving is to *gufa di-malka* (the body of the King), a term with various meanings.[100] One meaning is the divine itself, the essence of God without His cloaking symbols. Cleaving to the body of the King is connected also with the anthropomorphic, mythic perspective of the Zohar. The sefirot are classically arranged according to the structure of a man's body; and the sefirah *Tiferet* (which signifies the explicit name of God, the tetragrammaton) is "in the image of" the King. Cleaving to the body of the King also indicates connection with the entire sefirotic system, which signifies the "body" of the divine.

"Cleaving to the King" is usually described as the result of man's first cleaving to Shekhinah, the partner of this King, and of the arousal of Shekhinah to cleave to the King. In this way, the human being is able to participate in and cleave to the supernal *devekut*, the union of the divine male and female.[101] We have here, then, a chain of cleaving: Israel cleaves to Shekhinah, then Shekhinah cleaves to the blessed Holy One; and it is through their union that reality is blessed.

At one point, Rabbi Pinḥas suggests to Rashbi and the Companions a contemplative praxis to understand this "mystery" of the connection between the different dimensions of reality with one another. The praxis involves the contemplation of a candle (or lamp) and the different colors of the flame. Then he remarks: "Above them [that is, the people of Israel] glows the candle, lights merging as one, worlds glimmering, above and below in bliss. Then, *And you, cleaving to YHVH your God, are alive every one of you today.*"[102]

According to the Zohar, the covenant of circumcision is the essential precondition for cleaving to the body of the King. Only the circumcised can inherit the female attribute of the divine and thus cleave to the body of the King.[103] The way to cleave to the King is through cleaving to the Torah; and indeed the Companions define themselves as those who endeavor to cleave to the blessed Holy One through the Torah: "Happy are the Companions who engage in Torah day and night, whose companionship is with the blessed Holy One! Of them is written: *You, cleaving to YHVH your God, are alive every one of you today.*"[104] In expounding the word "alive" in that verse, the Zohar interprets *devekut* as the cleaving to the life that defines the divine. The human being yearns to cleave to God, the source of true life, the life of life.[105]

It is applying the knowledge of how to cleave to the King that arouses the divine power above to descend and dwell upon those cleaving below. Expressed differently, it is the act of human cleaving that causes holiness to dwell upon the kabbalist below, meriting him the "life" that comes from the very life of God.[106] The kabbalists (or the righteous) are therefore described as the ones who know the mystery of the cleaving of human will with the divine. As Rabbi Abba says: "Happy is the portion of the righteous who know how to affix their will to the Holy King! Of them is written: *You, cleaving to YHVH your God, are alive every one of you today.*"[107]

Devekut is also the main task of the mystic in prayer. The purpose of prayer is to connect the human being with God and to enable the union of the male and female within divinity.

It is precisely during the peak moments of prayer, when the highly fo-cused worshipper experiences the sacred union in his imagination, that *Tiferet* and *Malkhut* seek to ascend, to soar from the world of man upward to the hidden recesses of *Ein Sof*. It is in these moments that the kabbalists must endeavor to prevent disconnection between the world of man and the world of God. The *devekim*, those who cleave to God, are therefore the ones who guard the intimacy between the divine and the human.

The conception of *devekut* found here is distinct from the *devekut* whose outcome is death by divine kiss, or the soul's ecstatic cleaving with the divine leading to its separation from the body. Here, *devekut* signifies the endeavor to ensure that the divine remain as a stable presence in the world, as in "I held him, I would not let him go" (Song of Songs 3:4), rather than an expression of the soul's soaring upward to cleave with its divine source.

> While [King David] was arraying and arranging his praises for unification he said:
>
> *And You, O YHVH, be not far off* (Psalms 22:20).
>
> *And You, O YHVH*—the mystery of a single union without separation.
>
> *Be not far off*—When She ascends to be crowned by Her husband, and everything is in the upper world, [He] seeks to rise from there to *Ein Sof*, to bind all together, above and beyond; therefore [David says,] *be not far off* to de-part from us, to leave us.
>
> Therefore, when arranging praises, Israel must [be included there and must] cleave to Him from below. For if this glory seeks to ascend, then Israel below hold fast to it. . . . And therefore the prayer is recited in a whisper, like someone confiding a secret to the King. . . . and while he [abides] in the secret with Him, [the King] does not distance himself at all. . . . Because Israel below hold fast to Him and do not allow Him to slip away and leave them. . . .
>
> Therefore we must unite with the blessed Holy One and hold fast to Him, like someone drawing another down from above, so that He will not depart from a person even for an hour. . . . Therefore is written: *You, cleaving to YHVH your God, are alive every one of you today*. (Zohar 2:138b)

Like the entire experiential world of the Zohar, the experience of *deve-kut* is neither singular nor univocal. The different uses of the word *devekut* in the Zohar generated a formulation that recognizes the multi-vocality and diversity of the concept. Hence this anonymous teaching: "The whole time that the blessed Holy One walks, as it were, with Israel, He cleaves [to them] spirit to spirit, and therefore is written: *You, cleaving to YHVH your God*—with all kinds of cleaving, never separated from one another."[108]

In the Zohar's language of mystical experience, *devekut* signifies the unification of the soul with the blessed Holy One, and it is in fact a description of sexual union. This union transpires as a result of the soul's identification with the world of *Malkhut*-Shekhinah and its yearning to cleave to God. The yearning to join and unite between God and the feminine world, associated with both King David and the dimension of the soul, leads first to embracing and ultimately to sexual intercourse: in the words of the Zohar, "a single unification, a single bond." The union of David/ the soul/Shekhinah with the blessed Holy One is described as an experience of being filled with the divine plenty, like spring water sustaining the flocks of reality.

> Rabbi Ḥiyya opened, "*My soul cleaves to You, Your right hand supports me* (Psalms 63:9). One should contemplate this verse.
>
> "*My soul cleaves to You*—for King David constantly conjoined his soul to the blessed Holy One, unconcerned with other, worldly matters, only with joining his soul and aspiration to Him.
>
> "Since he cleaved to Him, He supported him, never abandoning him. From here we learn that when a person comes to cleave to the blessed Holy One, He grasps him, never abandoning him.
>
> "Alternatively, *My soul cleaves to You*—so that his rung would be crowned above. For when that rung cleaves to supernal rungs—ascending with them— the right hand grasps it, raising it, uniting it in single unification, fittingly as is said, *Your right hand will grasp me* (Psalms 139:10), and similarly, *his right hand embracing me* (Song of Songs 2:6). So, *Your right hand supports me*. Once this is grasped by the blessed Holy One, it is written, *His left hand beneath my head, his right hand embracing me* (Song of Songs 2:6)—single unification, single bond, whereupon that rung of his is filled and blessed. When it is filled, all those channels are filled in four directions of the world; all those flocks are watered, each in its own direction." (Zohar 1:163b; Matt 2004–2007, vol. 2, pp. 412–13, reformatted)

Here *devekut* describes the experience of reciprocal holding between the human being and God. When a person's soul cleaves to God, then God cleaves to that person. This is yet another illustration of the central zoharic principle of *it'aruta de-letata* and *it'aruta de-le'ila* (the arousal below and the arousal above), which establishes the arousal of the lower world as a precondition for that of the divine world.

As in the previous passages, the implication is that the purpose of such cleaving is not the complete merging with divinity through ecstatic death, but rather the enhancement of the sense of life without leaving the body. This passage presents an experience of "single unification, single bond" that does not cause the individual soul's dissolution, but rather leads to an experience of being filled with the blessing of the divine plenty that also waters the "flocks"—the various dimensions of reality that come to drink from the divine well.

Kiss, Embrace, and Intercourse

The kiss, the embrace, and sexual intercourse are in fact the different faces of the experience of *devekut*. In the Zohar, the kiss typically describes the desirable experience of the cleaving of spirit to spirit. This "spiritual" cleaving is sometimes understood as more exalted than the *devekut* termed *gufa be-gufa* (body to body). The kiss brings about the unification of the lovers' mouths and the commingling of their spirits. In the section *Midrash ha-Ne'elam*, in one of the most beautiful homilies on "O that he would kiss me with the kisses of his mouth" (Song of Songs 1:2; transl. Matt), the Zohar interprets the word פיהו, *pihu*, "his mouth" (an unusual grammatical form), as signifying the intertwining of both their mouths and their total intermingling at the time of the kiss:

> [O that he would kiss me with the kisses] of his mouth (pihu) (Song of Songs 1:2).
>
> Why does it say *pihu*, it should have said "his mouth" (פיו *piv*)?
>
> Rather, to comprise the two of them as one [for the *hei* signifies what is feminine, in addition to the "masculine" letter *vav*].
>
> *Pihu*—to show that She is ready for Him like a woman who prepares her mouth to receive her husband's kisses, and therefore sometimes it seems as though her mouth is his mouth. (*Zohar Ḥadash*, Song of Songs, 63d)

The kiss between the sefirot *Malkhut* and *Tiferet* is depicted as the stage preceding intercourse. During this kiss, Shekhinah receives the qualities of the kisser. Shekhinah prior to intercourse is "a lily of the Sharon" (Song of Songs 2:1) that is pale on account of her virginity and desire, while "after she has become united with the king, with those kisses," she becomes red and is called "rose of the valleys" (ibid.), as it is written, "His lips are as roses" (ibid. 5:13).

This kiss between *Malkhut* and *Tiferet* is the model for the relationship between human and divine reality, as well as for the mystical connection of the soul with God. The soul (grammatically feminine in Hebrew) is in the image of Shekhinah: she is the female yearning for her lover, and her deepest desire is that he "kiss me with kisses of the mouth." The lips of God are red like a rose, and contact with them through the kiss causes Shekhinah/soul to change, to vary, and to enhance her erotic qualities as she is transformed into the "rose of the valleys."

When the soul identifies with *Malkhut*, then the kiss is between the lips of the mystic (as female) and the lips of God (as male). Sometimes, though, as we have already seen, the gender of the lovers is transformed. The connection between God and Moses, for example, is a connection of mouth-to-mouth kisses, in which Moses' mouth signifies the mouth of the male, and the figure of God to which he cleaves through the kiss is Shekhinah. Speaking "mouth to mouth," as it appears in the Torah (Numbers 12:8), is transformed by the Zohar into a kiss in which the mouths and spirits of the lovers cleave and intertwine.

In the mystical kiss, the rose lips of both male and female divinity drip myrrh into the mouth of the loving and beloved mortal. In the passages discussing *devekut* that we saw earlier, the kiss does not signify ecstatic death—death by divine kiss—but rather an experience that intensifies the vitality of the kissers. The essence of this description of the kiss is mutuality, and the infusion of the kissers' lives into one another.

> The chamber of desire. . . . this is the chamber of Moses. Into this chamber Moses enters with love and he kisses kisses.
>
> In this chamber, *Moses spoke, and God answered him with a voice* (Exodus 19:19), when they cleaved kisses with kisses, this one with that.
>
> About this is written: *Let him kiss me with kisses of his mouth* (Song of Songs 1:2).

There are no kisses of joy and love unless they are conjoined, mouth and mouth, spirit and spirit; then they are saturated with the luxuries of all and with the joy of the supernal light.

Come and see: *Moses spoke*—as is written: *Ah, you are beautiful my darling* (ibid. 1:15); and *Your lips are like a crimson thread* (ibid. 4:3).

And God answered him with a voice—as is written: *And you, my beloved, are beautiful, beautiful indeed* (ibid. 1:16); and *His lips are like lilies, they drip flowing myrrh* (ibid. 5:13). (Zohar 2:253b–254a)

The language of the kiss is particularly appropriate for the Zohar's authors to depict their religious world, as the mouth is after all the most essential organ for fulfilling their spiritual paths and their interpretive endeavors. The words of Torah uttered by their mouths are their world's kisses to God, the object of their love; and if in the course of the kiss, the boundaries between his mouth and her mouth are sometimes blurred, so it is in their worship. This joining of the mouths, the kiss, is a connection of desire and not of judgment, and is the place for the *devekut* of love and the infusing of the spirit.

The kiss is important also in the context of the idea that reality as a whole is suspended from God's lips. According to the Zohar, the entire world originates from the lips of the divine, and it is with this awareness that the mystic wishes to kiss the rose lips of God, whose "mouth is delicacies."

And the lips are entirely red as a rose, as is written: *His lips are like roses* (Song of Songs 5:13)—the lips murmur might, they murmur wisdom. On these lips depend good and evil, life and death. From these lips are suspended the masters of arousal . . . judgment and mercy, and through these lips the mouth is seen when open.

From the breath that emerges from the mouth, myriads upon myriads are adorned, and when it [the breath] expands, the faithful prophets are adorned in it, and they are called the *mouth of YHVH*.

When words emerge from the mouth and are murmured by the lips, they illuminate all the eighteen thousand worlds, until they are all joined as one with eighteen roads and paths—and all await this mouth with a tongue that utters greatness. . . .

And about this is written: *His mouth is delicacies* (Song of Songs 5:16)—delicacies, indeed.

What is *his mouth*? As is written: *As the mouth tastes food* (Job 34:3).

And all of him is delightful—fire and water. . . . His mouth is inscribed with letters. . . . Happy is the portion of the one who is careful with the sweetness of the King and tastes Him as is appropriate! About this is written: *Taste and see that YHVH is good* (Psalms 34:9). (Zohar 3:295b, *Idra Zuta*)

The mystic is not to "enter the sanctuary" at any time or in any manner as he pleases (Leviticus 16:2), but rather he must prepare himself and cautiously approach the delights of the King's mouth. The world of mystical speech is in fact the intertwining of the mouth of the mystic with the delights of the divine mouth.

The sweetness of the kiss is connected in the exegetical tradition both with eros and with ecstatic death.[109] Death by kiss—death "by the mouth of God"—is considered a most desirable way of leaving the world.[110] Interestingly, in the Zohar we do not find many references to the kiss in the context of death, yet in one such passage we find the promise that he whose soul leaves the world with a kiss will cleave to the divine forever.

> The Assembly of Israel says: *Let him kiss me with kisses of his mouth* (Song of Songs 1:2). Why does it say *Let him kiss me*? It should have said "Let him love me!" Why *Let him kiss me*? We have taught as follows:
> What are kisses? The cleaving of spirit to spirit, and therefore the kiss is with the mouth, for the mouth is the outlet and source of the spirit. Therefore kisses are with the mouth, with love; and the spirits cleave to one another and they are not parted.
> And therefore, whoever's soul departs with a kiss, cleaves to another spirit, to a spirit that never leaves him. And this is called a kiss; and about this the Assembly of Israel says: *Let him kiss me with kisses of his mouth*, to cleave spirit to spirit, never parting. . . .
> *Then Jacob kissed Rachel and broke into tears* (Genesis 29:11). Why did he weep? Because his heart could not withstand the cleaving of the spirit, and he wept. . . . Whoever kisses with love conjoins spirit to spirit with the cleaving of love. (Zohar 2:124b)

The cleaving of spirit is liable to bring about an extreme and intense emotional response, so extreme that it borders on death. Here, Jacob weeps in response to his kiss with Rachel, a response that appears in many descriptions of intense religious emotion in the Zohar.[111]

Death by kiss as signifying ecstatic, mystical death appears at the end of the *Idra Rabba*. While the ten companions assemble with Rabbi Shim'on for this unique gathering, only the teacher and seven disciples emerge. Three of the Companions die during the Idra; the revelation of mysteries, or the intensity of intimacy with the divine, leads to the final separation of their souls from their bodies.

It is precisely here, at this pivotal event, that we should pay close attention to the Zohar's ambivalent stance regarding ecstatic death by divine kiss. The Zohar oscillates between polar views of such mystical death: positively, as a peerless mark of praiseworthiness and as a theurgic act affecting unification in the upper worlds; versus negatively, as a punishment for the over-disclosure of mysteries and secrets.[112]

> Before they left that threshing place, Rabbi Yose son of Jacob, Rabbi Ḥizkiyah and Rabbi Yeisa died. The Comrades saw holy angels carrying them off in a canopy. Rabbi Shim'on said a word and they settled down. He cried and said: Perhaps God forbid, a decree has been issued for us to be punished because through us has been revealed something not revealed since the day Moses stood on Mt Sinai?! . . .
>
> He heard a voice: Happy are you, Rabbi Shim'on. Happy is your portion! Happy are the Companions who stand with you! For something not revealed to all the powers above has been revealed to you!
>
> But come and see what is written: *At the cost of his firstborn, he shall lay its foundations; at the cost of his youngest, he shall set up its gates* (Joshua 6:26). All the more so, for by intense desire, their souls joined the Divine the moment they were taken. . . . While the souls of these ones were being sweetened with those words, their souls departed by a kiss and were bound in that canopy. The angels took them away and lifted them above. (Zohar 3:144a–b; Matt 1983, pp. 167–68)

While death by kiss is indeed understood here as a mark of distinction, the Zohar generally favors kisses of love and affection that bear the mark of life in this world, rather than the wish for ecstatic death by the divine kiss that plucks mortals from the world.

Altered Sense of Time

Another expression of mystical experience in the Zohar is that the sense of time differs from that of ordinary wakefulness. Numerous passages mention a loss of the sense of time during mystical experience: "they did not know if it was day or night." This atemporal (or meta-temporal) condition is depicted as accompanying ecstatic experience, and it marks an experience as extraordinary.

The origins of this formulation are found in the prophet Zechariah's words about the time of the redemption. He describes the "day of YHVH" as one that is "neither day nor night" (Zechariah 14:7).[113] In rabbinic literature, in the story that recounts Rabbi Eli'ezer ben Hyrcanus' initiation as a *talmid ḥakham* (sage), his first public exposition is characterized by quintessentially revelatory language: "Rabbi Eli'ezer was sitting and expounding matters greater than those revealed to Moses at Sinai, and his face was shining like the light of the sun, and his radiance went forth like the radiance of Moses; and no one knew if it was day or night."[114]

In the story of the Old Man of *Mishpatim*, we encounter the most widespread formulation of the paradoxical and indeterminable element of mystical experience expressed in the words "they did not know if it was day or night." Here, however, owing to the Companions' profound identification with the old man's teaching, we find narrated an even more acute formulation: "He was silent for a moment. The Companions were amazed; they did not know if it was day or night, if they were really there or not."[115] This conveys their loss of the sense of time, accompanied also by their loss of certainty regarding their very existence. The description of the Companions' experience as a paradoxical state is found as well in other places that seek to convey the difference between intense, religious experience and the more prosaic experiences of human life.[116]

The following passage describes the loss of the sense of time as part of a description of a revelatory experience similar to that of Mt. Sinai, experienced by Rabbi Shim'on and his son El'azar in the story of Rabbi Ḥiyya's initiation as a member of Rabbi Shim'on's circle:

> Rabbi Shim'on sat down, and his son Rabbi El'azar stood and expounded words of mysteries of wisdom; and his face shone like the sun, and his words spread out and soared in the firmament. They sat for two days and did not eat or drink, not knowing whether it was day or night. When they left, they realized that two days had passed—and that they had not eaten a thing. (Zohar 2:15a)[117]

In the continuation of the story, Rashbi expounds another verse as being about this experience:"And he was there with YHVH forty days and forty nights" (Exodus 34:28).[118]

The power of the intimate encounter between the human being and God alters (or perhaps even annuls) the sense of time. It offers instead an experience of atemporality and eternity. Alongside the amplification of certain senses, like vision and hearing, there is also the fluidity in the sense of time and an altered sense of light.[119]

In another story, a wondrous character expounds the difference between the prophecy of Moses and that of the other prophets. The lower grades of prophecy are characterized by physical or mental change or the departure from the human domain, whereas Moses' prophecy is distinguished by his capacity to stand before the divine, face-to-face, while remaining himself.

> With many honored and supernal rungs is Moses the faithful prophet distinguished from the other prophets of the world. . . . Face-to-face Moses raises his head, without fear he lifts his face and contemplates the splendor of the supernal glory; and his face and his mind did not change like the other prophets. For when they sought to contemplate, they departed from their domain and their minds, and the splendor of their face changed, and they knew nothing at all of this world. (Zohar 3:268b–269a)

The sense of time pertains to the knowledge "of this world," and its disappearance attests to the departure from the reality of *hai 'alma* (this world) to other dimensions of being.[120]

Fragrance

Reality in the world of the Zohar is suffused with fragrances:

- One's good deeds in this world produce pleasant perfumes for one's astral garment in the Garden of Eden.[121]
- The souls of human beings that ascend nightly to the Lower Garden of Eden bestow upon it the fragrance of their deeds, and they take in return the perfumes of that celestial realm.[122]
- Following his midrashic representation, the Zohar depicts the patriarch Jacob as bearing the fragrance of the Garden of Eden with him wherever he goes.

- Similarly, as the "man of God" (*Ish ha-Elohim*) the prophet Elisha also emits this Edenic fragrance from his body. It is because of this fragrance that the Shunammite woman is able to identify him as a messenger of the divine.[123]
- The Assembly of Israel, Shekhinah, is described as a fragrant field, a perfumed flower bed.[124]

Because of its ability to evoke a strong sensual experience without a physical presence, the "spirituality" of the sense of smell is particularly favored by the Zohar's authors. The pleasing aroma of the sacrifices, the incense, and indeed the deeds of human beings ascend to, and are inhaled by, God's nose—and they arouse Him to action.[125] In the description of God's nightly delight with the souls of the righteous in the Lower Garden of Eden, the quintessential activity is without a doubt the inhaling of the fragrance of the souls of the righteous and their *ḥiddushei Torah* (innovations of Torah).[126]

In extraordinary states of consciousness, as in the story of the Companions' celestial journey in the unit *Rav Metivta*, smell functions as a means of identifying a person's spiritual level.[127] And at the end of the *Idra Rabba*, fragrant aromas ascend in response to the Companions' mystical experience:

> They rose and walked on. Wherever they looked aromas arose.
>   Rabbi Shim'on said: This proves that the world is being blessed because of us!
>   Everyone's face shone, and human beings could not look at them. (Zohar 3:144b, *Idra Rabba*; Matt 1983, p. 168)

This description is both a paraphrase and a *tikkun* (healing) for the description of Rabbi Shim'on and Rabbi El'azar's two departures from their cave as recounted in the Babylonian Talmud.[128] In the talmudic account, upon first leaving the cave, both Rabbi Shim'on and his son are filled with anger and disdain toward people who engage in matters of this world (rather than Torah and the World to Come), and thus everything upon which the two sages cast their gaze is immediately burned. Here, however, upon leaving the great assembly, wherever they looked, aromas arose.

Indeed, perhaps the ascent of those aromas is actually a continuation of the talmudic story of their second departure from the cave, whereupon Rabbi Shim'on becomes a healing agent in the world. Although the faces of all who departed from the great assembly shone with a great light so that none could look upon them, this, it should be stressed, is not a destructive presence, but rather a force bestowing blessings upon the world. The fragrant aromas that fill the world as the consequence of mystical experience are testimony to the infusion of the divine reality into the human domain.

Fire

In various passages, the act of learning and expounding creates, at its peak, the appearance of fire surrounding the Companions. The fire that descends from heaven, like the altered sense of time, confirms the mystical experience and validates the connection between the human being and God.[129] The description of the descent of the heavenly fire into human reality usually resembles the descriptions of mystical experience in rabbinic literature. According to the Talmud, fire surrounds Rabban Yoḥanan ben Zakkai and his student, Rabbi El'azar ben Arakh, who together sit and expound *Ma'aseh Merkavah* (the Chariot Episode): "Rabbi El'azar ben Arakh immediately began expounding *Ma'aseh Merkavah*, and fire descended from heaven and surrounded all the trees in the field. They all opened and uttered song."[130]

We find this same fire in the story about the *tanna* Shim'on ben Azzai, who would engage the biblical text while fire burned around him. The fire is an expression of the joy of the words of Torah in their being restored to their original essence, as on the day they were given at Sinai:

> Ben Azzai was sitting and interpreting, and fire was all around him. They said to him, "Perhaps you are engaging in the inner rooms of the Chariot?" He said to them, "No, I was sitting and stringing the words of the Torah, and the words of the Torah to the Prophets, and the Prophets to the Writings; and the words of Torah were as joyful as on the day they were given from Sinai. Were they not originally given in fire—as is written: *And the mountain was burning with fire* (Deuteronomy 4:11)?"[131]

In moments of ecstatic experience in the Zohar, this fire returns and descends upon the Companions. Thus on the occasion of the Idra Rabba and also during the Idra Zuta, the Companions experience the divine fire: "For we are sitting in supernal holiness, supernal fire surrounds us."[132] Similarly, at the exegetical climax of another story:

> While he was speaking with them, fire came and surrounded him and they sat outside. They heard a certain voice that said: "O Holy One, *the King has brought me into his chambers* (Song of Songs 1:4), in all those rooms of old countenance. . . . when they saw this, they trembled and great terror descended upon them. They said: We are not worthy of this, let us go out from here. . . . They sat there the whole day and could not see him. (Zohar 1:90a)

In the tale of Kfar Tarsha as well, at the climax of the collective mystical experience, divine fire descends and surrounds the Companions. The participants' mystical expositions penetrate the divine world, drawing down some of its qualities upon the assembled mystics.[133]

The descent of heavenly fire bestows great sanctity and marks the mystical experience being described as part of the ultimate and collective mystical experience of the giving of the Torah at Mt. Sinai. The experience of fire has the quality of the experience of Sinai: it comprises the revelation and cognition of a new face of the divine.

Radiant Face

Another phenomenon accompanying mystical experience in the Zohar is the radiant face. The origin of this image is, of course, the biblical description of Moses' descent from the mountain after his face-to-face encounter with God,[134] as well as the desire to have God "shine His countenance" upon us, as in the priestly blessing ("May YHVH shine His face upon you").[135]

In rabbinic literature, Moses is portrayed as the model—whether for a prophet or a sage—of the perfect human being. He is radiant with the power of the divine light and fire with which he has come into contact. Of the priest Pinḥas, Rabbi Shim'on likewise said: "When the holy spirit descended upon Pinḥas, his face shone like a torch."[136] The *Heikhalot* literature is replete with descriptions of a man's transformation into light and fire in situations of great intimacy with the divine.[137]

In the ancient story recounting Rabbi Eli'ezer the Great's first public exposition, which we saw earlier, we noted that his face is explicitly compared with that of Moses: "Rabbi Eli'ezer was sitting and expounding matters greater than those revealed to Moses at Sinai, and his face was shining like the light of the sun, and his radiance went forth like the radiance of Moses; and no one knew if it was day or night."[138] This story places the generation of the sages on par with that of Moses and his generation, or perhaps even higher than them. Rabbi Eli'ezer is transformed from a well into a flowing spring; his face radiates like Moses—yet unlike Moses, his words are all innovations and not merely the transmission of words revealed. *Ḥiddushei Torah* (innovations in matters of Torah) generate an acute transformation both in the expounder and in his surroundings. The light that radiates from Rabbi Eli'ezer annuls ordinary time, measured by the changing light of the luminaries between day and night. It gives his exposition an atemporal quality. Such comparative reflexivity is found frequently in the Zohar as well.

This rabbinic story about Rabbi Eli'ezer serves as a model for the Zohar's protagonists and their innovative power. As we have already seen in our discussion of the figure of Rabbi Shim'on bar Yoḥai (Chapter 1), his radiant face during the Idra Rabba represents one of the peak moments in all zoharic literature. His awareness that his face is indeed shining is one of the signs of his superiority over Moses, and it characterizes the zoharic worldview, which places great value in mystical experience that maintains a high degree of reflexivity.

The zoharic expounder generates, in his own place and in his own time, an event of *Matan Torah* (the Giving of the Torah). The newly innovated words of Torah rejoice in their own revelation; and the light of innovation shines upon those who produced them. In the story of Kfar Tarsha, anonymous protagonists take part in a collective endeavor to innovate words of Torah, which leads ultimately to their enjoying a collective mystical experience. Rabbi Abba, who is present at the event and later recounts it, attains an experience of radiance: "So it was, for that day the Companions saw the face of *Shekhinah* and were encompassed by fire. Rabbi Abba's face blazed in fire from rapture of Torah."[139]

The "lighting up" of the face (*he'arat panim*) is a more moderate phenomenon than the "radiant" face (*krinat ha-panim*). In rabbinic literature, the lighting up of the face appears in the context of learning something new in Torah,[140] based on the verse from Ecclesiastes (8:1), "A man's wisdom lights up his face." In the Zohar, facial illumination appears in the context of unmistakable mystical experience. So, for example, in the story about Rabbi El'azar son of Rabbi Shim'on, we find: "Rabbi Shim'on sat down, and his son Rabbi El'azar stood and expounded words of mysteries of wisdom; and his face lit up like the sun, and his words spread out and soared in the firmament."[141]

In a number of places, the "lighting up" of the face appears following a vision (or the reception of knowledge) from the upper worlds, as this phenomenon is connected with the composition's quest to shine "like the radiance of the sky."[142] In the unit *Midrash ha-Ne'elam*, in the portion *Vayetse*, we read about Rabbi Abba who, while asleep, experiences the revelation of mysteries such that his face begins to shine while his companion Rabbi Yose is seated beside him:

> He saw that Rabbi Abba's face had become redder and that he was smiling, and he saw a great light in the house.
> Rabbi Yose said: This means that Shekhinah is here.
> He lowered his eyes and sat there until dawn broke and light illuminated the house. Before he raised his eyes, he saw the morning and the house became dark.
> Rabbi Abba awoke and his face was shining and his eyes were smiling.
> Rabbi Yose held onto him.
> Rabbi Abba said: I know what you seek. By your life! I have seen supernal mysteries, and when the Master of the Countenance took hold of my soul, he raised it to great and supernal rooms, and it beheld the souls of the other righteous who ascend there. . . . and I saw my [interpretations of] Torah, which was lying there—heaps and heaps like a huge tower—and therefore I am rejoicing in my portion, and my eyes are smiling. (*Zohar Ḥadash, Vayetse*, 28b)[143]

In the Zohar's commentary on the Torah portion *Va'ethanan*, it is Rabbi Yose who this time sees the upper worlds while lying prostrate and asleep.

Although, as he attests, he does not have permission to relay what he saw, his vision causes his face to shine.

> One day Rabbi Yose fell ill. Rabbi Abba, Rabbi Yehudah, and Rabbi Yitshak went to see him; and they saw him lying on his face asleep. They sat down. When he awoke, they saw that his face was smiling.
>
> Rabbi Abba said to him: Have you seen some new thing?
>
> He said to him: Certainly. For just now, my soul arose and saw the glory of those who have sacrificed themselves for the sanctity of their Master. . . . and the blessed Holy One delights in them. And I have seen what I am not permitted to tell. . . . My soul and my heart were illuminated with what I saw, and therefore my face is smiling. (Zohar 3:267a–b)[144]

General Characteristics of Zoharic
Mystical Experience

In the previous chapter, we examined the components comprising mystical experience in the Zohar. Each component—radiance, saturation, delight, cleaving, etc.—affords a unique perspective in understanding mystical experience in the Zohar. Having analyzed these experiential components in their own terms, we seek now to determine the shared contours that produce the special quality of zoharic mystical experience. That is, we seek to discover the appropriate language for describing mystical experience in the Zohar as a whole.

The Mystical Wave

Repeated and sustained reading of those Zohar texts describing mystical experience has brought into sharp relief a form of mysticism that, despite its connection with earlier mystical systems prevalent in its own environs, nevertheless stands as unique.

In order to extract a general structure from those passages, I employ the term "experiential wave." It is not a mystical world at whose center stands a clearly defined ladder of ascension. Nor is it a mystical world that outlines a marked path with well-known stations, leading the practitioner to a particular and well-known end. Rather, the zoharic wave begins with the unique contemplation of biblical verses, undertaken with a special intention. Amid the exegetical process, in which the verses are expounded by different speakers, this contemplation intensifies. The accumulated tension generates moments of mystical ecstasy—moments of insight, innovation, exaltation of the soul, powerful emotional responses, and sometimes even the experience of contact with the divine world. After these peak moments there follows a conscious closure, a quieting and sealing of the experience. In many instances, the experiential wave is sealed with a general statement about the people of Israel, God, or the Companions.

The wave metaphor is fitting for the subject of our inquiry, whether by "wave" we imagine water in the world's oceans and rivers, or whether the reference is to the erotic and sexual dynamic in the "oceans and rivers" of human senses and emotions. In any case, a crucial consideration in the choice of this model is the wave's dynamism: the calm surface, the slow rising of the wave, the peak, and then the subsequent calm, all in continuous movement. However, just as the ocean contains eddies, rips, and ripples that alter the general wave pattern, so the mystical wave in the Zohar appears with an array of qualities within the ocean of the Companions' consciousness.

The ideas and concepts of the French philosopher Henri Bergson were most instructive in my attempt to articulate the special flavor of zoharic mysticism. Bergson speaks of true or ultimate reality as the *durée* (duration).[1] According to Bergson, the *durée* is identical with the "deep self" and perhaps also with God. The dynamic foundation of this *durée* is flowing time, this flow stemming from a vital internal movement that he terms the *élan vital* (vital impetus).[2]

Bergson argues that there are two ways to comprehend reality: the first mode of knowing is that of *analysis*, which seeks to break things down into component parts that are then described in well-known terms. The second mode is *intuition*, a form of "sympathy whereby one carries oneself into the interior of an object to coincide with what is unique and therefore inexpressible in it."[3] Intuition is able to accomplish what reason and rationality cannot, namely, it enables direct, unmediated apprehension of reality as the *durée* of consciousness.

Intuition, says Bergson, can apprehend reality in such a way only when liberated from the shackles of rational cognition.[4] He sought to demonstrate that through intuitive empathy, it is indeed possible to discover absolute reality, in all its splendor, without the distortions imposed by reason's practical and functional considerations.

Intuition is man's tool for achieving contact with the *élan vital* (the eternal, creative font of existence) and with the divine impulse in evolution. Intuition enables one to see things "from the inside," to integrate with the time-dimension of the object of contemplation and thereby penetrate into the grand, creative flow of life emerging from and generated by the divine power: "Then by the sympathetic communication which is established between us and the rest of the living, by the expansion of our consciousness which it brings about, it introduces us into life's own domain, which is reciprocal interpretation, endlessly continued creation."[5]

For Bergson, intuition is an act of identification with the time of the object, and he sees intuition as a developed instinct that has self-consciousness and whose manifestations can be processed and evaluated by the mind.

> These fleeting intuitions, which light up their object only at distant intervals, philosophy ought to seize, first to sustain them, then to expand them and so unite them together. The more it advances in this work, the more will it perceive that intuition is mind itself, and in a certain sense, life itself.[6]

The heroes of the Zohar are, to borrow Bergson's terminology, masters of intuition. Their mystical experience traces an arc (or we might say: a wave) from their initial spiritual, empathic listening to the rustling of divinity within reality; to their descent (or ascent) into the divine, which for them constitutes ultimate being; and to their subsequent return to the world of reason and speech.[7] They seek to recount and describe that which they discover in the oceans and rivers of divinity, and thereby rectify and illuminate finite, physical reality and the world of reason and speech.

We have already explored the zoharic protagonists' intensive engagement with the consciousness of the divine river that flows from Eden to water reality. This river is, as we have seen, the object of their deepest quest, and for the Zohar's heroes constitutes the divine *durée*, continuously flowing within all dimensions of reality—physical, emotional, and linguistic—as well as in the dimensions of their own consciousness. It is with this river that they seek to connect, and within its flow that they create their waves.[8]

Within the Zohar's experiential wave, including during peak moments of mystical experience, the mystic practitioner generally does not lose his individual or personal human identity. Even in rare and precious moments of revelation, or of contact with the divine presence, the duality (however soft) between man and God, between the lover and the beloved, remains intact. To be sure, there is cleaving (*devekut*) in the Zohar: the divine spirit within a man cleaves to God's spirit, and such cleaving of spirit to spirit is described as a kiss. Even so, the Zohar's protagonists do not disappear in the divine light, nor do they drown in the divine river that flows from Eden. Rather, they bathe and soak in that river—and even expound creatively as a result of their contact with it.

Zoharic mystical experience is essentially an experience of *participation* (communion) rather than *unification*. Given the erotic meta-structure that underpins zoharic mysticism, however, we do indeed find in the Companions' mystical experience moments of intermingling and unification; yet these moments are only part of the zoharic mystical enterprise, part of the love-act in its entirety.

What remains now is to find the appropriate terminology for the peak experiences described by the Zohar. Let us test the suitability of the concept "ecstasy" for these experiences.

Ecstasy

The concept "ecstasy" has been defined and employed in a great variety of ways both in the research of mystical phenomena in general and in Jewish mysticism in particular.[9] Arvind Sharma defines ecstasy as a heightened state in which a person experiences himself as outside himself or beyond himself.[10] The experience can be of being penetrated, and taken hold of, by an external force. Or it can be an experience of the exaltation of the soul and its ascent from its usual residence in the body, as in the original meaning of the Greek word *ekstasis*—standing outside.

Sharma cites Mircea Eliade's essentialist approach to ecstasy. Eliade claims that ecstasy is a condition of the human being *qua* human being, and consequently, his research focuses on ecstasy as a human phenomenon and not, for example, as an historical phenomenon. According to this view, the ecstatic experience itself is universal, while its contours and the meaning bestowed upon this experience are culturally and historically determined.

Sharma discerns among the history of the world's religions two kinds of ecstasy: the ecstasy of communion, in which one who takes part in the divine still experiences herself as a separate and individual entity; and the ecstasy of union, characterized by an experience of true merging with the divine.

Ramakrishna, the great Indian Tantric teacher of the nineteenth century, describes the difference between these two kinds of mystical ecstasy as the difference between "tasting sugar," the focus of the Bhakta devotee, and "becoming sugar," the deep desire of the yogi seeking the unification of Advaita. Significantly, Ramakrishna does not claim that these two definitions are mutually exclusive.[11]

The experience of ecstasy and techniques for attaining this state have merited special and detailed attention in most of the world's religions. As an experience of the soul's flight from the body, ecstasy can manifest through dramatic external movements or through a profound quieting, nearly unto death, of the physical body.

In the context of research into Jewish mysticism, Gershom Scholem distinguished between the ecstatic and theosophical trends in Kabbalah.[12] Scholem established that these two approaches produced different "schools." He added that despite the differences between them, these two mystical phenomena properly belong alongside one another, insofar as only an understanding of both enables us to produce a comprehensive picture of Jewish mysticism in Spain in the thirteenth century. In his chapter on the Kabbalah of Rabbi Abraham Abulafia, Scholem discussed the definition of ecstasy as well as its suitability as a description or name for that mystical school. In his view, Abulafian ecstasy does not involve the intoxication of the senses, but rather is a state that appears suddenly, albeit after the structured preparation of the body and the soul in order to receive the divine bounty.[13]

More recently, Moshe Idel has researched, developed, and refined the distinctions between the trends he terms "theosophical-theurgical" and "ecstatic," in an effort to define phenomenologically the vectors of Jewish mysticism across the ages. The theosophical-theurgical trend, he writes,

> encompasses two central subjects: theosophy—a theory of the elaborate structure of the divine world—and the ritualistic and experiential way of relating to the divinity in order to induce a state of harmony. This is a highly theocentric form of religiousness that, while not ignoring the needs of the human being, tends to conceive of religious perfection as instrumental for exerting effective influence on high. On the other hand, ecstatic Kabbalah is highly anthropocentric, envisioning the mystical experience of the individual as itself the *summum bonum*, regardless of the possible impact of this mystical status on the inner harmony of the divine.[14]

Idel has simultaneously explored the ecstasy of mystical experience and its general characteristics, as well as the historical and literary phenomena of the ecstatic Kabbalah, embodied in figures like Abraham Abulafia. Idel's conclusions have generated a particularly fruitful exchange among Kabbalah scholars.

Meanwhile, Elliot Wolfson has highlighted the impossibility of separating theory from praxis, and gnosis from ecstasy, in the mystical world of the Zohar. He has emphasized the organic connection between theurgy and ecstasy.[15] In fact, he seeks to evaluate anew Scholem's original division of the theurgic and ecstatic schools in Kabbalah, as well as Idel's suggestion that we distinguish phenomenologically between theosophical-theurgical trends and ecstatic trends.

Wolfson has focused on the religious phenomenon of ecstasy in zoharic texts in order to demonstrate that the sharp dichotomy between the two schools does not satisfactorily explain at the experiential level the shared and different features of these two trends. He therefore suggests that if we isolate the ecstatic element and study it as a phenomenon in itself, we will find much in common between certain experiences described in zoharic texts and experiences characteristic of the trend termed by scholars the ecstatic Kabbalah.

It is, then, important to distinguish between the use of the term "ecstasy" to refer to an experience (or as a characteristic of a particular kind of experience) and its use to denote a unique historical, religious phenomenon. In his research, Wolfson speaks of ecstasy in the former sense of religious experience, more than in reference to the historical phenomenon of the prophetic Kabbalah of Abraham Abulafia.

In her research into the prophetic-ecstatic patterns of the earliest kabbalists, Haviva Pedaya has shown that in the contours of their experiential-religious continuum, ecstasy and theurgy actually appear as two attitudes. The first leads to an extreme personal pleasure, while the second leads to an experience of influence on high. Significantly, these two modes are sometimes integrated with one another. It should be noted that Pedaya explored the experiential-ecstatic aspects of kabbalists belonging, according to Idel's classification, to the theosophical-theurgical stream.[16]

In seeking to understand the mysticism described in the Zohar, we must address the degree of suitability between the mystical-experiential world it describes and the model suggested by Idel. Yet before doing so, let us recall some important points about models in general and this model in particular.

Models furnish us with outlines as well as content for religious-mystical phenomena, in order to enable the latter's comparison and classification. While the model does not ignore the unique aspects of religious phenomena, it focuses on the general and basic structures that characterize the distinct phenomena, and the structures of consciousness that in turn characterize them. The model is predicated on abstraction; its language is not that of the phenomenon that it seeks to explain.

We must therefore be attentive to the degree of resonance or discord between the theoretical terminology and the internal language of the phenomena examined: the model is conceptual and analytical, which we must bear in mind as we apply it to the zoharic material, which is anti-didactic and non-analytical.

In the Zohar, no one guides the student in an organized, structured manner into the orchard of divinity or into the divine sefirot. Didactic systematization is foreign to this composition's spirit. The Zohar leaves to other kabbalistic compositions the detailed and highly ordered description, classification, and cataloging of the map of the divine world—including the defined paths to enter it. The spirit of the composition tends rather to poetic, mythic, imaginative, experiential, and mystical forms of expression. Thus we do not find in the Zohar conceptual analyses of different mystical systems—as we find, for example, in the writings of Abraham Abulafia or in the systematic writings of the "theosophical" kabbalists.[17]

At first glance, the place of zoharic mysticism would seem to be firmly in the "theosophical-theurgical" stream. Close analysis of the text, however, reveals that in terms of the way the composition presents itself and de-scribes religious-mystical experience, it is in fact very difficult to distinguish between theurgy and ecstasy (in the sense of the desire to attain a powerful, personal, and unmediated experience of the holy), as they are interlaced one with another.

What if we adopt a broader definition of ecstasy? Let us say that it refers to an extreme deviation from the perception of reality as experienced in ordinary states of wakefulness by consciousness, the body, the senses, and the emotion. It can be experienced either as a terrifying or pleasurable depar-ture from the "human domain."[18] If so, then the Zohar documents many such events.[19] In moments of this kind of ecstasy, the Zohar's protagonists experience a state of atemporality, accompanied by the dramatic enhance-ment of certain senses, and also by a mythical-mystical connection with different divine grades.

It should be emphasized that ecstasy is but one component—even if the peak component—of the total course of the zoharic mystical wave. In zo-haric mysticism, theurgic ends serve as the vehicle for ecstatic experiences, while the ecstatic quest and the ecstatic experience serve theurgic ends.

In contemplating the Zohar's heroes and their religious practice, it emerges that they do indeed fit Idel's definition of the theosophical-theurgical mystic. They engage in Torah in order to recognize and behold,

in a more daring way, the divine world, and as such they are faithful theoso-
phists. Such knowledge serves as a tool enabling them, through their mystical worship, to balance and rectify the inner divine world, and as such they
are quintessential theurgists.

The endeavor is theurgic; yet, as Idel himself has discerned, it is not understood in material terms, but rather in terms of the experience of contact
between the divine and the human. The deep desire of the Zohar's protagonists in rectifying the divine world is to bring about the condition in which
the divine bounty flows and pours forth its goodness and blessings upon
the human world. Thus their mystical service is of the "ascent for the sake
of descent" kind, as Haviva Pedaya has termed the mystical worship of the
earliest kabbalists.[20]

In addition to all these characteristics, however, there can be no doubt
that the heroes of the Zohar also yearn with all their might for a powerful,
personal, religious experience, for an unmediated connection with divinity—"to behold the *no'am* of YHVH," to participate in the divine delight,
to be illuminated by the light of God, and to take pleasure in its splendor—
and thus we find among them clear ecstatic character traits. The zoharic
world, then, cannot be easily defined or placed solely in the theurgic or
ecstatic side of the mystic field.

Within the zoharic circle's exegetical act, which as we have seen constitutes its central vehicle for generating mystical experience, we frequently
find moments of ecstasy. There is no doubt that these are moments of contact and connection between the speaker's soul and the objects of her love—
Torah and God. From a theurgic vantage, these are the ideal moments for
human action on the world of divinity; the meta-temporal moments in
which every gesture, word, and insight is brimming with its latent potential;
the moments that produce the *mayin nukbin* (female waters) necessary for
the union of the male and female within divinity. In these moments, the
mystic actively takes part in the world of divinity that he expounds.

While it is possible, perhaps, to perform such theurgic acts without ecstasy
(in the narrow sense of the term), such moments are in fact the great accel-
erator in the process of generating blessings throughout all the dimensions of

reality. Zoharic mysticism is distinguished by the "flowing" weaving (in the Bergsonian sense) of theurgic and ecstatic elements with one another.

In concluding this discussion, let us return to Idel's methodological framework, which distinguishes between the theurgic and the ecstatic, in order to differentiate between the "hard" ecstasy of Abraham Abulafia and the "soft" ecstasy of zoharic literature. For the Zohar's protagonists, the ultimate end of religious-mystical worship is not personal, ecstatic experience on its own. The energy of the experience is immediately and responsibly harnessed for the broader purpose of drawing down blessings for the well-being of God, the world, and for humanity. While the mystic can indeed seek, at the personal level, to behold the pleasantness of God, his ultimate purpose and destiny is to channel and regulate the divine delight for the benefit of all reality.

A Multifaceted Experience

Descriptions of mystical experience in the Zohar typically comprise a number of intertwined characteristics.

> So it was, for that day the Companions saw the face of *Shekhinah* and were encompassed by fire. Rabbi Abba's face blazed in fire from rapture of Torah. It has been taught: All that day, none of them left the house, and the house was swathed in smoke. Words among them were fresh and ecstatic as if they were receiving Torah that very day from Mount Sinai! When they departed they did not know if it was day or night. (Zohar 1:94b; Matt 2004–2007, vol. 2, p. 98)

Seeing the face of Shekhinah, the appearance of fire, the blazing and radiant face, the experience of standing at Mount Sinai, and the loss of the sense of time are here integrated. Elsewhere in the Zohar, we find the integration of saturation by water, delight, and the experience of receiving divine blessings.[21] The different components combine organically to produce the complex whole that is mystical experience. We are not dealing here with a single, recurring experience but rather with a multifaceted experiential reservoir, in which a number of characteristics appear in different configurations each time.

A Pleasurable Experience

We have already examined the details of delight and pleasure, and their place in zoharic mystical experience,[22] and therefore here I will observe only that another common feature in all the Zohar's descriptions of mystical experience is the pleasurable and joyous experience of the mystic. Descriptions are rare of revelation in which the human response is fear and trembling alone.

In contrast, in descriptions elsewhere of prophecy, revelation, and mystical experiences, the divine presence is often portrayed as shaking the very foundations of man. We find such accounts in the Bible (for example, in the description of the giving of the Torah at Mount Sinai, and in the prophetic revelations of Ezekiel and Daniel); in the descriptions of the *Heikhalot* literature;[23] and in the writings of Abraham Abulafia in his account of the entry into prophetic experience.[24] But the Zohar emphasizes the emotional spectrum of joy, satisfaction, pleasure, delight, expansion, illumination, crowning, and saturation. Its descriptions of human contact with the divine are saturated with hues and shades of erotic experience, and their language is the language of love.

There are, however, also dramatic moments in which the heavenly herald calls out to the people of the world with a terrifying and frightening voice, to awaken from their slumber and fulfill their destiny. Yet, as we have already seen, these voices of calling are directed not to the Companions, who are awake—and aware of their wakefulness—but rather precisely to the sleeping masses, who do not wish to listen at all.[25]

In zoharic literature, we do find terrifying encounters between the human being and the forces of judgment in divinity, and confrontation with the forces of evil. Just as divinity directs its pleasure-filled countenance toward reality, it also directs a countenance saturated with judgment. Divine judgment and mythical evil are strong presences in the Zohar's world. Yet the encounter between the Zohar's heroes and the divine is nearly always an encounter of love, pleasure, and "spiritual sensuality"; and awe, when it does exist, is the awe of lovers.

Whether mystical experience is described with images of light, water, fire, or fragrance, pleasure and delight are always involved. Delight and joy appear in the Zohar in a rich and diverse range—from the smile of the one undergoing mystical experience or of the Companion listening to his fellow, to the physical and spiritual delight beyond which there is no higher.

Softening of the Boundaries between the Divine and the Human

The awareness of the softening of the boundaries between the divine and human world, and the commingling and merging of these dimensions, is common to the various descriptions of mystical experience in the Zohar. Religious thought has long pondered the question of the proximity or distance between the divine and human realms, with some portraying God as transcendent and sublime, and others seeking to emphasize God's immanence and presence.[26]

This argument is found already in rabbinic literature, and the Rabbis' interpretations of the giving of the Torah at Mount Sinai demonstrate sharp differences between those who claim that "the blessed Holy One bent the lower heavens and the upper heavens onto the mountain and His glory descended," versus those who claim that "neither Moses nor Elijah ascended to Heaven nor did the Glory of God descend [to earth]."[27] The Zohar's understanding of the degree of merging and commingling between the divine and the human owes a great deal to the figure of Rabbi Akiva, whose life and religious-mystical endeavors express a vision of reality in which divine and human dimensions are essentially interconnected.[28]

The Zohar seeks to inculcate a complex conception of the divine, at once transcendent (beyond the horizons of human cognition) and present (active in the world of humanity). The possibility of achieving live contact with divinity active in the world, of attaining knowledge and experience of the divine, constitutes the deep quest of this literature. The Zohar emphasizes the structural affinity between the divine world and the world of the human body and soul; therefore, its descriptions of mystical experience testify to intimate interfacing between these two worlds. Such tropes as the

radiance of the face, or the loss of the sense of time, express states of extraordinary intimacy between the human and divine world.

The softening of boundaries is the most widespread model for divine-
human relations in the Zohar. The human being interacts with the divine
world, participating in intra-divine events, for example, during prayer, yet
usually he does not lose his personal identity, even during peak moments.
In contrast, when the Zohar speaks of Rabbi Shim'on, we find descriptions
approximating the total merging of the divine and the human. In the passages recounting Rabbi Shim'on's adornment or crowning with the sefirah
Yesod, we find descriptions that convey a mythical-spiritual move in two
directions: a human partakes in the life of a divine attribute, and a divine
attribute is embodied in a particular human being.[29]

A Contained Experience

Zoharic mysticism is distinguished by its contained rather than eruptive
quality.[30] In other words, this is a mysticism circumscribed by an agreed-
upon language of expression and by accepted guidelines of intention and
action. The unique collective study of Torah during special times of the day
and similar special circumstances furnishes the context in which the experience transpires. These conditions have implications for the very character of
the experience and the language with which it is described.

The framework in which the mystic operates encourages the creation of
the experience. It generates and contains that experience. It even serves as a
safety net protecting the practitioner from the total loss and disintegration
of boundaries. The guidelines in which this mysticism transpires are not laid
bare in the Zohar; they must be extricated from the flow of the zoharic
text. It is the recurrence of patterns that enables identification of the structure in which the experience occurs.

In discussing the general qualities of mystical experience in the Zohar,
I have drawn upon "containment" and the "container-contained relationship," concepts from the field of psychoanalysis,[31] in order to show that its
experiential-mystical world is neither chaotic nor lacking boundaries. On
the contrary, particular structures and conventions bestow upon this world

a contained quality. This quality produces, structures, and ensures the well-being of the participants in this experiential world. The role of the teacher and the zoharic circle (the Companionship), as well as the times and means by which the Zohar's spiritual life unfolds, all contribute to this special zoharic quality.

To illustrate the importance of containment in zoharic mystical experience, we turn now to a unique and long story, spanning some twenty pages in the commentary to the Torah portion *Terumah*. The story takes place within a single day. It is a wonderful example of the interweaving of rather minor happenings with extended and complex expositions, with the Companions' innovations of Torah and revelation of secrets intensifying during the day.

This particular story contains neither miraculous or supernatural events nor encounters with wondrous characters. Within the "ordinary" framework of midrashic language, the Companions attain such a unique mystical experience and state of mystical consciousness that their great teacher, Rabbi Shim'on bar Yoḥai, in a moment of intense emotion, attests that such a day will not return until the coming of the Messiah. The Companions' actions in this story represent a mystical-symbolic construction of a new tabernacle and Temple of the spirit.

The first part of the story takes place in the plain of Ginnosar, at the edge of the Sea of Galilee, with the Companions sitting in the shade of some trees. As a gesture to the trees and their pleasant shade, Rabbi Shim'on begins an exposition about the symbolic trees that comprise the great sefirotic tree, in which God dwells as in a palanquin. At the end of his exposition, Rabbi Shim'on says:

> One who attains the Palanquin is entitled to everything. He is worthy of sitting in the comfort of the shade of the blessed Holy One, as it is said, *I delight to sit in His shade* (Song of Songs 2:3).
>
> Now that we are sitting in this shade of comfort, we should be aware that we are sitting in the shade of the blessed Holy One within the Palanquin! We should crown this place with crowns so high that the trees of the Palanquin will be swayed to cover us with another shade. (Zohar 2:128a; Matt 1983, p. 128)

This is an example of the moment of entry into mystical consciousness. In this moment, the teacher experiences a change in consciousness that he then evokes for his students. The palanquin is no longer the metaphysical or theosophical topic about which the Companions speak, but rather is described here as an experience that, if attained, entails sitting in the desired shade of the lover, the blessed Holy One. Having clarified that the palanquin is in fact an experiential event available to humanity, Rabbi Shim'on now switches to the present tense. Not only is the palanquin an experience, but it is being experienced right now, in the present, by Rabbi Shim'on and his disciples, who are now seated in the shade of the blessed Holy One, within His palanquin.

Rabbi Shim'on explains here to his students the experience of transition from the shade of one domain to the shade pertaining to another order altogether. This is the moment of the expansion of consciousness: "Now that we are sitting in this shade of comfort, we should be aware . . . !" The Companions seated beneath the tree now experience two kinds of shade: the shade of the trees, and the deeper, encompassing shade of the blessed Holy One.

Rabbi Shim'on even defines the purpose of the homilies to follow: "so . . . that the trees of the Palanquin will be swayed to cover us with another shade." The purpose is to experience yet another deeper level of the blessed Holy One's shade, a shade produced through the active arousal of the "trees of Lebanon" that comprise the palanquin. The quest is to intensify the experience, so that the Companions' experience will not merely be one of sitting in a static palanquin, but in a palanquin whose trees (the sefirot) are in an aroused, dynamic state.

The teacher here both encourages the expansion of the Companions' consciousness and contains it. He at once gives voice and determines boundaries for the experience. Throughout the experience, Rabbi Shim'on serves as the participants' reference point. His very presence ensures that the experience remains bounded. At the shore of the Galilee, the Companions build a glorious, mystical palace—a divine palanquin in which they sit, and which they strengthen, maintain, and arouse to action.

The Companions' experiences of being in the Garden of Eden and of contact with the Tree of Life prompt them to continue to expound even after leaving the water's edge and the trees' shade, en route to Rabbi Shim'on's home in Tiberias. The entire journey is the story of the endeavor to deepen and intensify the presence of the divine shade in the midst of the Companions, and "to walk in the paths of the guardians of the Tree of Life."[32]

At day's end, Rabbi Shim'on dramatically proclaims the uniqueness of the daytime that illumined the Companions' way, and in which they attained the world that is coming. He declares that the coming night, too, should illumine the Companionship—and thus enable them to join the words of the day with the words of the night in the presence of *Atik Yomin* (the Ancient of Days).

The Companions continue with their expositions; and after midnight, one of the Companions expounds, "for your love is more delightful than wine" (Song of Songs 1:2). The mystical homily unfolds and accumulates ecstatic tension. Another transformative moment arrives, and the Companions experience and understand that the "wine" that they are interpreting—and thanks to which they are so filled with joy—is in fact God Himself. Rabbi Shim'on responds with ecstatic weeping, and his words serve to confirm the experience undergone by the Companions.

> Rabbi Shim'on cried and said: Now I know for sure that High Holy Spirit is vibrating within you. Happy is this generation! A generation like this will not arise until King Messiah appears! Torah has been restored to her antiquity! Happy are the righteous in this world and the world that is coming! (Zohar 2:147a; Matt 1983, p. 131)

As in many other zoharic stories, Rabbi Shim'on, the great teacher, appears in order to clarify both for the Companions and for readers the deep meaning of the story. The uniqueness of the day, in the words of the teacher, lies in the Companions' success in restoring the Torah to her antiquity.[33]

This story illustrates the special character of zoharic mysticism, which, as we have seen, takes place within certain structures whose purpose is to contain the experience and ensure that it does not overflow or burst forth without boundaries. The story as a whole, with all its pieces, constitutes a single experiential-mystical wave. The mystical experience in the story is not merely that of the peak experience after midnight. The story documents the way in which the Companions experience a change in consciousness, leading them to experience an ever-intensifying process of connection with the divine, until they join with the Torah "in her antiquity," as she is present in the ancient and undifferentiated divinity. The experience is dependent on the narrative; and the narrative is the vessel through which the experience unfolds.

Throughout the entire day, the Companions' consciousness continues to expand; and they experience dimensions previously concealed from them on the shore of the lake. Their journey attests to their endeavor to see that which cannot be seen with the ordinary gaze, and to know experientially the divine reality in the place where previously had been only the shade of trees.

This is a story about the endeavor to find the divine in nature, to find the concealed in the revealed, and to experience theosophical truths rather than merely to know them as theoretical knowledge alone. The claim that "all is God" can be entirely theoretical, yet Rabbi Yose's realization that the wine about which the Companions have been expounding throughout the night is in fact the blessed Holy One Himself is no longer just a theoretical claim. This is the insight at the moment of its experiential revelation in the story's present; this is a zoharic secret, and this is the composition's mystical mode.

Further, the story illustrates how mystical experience in the Zohar is akin more to flowing honey than to a wild river bursting its banks. It is characterized more by a thread of grace than a torrent of light and fire. Generally, it contains the humorous eroticism, play, and yearning characteristic of courtship and seduction—and not simply the rupturing power of eruptive ecstasy.

Despite the power of the experience, the zoharic mystic does not abandon the "human domain," nor is his personal identity annihilated. To be sure, his consciousness expands, and sometimes even his gender identity can be fluid, yet the mystic remains who he is even when in a state of cleaving, radiance, saturation, and delight.

Zoharic mysticism, therefore, involves the subtle *contact* of human consciousness with the Holy, more than *union* with it. This is a mysticism of kisses, "the cleaving of spirit to spirit," more than a mysticism of sexual union, "the cleaving of body to body"; and sometimes, as we have seen, the Zohar prefers the spiritual connection to the physical. Mystical speech, the mystical word, represents the human kiss on the sweet mouth of God, on which all reality depends.

Two lovers do indeed have a powerful desire to connect, yet this connection does not negate each one's separate existence. The kiss is the merging, commingling, and unification of the mouths—as we saw in the Zohar's interpretation of the word *pihu* (his mouth) in "O that he would kiss me with the kisses of his mouth" (Song of Songs 1:2; transl. Matt)—yet there can be no kiss without two entities.[34]

Elements of Contained Mystical Experience

The question now arises: what is it that creates this containment and moderation in zoharic mysticism? What are the characteristics, conditions, and practices that enable the mystics of the zoharic circle "to enter and exit"—to expose supernal secrets yet survive their exposure, to attain experiences of a different order of consciousness and return to ordinary consciousness, and to simultaneously participate in human and divine realms of being? How are the members of the zoharic circle able to live a sane and lucid life within a society that does not necessarily share their worldview? And how is it that they do not die, go insane, or "cut the shoots"?

We must of course explore these questions from within the Zohar's own internal world, from within the horizons of its own self-understanding and narrative framework. At the same time, however, we seek to answer these questions by momentarily stepping outside the narrative framework. Let us contemplate the possibility of the historical existence of a mystical group in Spain in the thirteenth century, whose experiences provided part of the inspiration for the writing of the Zohar, and whose practices and worldview are imprinted in its words. In any case, we shall see that some of the answers will be found in the structures by which the Zohar chooses to fashion states of intensified mystical consciousness.

TIME

The Zohar establishes a special time frame—the hours from midnight till dawn—in which the Companions generate mystical experience. The very fact of this circumscribed time frame bestows upon their mystical life a contained and moderate quality. The kingdom of night, with its many sparkling lights and secrets, is favored by the Companions above that of the kingdom of day and its stark, powerful light.

Like King David, the zoharic mystics are filled with sorrow in the face of the ascending light of day, which heralds the disappearance of the night's magic, the separation of the earthly and divine lovers, and the onset of the kingdom of day and its laws.[35] With all its sorrow, this alternation between the reality of the night and the reality of the day is of course necessary as we learn from the Zohar's legends about King David, as well as the stories that the Zohar tells about its protagonists. Night is the time of song and experience, while day is the time of commandment and law.[36] The Zohar's special time frame for mystical experience serves to limit and channel the yearning to live only a life of encounter with the divine. It creates a balance that enables the mystic to enter and exit the orchard in peace.

In the fairy tale of Cinderella, a royal chariot appears at night to take the miserable young woman from her wretched place in the kitchen to a ball in the palace; with the aid of a magic wand, she is transformed into a beautiful princess. At the stroke of midnight, after delighting in the royal ball, the chariot and royal finery in which she was adorned disappear, and she finds herself once again covered in dirty rags in the poor and sorrowful world of her enslavement in the kitchen. Similarly in the Zohar—although the order, of course, is inverted: at midnight, the mystic strips off the clothes of his human existence and adorns himself with the festive, splendor-filled garments of the divine world, only to return, with the rising of the sun, to his scattered and gray earthly reality.

An analogy may be found in Jewish attitudes regarding the relationship between the Sabbath and the remaining days of the week. On the Sabbath, when people rest from their labor and are freed from their obligations, they ascend to the degree of angels, abide in the world of souls, enjoy the splendor of Shekhinah, and experience a foretaste of the World to Come. Then, with the Sabbath's end, they return once again to the profane and laborious reality of the six days of labor.

Our comparison of Cinderella, the Jew's experience of the Sabbath, and the zoharic mystic's participation in the nocturnal delight raises the question: which level of reality would they all consider to be more "real"? Is not the natural place of the human being and of Cinderella in the king's palace and in his presence?

The fairy tale, of course, concludes with a "happy ending": the unjust world of sorrow disappears and Cinderella gets to live out her true, royal identity in the palace; the World to Come is depicted as a world entirely Sabbath; and the world of the nocturnal delight, which perhaps sounds fantastic and imaginary, is in fact the authentic reality for the true nature of human beings, created in the divine image, as they were in the Garden prior to the sin. Perhaps the desire to live in a harmonious reality, devoid of death, to experience the continuous presence of the divine, and the recognition that this reality is how things really ought to be, lies at the heart of all quests and visions of redemption.

The delineation of time serves to channel and modulate the flow of the mystical life of the zoharic circle. With the rising of the sun, after a night of collective mystical endeavor by the light of candles, moon, and stars, the Companions depart for their daily tasks. They touch once again profane reality with all its hardships and obligations; and from the power of their nocturnal experience, they preserve during the day only a symbolic thread of grace—like mystical *tsitsit* (tassels; Numbers 15:38), which reminds them not only of their obligations, but also of their true essence.

THE MYSTIC CIRCLE—THE COMPANIONSHIP

The fact that the Zohar focuses on the life of a group rather than an individual contributes to the balance that enables its Companions to peacefully enter and exit the orchard of encounters with the divine. As we have already shown, the life of the circle requires cooperation and communication among the Companions, which serves to moderate the boundaries of personal experience. The collective endeavor to expose the divine dimension in the Torah, and the desire to relate this dimension to one's companions in an accepted language and in such a way that they will understand, together reduce the possibility of mystical vertigo and the loss of communicability. In the inner circle of the zoharic story, the needs of the group and the bonds of love between the Companions bestow a moderating influence on the experience.

The Zohar is full of stories in which an emotional or religious "concern" of one of the Companions, such as the fear of death or a new spiritual insight, becomes the topic for discussion, consultation, and mutual consideration. It might be argued that the mere fact of transmission and the reflection on the experience diminishes its authenticity and thins it out, yet it is precisely this social dynamic and the need for cooperation that brings about the disclosure of mystical experience, both for the protagonists of the Zohar and its readers.

If we consider yet another layer of the composition, namely, the world of the work's hidden authors, and assume that the Zohar reflects in some way the life of real mystics, we might suggest that the social character of the group encourages its members to intensify their religious world and to experiment with mystical experience, while at the same time preserving the mystic's connection with normative reality. Presumably the spiritual, artistic, and literary effort involved in the creation of the composition's pseudepigraphic disguise also gives its authors a certain distance, which by its nature modulates the sense of ecstasy. While it is true that a disguise can grant one greater freedom to play, this tendency is tempered by the composition's reflexivity. The extraordinary reflexivity of this circle regarding the course of its pseudepigraphic enterprise—the effort to fabricate and assume thousand-year-old identities in a land two thousand miles away—prompts awareness of the distance between the creators of the Zohar's literary frame and the figures that populate its pages. Such distance helps them to enter the orchard of divine experience and also to exit from it in peace.

THE TEACHER

The existence of the figure of the teacher and his centrality give the text a special focus. The very fact of the teacher's existence as a point of reference may protect the Companions (or the Zohar's authors) from mystical disorientation. The Companions' adventures are measured in relation to Rabbi Shim'on bar Yoḥai, the man of God, the omniscient master, from whose mouth the Companions learn the ultimate meaning of all that befalls them. The disciples' experiences are brought before the great teacher for clarification, criticism, and articulation.

Just as there are stories in which Rabbi Shim'on encourages mystical experience (as in the commentary to the Torah portion *Aḥarei Mot*, and in the *Idra Rabba*), there are also instances where he criticizes the experience or its boundaries (as in the story of Kfar Tarsha), and other occasions where he expresses ambivalence about ecstatic experiences (as in the end of the Idra Rabba). Every personal experience in the Zohar has a boundary, and this boundary is produced from the teacher's very existence and presence, be that teacher external or internal, real or spiritual, historical or fictional. This figure, who, significantly, is not portrayed as the divine madman, but rather as the teacher responsible both to his disciples and to the broader community, contributes greatly to the moderation of ecstatic experience.

THE TORAH AND THE EXEGETICAL STRUCTURE OF MYSTICAL EXPERIENCE

Another factor that may contribute to the contained quality and moderation of zoharic mysticism is its dependence on interpretation and exegesis. As we have seen, the ever-intensifying expositions of the Companions are indeed capable of generating ecstatic experience. At the same time, the zoharic homily has a wave structure: the homily (and the speaker) accumulates tension, culminating with the newly uncovered *ḥiddush* (innovation in Torah) or secret revealed through the words of the Torah, and then this wave subsides. The structure of the homily itself concludes the ecstatic experience.[37]

The mystics of the zoharic circle invest great intellectual effort in the intensive enterprise of exposing secrets in the Torah. This mode of generating mystical experience involves an entirely different enterprise from the techniques of, say, Abraham Abulafia, whose purpose (as Moshe Idel has demonstrated) is to generate mystical experience via (over)loading the kabbalist's consciousness with a huge quantity of linguistic combinations lacking semantic meaning.[38] The zoharic mystic is required to possess a high and multidimensional capacity for concentration vis-à-vis the sacred text. As we saw in our discussion of the Companions' entry into the dimension of the secret,[39] contemplation of the text begins with the *peshat* (simple meaning), followed by the citation of a range of interpretations and associated ideas from Jewish exegetes across the generations. The next stage, which serves as preparation for the mystical ascent, involves a heightened contemplative effort superseding the known, usual, and obvious interpretation. This contemplation weakens the control of common sense in the interpretive act. It heightens instead a rarer sense, permitting a higher level of association in seeking the verse's gateways to the mystical homily. The exegetical enterprise is predicated on an acute and powerful set of intentions, the focus of which is not merely another understanding of the text possessing a discursive meaning alone (as the talmudic saying puts it, "the Torah speaks in the language of human beings"). Rather, it seeks to expose the live divine world hidden within the holy text, as well as a connection with this world.

The world revealed through such interpretation, which engenders emotional and mystical ecstasy, is neither a private world nor an arbitrary dimension of reality lacking all form. It is complex and filled with dynamic dimensions, differentiated from each other yet always interconnected. Only certain aspects of the mystery of divinity are open to cognition and can be spoken about, experienced, and known. Other aspects, however, are, as the Zohar says, open to questioning and wonder alone. They may be experienced, yet they cannot be fathomed by human intellect. Beyond these lie aspects of divinity of which not even a human question can be formulated, a world of mystery open only to experience, where symbols do not point to discursive ideas, but rather to the ultimate ground of reality:

> "*Lift your eyes on high and see: Who created these?* (Isaiah 40:26). . . . To which site? The site toward which all eyes gaze. Which is that? *Opening of the eyes.* There you will discover that the concealed ancient one, susceptible to questioning, *created these.* Who is that? *Who.* . . . Since it can be questioned, yet remains concealed and unrevealed, it is called *Who.* Beyond there is no question. (Zohar 1:1b; Matt 2004–2007, vol. 1, p. 5)

The search for the divine reality within Scripture does not nullify the intellect but rather harnesses it for new aims. Furthermore, the artistry of zoharic *midrash*, by its nature, necessitates coherent interpretation and the clear identification of the exegetical course, beginning with the verse's words and extending to the mystical experience born of their new meaning. Sometimes it is even possible to see the exegete's effort to ascend—the trace of his mystical chariot of fire before its heavenly ascent.

Moshe Idel has commented on the conservatism characteristic of the experiences of mystics possessing an excessive sense of fear and awe toward the canonical texts that they interpret.[40] There is no doubt that a similar acute awareness of the developing process of the exegetical enterprise, as well as the speaker's intellectual alertness—which, as we have seen, does not recede in the course of the mystical homily—together contribute to the moderate flavor of mystical experience in the Zohar.

EXILE AND MYSTICAL REVELATION

The powerful exilic consciousness that resonates among the Zohar's protagonists is yet another element contributing to moderation in its mystical experience. While the Zohar accepts the view that the ultimate locus of prophecy is the Land of Israel, its authors develop the daring idea that every place in which flows the River Kevar (the locale in Babylonia of Ezekiel's great vision), some kind of experience of revelation is indeed possible. For this river is the current that "already" bears the divine bounty from the supernal Eden into reality.

> *In the land of the Chaldeans by the River Kevar* (Ezekiel 1:3)—in a place where exile prevails. Even so, *al Nehar Kevar, by the River Kevar.* What is *Nehar Kevar,*

the River Kevar? That was *kevar*, already—previously, for *Shekhinah* dwelled on it, as it is written, *A river flows from Eden to water the garden*. . . . (Zohar 1:149a–b; Matt 2004–2007, vol. 2, p. 331, modified)

The experience of prophecy in the Zohar is not confined to the past, but rather it is a living possibility in the present. In his introduction to the critical edition of Moses de León's *Shekel ha-Kodesh*, Charles Mopsik convincingly demonstrated the living presence of prophetic experience in the consciousness of Moses de León and Joseph Gikatilla, both of whom were among the central members of the zoharic circle.[41]

The reality of exile is indeed far removed from the sacred center in the Land of Israel; nevertheless, Moses de León has bequeathed to us a most daring interpretation, where he claims that it is precisely in exile that it is possible to behold that which was concealed in the Land of Israel when the Temple still stood. In his commentary on Ezekiel's vision of the Chariot, he interprets the first verse—"the heavens (*shamayim*) opened and I saw visions of God" (Ezekiel 1:1)—as the key to understanding the arousal and intensification of mystical consciousness, especially in exile. When the Temple still stood, de León writes, there prevailed a condition of perfect union between the male and female aspects of divinity. The lover and the beloved, the blessed Holy One and His Shekhinah, were in state of permanent coupling, which in turn bestowed stability and balance upon all reality. This was, however, a closed perfection, such that nothing could be known of it, for the *mysterium* was hidden deep within the lovers' embrace.

Destruction and exile brought about the end of this condition: the lover and the beloved parted, the sanctuary was destroyed, the male aspect of divinity ascended on high, and Shekhinah went forth with Her children into exile. In the words of Ezekiel: "The heavens opened"—the divine couple separated and were parted. Paradoxically, it was the breaking of this enclosed harmony that allowed "visions of God." The possibility of discovery and inquiry are dependent on the disintegration of the primal, monolithic world; it was the crisis that enabled the capacity to see.

The heavens opened (Ezekiel 1:1)—From here you can know of the union of the place in the mystery of *shamayim* (heavens) that unites all. . . . and now, because of the exile and the destruction, the building has been moved and uprooted from its place. . . . And that which was in a special union bound in a strong bond in the mystery of *shamayim* [the heavens], certainly opened, [and all the building] and the bond was uprooted from its place. . . . and for this reason that which was concealed became seen, for there is nothing *protecting it* (Deuteronomy 33:12) as at first. And therefore, *I saw visions of God* (Ezekiel 1:1)—*visions (mar'ot)* is written [defectively,] without the *vav* [so that its consonants resemble and hint at the phrase *mar'at elohim,* "a mirror of God"], like a man who looks in a mirror [*mar'ah*] that shows the whole form. And She who was covered *like a fruitful vine in the recesses of your house* [that is, the Temple] (Psalms 128:3) went forth outside and is seen and revealed in another land on this day; and She descended to Babylonia outside of Her domain and is seen there.[42]

But who is it who sees Her? The preceding text is saturated with the consciousness of the observer, namely, the son, the people, the child whose parents are now divorced; and that which is seen is connected with *gilui arayot* (literally, the exposure of nakedness, which is classically understood as incest) and all its associated dangers. The separation and dissolution of the union, like the purported removal of the cherubim from the Holy of Holies to the marketplace, implies the painful and violent exposure of an intimacy that ought to have remained concealed, private, and sanctified. It is transformed into a spectacle now seen outside, in the public space of the market in the light of day. In the Zohar we find a most harsh image of *gilui arayot* as the condition created by the separation of the united lovers, leading to the exposure of their genitals, which ought to have remain concealed by the very act of lovemaking.

> *And a querulous one alienated his friend* (Proverbs 16:28)—that is to say that the King separated from Matronita, as is written: *The nakedness of your father and the nakedness of your mother you shall not uncover* (Leviticus 18:7). . . .
>
> On the day that Solomon erected the house below, Matronita prepared a house for the King, and they set up their abode together, and Her face shone with perfect joy. . . . And when this son, as I have said, does not behave according to the King's desire, then She is the nakedness of all, naked on all sides, for the King separates from Matronita and Matronita leaves His palace, and therefore She is the nakedness of all.
>
> Is there not nakedness when the King is without Matronita—and Matronita without the King?!

> Therefore it is written: *The nakedness of your father and the nakedness of your mother you shall not uncover; she is your mother* (Leviticus 18:7). . . . When the King departs from Matronita and blessings are not found, then it is woe: woe for all, for the upper and lower realms. (Zohar 3:74a–b)[43]

According to this reading, *gilui arayot* is always the result of the dissolution of the ideal union that establishes the appropriate (hidden) state of nakedness. The Zohar draws this bitter image as a description of the separation of Shekhinah from her union with her lover, the blessed Holy One—a separation that exposes, both literally as well as metaphorically, the nakedness of the separated lovers. (It is for this reason, says the Zohar, that it is forbidden to gaze upon the rainbow: it is an expression of the nakedness of the male genital organ on its own, instead of its being united with, and thereby hidden within, the female's body.[44]) The exposure of nakedness is therefore the exposure of the incompleteness of each side, of each genital organ by itself, which has not been made whole by its partner.

There is, however, another aspect to this picture. Suddenly, because of the circumstances, it is now possible to see that which had always been hidden within, to discover and grasp aspects of the divine previously concealed.

In an equally harsh picture, the Zohar describes the exposure of the nakedness of Shekhinah through an interpretation of the commandment to send forth the mother bird.[45] In the ideal state, the mother bird rests upon her chicks; similarly Shekhinah, the mother of Israel, nourishes and suckles her children, the children of Israel, and protects them. Yet, when she is sent forth or divorced, amid her flight her nakedness is revealed, which in the ideal state covered and nourished the offspring.

The Zohar expounds here the tension between two senses of the Hebrew infinitive *legalot*: "to go into exile" versus "to expose." The exiled Shekhinah is revealed and exposed in exile. This wordplay is important for understanding the Zohar's ambivalence regarding the secret and the revelation of secrets. Exile is brought about by human misdeed, and Shekhinah goes forth into exile with her children and is thereby exposed. In other words, the tremendous experience of revelation that the Companions (or the zoharic authors) experience is the result of the condition of exile. This condition of exile contains an element of the exposure of the nakedness of the mother by the children, an exposure—and revelation—that creates a unique yet dangerous situation.

The rectification (*tikkun*) of mother Shekhinah—the restoration of her exiled condition—is possible only through the deeds of the children. The mystics act for the sake of *tikkun* in two ways. The first is as arousers of female waters, *mayin nukbin*, so as to create anew the union between She-khinah and the blessed Holy One.

The second way of *tikkun* is the path of *teshuvah* (repentance/restora-tion): the mystics are the ones who restore Shekhinah to her appropriate place. Yom Kippur, the Day of Atonement, is the opportunity for ultimate *teshuvah*, insofar as only then is there both the restoration of Shekhinah to her abode as well as *kippur*, in the sense of covering her exposed nakedness.

Particularly striking here is the profound awareness that following the revelation and exposure of secrets is the need for their re-cover-y, and that such covering is indeed appropriate and necessary for them. Here then we encounter the deep zoharic paradox: The active state of the human being takes place precisely in the context of a compromised and exiled divine reality, and it is here that the mystic is at his most potent: he reveals secrets and rectifies divinity. In the harmonious state, the secret is covered and con-cealed, the divine union abides and blessings descend upon the world, not by virtue of revelation and exposure, but precisely because of the restora-tion of the secret once again to a state of concealment, hidden from view.

> Rabbi Yose said: It is written: *The nakedness of your father and the nakedness of your mother you shall not uncover* (Leviticus 18:7); and it is written: *she is your mother, you shall not uncover her nakedness* (ibid.). We have taught: *she is your mother*, indeed. If her nakedness has been uncovered, who has to restore her and rectify her? The one who exposed her.
>
> We have taught: The evil inclination in man is strengthened only through those *arayot* (incestuous desires) and all the sins cling to those *arayot*; and it is written: *you shall not uncover.*
>
> When it [the evil inclination] is mended, it is mended in relation to the one who revealed; and this is called *teshuvah* (restoration, return).
>
> Rabbi Yitsḥak said: All the sins of the world cling to this, until Mother was

exiled/revealed because of them. And when She is exiled/revealed, all the children are exiled (because of Her); and it is written: *do not take the mother together with her children* (Deuteronomy 22:6). And when the world is restored below, all is restored until the restoration ascends to Holy Mother, and She is restored; and what was exposed is covered. . . . And when is She called *teshuvah*? When Mother is covered and abides in joy over Her children, as is written: *the mother of children is happy* (Psalms 113:9); and She returns to Her stature, and whatever was closed returns to its place. (Zohar 3:15b)

These two images are quintessential expressions of particularly daring and creative zoharic exegesis—the central mode of which is, as we have seen, the hyper-imaginative drawing forth of the power latent in Scripture's words. The passage displays a profound reflexive awareness that in exposing the secrets of divinity and in expounding the Chariot Episode, the mystics of the Zohar constantly risk straying from the warning found in Mishnah Ḥagigah, namely, to protect the glory of God.

The mystic must know the boundary between the desire to cleave to God and to affect *tikkun* (restoration) in the world of divinity and the catastrophic over-exposure of the divine-father and the divine-mother. It is not for nothing that, in the Zohar, the exposure and concealment of the secrets of divinity are bound with the acute awareness of the dangers inherent in disclosure. Correct or appropriate revelation, according to the Zohar, does not reveal in order to expose and gaze upon the nakedness, but rather to rectify it and create for it a garment, a covering, and protection.

Moreover, the purpose of revelation is to bring about, in special hours of grace—through the mystical meditation on the words of the Torah or through the mystically intentioned performance of the commandments—the lovers' renewed unification, and thereby the concealment of their nakedness, which is simultaneously the source of all blessing and the source of all danger. We have already seen something similar in the Zohar's interpretation of "He covered it with pure gold" (Exodus 37:2), which describes the necessity of covering and overlaying the light of the sefirah *Yesod* with the mystic's soul as being also the necessity for intercourse in which the phallus is concealed, contained, and softened in the body of the female.[46] We find this idea, too, in the Zohar's exposition of the need to guard the purity of the female genital opening, the Holy of Holies, and to prepare it such that only the High Priest can enter, so that it will not be defiled through its exposure to the forces of evil.[47] And yet again in the description of mystical experience as the opening of a well, we find the demand to return the great stone to the mouth of the well, which, while covering the well, also preserves its purity and clarity.[48] While exile does indeed enable contact with divinity, it is imperative that this contact be moderate so that blessings will abide and abound.

We can find this connection between the Zohar's moderate mysticism and the consciousness of exile in a fascinating homily about the different forms through which divine revelation takes place. Although it occurred in the wilderness and not in the Land of Israel, Moses merited the great revelation of face-to-face speech with God (Deuteronomy 34:10), "plainly and not in riddles" (Numbers 12:8; transl. NJPS). Beneath this degree of revelation are various other possibilities of revelation.

One of these lesser degrees is called *massa* (pronouncement/burden), and the Zohar points out that *massa* is the form of revelation that comes little by little and with great difficulty. It seems to me that its authors are hinting here at the way in which God is present in the exile imposed by Seir, that is, Edom, the world of Christendom. In such a reality one can encounter the divine presence only after concerted effort and only in the secrecy of the whisper. Perhaps this is yet another explanation for the moderate mysticism of the Zohar and its complex means for generating mystical experience, which usually are not accompanied by overwhelming flooding of the divine voice and light.

> Through six degrees of prophecy [did God] speak to the prophets: *maḥazeh, ḥazon, ḥezyon, ḥazut, davar,* and *massa.* The [first] five are all like one who sees a light shining behind a wall, and some of them are like one who sees the light of the sun through a lantern. But *massa*, burden, is when that light reaches him with great difficulty, and the word is difficult for him and is barely revealed. . . . and here: *Massa Dumah* [*the pronouncement/burden of silence*]; *he calls to me from Seir* (Isaiah 21:11).
>
> *Massa Dumah*—a great burden that cannot be revealed; and this is prophecy in a whisper and abides in a whisper.

> *He calls to me from Seir*—Here it is not revealed who said *he calls to me from Seir*, whether the blessed Holy One or the faithful prophet. But this prophecy certainly abides in a whisper within the supernal mystery of faith. (Zohar 2:130b)

We conclude our discussion with the words of Rabbi Moses de León about the possibility of prophecy in his own day. While acknowledging the decline in generations in terms of prophetic capacity, he nevertheless maintains that prophecy does in fact exist in his generation, even if it is only a spark:

> And the least and the last of all, those in our generation now, are lesser in their knowledge and in their prophecy, for prophecy has ceased from them. But because of the Torah in which they engage, the light of Torah shines in their intellects; and it is nearly a spark of prophecy. And this is what our sages of blessed memory said: "a sage is superior to a prophet, as is said: *and the prophet is the heart of wisdom* (Psalms 90:12)"; that those who were first in the days of our teacher Moses, peace be upon him, received divine help and assistance, both because of their virtue . . . and because of their preparation in having eaten the fine intellectual and spiritual food that emanated from the supernal light.[49]

Moses de León's words here, while seemingly bowing humbly before the greatness of the past, in fact posit prophecy as an existing and living reality in his own generation; and in expounding the matter of "a sage is superior to a prophet," he firmly establishes prophecy as the "heart" (that is, the core) of wisdom. The humility in relation to prophecy in his time perhaps also contributes to the moderate and contained character of mystical experience in the Zohar.

The Zohar's Three Main States
of Mystical Consciousness

Mystical experience in the Zohar comprises different modes of connection between the human being and the divine. Diversity notwithstanding, it seems to me that it is nevertheless possible to attempt to define, even if only schematically, the three main states of mystical consciousness in the zoharic world, and thereby gain a deeper understanding of the dynamism that characterizes the spiritual practice of the Zohar's mystics.

These three states constitute archetypal states of consciousness and contain within and between them a range of additional experiences. The Zohar is rarely didactic or methodical, and so these states of consciousness are not presented to the reader in a systematic fashion. Nevertheless, alongside the Zohar's extraordinary diversity and richness, we also find clear conceptual paradigms that recur in different contexts.

The Zohar has its own unique language for expressing and discussing mystical experience. In seeking to explore the characteristics of the states of consciousness involved, it is very difficult to rely on any one of the models employed by scholars of religion outlining the contours of mystical experience. A phenomenological approach to mystical experience, therefore, requires that we first pay close attention to the Zohar and its unique language, and only afterward look for similarities with other models.

I call the three foundational states of mystical consciousness in the Zohar by the names of the sefirot that represent them: the experience of *Malkhut*, the experience of *Tiferet*, and the experience of *Atika*.[1] While these states do not appear as a clearly articulated ladder of ascension, there is no doubt that they stand in a hierarchical relationship; the consciousness of *Atika* is the highest and most exalted of the states, while the consciousness of *Tiferet* is higher than the state of consciousness of *Malkhut*.[2]

The Malkhut *Experience: Rose Consciousness*

This state of consciousness is concerned with the wonder of differentiated, dualistic reality, and through it one experiences the dynamic, continuously changing quality of being. This is an experience whose locus is within time. Here the mystic is aware of the transience of all phenomena, of the change inherent in differentiated reality, and of the law of birth, growth, decline, and death that governs all beings found in time.

At the root of this state of consciousness lies the yearning and longing to mingle with another, complementary quality of the divine reality—to receive and be influenced by that other. This is a colorful, erotic state of consciousness, filled with movement and capable of being described in words.

Malkhut consciousness is characterized by a sensory and emotional intensification. In this state, speech is heightened, overflowing, and is similar to the speech of lovers. *Malkhut* consciousness stimulates the poetic imagination and free association, symbol and metaphor being the key building blocks of its language.

According to the kabbalists of the Zohar, this mystical consciousness is considered an opening or portal through which one must pass in order to reach the other domains of consciousness and aspects of the divine. The qualities outlined here all derive from the cosmic law of the sefirah *Malkhut*, in all its varied meanings. This is a state of connectedness with the feminine as a divine-cosmic quality, symbolized by the rose, by female eros, as well as by the night and its varied, mysterious lights, and especially by the moon—waxing, waning, and always changing.

This consciousness defines the foundational experience of the zoharic mystic's soul. This state, which exists within the duality of human consciousness, acknowledges—and indeed uses—this duality as a launch pad for mystical experience. It has many parallels with the concept and practice of *Bhakti* in Hinduism, where the recognition of the soul's separation from the divine generates the yearning for union.[3] It is also interesting to compare this state with the results of Masters and Houston's research into expanded states of consciousness, undertaken in the 1960s and published in their book *The Varieties of Psychedelic Experience*. Their research included experiments with psychedelic drugs, as well as experiments without the use of drugs. Their findings suggested a continuum of four main states of consciousness, with the number of people capable of experiencing these states diminishing as we ascend from the first to the fourth state:

(a) "Sensorium," the state of heightened sense perception.

(b) The "ontogenetic" state, in which the subject remembers his/her personal history. (This state parallels consciousness as described in the process of Freudian psychoanalysis.)

(c) The "phylogenetic," or symbolic, state, in which the subject experiences the great myths and foundational rituals of human culture. (This state parallels Jung's collective unconscious.)

(d) "Mysterium," the state of integrated and deep, mystical consciousness, as documented in mystical testimonies in many of the world's religions.[4]

The Rose Consciousness of *Malkhut* is similar in broad outline to the sensorium as described by Masters and Houston.

This state of consciousness is not foreign to the reader: we are likely to experience it in situations of great excitement, inspiration, love, and erotic arousal; in moments of wonder in the face of the majesty and power of nature; or when taking intoxicating drugs. In this state of consciousness everything is intensified and amplified. The details of reality connect with one another in surprising and novel ways; everything is interesting. The mind and the imagination are in a state of excited and colorful intensity. In this state, reality can be experienced as brightened or darkened, but never as insignificant or pale. We perceive things that we never sensed before.[5]

The Tiferet Experience: Tree of Life Consciousness

This multifaceted state of consciousness is characterized both by qualities of eternity and atemporality as well as qualities of movement and eros. Associated with them is the experience of centeredness or concentration, comprising all the different vectors operative in this state. This is the consciousness of the center, positioned between the deep and concealed state of consciousness above (Atika, with which one must make contact) and the active, dualistic state below (Malkhut, with which one must connect—and upon which one must act).

Additional characteristics of this state of consciousness include: stable clarity; an experience of radiance; overarching structure (rather than particular narrativity); full presence; focused intention; total knowledge; and the desire to influence and create. The consciousness of the sefirah Tiferet is identified by the kabbalists of the Zohar as a consciousness whose quality is quintessentially masculine.

Compared with Malkhut consciousness, this state of consciousness is more difficult to define. The layers of the Zohar describe this reality variously. Excessive harmonization of those descriptions would cause us to miss both the variegated nature of the composition as a whole, and the diversity of experiences described among its pages.

In the main corpus of the Zohar, we find Tiferet representing center, stability, and lawfulness. Tiferet is symbolized by the day, the written Torah, the Tree of Life, the sun, the King, the blessed Holy One—that is, the aspect of God that establishes law and order. The attitude toward this dimension of reality is positive and favorable, as both Shekhinah and the human soul seek to unite and cleave with this divine dimension.

In the Idrot, the situation is far more complex. The Idra Rabba and the Idra Zuta present the dimension of divinity and the dimension of the human soul under the broad heading of Ze'eir Anpin. That is the mythic image of

God, religion, the soul, and consciousness, as recognized in differentiated reality. In sefirotic language, the "countenance of Ze'eir Anpin" comprises the sefirot from Ḥesed to Yesod. Employing bold, anthropomorphic language, the Idra Rabba details the contours of that countenance, with every limb paralleling a particular mode of divine action in reality. This image of God—and its parallel image of human consciousness—is described as lacking a balanced relationship between love and judgment. Indeed, it is described as suffering from an excess of judgment.[6]

The Idra Rabba states the reason for this imbalance in Ze'eir Anpin: a misalignment of this consciousness with that of Atika Kadisha (or Arikh Anpin). Speaking less mythically and more abstractly, we are dealing here with a lack of the appropriate connection between dualistic consciousness and its unified and undifferentiated source. In the Zohar, Rabbi Shim'on explicitly identifies the state of consciousness (or state of attainment) of "the righteous" as located in Ze'eir Anpin, pointing to a need to align this consciousness with the divine countenance of Atika: "The desire and delight of the righteous who are in Ze'eir Anpin is to behold and cleave to the adornments of Atika, concealed from all."[7]

This state of Ze'eir Anpin, even though containing great clarity, is not stable—and certainly not static. The Idra Rabba opens with a statement to the effect that there is an imbalance in Ze'eir Anpin, and the Companions assemble in order to act for this divine countenance's sake, citing "it is time to act for YHVH" (Psalms 119:126).[8] Nevertheless, even while unbalanced, the consciousness of Ze'eir Anpin contains the capacity to be rectified and stabilized—and thereby to constitute the "center bar" at the heart of consciousness.

Although difficult to define precisely in terms of consciousness, the essential qualities of this state remain the same whether we are discussing Tiferet or Ze'eir Anpin. In this masculine state of consciousness, the mystic shines and is radiant. He is at the peak of his potential to bestow and fertilize. This is the solar, radiant, and atemporal state with which Rabbi Shim'on describes himself in the Idra Rabba.

In a particularly beautiful zoharic passage in which Rabbi Shim'on expounds "I am a lily of Sharon, a rose of the valleys" (Song of Songs 2:1), we find a detailed and unique description of the two states of consciousness of *Malkhut* and *Tiferet*. This homily describes the erotic relations between the Assembly of Israel and the blessed Holy One. In so doing, it describes also the difference between the two states of consciousness through which a human being is able to come into contact with the world of divinity: the first is a dualistic, changing state of consciousness, whereas the second is stable, concentrated, and unchanging.

This homily is one of the most outstanding illustrations in the entire Zohar of the composition's ability to speak through a midrashic-symbolic-mythic language about the two different states of consciousness of *Malkhut* and *Tiferet* and the hierarchical, complementary relations between them. The consciousness of *Tiferet* is presented here as the difficult to attain, elusive, fleeting ideal; the consciousness of *Malkhut*, with all its complexity and instability, is portrayed as much loved and desired.

> Rabbi Shim'on opened: *I am a lily of Sharon, a rose (shoshanat) of the valleys (amakim)* (Song of Songs 2:1).
>
> *I am a lily of Sharon*—who wishes to be watered by the streams of the deep river, the font of the rivers. . . .
>
> *A rose of the valleys*—who stands in the depths (*amikta*) of all. . . .
>
> Come and see: At first, green like a *lily* whose leaves are green; afterward, *a rose*—red with white hues.
>
> *A rose (shoshana)*—with six (*shisha*) leaves.
>
> *A rose (shoshana)*—because She changes (*ishtaniyat*) from color to color and varies (*shaniyat*) Her colors.
>
> *A rose*—at first a *lily*; when She wishes to unite with the King, She is called *lily*. After She has cleaved to Him—to the King—with those kisses, She is called *rose*, since it is written: *His lips are as roses* (Song of Songs 5:13).
>
> *A rose of the valleys*—for She changes Her colors; sometimes for good, sometimes for evil, sometimes for mercy, sometimes for judgment.
>
> *And the woman saw that the tree was good for eating and a delight to the eyes* (Genesis 3:6).
>
> Come and see: Human beings do not see, do not know, and do not consider. When the blessed Holy One created Man and adorned him in supernal glory, He desired that he would cleave to Him so as to be unique and of single heart at the singular site of cleaving that never changes or turns, with the single bond that bonds all together, as is written: *the Tree of Life in the middle of the garden* (Genesis 2:9).

Afterward they strayed from the way of faith and abandoned the singular tree that looms high over all trees, and cleaved to the place that changes and turns from hue to hue, from good to evil and from evil to good, and descended from on high and cleaved below to the ever changing; and they abandoned the singular tree that looms high over all the trees, as is written: *God made man straight, but they have sought multiple accounts* (Ecclesiastes 7:29). Certainly, then, their hearts changed to that side, sometimes for good, sometimes for evil, sometimes for mercy, sometimes for judgment. According to that to which they cleaved, they certainly *have sought multiple accounts* and cleaved to them.

The blessed Holy One said: Man, you have abandoned life, and to death do you cleave! (Zohar 1:221a–b, 3:107a)

The first part of the homily, without the interpretation of the sin of eating from the Tree of Knowledge of Good and Evil, presents us with a description of the state of consciousness of *Malkhut*, in all its glory. This consciousness is described through a mythic and erotic secret of the lily and the rose. Presented for us here is the process of the perfection and ripening both of the mythic image of Shekhinah and the feminine consciousness-soul of the human being, which yearns to unite and join with the blessed Holy One in kisses of love.

Significantly, it is precisely this erotically ripe condition—the state that follows knowledge of the king, or kisses with God—that generates a condition of continuous movement and change. The Rose Consciousness of *Malkhut* is in essence "sometimes for good, sometimes for evil, sometimes for mercy, sometimes for judgment."

The homily expounded by the great teacher (about the verse uttered by the beloved in the Song of Songs in the first person) sounds like Rabbi Shim'on's description of his own state of consciousness during the exposition. That is to say, it is about himself—about the state of consciousness in which he finds himself—that he expounds "I am a lily of Sharon, a rose of the valleys." In this state of consciousness, the more the experience intensifies, the more complex and diverse it becomes.

The second part of the homily, which interprets the eating from the Tree of Knowledge in light of the first part of the exposition, amplifies the complexity of the kabbalist's relationship with *Malkhut* consciousness.

According to this second part, the very fact of the existence of Rose Consciousness attests to the straying from the original divine plan when God created humanity in the divine image. The ever-changing consciousness is the consequence of eating from the Tree of Knowledge of Good and Evil, which serves here as a symbol for humanity's opting for knowledge, complexity, time, and movement—despite the inevitability of death bound up with that choice.

But God's intention, it seems, had been otherwise. God made human beings straight (*yashar*), and His hope had been to create a being capable of living in permanent, uninterrupted connection with the divine—a stable connection, never changing or alternating. This is a description of the ideal state of consciousness according to the Zohar: a stable and permanent state of *devekut*, which expropriates the mystic from the experience of time and its laws. Straightforward access to that state of consciousness, however, has been lost through humanity's choice to place itself—and indeed all of reality—under the domain of *Malkhut*. The ever-turning flaming sword of duality (Genesis 3:24) guards against direct access to the experience of an eternity of unmediated contact with the Tree of Life.

As noted above, Tree of Life Consciousness is considered quintessentially masculine, and thus the rich zoharic language of masculinity, maleness, and male sexuality, as well as the description of the relations between the sefirot *Tiferet* and *Yesod*, are the foundational language for understanding this state. The figure of Elijah the prophet in the Zohar furnishes a glimpse of this consciousness in its extreme. The Zohar views Elijah as the most masculine of all men, connected exclusively to the Tree of Life, eternity, and the phallic maleness of this tree, without any contact whatsoever with the other necessary component of human personality—namely, the connection with the Tree of Knowledge of Good and Evil, or feminine consciousness. Elijah is caught in the paradox of his absolute masculine personality. He cannot die like other mortals, as he has no contact with the feminine, "whose feet descend to death" (Proverbs 5:5); and even the angel of death, also bound by time, is unable to subdue him. At the same time, because of his lack of contact with the feminine, the world cannot endure him. (From here we learn that it is the feminine consciousness that is communicative and that is able to bring about change on the learner's part.) Elijah has to be taken from the world of mortals to the world of angels, as this world is unable to withstand his absolute masculinity.[9]

Tree of Life Consciousness is not necessarily characterized by any external characteristic or movement. In this state, consciousness is so concentrated that there is no room for error or stumbling. Any movement or action associated with it will be precise and correct.

This state of consciousness is familiar to us in states of breath meditation or concentration, sometimes in prayer, and sometimes in particularly concentrated moments in writing or some other such activity where the ordinary sense of the dimension of time disappears. This state is also familiar to us in states of performance—for example, virtuoso musicians or talented dancers during a recital, or Olympic sprinters during a race. In this state, there is an element of "majesty"; and the quality of the ego is experienced as more expansive or united with something larger than itself.

The Atika Experience: White Light Consciousness

Finally we come to the ultimate state of consciousness, beyond which there is no higher during corporeal life. In contrast with the other two states, in this state are experienced the oneness and unity at the heart of being. Consciousness comes into contact with the root of all reality, with the most ancient countenance of the divine.

Atika, or *Arikh Anpin* in the language of the *Idrot,* is an epithet for the divine in its original arousal of will, the beginning of its emanation outside itself in order to create reality. The experience of *Atika* is one of contact with the most archaic. Its world is found beyond the horizons of language, beneath the ordinary threshold of consciousness. Thus it is described only through the language of images.

In this state of consciousness, a deep mythic layer of the soul is exposed—a reality experienced not through concepts but rather through pictures and images, usually of a most primal kind. As opposed to the other two states of consciousness, the state of *Atika* is not differentiated in terms of gender. This state of consciousness is not sexual—neither masculine nor feminine—but is rather unified.

We find this experience, for example, in the Zohar's description of the genesis of reality and the emergence of being from infinity. That experience is described through images of singularity, incapable of being defined in language. In the passage that opens the Zohar's expositions on the first verse of Genesis, we find an account of pre-differentiated being prior to its emergence from *Ein Sof*:

> A spark of impenetrable darkness flashed within the concealed of the concealed,
>   from the head of Infinity,
> a cluster of vapor forming in formlessness, thrust in a ring,
> not white, not black,
> not red, not green,
> no color at all.

Zohar 1:15a; Matt 2004–2007, vol. 1, pp. 107–8, reformatted

The multiplication of negations here expresses the desire to describe an amorphous dimension that precedes order and language, more than a philosophical attempt to preserve the transcendence of divinity through negative descriptors alone. This description is, therefore, a gateway into an experiential dimension more than a speculative endeavor. This state is familiar to us through the attempt to describe the genesis of thought in human consciousness, the state prior to birth or the origin of being.

An additional experience of the presence of *Atika* consciousness is found in the Zohar's account of the deliverance at the Sea of Reeds, depicted by Rabbi Yitsḥak as a mythical, archetypal event of the exposure of all reality to the original light of Creation: "At that time, *Atika Kadisha* was revealed and favor (*ratson*) was found in all the upper worlds. Then illuminated the illumination of all!"[10] The presence of the absolute light throughout all reality in this meta-temporal moment returns the world to its foundation. It alters the laws of nature so as to enable the birth of the people of Israel.

In the same place and context, we find yet another primal picture, also on the threshold of linguistic consciousness. This imagery parallels the description of the absolute light a moment prior to the change in reality. It is the picture of the serpent, the emissary of *Atika*, who bites the genitals of the hind, thus enabling her to give birth. The imagery of the dragon biting the hind's genitals is indeed found in rabbinic literature, yet the mythical context of the hind in distress prior to giving birth and the nation standing at the entrance of the birth canal at the Sea split in two, transforms the picture of the biting serpent into a particularly archaic image.

The connection between the two pictures is fundamentally experiential. It engenders in the reader a sense of the primordial.

White Light Consciousness is described in the Zohar with a panoply of images. The Zohar employs such imagery to evoke the experience of being filled with the divine bounty without condition or limit—an experience of infinite security and love stemming from the encounter with the undifferentiated divinity of *Arikh Anpin*.

For example, the *Idrot* invite the reader to come and see a continuum of grand mythical images, which remain unexplained and which do not stand in any systematic order, and whose sole common denominator is precisely this experience. At first the Zohar draws an image of a skull being filled with crystal dew that trickles unceasingly from a white skull. Afterward, the Zohar describes gazing into a face that has one eye constantly open, from which flows a white light, which in turn bathes the eyes of the one gazing. Then the image of fish in the depths of the sea, whose eyebrow-less eyes are always open. And then yet another image of the unceasing flow of milk from the mother's breast.[11]

We readers are thus invited to contemplate a collection of images, different from one another yet connected in their experiential depth, in the hope that one of these images (or a combination of them) will resonate within us. These primal pictures lie beyond the world of differentiation, both conceptually and morally. They are non-narrative and their dynamism is limited. These are images of the depths of the ocean, pictures belonging to the dawn of reality and consciousness. Thus they reveal the mysterious and enigmatic connection between death and life: from one perspective, they are images of annihilation and death; seen from another vantage point, they are pictures of conception, fertilization, and the genesis of life.[12]

The mystical state of White Light Consciousness is connected more with being than with either cognition, contemplation, or intention. Like the Neo-platonic conception of the origin of being, so in the Zohar the single eye of *Atika* pours forth continuously: Eden flows forth from itself and influences the divine river un-reflexively, without ceasing or changing intention.

The Zohar emphasizes not only this dimension's continuous presence within reality, but also that ordinary human consciousness is not sufficiently cultivated to absorb it. As we have already seen, the Zohar attributes many of the defects of reality to the absence of connection with this dimension. The Zohar's desire to act for the sake of this ancient divinity (*Atika*), and to restore the Torah to its ancient state, applies its foundational religious experience at the programmatic level: through an ancient-new connection, one must find a way to reconnect Jewish religious culture—a culture of distinctions, laws, analysis, and structure—with its more ancient, mythic, and unified source.[13] Such an experience is associated with a strong sense of pleasure and delight, experiences that according to the Zohar have their origins in the White Light of *Atika*.[14]

.   .   .

The three states of consciousness outlined above are all mystical states of consciousness. In each one is a unique experiential connection, beyond that of ordinary states of human consciousness, with distinct divine dimensions.

The love of wandering that characterizes the zoharic circle mirrors the way that these states are attained or experienced, as well as the way they are described. They do not appear in one fixed and binding form or structure; and their manifestation can be sudden—divorced from any systematic order or ascent of a ladder of consciousness.

We can also speak of these three states by using the zoharic language arising from the code verse "A river flows from Eden to water the garden." The three components of that verse—Eden, river, and garden—parallel the states of consciousness of White Light, Tree of Life, and Rose. These states of consciousness, and the encounters that they engender with the world of divinity, lie at the heart of the Zohar's language of mystical experience. They bestow upon the composition its richness and uniqueness.

The Ability to Express Mystical Experience

A key aspect in any discussion of mystical experience in the Zohar is the composition's profound awareness of the relationship between language and experience. Indeed, one of the distinguishing features of the Zohar's mystical-experiential world is the centrality of dialogue and the spoken word. Its protagonists do not stand dumb and mute in the face of their unmediated encounter with the divine world; on the contrary, generally their experiences cause them to speak, to describe and expound.

In the Zohar, speaking about the experiential world is done through a symbolic language. As Moshe Idel has beautifully demonstrated, the employment of such symbolic language does not serve to express the inexpressible, but rather to illustrate the dynamism of the divine world, which cannot be defined through ordinary language.[1] Sometimes it seems that zoharic speech overflows in a celebration of verbal expression; on other occasions, we find firm statements on the inability to describe, because of their very nature, the divine dimensions beyond language.

The protagonists of the Zohar do not naively speak about their experiences; they are, rather, acutely aware of the limits of language that they repeatedly lay bare before the reader. In this regard, the Companions' self-awareness—as the ones capable of crossing the boundary of the inexpress-ible—functions as one of the Zohar's key performative techniques in entic-ing and drawing the reader into its world. This linguistic limit, then, whets the reader's appetite. It serves the composition's understanding of itself as comprising a mystic circle, which, unlike other groups, found a way to utter the mystery of faith.[2]

What is it, though, that enables the Zohar's protagonists to express the inexpressible? How do they overcome the limits of language as described in so many mystical testimonies around the world, as well as in various schol-arly models that have sought to define the foundational characteristics of mystical experience?[3]

The heroes of the Zohar answer such questions with a range of sugges-tions. While it is true that there are divine dimensions open only to question or experience,[4] there is in fact a special process that enables the mystic to utter the inexpressible, and through which the ineffable is reflected within the effable world.

This question arises, for example, in the zoharic homily on Psalm 19. This psalm is a song in praise of the mighty acts of God, as recounted by the heavens and their host but without words. Nature is described as a win-dow and mirror for the divine: "Heaven declares the glory of God, and sky proclaims His hands' work" (v. 2). The zoharic homilist wonders about the divine story that the heavens "declare" throughout the day, as the Psalmist has seemingly paradoxical things to say about them. On the one hand, the grand narrative transpires without words: "There is no utterance, there are no words, whose sound goes unheard" (v. 4). Yet on the other hand, this story—their words—is indeed known in the world: "Their voice carries throughout the earth; their words, to the end of the world" (19:5).

It is in the space between the "no utterance" and the "words to the end of the world" that the zoharic homily unfolds. The celestial bodies and the heavens themselves are interpreted as sefirot that declare and proclaim the divine story to the world.

The Zohar's question is: How can it be that the people of the world speak the mystery of faith of the blessed Holy One if this secret abides in a realm above and beyond words? How is this silent story transformed into something that all the wise of heart, the mystics across the world, speak about constantly? What is it that enables the mystics to give voice to the experience of the divine?

The answer, according to this homily, is that the story recounted with "no utterance" and "no words" is transformed into a story capable of being spoken by all because the boundary between the upper and lower worlds is not sealed.

To be sure, such matters are beyond the boundaries of linguistic expression, yet something of the beyond is nevertheless filtered and reflected in the droplets within language. The upper world flows and pours forth into the lower world; and the wise of heart are the ones who know how to capture in their heart's eye the sparks of the silent story found in their world, and to give this story voice.

The continuation of the homily describes the required state of consciousness for experiencing the upper world in the lower. "He placed in them a tent for the sun" (v. 5) is interpreted as referring to the way in which the higher sefirot, those that hail from the world of "no utterance," are gathered and reflected in the shining speculum of the sun, the sefirah *Tiferet*, thereby enabling a part of them to reach the world expressed in "words." According to this homily, whoever can draw down the reality of "no utterance" into "words" attains the state of consciousness of *Tiferet*. This state, as we have already seen, is beyond time and is concerned with center—a state of consciousness highly concentrated and directed toward that reality between the singular, primal source and the dualistic world of phenomena.

It is through *Tiferet* (Tree of Life) consciousness that the world of "no utterance" is experienced. And it is from here that the ability to transform mystical experience into words is created.

> *Day to day makes utterance* (Psalms 19:3)—Because this utterance is a supernal mystery and is unlike other utterances, the [next] verse reiterates and says *there is no utterance, there are no words*, as is the case with other utterances in the world. Rather, this utterance is a supernal mystery of the upper levels, where there are no utterances and no words, and they [these levels] are not heard like the other levels that are the mystery of faith, which are the sound

that is heard. Yet these are never heard, as is written: *whose sound goes unheard* (ibid., 4).

Their voice carries throughout the earth (ibid., 5)—even though they are concealed above and have never been known, their bounty and flow pours forth and flows below. And because of this flow we have perfect faith in this world, and all the people of the world speak of the mystery of faith of the blessed Holy One, of those levels, as though they had been revealed and were not hidden and concealed.

And this is the meaning of *their words to the end of the world* (ibid.)—from one end of the world to the other, those wise of heart speak of those hidden levels, even though they are unknown. (Zohar 2:137a)

The Zohar contains numerous expositions that explore the dynamic structure of the relationship between thought, voice, and speech as paralleling the movement of emanation within the divine world.[5] The ability to utter the "mystery of faith" is in fact an expression of the appropriate connection between voice and speech. Human thought, as a model of divine thought, signifies the beginning of the process of the manifestation of reality, which ultimately will receive expression through appropriate speech.

The beginning of thought stems from, and is dependent upon, the arousal of will, which is represented by the sefirah *Keter*. Will is the primary stirring, the first arousal—nondiscursive and linguistically undifferentiated—toward something other, to a relation beyond that of consciousness with itself, an attitude toward something external. Will indicates the beginning of the passage from the divine nothingness to the very beginnings of being.

Thought is the human representation of the divine quality of the sefirah *Ḥokhmah*, or *Ḥokhmah* in combination with *Binah*. It is the conceptual Eden from which the river of voice flows forth. Sometimes, this division is softened by the mediation of a secret, inner voice, on the pattern of the sefirah *Binah*, that precedes the appearance of the audible voice.

Voice comprises the totality of emotions, thoughts, and intentions that together create experience, prior to its articulation in speech. Voice is considered a masculine element, whereas speech—which pronounces, clarifies, and articulates voice through the organ of the mouth and transforms it into meaningful sound—is considered by the Zohar a quintessentially feminine element.[6]

This structure of the appropriate and balanced flow from the abstract to the differentiated is repeated many times in the Zohar. It represents both the dynamic structure of the divine world and its creative, generative power, as well as the generative force of sexuality in the human world below.

This parallel between the dynamic structures of the creation of reality, the creation of human beings, and the production of language is also the basis for Rabbi Shim'on's stern demand of his disciples to be extremely careful regarding every word that leaves their mouths—for the word, in its very essence, is potent and constitutive of reality. This reality can be either blessed or distorted and destructive. Because of the human partnership with the divine through the creative power of the word, mystical speech must be aware of its awesome power in order to be blessed and beneficent.

Already in *Sefer Yetsirah* (the Book of Creation) we find the mouth and the genitals as the two organs of the Covenant in man. The order of the creation of the word is identical to the process of the creation of life. The Zohar, in turn, based on the science of its day, describes the way that sperm is produced in the brain, traverses along the spinal column to the genital organ, from where it enters the womb of the female to begin the creation of the newborn. Mystical speech is, then, also an erotic expression—the appropriate pairing of the gushing, guiding power of the masculine voice with the separating or articulating capacity of the feminine mouth, a pairing that brings about the creation of "true" and rich speech.

Thus, a condition for correct mystical speech is the attainment of the state of consciousness of *Tiferet*, the world of voice that draws its content or images from the world of thought. This process is connected to the description of the three main states of consciousness in the Zohar discussed in the previous chapter: that of *Atika* (also known as *Keter*), the unitary and undifferentiated state, whose precise alignment with the states of consciousness of *Tiferet* and *Malkhut* engenders appropriate speech.[7]

One of the most beautiful descriptions of the eros-laden creation of speech is found in Rabbi Shim'on's homily in the Zohar's commentary to the Torah portion *Shemot*. Rabbi Shim'on expounds a yearning and love-filled verse from the Song of Songs (4:8; "With me from Lebanon, bride; with me from Lebanon come! Descend from the peak of Amana, from the peak of Senir and Hermon, from the dens of lions, from the mountains of leopards!") as describing the mystery of faith. According to Rashbi, the verse refers to the shared and singular source of speech in the whiteness (*loven*) of *Keter*, the divine "Lebanon." At the same time, it bespeaks the mystery of the calling of the masculine forces within divinity to the feminine forces, so as to achieve unification. The verse describes the yearning that generates the birth of the word through the tongue, teeth, and lips.

On one level, the verse is expounded about the divine world, while on another level, it describes the birth of the poetic-erotic language of the Song of Songs. The thought and speech that flow from the Lebanon through the lips in the appropriate manner create appropriate speech, which, at its peak, is represented by the language of the Song of Songs. According to the Zohar, it is in the Songs of Songs that we find the ultimate, truest, and most complete speech; speech in which are intertwined different levels of reality, and in which abides the perfect symmetry between human eros and the mystery of divinity.

> Rabbi Shim'on said, "This verse was uttered concerning the mystery of the union of faith. *With me from Lebanon, bride.* Voice said to speech, *With me*, for this voice comes to speech, conducting it—becoming one, completely inseparable. Because voice is general and speech is particular; so the general requires the particular, and the particular requires the general. For there is no voice without speech, and no speech without voice. *So, with me from Lebanon*—since the essence of both of them derives *from Lebanon*.
>
> "*Descend from the peak of Amana*—the larynx, from which issues breath, consummating all, from the mystery of Lebanon, concealed and treasured away.
>
> "*From the peak of Senir and Hermon*—the tongue, tip and middle, articulating speech.
>
> "*From the dens of lions*—the teeth.
>
> "*From the mountains of leopards*—the lips, consummation, by which speech is consummated." (Zohar 2:3a, Matt 2004–2007, vol. 4, pp. 7–8)

Even in those places in the Zohar where silence may clarify the experience or mystical attainment, the experience does not remain buried silently

in the heart of the mystic. Rather, it is transformed into knowledge transmitted to one's companions.

The question of silence and speech in religious worship, and the awareness of the mystic's great endeavor to draw down a world beyond words
into language, arises in the story appearing in the Zohar's opening pages
(1:1b–2b). Rabbi El'azar (son of Rabbi Shim'on) opens the verse "Lift your
eyes on high and see who created these" (Isaiah 40:26), through which he
expounds the inevitable frustration of the mystic who seeks to climb the
ladder of divine attainment. Rabbi El'azar describes the attempt to climb
from the state of consciousness of *Malkhut*, termed "What" (*Mah*)—the
world that can be indicated, apprehended, and discussed in words—to the
world of *Binah*. This is a higher divine world, the world of "Who" (*Mi*), a
world that cannot be apprehended intellectually, open to questioning yet
beyond answers and discourse. Rabbi El'azar expounds the connection between these two ends of the divine world, between the What and the Who,
and the role of the sefirah *Tiferet* that stands between them.

His father, Rabbi Shim'on, then tells him: "My son, cease your words,
so that the concealed mystery on high, unknown to any human, may be
revealed." Rabbi El'azar stays silent; and Rabbi Shim'on weeps and recounts the wonderful story of how, with the help of Elijah the prophet, he
learned the deep secret of the verse interpreted by his son.

That secret of the verse lies in understanding the essence of religious worship as determined by the necessary tension between the ineffable and inexpressible, the world of *Binah* called "Who" (*Mi*) on the one hand, and
the divine world capable of being expressed and explored verbally, termed
"These" (*Elleh*) on the other. Only the integration of the *Mi* and the *Elleh*
can complete the divine name *Elohim* ("God"). (In Hebrew, the letters of the
word *Elohim* are the same as those of the words *elleh* and *mi*.)

According to Rabbi Shim'on, the mystics, those who raise their eyes
on high, must see and understand that the source of the world capable
of being comprehended (designated by the term *Elleh*) lies in the world
only open to wonder, the world of the higher sefirot that emerge from *Ein
Sof*—namely, *Keter*, *Ḥokhmah*, and especially *Binah* (signified by the term

Mi). Appropriate and balanced religious worship, then, is that which consciously comprises these two qualities: the quality of wonder and silence as well as that quality capable of being defined, analyzed, and translated into religious norms.

The separation of these two qualities and the forgetting that the source of the *Elleh* lies in the *Mi* leads to the mystical sin of splitting the divine name *Elohim*. This is the sin of pointing at the *Elleh*, the concrete aspects of religious life, and seeing them as ultimate reality at the expense of the necessary and elusive quality of the world of wonder. This is, according to elsewhere in the Zohar, the children of Israel's sin with the golden calf, for as they pointed at their idol they cried out: "These (*Elleh*) are your gods, O Israel" (Exodus 32:4), and thereby expressed their preference for the world of *Elleh* devoid of the world of *Mi*.[8]

The question of the ability to express the ineffable emerges here once again. The mystic has a duty to find a way to express the inexpressible, as the undifferentiated worlds of question must be related to the differentiated, dualistic worlds. The son's silence in this story clears the space for his father to enter and to transport the listeners to a deeper dimension of interpretation. Rabbi Shim'on's homily is not merely a theosophical exposition describing the chain of divine emanation; it is rather an exposition describing the mystical endeavor to draw down the experience of the world of the question into the world of voice and speech.

The world of "What," the world of *Malkhut*, cannot be composed without the drawing down of the "letters" or elements from the higher worlds. The upper world seeks to be revealed in the world of speech; and to this end, *Binah*, the great mother of all being, lends her power to the world of expression and speech. The passage to expression takes place at the moment of the encounter between the mystic and female divinity. Rabbi Shim'on expounds this through the connection between "Three times a year all your males shall appear before the Sovereign, YHVH" (Exodus 23:17)—where the Sovereign YHVH is interpreted as referring to the sefirah *Malkhut*—and "These I remember, I pour out my soul, how I walked with the crowd, conducting them to the House of Elohim with joyous shouts of praise, the festive throng" (Psalms 42:5). The world of appropriate mystical speech ("joyous shouts of praise") bursts forth when the male appears before feminine divinity ("the Sovereign of all the earth").

This encounter, however, is not between males and the feminine aspect of the divine in and of herself, but rather the feminine when adorned in masculine clothing. *Malkhut* adorns herself in the letter *yud*, the symbol of *Yesod*; then she is called *Mi* (Who) and thus she appears before the male. This is Shekhinah in a special erotic mode, whereby she appears as female adorned with the signs of the male.[9] As Elliot Wolfson has shown, this condition of union, where the feminine incorporates the masculine, is not common in the Zohar—where we more generally find the masculine incorporating the feminine. This is a most unique and potent appearance of the feminine, adorned with the masculine genital organ.[10]

We are not, it should be stressed, dealing here with an essentially androgynous figure, but a figure defined as female, which when seen by males appears as the phallic feminine, wrapped in masculinity, perhaps even for reasons of modesty to prevent exposure of the genitals. In this condition of appearing, in the encounter between the mystic and Shekhinah, the letters from the heights of the world of divinity are drawn to the voice that is heard in the House of *Elohim*, the world of *Malkhut*, from which mystical language bursts forth.

> "For *Mah* (What) was not so, is not composed until these letters—*Elleh*—are drawn from above to below and Mother lends Daughter Her garments, and adorns Her in Her adornments.
>
> "When does she adorn Her fittingly? When all males appear before Her, as is written, *All your males shall appear before the Sovereign, YHVH* (Exodus 23:17). This one is called Sovereign, as is said: *Behold, the ark of the covenant, Sovereign of all the earth* (Joshua 3:11).
>
> "Then the letter *he* departs and *yod* enters, and She adorns Herself in masculine clothing in the presence of every male in Israel. Other letters Israel draws from above to this site: (*Elleh*) *These, I remember* (Psalms 42:5). 'With my mouth I mentioned them, in my yearning I poured out my tears, drawing forth these letters.[11] Then, *I conduct them* from above *to the house of Elohim*, to be *Elohim*, like him.'
>
> "With what?—*With joyous shouts of praise, the festive throng.*" (Zohar 1:2a; Matt 2004–2007, vol. 1, p. 9, adapted)

In the course of the homily, Rabbi Shim'on identifies completely with David, the author of the Psalm. The words of the Psalm, "I pour out my soul," are described here as a mystical activity—"with my mouth I mentioned them, in my yearning I poured out my tears"—whose purpose is to draw down the divine "letters" from above to below with joyous shouts of praise. In fact, this very mystical activity informs Rabbi Shim'on's exposition.[12]

In this context, it is fitting to mention the homily that we encountered earlier about the verse "at daybreak I prepare for You and wait (atsappeh)."[13] That homily deals with the way in which the mystic, in this case King David, encompasses within himself the divine light that he covers over, so that through him this light might reach the world in a positive and beneficial way. The divine light is not narrated but is experienced; and this experience pertains to the domain of the ineffable. Nevertheless, the ability to convey and speak the experience flows from the power of the receiving vessel, which covers and gilds (metsappeh) the light. The mystical experience that the Companions describe in language is, in fact, an expression of the mystic's artistic power to gild the light in words; and this endeavor is understood as a quintessentially feminine activity.

The complex relationship between the effable and the ineffable raises the question of the mystic's state of consciousness during mystical experience. In the opening of the unit Rav Metivta (Master of the Academy) that we have already seen, we witness the transition from a condition characterized by an inability to utter words to a condition in which a new capacity for expression is born due to the change in the speakers' state of consciousness.[14] Something in the transition (from an ordinary state of consciousness to the new state of consciousness in the spiritual realm that the Companions are visiting) removes what blocks speech, enabling words to be spoken. Among the speakers is created a new intimacy that encourages speech.

As a rule, the circle of Rabbi Shim'on encourages the Companions' speech. Thus we read: "Rabbi Shim'on was silent for a while. He said, 'Silence is necessary everywhere—except for silence of Torah.'"[15] It is as though the Zohar is claiming (contrary to Psalms 19), "There is utterance; there are words!" even for matters that pertain to a world of no utterance.

This encouragement is connected with the assumptions that there is someone to speak with and something to speak about, and that it is possible, permissible, and desirable to speak about the divine world that appears through the interpretation of the words of the Torah. We are told that in Rabbi Shim'on's generation a person says to his companion, "Open your mouth so that your words may shine forth."[16] Such a statement is laden with profound optimism regarding the capacity of language. Language here expands the boundaries of what it is capable of being expressed.

Speech and the ability to speak mystical experience are also connected with the self-perception of the Zohar's protagonists, who see themselves as belonging to a group in which the Holy Spirit (*Ruaḥ ha-Kodesh*) pulsates and resounds. As Haviva Pedaya has shown, among the first generations of kabbalists the experience of the Holy Spirit was connected with automatic speech, in some cases even against the mystic's will. The descent of the Holy Spirit leads to the outpouring of what Pedaya terms *dibbur ha-mitpa'el* (ecstatic speech).[17] In the story appearing in the weekly portion *Terumah* in the Zohar, Rabbi Ya'akov bar Iddi, who sees himself as a temporary guest in the circle of the Companions, opens with a homily about the relationship between the Holy Spirit, prophecy, and the spirit of understanding and insight. In his homily he claims that there are people who, like King Saul, discover the ability to prophesy only when in the company of a group of prophets; and who, upon leaving such company, lose their prophetic capacity. That is, the connection with people occupied with prophecy bestows upon the participants their prophetic ability.

Then, in a leap from the homily to the immediate narrative context, and applying what he has just said about King Saul to himself, Rabbi Ya'akov bar Iddi relates to the companions of Rabbi Shim'on's circle as "faithful prophets" and to his own ability to expound mystical matters as arising from his entry into a circle of students among whom the Holy Spirit pulsates:

> As long as [Saul] was in the company of those prophets, prophecy alighted upon him. After he separated from them—he no longer prophesied.
>
> As for me, who gave me the arousal of the Holy Spirit? [It came about] through my being in the company of faithful prophets, the students of Rabbi

Shim'on bar Yoḥai, for whom the upper and lower worlds tremor. So too [they tremor] for me, when I am among you! (Zohar 2:154a)

It is the self-image of the circle, as a group among whom the Holy Spirit and spirit of prophecy dwells, that enables the Companions to utter what usually cannot be spoken.

The ability to express mystical experience in language is nevertheless limited, and the Zohar frequently points to these boundaries: there are things that can only be seen and not spoken, matters that can be known but are incapable of being uttered, and matters that can only be sensed in the mind without being fully comprehended.

The Zohar creates liminal linguistic situations that undermine or challenge ordinary, everyday consciousness and that serve the function of creating a new intellectual, imaginative, and emotional expanse. One of these linguistic limits is the use of paradox in order to describe situations at the edge of language's capacity of expression.[18] Thus, when the Zohar's protagonists describe certain of their insights or visions, they employ terms like: "touches and does not touch," "shines and does not shine," "is found and is not found," "exists and does not exist." These linguistic devices serve a performative function. We readers immediately understand that we are dealing with a reality, a domain to which dichotomous distinctions do not pertain.

In the reality of the world of separation, a thing exists as itself; it is not at the same time something else. The meaning of expressions like "touches and does not touch"[19] is not temporal sequence—that is, at first there was touching and then there was not—but rather that the touching is so subtle that it cannot really be defined as touching at all. This is also true of knowledge that "is known and not known"[20] or a presence that "is found and not found."[21]

Linguistic devices of this kind are generally employed by the Zohar in describing the earliest stages in the emergence of differentiated reality from within *Ein Sof*. Such paradoxical language is fitting for the inherent ambiguity of this primal situation. It prompts us readers to expand our consciousness to encompass this kind of reality.

Furthermore, in these descriptions we often find long strings of negation, the purpose of which is to interrupt the reader's capacity for clear discursive comprehension of the topic under discussion. From an experiential perspective, this language serves as an active invitation to enter the portal of visionary, dreamlike, and poetic seeing—a seeing in which it is possible to say:

> A spark of impenetrable darkness flashed within the concealed of the concealed, from the head of Infinity—a cluster of vapor forming in formlessness, thrust in a ring, not white, not black, not red, not green, no color at all. (Zohar 1:15a; Matt 2004–2007, vol. 1, pp. 107–8)

In describing the process of emanation, the Zohar frequently employs superlative doublets, like "*Atika de-Atikin*" (the Most Ancient of Ancients), "*sitra de-sitrin*" (the secret of secrets), "*tamir de-tamirin*" (the most hidden of the hidden).[22] More than a theological-philosophical attempt to express God's transcendence, such constructions—like the Zohar's strings of negation or its paradoxical formulations—create, through their exaggeration and their rhythm, a hymn-like, mythic atmosphere appropriate to the profound and primal subjects being discussed.

For example, in the *Idra Rabba*, an anonymous teaching is quoted in the description of the *tikkun* (arraying) of the beard: "The *tikkun* of the beard is hidden and concealed, hidden and not hidden, concealed and not concealed, in his adornments known and not known."[23] Here the paradoxical language creates an experience of complexity and at the same time a desire to capture the sparks of the "not hidden," the "not concealed," and the "known."

Expressed differently, the object of inquiry is of its essence all these things and their negation; and the one apprehending these mysteries is caught in the tension between contact with the present and not-present aspects of this divine dimension. The continuum of opposites is therefore simultaneously a recognition of language's limits and the overcoming of them. Sentences of this kind leave behind them a trail of mystery saturated with emotions and sensations. They invite the reader to apprehend this mysterious dimension by joining the grand endeavor of the zoharic circle.

16

On Books and Writing

Our exploration of the Zohar's attitude toward expressing mystical experience as well as of the work's self-perception requires also a special discussion about the place of the book and the role of writing in the composition. Can we find in the zoharic text itself statements or clues alluding to
the transformation of the Companions' oral world into a text or book? In
particular, does the Zohar refer to a "book" of secrets?[1]

In a number of passages, we do encounter a myth about a book—the
ultimate book, containing all the world's secrets—usually referred to as *sifra
de-Adam* (the Book of Adam) or *sifra de-Ḥanokh* (Book of Enoch).[2] According to the Zohar, this book was first given to Adam, from whom it passed
to Enoch, and then to Moses and Solomon. The Companions along with
Rabbi Shim'on repeatedly take pride in their knowledge of the contents of
this wondrous work.

This myth appears in the Zohar in numerous formulations and in different stories. Interestingly, it is Rabbi Shim'on himself who articulates the
dangers posed by such a book's very existence. The book of secrets is dangerous, Rabbi Shim'on says, because incorrect or inappropriate readings of

it are likely to cause—and indeed have caused—its readers to abandon the domain of holiness for the domain of evil and impurity.

Expressed differently, it is the very existence of the written work that is at the root of the seductiveness of external cultures and wisdoms—for example, magic, astrology, and the like. This is an extremely harsh statement about the dangers associated with writing and uncontrolled publication.

In order to maintain a proper relationship with the secret, it is imperative that the secret remain oral, and that it be transmitted through the living tradition of teachers and disciples. Rabbi Shim'on attests that in his own day, while the wise of the world do indeed know the secrets of the world and the secrets of divinity, they do not disclose them.

> Rabbi Shim'on said: "If I had been present in the world when the blessed Holy One issued *The Book of Enoch* to the world and *The Book of Adam*, I would have objected to their presence among human beings, because all the wise did not contemplate them carefully and strayed in strange words, abandoning the supernal domain for the other domain. But now the wise of the world know words and conceal them, invigorating themselves in the service of their Lord." (Zohar 1:72b; Matt 2004–2007, vol. 1, pp. 429–30, adapted)

This last statement is more than a little ironic if we understand the "book of secrets" as referring to the Zohar itself!

This book of secrets is elusive, difficult if not impossible to grasp; in a number of stories in the Zohar, the book disappears in fire and wind from the hands of its finder.[3] Rabbi Abba, the most senior of the Companions, is depicted as the great expert in such books. On one occasion, he explains the book's chain of transmission from Adam to Enoch, and on to the wise of each generation. Of particular significance for us in his account is the fact that the Zohar's protagonists claim access to this book.

> Rabbi Abba said, "An actual book was brought down to Adam, from which he discovered supernal wisdom. This book reached *the sons of Elohim*, who contemplate and know it.... *Ḥanokh* [Enoch] had a book—a book from the site of *the book of the generations of Adam*, mystery of wisdom.... Happy are the devout of the world, to whom supernal wisdom is revealed, never to be forgotten, as is said: *The secret of YHVH is for those in awe of Him; to them He reveals His covenant* (Psalms 25:14). (Zohar 1:37b; Matt 2004–2007, vol. 1, pp. 237–39)

In a different story, the Companions attest that they indeed have knowledge of this book, and that it is concealed among them; the book is thus characterized by a doubled esotericism—a book of secrets that is kept secret.

This book is in fact condensed light from the supernal radiance given to Adam. According to the account found in *Zohar Ḥadash*, Enoch is deemed worthy of having this primal luminescence illuminate within him. Thus he receives from the angels supernal wisdom together with a book that had been concealed within the Tree of Life: "One day he entered the Garden of Eden and they showed him the secrets (or: mysteries) of the garden, and he left that book and all that he had seen outside; and it is concealed among the Companions."[4] When God takes Enoch (soon to be transformed into the angel Metatron), he leaves behind the supernal book together with all that he has seen and learned of the world and steps into paradise. In this way, the Companions now have access to that wondrous Book of Enoch—whose essence is light, and whose natural place is among the branches of the Tree of Life—images that of course also recall the Torah (identified as "a Tree of Life for those who cling to her"; Proverbs 3:18).

Another story in the Zohar recounts how Rabbi Abba, together with Rabbi Yehudah of Akko, finds an ancient book hidden in a cave in the desert, containing the secrets of the soul and its peregrinations after death.[5] Rabbi Abba relates that he began reading the book, until the book itself called out "Till here, be silent!" at which point the remaining letters on the page were magically erased. Later in a dream, Rabbi Abba recalls, he was instructed not to reveal what he had read in that hidden book save to the mighty rock, Rabbi Shim'on bar Yoḥai.

The Zohar also cites the "Book of Rabbi Yeiva Sava" and the "Book of Hamnuna Sava," both of which contain secrets and mysteries. All told, in the Zohar's consciousness there do exist alongside the Torah various additional books of secrets.

Rabbi Abba is without doubt the central figure in matters pertaining to writing in the Zohar, as well as to allusions to the very act of the Zohar's writing found in the composition itself. One of the most interesting stories in the Zohar exploring the theme of the great teacher's legacy after his death is found in its commentary to the Torah portion *Vayeḥi*. The story begins with Rabbi Yose lamenting the cessation of knowledge among the Companions after Rabbi Shim'on's death. It continues with a description of Rabbi Yehudah's nightmarish hallucination, the entire scene imbued with a profound sense of loss and confusion.

> "One day he fell asleep under a tree, and in his dream he saw four wings arrayed, and Rabbi Shim'on ascending on them with a Torah scroll. He left behind no book of mysteries or aggadah, but took them away with him. They took him up to heaven, and he saw him disappear from sight, revealed no more.
>
> "When he awoke he said: 'Surely, ever since Rabbi Shim'on took his final sleep, wisdom has departed from the earth. Woe to the generation that has lost this precious stone, joining upper and lower pillars!'" (Zohar 1:217a; Matt 2004–2007, vol. 3, p. 308)

With Rabbi Shim'on's death, all wisdom departs from the world, for he carries with him to the uppermost heavens the Torah, the books of secrets and mysteries, and the aggadah. Rabbi Yehudah tells Rabbi Abba about his dream; and in Rabbi Abba's response we can discern the beginning of the Zohar's self-consciousness as a written work:

> Rabbi Abba raised his hands to his head and wept and said: "Rabbi Shim'on, the millstones with which fine manna is ground every day, and then gathered, as is written: *The one with the least gathered ten ḥomers* (Numbers 11:32)![6] Now millstones and manna have disappeared; nothing remains of them in the world except what is written, *Take one jar and put in it a full omer of manna and set it before YHVH for safekeeping* (Exodus 16:33)—it is not written *revealed* but rather *for safekeeping*, for concealment. Now who can reveal secrets, and who will know them?" (ibid.; Matt 2004–2007, vol. 3, pp. 308–9)

The manna, according to the Zohar, is the spiritual nourishment that trickles from the skull of *Atika Kadisha*, and the millstones that grind this manna are Rabbi Shim'on himself. Rashbi's death, therefore, signifies the end of the ability to be nourished by the spiritual food from the world of *Keter*, as there is no longer anyone to mediate and process the manna to render it consumable in this world. Just as Moses' death signifies the end of the wilderness wanderings and the cessation of the manna, so Rabbi Shim'on's death concludes the period of disclosure and innovation in which the Companions enjoyed the spiritual delicacies that Rabbi Shim'on revealed.

As Rabbi Abba's homily proceeds, he outlines what can nevertheless be preserved of the special quality that Rabbi Shim'on inspired in the world. Rabbi Abba cites Moses' command to his brother Aaron to place an *omer*'s worth of manna in a jar as a keepsake in the sanctuary (Exodus 16:33). In its biblical context, the need to preserve a small quantity of manna arises from the recognition that the miraculous era in which the people ate "bread from the sky" is about to end. The jar of manna is to serve as a reminder of the celestial food with which God, through his prophet Moses, fed the people in the wilderness.

As we will see below, Rabbi Abba's exposition about the jar of manna in fact relates to the question of the recording—the rendering into writing—of the world of the Companions and the teacher, a world that inspired the Zohar's composition. In the context of the homily, Rabbi Shim'on is Moses, and Rabbi Abba is Aaron. Rabbi Abba is the one who receives and executes Rabbi Shim'on's command to store "manna" as a keepsake, for it is he who creates the jar—namely, the book that contains the preserved essence, a tiny fragment of the divine bounty that inundated the world while Rabbi Shim'on was alive.

After the great teacher's death, all that remains is one jar of manna in which is preserved a memory of the experience of Rabbi Shim'on's generation, the new *dor de'ah* (generation of knowledge). Like the manna in the wilderness, the teachings of Rabbi Shim'on are by their very nature unable to be stored—they can only be experienced. The miracle of the sanctuary's jar was that only in that specific container did the stored manna not spoil.

Just as the sanctuary's jar succeeded in preserving an *omer*'s worth of manna, so it was necessary to create a vessel capable of preserving the teachings of Rabbi Shim'on. As Yehuda Liebes has already suggested, the Zohar is that miraculous jar of manna.[7] Seen in this light, then, Rabbi Abba's homily is a unique *ars poetica* statement about the very enterprise of the writing of the Zohar itself. The book is therefore the concealed jar of manna, in which is preserved the essence of the zoharic circle's experience, the generation that created a "live Zohar," which then served as the inspiration for writing the composition.

The Zohar as a book, however, is not like Rumi's "wine poured without glasses" or the psalmic "knowledge covering the earth like the sea," as was the case in the generation of Rabbi Shim'on, which experienced the abundance of divine wisdom. It does, though, contain an essence, a trace of experience, which, when inhaled or tasted, enables the reader to return and enter the lost world of the Companions.

Rabbi Abba's remarks bespeak a measure of sobriety regarding the relationship between life and art. The creation of the container, whether it be a jar or a book, is born from the acknowledgment of the passing of experience itself. Thus it is more about conservation and memory than about the continuation of creativity.

Nevertheless, the genius of the Zohar as book lies precisely in its ability to capture the life of the experiences in Rabbi Shim'on's circle. As I have already noted, it is my view that the Zohar was composed in the aftermath of the live experience of a teacher and circle of disciples, following the great mourning of the end of this experience; and it was perhaps the loss of this live experience, the ensuing grief and need to work through this grief, that generated this most sublime literature and poetry.

It is possible that Rabbi Abba is the disguised figure of Moses de León, whose hand is readily discernable in the writing of the Zohar. Significantly, Rabbi Abba is not the teacher but rather the outstanding student. If my speculation is correct, then de León's decision to appear not as the teacher, the hero, but rather as a secondary character distinguishes him from, for example, the author of *Tikkunei ha-Zohar* and *Ra'aya Meheimna*, who identifies himself with the hero of the composition, Moses.[8]

The decision to appear in the composition as Rabbi Abba would have given its author great room in which to maneuver. It would have enabled him to occupy the space of observer and to adopt an ironic perspective that would be very difficult if he identified totally with the composition's hero. From his vantage point as student and disciple, he would be able to reanimate the group's experience—the love, the tension, the thrill of creativity, the adoration of the teacher, and the intensity of the circle's religious, mystical, and mythical life. Perhaps, unlike the other disciples and even the teacher himself, he was endowed with a unique literary artistic genius, for after all, the book produced by Rabbi Abba—whoever he may be—is no mere dull account of the group's life, but an imaginative, literary marvel.

Perhaps most fascinating of all in this context would have been the decision on the part of the author, through the character of Rabbi Abba, to create a myth about himself explaining how he assumed the freedom to write his artistic version of the group's life. The need for justification of the very enterprise of writing the Zohar attests to the fact that this endeavor was not a given, a fait accompli, but rather was riddled with ambivalence. Even among the Rabbis of the Mishnah and Talmud, the writing down of the Oral Torah came about only after considerable debate and polemic, and there are explicit prohibitions against writing and recording the oral word.[9] How much more problematic, then, is the inscription of the Torah's secrets, bound as they are by the severe restrictions against expounding *Ma'aseh Bereishit* (The Creation Episode) and *Ma'aseh Merkavah* (The Chariot Episode).

On the personal-artistic level, this ambivalence would also have been informed by, on the one hand, the desire to preserve, and on the other, the question of whether it would indeed be possible to convey the world of the Companions without annihilating the life that pulsated through it. It may be that the need to find or invent a myth of legitimacy for the writing of the work stems from the internal politics of the generation of the Zohar's authors. We might further speculate that the teacher's command to his student to write reflects the struggle for inheritance of the group's true tradition, and that this myth at once bestowed authority on one man or group, while denying such authority to others, who may have already begun writing their own version of events.[10]

In another passage where the Zohar discusses the desolation destined to befall the world after Rabbi Shim'on's death, Rabbi Abba once again figures prominently:

> Rabbi Abba raised his hands upon his head and wept. He said, "Rabbi! Radiance of Torah ascends now to the highest heaven of the supernal throne. Afterward, who will illumine the radiance of Torah? Woe to the world that will be left orphaned! However, words of the Master will shine in the world until King Messiah arrives, for of then is written *The earth will be filled with knowledge of YHVH as waters cover the sea* (Isaiah 11:9)." (Zohar 2:68a; Matt 2004–2007, vol. 4, p. 376)

Rabbi Abba's words are uttered before Rabbi Shim'on's death, yet even here we find him assuring us that even though Rabbi Shim'on will disappear, his words will endure and continue to shine forth until the coming of the Messiah. The way to guarantee this, it would seem, is in the writing of the Zohar.

In the *Idra Zuta*—the description of Rashbi's departure from the world—Rabbi Abba appears unmistakably in the role of the scribe.

> Everyone left; Rabbi El'azar, his son, Rabbi Abba, Rabbi Judah, Rabbi Yose and Rabbi Ḥiyya remained. Meanwhile, Rabbi Yitsḥak came in. . . . Rabbi Abba sat behind him and Rabbi El'azar in front. Rabbi Shim'on said: Now is a time of favor! I want to enter without shame into the world that is coming. Holy words, until now unrevealed, I want to reveal in the presence of Shekhinah. . . . Until now they were hidden in my heart as a password to the world that is coming. I will arrange you like this: Rabbi Abba will write; Rabbi El'azar, my son, will repeat; the other Companions will meditate within. (Zohar 3:287b; Matt 1983, p. 183)

Rabbi Shim'on reveals, Rabbi Abba records, and we read the secrets of the *Idra Zuta*.[11] After Rabbi Shim'on leaves his body and unites with Shekhinah, Rabbi Abba abandons his role as scribe and assumes the role of narrator and witness, saying: "Before the Holy Spark finished saying 'life,' his words subsided. I was still writing, intending to write more but I heard nothing. I did not raise my head: the light was overwhelming; I could not look."[12]

As the most senior of the disciples, Rabbi Abba also merits attending to Rabbi Shim'on's miraculous burial.[13] Another assembly that takes place after Rabbi Shim'on's death,[14] recounted in the Zohar's commentary to the Torah portion *Mishpatim*, includes yet another discussion about writing. Here, too, Rabbi Abba appears as the central protagonist. Following an extensive account of the mysteries of emanation, the Zohar describes the strengthening of the forces of judgment in the world and in divinity, brought about through improper intention and focus in the behavior of human beings. This is a description of the harsh face of the absence of positive theurgy.

The passage focuses on the complex connection between Shekhinah's role as a mother toward her children and her sexual relationship with her partner (the blessed Holy One). When the forces of judgment are strengthened in the world, Shekhinah is severed from her children and is unable to nurse them, as she does not enjoy the bounty-producing union with her partner. Shekhinah loses her capacity to bestow as she does not receive the very substance that enables her to give. The juxtaposition of the sexual image alongside the motherly image establishes a dense, highly compressed mythic mystery; and it is in this context that Rabbi El'azar responds with a question: "Father revealed all these *tikkunim* (expositions) so as to enter without shame into the world that is coming. Now, why should they be revealed?"[15]

Rabbi Abba's reply is in fact the continuation of the story in the *Idra Zuta* that we saw earlier. He explains to the Companions, and to the readers as well, why he has recorded the secrets.

> Rabbi Abba said to him: What I have written from the Holy Spark I have said to the Companions, for they know matters and knowledge is required, as is written: *that you will know that I am YHVH* (Exodus 10:2); and it is written: *and they will know that I am YHVH* (Exodus 29:46), so that matters will be established in our hearts. From here on, the matters are concealed among us. Happy is our portion in this world and in the world that is coming, for till now the Holy Spark was crowned with matters among us! (Zohar 2:123b)

This dialogue between Rabbi El'azar and Rabbi Abba reveals the tension between the two senior disciples of the circle after Rabbi Shim'on's death. Rabbi El'azar, the son, expresses doubts about Rabbi Abba's enterprise; and Rabbi Abba, for his part, defends his undertaking. The purpose of writing, Rabbi Abba explains, is to enable Rashbi's words to be established in the hearts of the Companions. That is, the text is intended for the inner circle alone, and it is subject to the laws of strict esotericism: "from here on the matters are concealed among us."

We must, however, ask whether this esotericism is not in fact one of the composition's strategies of seduction. After all, we readers understand that we are becoming a party to the secrets of an esoteric group, and Rabbi Abba's words serve as a lure to enter and discover what has been concealed.

Just as disclosure requires consent, so writing requires approval. In an encounter between Rabbi Shim'on and the prophet Elijah in the Zohar's commentary to the Song of Songs, we find a more direct expression of the need for authoritative consent in the act of writing:

> Rabbi Shim'on rejoiced. Elijah said to him: Rabbi, say your words and I will say after you, for through you and through me the matter will be completed. And permission has been granted us from the most ancient of all, that these secrets be revealed below and above. You below and I above. By your life, Rabbi, you are of supreme importance, because all your words will be written above before the Ancient of Days; and my words will not be written above, but my words will be written by you in this world. Your words will be written above, and my words written below. Happy are the righteous, in this world and in the world that is coming! (*Zohar Ḥadash*, 62c)

As Boaz Huss has already shown, this passage implies that while Rashbi's words have indeed been committed to writing, they are not to be found in this world but rather in the upper worlds, before the Ancient of Days (alluding to the famous passage in the Introduction to the Zohar, 4b). On the other hand, Elijah's words, which are indeed found in this world, are written below by Rabbi Shim'on bar Yoḥai!

Here, it seems, we have for the first time a description of a work—found in this world—written by Rabbi Shim'on containing the secrets revealed to him by Elijah the prophet. However, this passage also bespeaks a certain reticence regarding this composition, presented here as being of a lower order than the innovations of Rabbi Shim'on himself, which are inscribed above.[16]

Only in one passage do we find Rabbi Shim'on himself engaged in the act of writing. In the literary unit *Rav Metivta* (Master of the Academy), a spirit guide of the celestial academy instructs Rabbi Shim'on to record all that he sees by the light of a lamp (in other words, at night): "O holy, pious one, light of the world, take a notebook from this satchel; and take a lamp and write [down] these matters."[17]

Rabbi Shim'on himself undergoes an ecstatic-prophetic experience, weeps bitterly, and composes a love poem in honor of the Torah.

> He cried and placed his head between his knees and kissed the earth. In the meantime, he saw numerous images of the Companions circling around him. They said to him, "Do not fear, bar Yoḥai! Do not fear, Holy Spark! Write and rejoice in the joy of your master!"
>
> He wrote [down] all the things he heard that night; he learned them and repeated them and did not forget a thing. And the lamp shone before him all that night until morning came. (Zohar 3:166b)

Although not explicitly referring to the act of writing, there are other passages in the Zohar where the appearance of the word *zohar* seems to allude to the composition of the work itself. Here, for example, is a passage from the unit *Sitrei Torah*:

> Inside the hidden nexus, from within the sealed secret, a *zohar* flashed, shining as a mirror, embracing two colors blended together. Once these two absorbed each other, all colors appeared: purple, the whole spectrum of colors, flashing, disappearing. Those rays of color do not wait to be seen; they merge (*itḥabran*) into the fusion (*ḥibura*) of *zohar*. In this *zohar* dwells the one who dwells. It provides a name for the one who is concealed and totally unknown. (Zohar 1:147a–b; Matt 1983, p. 75)

The key phrase alluding to a written work is: "they merge (*itḥabran*) into the fusion (*ḥibura*) of *zohar*." Yehuda Liebes has suggested that word *ḥibura* hints at a written composition, and that the entire passage alludes to the Zohar itself.[18] For his part, Daniel Matt has argued that the passage "In this *zohar* dwells the one who dwells, it provides a name for the one who is concealed and totally unknown" refers to the pseudepigraphic disguise of Moses de León.[19]

Matt also highlights another passage in which we can discern both an allusion to the Zohar as a written work and the author's play with his pseudepigraphic persona.[20] The passage interprets the "motto verse" of the entire composition: "The enlightened will shine like the *zohar* of the sky" (Daniel 12:3).[21]

> "It is written: *The enlightened will shine like the radiance of the sky, and those who turn many to righteousness, like the stars for ever and ever* (Daniel 12:3). *The enlightened will shine.* Who are *the enlightened*? The wise one who contemplates, on his own, things that human beings cannot utter. . . .
>
> "*Will shine like the radiance of the sky.* What is *the radiance of the sky* (*zohar ha-rakia*)? The sky of Moses, standing in the middle; this *radiance* (*zohar*) is concealed and not revealed, standing above that sky in which colors can be seen. Although those colors can be seen within it, they do not glow with the radiance of the concealed colors. . . .
>
> "Of this we read: 'Moses attained the speculum that shines,' which stands above the one that does not shine." (Zohar 2:23a–b; Matt 2004–2007, vol. 4, pp. 79–81, adapted)

Matt sees in the words "this *zohar* is concealed and not revealed" the author's allusion to the concealed or pseudepigraphic form of his composition. The enlightened are the kabbalists who shine like the radiance of the sky, which is the sky of Moses, which in turn alludes to the Zohar. The enlightened, then, are the ones who shine with the mystical radiance of the composition.[22]

Again, these passages about writing in general and the composition of the Zohar in particular are neither clear nor explicit. As is the Zohar's custom, such matters are subtly alluded to and deftly intertwined within expositions of Scripture and enigmatic stories. The need to find or to invent earthly and divine consent for the writing of the Zohar appears already in the epic layer of the Zohar, though such references are usually enigmatic and allow numerous interpretations.

This is not the case, however, in the later strata of the Zohar.[23] In *Ra'aya Meheimna* and *Tikkunei ha-Zohar*, both of which were written at the beginning of the fourteenth century by authors already familiar with the Zohar as an existent work, the question of the legitimacy of the composition of the Zohar is discussed explicitly. In these strata, the role of divine consent in the composition of the work is of paramount importance and is stated so categorically.

> [*And none of the wicked will understand (yavinu)*], *but the enlightened will understand (yavinu)* (Daniel 12:10)—from the side of *Binah*, which is the Tree of Life. About them is written: *and the enlightened will shine like the radiance (zohar) of the sky* (Daniel 12:3)—through this book of yours, the book of radiance (*Sefer ha-Zohar*), they will shine from the radiance (*zohar*) of the supernal mother—*teshuvah* (repentance/return). These do not need to be put to the test. And since Israel are destined to taste of the Tree of Life, which is this book of radiance (*Sefer ha-Zohar*), through it they will emerge from exile in love and mercy. (Zohar, *Ra'aya Meheimna*, 3:124b)

> It is written: *the enlightened will shine like the radiance (zohar) of the sky* (Daniel 12:3)—these are Rabbi Shim'on bar Yoḥai and his Companions, who radiated radiance of above. . . . *Like the radiance (zohar) of the sky*—what does it mean *like the radiance*? It means that when they composed this work, the upper realms consented and called it the Book of Radiance (*Sefer ha-Zohar*).[24] (*Tikkunei ha-Zohar* 17a)

In a passage in *Tikkunei ha-Zohar* appearing in *Zohar Ḥadash*, a prayer comprises what we may term a quasi-nostalgic reading of the myth of the Zohar's composition. In it we find a deep desire that the book of the Zohar will activate the reader, expand his consciousness, and cause him to shine. While it is true that this prayer was composed by authors who already related to the Zohar as a written work, their words nevertheless attest to the way in which they understood its force in terms of its unique capacity to bring to the life of the reader the fullness of the zoharic world. For the author of this prayer, the Zohar is a work that invites the reader to participate in and innovate through this world, and finally, by virtue of that world's sheer power, to restore Shekhinah:

> Master of the Worlds, may it be Your will to comprise the upper and lower [realms] with this book, and may everyone be found in it, whether in writing or in speaking [through] the power of Your name YHVH, and all the entities that shine from it. . . .
>
> May all who are mentioned in this book, the upper and the lower, radiate from Your name and all the entities of it like the radiance that shines in the sky. And grant permission to all who are mentioned in this book, through

the power of Your name, the opportunity to appear immediately, in a blink of the eye, that each and every one of them may reveal precious matters, concealed mysteries before Shekhinah, who is alone in exile, that she may be illumined from Your name in this composition, and to unite with You through this composition, to connect with it and be adorned to you with many adornments, and so fulfill [Your promise], *I will see her and remember the eternal covenant* (Genesis 9:16). (*Zohar Ḥadash* 104a)

According to this prayer, the Zohar arouses a condition of revelation and disclosure of secrets. Reading and studying the Zohar are understood here as a way to connect with the power of innovation and the revelation of mysteries, both of which flow to the student via the Zohar's characters who are revealed in and act upon the reader's soul. By innovating secrets of Torah, the Zohar's reader is able to adorn the exiled Shekhinah so that she will be remembered and loved once again by her beloved—the blessed Holy One.

From the moment of its first appearance and circulation, the Zohar assumed the status of "written Torah,"[25] thus beginning the process of its crystallization into a book. At the same time, the Zohar underwent a process of sanctification and canonization, which on the one hand stifled the very creative adventure to which the Zohar invited the world, but which on the other hand inspired the continuation of zoharic creativity through creative exegesis, interpretation, and research.[26]

Concluding Remarks

In the Zohar's parable of the beloved in the palace, we readers follow the lover's exhilarating journey, during which the lover's veils and coverings are piece-by-piece removed, until the lover reaches the realm of the beloved's secrets. After the Zohar reveals that this parable of desire, courtship, and love alludes to the ideal relationship between the scholar of Torah and the Torah herself, we find the following surprising ending:

> [The Old Man said:]
> "Now he sees that nothing should be added to those words
> and nothing taken away.
> Now the *peshat* of the verse, just like it is!
> Not even a single letter should be added or deleted.
> Human beings must become aware!
> they must pursue Torah to become her lovers!"
>
> Zohar 2:99b; Matt 1983, pp. 123, 125

The lover of Torah acknowledges that only after the different dimensions of Torah have been revealed, only then can he stand in astonishment, wonder, and appreciation of her form, "just like it is."

This is no longer the simplicity of Torah that the simpleton might experience standing for the first time at her gate. It is, rather, a newly discovered appreciation of the way in which deep and profound secrets of Torah are present within the simple meaning of Torah, subtly illuminating their radiance unto her knowers and lovers. The long voyage into her mysteries allows us to stand filled with awe at the perfection of form that contains endless worlds of meaning.

Such is the experience of seasoned lovers of Torah, and like them the lovers of the Zohar stand in wonder and appreciation at the beauty of the Zohar's stories, homilies, and parables, for they have delved into—and have been touched by—the secrets and profound insight that are embedded in them, and which shine through them.

May we merit the joy of experiencing deep simplicity.

REFERENCE MATTER

Notes

Introduction

1. In deciding to focus on the *expressions* of mystical experience rather than making claims about the *inner essence* of such experience, I am following Moshe Idel. Focusing on the forms of mystical expression gives priority to historical, literary, and phenomenological tools of analysis over and above psychological tools of analysis. On the difficulties associated with the endeavor to recreate mystical experience itself, see Idel, *Kabbalah: New Perspectives*, pp. 35–38.

2. De Certeau, *Mystic Fable*, p. 3. For his unique definition of mysticism and mystics, see De Certeau, "Mysticism," pp. 11–25.

3. Particularly instructive for me was a fascinating and humorous chapter on the methodology of the study of myth, written by a scholar of Indian mythology, Wendy Doniger O'Flaherty. See O'Flaherty, *Sexual Metaphors*, pp. 1–14.

4. Sontag, *Against Interpretation*, p. 14.

5. See Idel, *Kabbalah: New Perspectives*, p. 213.

6. See Liebes, *Perakim be-milon Sefer ha-Zohar*, p. 6.

7. The methodological chapters in Yair Lorberbaum's study clearly articulate the ideological and interpretative meta-assumptions informing academic scholarship. See Lorberbaum, *Tselem Elohim*, pp. 127–69.

8. On the function of study as constitutive of experience and life-practice rather than theoretical knowledge alone, see Idel, "Models of Learning." On the interconnections between interpretive study of sacred texts and mystical experience, see Wolfson, *Speculum That Shines*, pp. 326–97.

9. In this book, I focus mainly on the literary unit termed by Zohar scholars *guf ha-Zohar* (the main corpus of the Zohar). This refers to zoharic homilies on the biblical text from Genesis through Deuteronomy, with the zoharic stories of Rabbi Shim'on and his companions embedded within them. My investigation will generally not cover the later strata of zoharic literature, that is, *Tiqqunei Zohar* and *Ra'aya Meheimna*, which are viewed in Zohar scholarship as written by a kabbalist in the fourteenth century who knows the Zohar as an existing book and sees himself continuing and developing it. See Liebes, "Zohar and Tiqqunei Zohar: From Renaissance to Revolution"; Tishby, *Wisdom of the Zohar* 1:1–7, 9–12.

10. The Zohar is a Midrash in that it is a running exposition, and in that its reading

of the biblical Hebrew text is not constrained by normal rules of grammar and syntax. The editing of the zoharic text, its preparation for printing, and the way in which it was received all support its characterization as a midrashic composition following the order of the Torah as sectioned by the weekly portion—even if the Zohar's present form does not reflect the mode of composition and distribution prior to its printing. On the mode of the Zohar's distribution, see Tishby, *Wisdom of the Zohar* 1:13–17, 91–99. On questions associated with the Zohar as an edited work and on the manner of its editing and printing, see Abrams, "Eimatai ḥubberah ha-hakdamah." On associated questions regarding the mode of the composition of the work, see Liebes, "How the Zohar Was Written"; Meroz, "Zoharic Narratives."

11. See Liebes, "Messiah of the Zohar"; and idem, "Zohar ve-eros." On the narratives of the Zohar, see Oron, "Me-omanut ha-derush"; Pechter, "Between Night and Day"; Tene, "Darkei itsuv ha-sippur."

12. On the centrality of the visionary motif in theosophic kabbalah, see Wolfson, *Speculum That Shines*, pp. 270–393; idem, "Forms of Visionary Ascent," pp. 209–35.

13. On this verse from Daniel as employed in the Zohar, see Liebes, "Zohar ve-eros," pp. 70–80; Wolfson, "Forms of Visionary Ascent," p. 210.

14. See Liebes, "Ha-Zohar ke-renesans."

15. For the adorning of the bride, see Zohar 1:8a–b. Also see Liebes, *Het'o shel Elisha*, pp. 107–9; Liebes, "Messiah of the Zohar," pp. 74–82 (Appendix 1).

16. In this connection see Scholem, *Major Trends*, pp. 156–243 (chapters 6,7); Kadari, *Dikduk ha-lashon ha-Aramit*; Liebes, *Perakim be-milon Sefer ha-Zohar*; Wolfson, "Left Contained in the Right"; Wolfson, "Light Through Darkness"; Wolfson, "Hermeneutics of Visionary Experience"; Liebes, "How the Zohar Was Written"; Wolfson, "Dimui anthropomorphi ve ha-symbolica," pp. 141–81; Wolfson, "Letter Symbolism and Merkavah Imagery"; Wolfson, "Hai Gaon's Letter"; Wolfson, "Beautiful Maiden"; Matt, "New-Ancient Words"; Green, "The Zohar"; Ta-Shma, *Ha-nigleh she-ba-nistar*; Liebes, "Ha-Zohar ke-sefer halakhah"; Liebes, "Zikkat ha-Zohar le-erets Yisra'el"; Meroz, "Der Aufbau des Buches Sohar." See also Mopsik, *Le Zohar*, introduction, pp. 7–58.

17. On the question of the Zohar's composition, see below, pp. 23–28; Scholem, *Major Trends*, pp. 156–204; Liebes, "How the Zohar Was Written," pp. 85–90; Idel, *Kabbalah: New Perspectives*, pp. 210–18; Meroz, "Zoharic Narratives"; Meroz, "The Path of Silence"; Meroz, "'Va-ani lo hayiti sham?'"

18. See Liebes, "How the Zohar Was Written," pp. 135–38.

19. My teacher Moshe Idel has remarked that it is difficult to believe that a group of Kabbalists would meet regularly without arousing curiosity and without any record of such a group appearing in the writings of the members of the circle.

20. In his article "How the Zohar Was Written" (pp. 85–89), Liebes notes that Moses de León's style is particularly discernable in the main corpus of the Zohar. Recently, however, Liebes has expressed reservations about the centrality he accorded de León in that article.

21. Bialik, "Halachah and Aggadah," in *Revealment and Concealment*, p. 79.

22. Scholem, *Reshit ha-kabbalah ve-Sefer ha-Bahir*, p. 2.

23. Idel, *Kabbalah: New Perspectives*, p. xviii.

24. See Hollenback, *Mysticism*, p. 298.

25. See Wolfson, *Speculum That Shines*, pp. 52–58. Recently, Ron Margolin has surveyed the history of scholarship of mysticism and its various definitions; see *Mikdash Adam*, pp. 33–39, 51–52.

26. See Hollenback, *Mysticism*, pp. 40–41. Hollenback wrote his book out of a perceived need to update the research of William James and Evelyn Underhill, and also with the methodological aim of proving that the contextual aspects of mystical experience are greater than its essentialist ones. In the context of academic scholarship, Hollenback's study lies firmly on the side of those who argue for the centrality of the cultural-religious context in the production of mystical experience. (For a survey and critique of Hollenback's book, see Garb, "Paths of Power.")

In his introduction, Hollenback highlights the antiquated methodology of phenomenological studies of mystical experience, in particular the 1902 seminal study of William James, *The Varieties of Religious Experience*, which argues that mystical experience is essential rather than dependent on cultural or personal variables. James outlines four characteristics of mystical experience: (*a*) *Ineffability*, insofar as mystical states are more like states of feeling than of intellect; (*b*) *Noetic quality*—to those who experience them, mystical states are authoritative states of knowledge and insight into the depths of truth that are unplumbed by the discursive intellect; (*c*) *Transiency*—mystical states cannot be sustained for long and are susceptible to continuous development; and (*d*) *Passivity*—although the oncoming of mystical states may be facilitated by preliminary voluntary operation, once set in, mystics feel as if their own will is in abeyance and indeed sometimes as if they are grasped and held by a superior power. See James, *Varieties of Religious Experience*, pp. 379–429.

To my mind, James's first and fourth posited characteristics are not appropriate for the contours of mystical experience in the Zohar. For the Zohar is distinguished by an extraordinary capacity to describe mystical experience. Further, perhaps owing to the limitations of language, any experience that is not verbal is not capable of full expression. As for passivity, the experience of joy in the presence of the divine is far more apparent in the Zohar than is the experience of annihilation or passivity. (In my view, James's discussion of the diversity of mystical testimonies is far more interesting and fruitful than his attempt to define mystical experience.)

For another survey and analysis of the arguments associated with the definition of mysticism and mystical experience, see Merkur, "Unitive Experience," pp. 125–53. On the terms "mysticism" and "interiorization," see Margolin, *Mikdash Adam*, pp. 33–39, 51–52, 57–59. See also De Certeau's unique approach to defining mysticism: De Certeau, "Mysticism," pp. 11–25.

27. According to Hollenback, each mystic brings to the world of mystical experience certain religious and conceptual beliefs and worldviews; the content of the experience generally bestows authority and legitimacy on the mythic and metaphysical conceptions to which the mystic is already loyal. The mystical experience is not merely context-dependent in its essence. Rather, the beliefs that characterize the mystic's interpretation of experience and the content of that experience are interdependent, such that we cannot attribute epistemological priority to the experience over the interpretation or vice versa.

See also Wolfson's summary treatment of the relationship between mystical experience and culture-dependent variables: Wolfson, *Speculum That Shines*, pp. 393–97.

28. See Liebes, "Zohar ve-eros," pp. 67–70.

29. Ben Yisrael, *Ge'ulat Yisra'el ha-shalem*, p. 41, paragraph 72.

30. See Zeitlin, *Be-pardes ha-ḥasidut ve-ha-kabbalah*; *Sifran shel yeḥidim*; *Al gevul shenei olamot*.

31. See Ashlag's comments about the Zohar in the introduction to his Sulam commentary, 1:16–20, and in his comments on the Zohar's own introduction, 1:21–30.

32. For a more extensive survey of scholarship, see the Hebrew version of the present book, pp. 36–38.

33. For a dynamic picture of developments in the field of Zohar research, I suggest the bibliography that Daniel Matt presents at the end of every new volume of the Pritzker edition of the Zohar, where one can find an updated list of zoharic scholarship (as it relates to the contents of that particular volume).

34. In this study, I will be discussing and citing the printed Aramaic edition of the Zohar as edited by Reuven Margaliot, 4th edn. (Jerusalem: Mossad ha-Rav Kook, 1964). Of the renderings into English herein, they are by Daniel Matt where such are available, usually from the Pritzker edition, vols. 1–4, which translates Matt's own critical edition of the Aramaic text. (When quoting from the Pritzker edition, however, the present book employs simpler typography: it does not reproduce the Hebrew terms that are interspersed in that translation, nor does it convey the transliterated terms in a distinct typeface. In the absence of those features, some terms have been re-ordered for clarity. Occasionally, too, this book uses another English rendering for key terms, or it lays out the translation in a slightly different format. Such changes are indicated by the notice "adapted" or "reformatted.") The remaining translations of Zohar passages have been rendered by Nathan Wolski (the translator of this book) directly from the Margaliot edition.

Chapter 1

1. The Zohar's depiction of the disciples' separation from the teacher as the separation from life itself originates from the description of Rabbi Akiva in tannaitic literature: *Sifra* 4:5; *Sifre Devarim, Ve-ethanan* 17; *Sifre Bemidbar* 5; *Tosefta Mikva'ot*, toward the end of chap. 1; *Tosefta Korbanot* 1: "[Rabbi Akiva,] whoever separates from you is as one who separates from life."

2. On the literary unit known as the "main corpus of the Zohar," see my introduction above, note 9. On the "epic layer," see Meroz, "Der Aufbau des Buches Sohar."

3. Many zoharic stories end with the Companions coming to Rabbi Shim'on to recount all their adventures, at which point Rabbi Shim'on explains, from a new and broader perspective, the meaning of that which befell them. See, for example: the end of the story of the Cave of Ramification in *Vayetse* (1:149a); the end of the story of Rav Hamnuna Sava in the Introduction to the Zohar (1:7a–8a); and the end of the *Sava de-Mishpatim* (2:114a).

4. On the blessed Holy One and the Assembly of Israel as the father and mother of human beings, see BT *Berakhot* 35b, "whoever [eats/drinks] without a blessing is as one who steals from his father and mother."

5. On the sefirah *Yesod* in the Kabbalah in general and in the Zohar in particular, see the chapter on the *Tsaddik* in Scholem, *Mystical Shape of the Godhead*, pp. 88–139; see also Liebes, "Messiah of the Zohar," pp. 12–19.

6. Zohar 3:295b–296b. See Liebes, "Messiah of the Zohar," pp. 63–65.

7. On the sefirah *Malkhut*, see the chapter on Shekhinah in Scholem, *Mystical Shape of the Godhead*, pp. 140–196. See Green, "Shekhinah." See Idel, *Kabbalah and Eros*, pp. 107–8, 137–45.

8. On Rashbi as Shekhinah and as the mouth of Shekhinah, and on the connection between the epithet *botsina* and "mouth," see Liebes, "Zohar ve-eros," pp. 105–6. See also the Zohar passage on the meaning of the mouth and speech (both cosmically and for the human being), in which *botsina* appears as the mouth that furnishes form and limit to the river of plenty coming from thought: *Zohar Ḥadash, Tikkunim* 103c–d. On Rashbi as *penei ha-adon* (the face of the Lord) in the sense of Shekhinah, see Zohar 2:38a.

9. This epithet appears dozens of times. See for example: Zohar 1:156a, 197b; 2:114a; 3:159a. See also the entry for *botsina* in Liebes, *Perakim be-milon Sefer ha-Zohar*, pp. 131–60.

10. On Rashbi and the image of light, see Zohar 2:200a; 1:4a. See also below, pp. 260–61.

11. Zohar 2:201a; 3:265b; 2:68a. On Rashbi as illuminator of the light of Torah, see Zohar 2:68a.

12. Zohar 2:86b. See below, pp. 51–55.

13. Zohar 2:149a. On Rashbi as provider of nourishment, see Hecker, *Mystical Bodies, Mystical Meals*, pp. 86–87.

14. Zohar 1:225a. See Liebes, "Messiah of the Zohar," pp. 14–16.

15. See, for example, the story about Rabbi Shim'on, Rabbi Yitsḥak, and the angel of death: Zohar 1:217b–218a, and what follows in this chapter. See Wineman, *Mystic Tales from the Zohar*, pp. 67–82.

16. Zohar 2:87a.

17. That Rashbi is a new Moses revealing a new Torah was noted by Elliot Wolfson, *Speculum that Shines*, p. 391. Boaz Huss has argued that emerging from the comparison between Moses and Rashbi, and from the claim that Rabbi Shim'on exceeds even Moses, the Zohar presents itself as completing the Torah, and indeed as being superior to it; "Hakham adif mi-navi," p. 125.

18. See Liebes, "Ha-mashiaḥ shel ha-Zohar," pp. 105–7 and notes there. See also Wolfson, "Hermeneutics of Visionary Experience," p. 324.

19. In BT *Yevamot* 49b, Moses is mentioned as one who saw through a "speculum that shines"; and in BT *Sukkah* 45b, Rabbi Shim'on and his son are mentioned as seeing through a "speculum that shines." On the comparison between the figure of Moses and figure of Rashbi in the Zohar and on the reasons for the choice of Rabbi Shim'on as the hero of the composition, see Huss, "Hakham adif mi-navi," pp. 103–39. On the "speculum" and its meaning, see Huss, "Hakham adif mi-navi," pp. 109–14.

20. Liebes, "Messiah of the Zohar," pp. 4–5. See also Huss, "Hakham adif mi-navi."

21. Zohar 3:1a. See also the comparison between the generations of the two leaders, Zohar 3:149a.

22. Huss, "Hakham adif mi-navi," pp. 114–19. Liebes already commented on this; "Messiah of the Zohar," pp. 21, 174, n.93.

23. Zohar 3:15a. The most acute image that places Rabbi Shim'on above Moses is found in the story of Hamnuna Sava, where a wondrous figure, the son of Hamnuna—cast in the image of Rabbi Shim'on—presents himself as the biblical Benayahu son of Yehoyada, who slew "an Egyptian man" (2 Sam. 23:21), namely, Moses! See Zohar 1:6b.

According to Huss, the figure of Moses—humble and reluctant—represents in the eyes of the Zohar the conservative figure of Rabbi Moses Naḥmanides (Ramban), who championed the cautious and conservative transmission of kabbalistic secrets and opposed innovations in Kabbalah. See Huss, "Ḥakham adif mi-navi," pp. 129–33.

24. Zohar 1:223a; Matt, Pritzker edn., vol. 3. On *Ra'aya Meheimna* and *Tikkunei ha-Zohar*, see Tishby, *Wisdom of the Zohar* 1:12; Liebes, "Ha-mashiaḥ shel ha-Zohar," pp. 105–6; Goldreich, "Beirurim bi-r'iyyato ha-atsmit"; Giller, *Enlightened Will Shine*.

25. Rabbi Akiva ordained Rabbi Shim'on. See JT *Sanhedrin* 6a–b. On Rashbi going to learn from his teacher Rabbi Akiva while the latter was in prison, see BT *Pesaḥim* 112a.

26. Avot de-Rabbi Natan (B) 12; (A) 6; BT *Sanhedrin* 86a.

27. Avot de-Rabbi Natan (B) 12.

28. Zohar 3:79b; see below, p. 49.

29. In an esoteric work from late antiquity, *Heikhalot Zutartei*, we read about Rabbi Akiva as a member of *yordei merkavah* (those who descend to the chariot): "God . . . who is hidden from the eyes of all creatures and is concealed from the ministering angels was revealed to Rabbi Akiva" (MSS Oxford, *Heikhalot Zutartei* 45b, *Sidrei shimusha rabba ve-sidrei heikhalot*). On Rashbi and the Torah, see Zohar 3:166b, 288a.

30. Adam sees Rabbi Akiva and his death while still a mere lump of clay: *Yalkut Shim'oni, Bereshit*, 247:41; a parallel to this midrash is on Zohar 1:55b. See also Zohar 3:61b.

31. BT *Menaḥot* 29b.

32. BT *Shabbat* 112b.

33. *Pesikta de-Rav Kahana* 4. For additional references of comparisons between Rabbi Akiva and Moses, and the privileging of Rabbi Akiva, see Huss, "Ḥakham adif mi-navi," p. 128.

34. Liebes, "Ha-Zohar ke-renesans."

35. Zohar 2:253b–254b.

36. Huss, "Ḥakham adif mi-navi," p. 129, note 97.

37. BT *Sukkah* 45b; *Sanhedrin* 90b; Midrash Genesis Rabbah 35.2. See also BT *Megillah* 17b; JT *Berakhot* 6b, 65a.

38. On the humility of Rabbi Akiva, see Liebes, *Ḥet'o shel Elisha*, pp. 98–105.

39. Zohar 3:16a.

40. Liebes, "Messiah of the Zohar."

41. BT *Ḥagigah* 12b. On the tsaddik, see Jacobs, *Holy Living*; Green, "Zaddiq as Axis Mundi," pp. 295–302.

42. Zohar 3:127b, *Idra Rabba*. On Rabbi Shim'on as "tsaddik yesod olam," see Liebes, "Messiah of the Zohar," pp. 12–23.

43. On the definition of the shaman and his functions, see Meged, *Sha'arei tikvah ve-sha'arei eimah*, pp. 27–31.

44. Zohar 3:15a; *Zohar Ḥadash* 41d.

45. Zohar 1:217b–218a.

46. On this story, see below, pp. 245-49. See also Liebes, "Zohar ve-eros," p. 109.

47. Zohar 1:223a, citing Deut. 9:9.

48. See below, pp. 225–28. Elliot Wolfson dedicated a book to the analysis of this theme in medieval Kabbalah: *Through a Speculum that Shines: Vision and Imagination in Medieval Jewish Mysticism*.

49. For a discussion on the extent of Rashbi's self-awareness as opposed to Moses, see Liebes, "Messiah of the Zohar," p. 174, n.93; Huss, "Ḥakham adif mi-navi," pp. 112, 118–19.

50. In his unique later reading of this event, Rabbi Moses Cordovero views the figure of Moses as more exalted than that of Rabbi Shim'on: "Regarding Moses—the skin of his face shone while sitting, standing, walking on the way, and when lying down, whereas Rabbi Shim'on's attainment was precisely when he was engaged in *Ma'aseh Merkavah* (The Episode of the Chariot, alluding to the divine revelation in Ezekiel 1)." According to this reading, Rashbi needs to attest to the light radiating from him, while Moses radiates light continuously in the eyes of all. See Cordovero, *Or Yakar* 22, p. 29; Sack, *Be-sha'arei ha-kabbalah*, pp. 42, 47, note 80.

51. Huss, "Ḥakham adif mi-navi," p. 125. In his note 80, Huss contests Scholem's view that the Zohar's author did not intend to produce a work that would attain such status.

52. The source of this parable is perhaps to be found in the legend of Rabbi Akiva and Turnus Rufus regarding circumcision; see *Tanḥuma, Tazria* 5; *Tanna de-Bei Eliyahu Zuta* 2. On this parable, see Hecker, *Mystical Bodies*, pp. 103–4.

53. See Matt, "New-Ancient Words"; Zohar 3:166b; 2:183b; Wolfson, "Beautiful Maiden Without Eyes."

54. See below, p. 149–50.

55. See Liebes, "Zohar ve-eros," pp. 87–98; Oron, "'Simeini kha-ḥotam'"; Giller, "Love and Upheaval," pp. 1–30; Yisraeli, *Parshanut ha-sod ve-sod ha-parshanut*.

56. Hellner-Eshed, "Nefesh ha-kanah ba-Zohar," pp. 114–16.

57. See Liebes's suggestion: "How the Zohar Was Written," pp. 85–90, 135–38.

58. On this passage and on the idea that it expresses opposition to the kabbalistic approach of Rabbi Moses Naḥmanides (Ramban) and his school—which advocated the restriction of secrets and which was reluctant to disclose them—see Liebes, "Messiah of the Zohar," p. 29.

59. Maimonides, *Guide of the Perplexed* III: Introduction; Vol. II, pp. 415–16. Trans. Shlomo Aires.

60. Regarding the verse from Psalms and the revelation of secrets, see Mishnah *Berakhot* 9:5; Maimonides, *Guide* I:9b (Pines transl., p. 16); Zohar 3:128a. As for the verse from Proverbs, the Zohar (2:98a) uses it to argue in favor of revealing secrets to those who are qualified to receive them, in order to avoid what Maimonides phrases as "robbing one who deserves the truth of the truth." On Maimonides's self-understanding, see Moshe Halbertal's comments in his *Concealment and Revelation*, pp. 60 68.

61. Midrash Song of Songs Rabbah 1.

62. Zohar 2:86b; Matt, Pritzker edn., vol. 4, p. 487, adapted. See above, p. 31, note 1.

63. See Idel, *Kabbalah: New Perspectives*, pp. 210–18, for a discussion of this generation and its short life.

64. Significantly, it is precisely the nonchronological and nonlinear editing of the Zohar's stories, as they appear in printed editions of the Zohar, which engenders a certain ambiguity surrounding the question of the life and death of Rabbi Shim'on; in one story, for example, we encounter his disciples after the death of the great teacher, while on the following page, Rabbi Shim'on is alive and teaching.

65. In this connection, Rabbi Shim'on's essence and character seems closer to that of Jesus (as depicted in Christian writings) than to that of the great heroes of rabbinic culture; he is human and divine, exists and yet is concealed, possesses supernatural powers, and is the son of God. See Liebes, "Christian Influences on the Zohar," pp. 146–52; Huss, "Ḥakham adif mi-navi," p. 127.

66. In its biblical context and according to its simple meaning, this verse has a positive valence and describes the end of the Flood. The Zohar expounds the words of this verse on their own and out of their context.

67. Judah Halevi, Laments 14. For alternative translation, see T. Carmi, *The Penguin Book of Hebrew Verse,* p. 339.

68. On this narrative, see Wineman, *Mystic Tales from the Zohar,* pp. 19–32.

69. One example is the deep personal identification of Rabbi Isaac Luria with Rabbi Shim'on, and Luria's decision to conduct his life and the life of his circle in the spiritual presence of Rashbi and his circle. On Luria and other figures who identified with Rabbi Shim'on, see Liebes, "Ha-mashiaḥ shel ha-Zohar," pp. 105–18.

70. See the talmudic story on the body of R. El'azar the son of R. Shim'on that does not decay, BT *Bava Metsia* 84b; on the bodies of the righteous, see BT *Bava Batra* 17a.

71. From this description, Rabbi Moses Cordovero later discerned a special praxis for the spiritual raising of the figure of the teacher in order to learn secrets; *Or Yakar* 8:263. See also Sack, *Be-sha'arei ha-kabbalah,* p. 45.

72. Zohar 3:284a.

73. See BT *Ta'anit* 5b.

74. Liebes, "Messiah of the Zohar," pp. 63–74.

75. Liebes, "How the Zohar was Written," pp. 85–90, 135–38.

Chapter 2

1. BT *Ḥagigah* 14b. On the story of the Four Who Entered the Pardes, see Urbach, "Ha-masoret al torat ha-sod"; Liebes, *Het'o shel Elisha*; Halperin, *The Faces of the Chariot,* pp. 199–210; Idel, "Perush al ha-kenisah le-Pardes"; Idel, *Kabbalah: New Perspectives,* pp. 90–91; Idel, *Hasidism,* p. 305, note 2; Elior, *Heikhalot Zutartei,* pp. 23, 62. On *pardes* as referring to a hermeneutic system, see Idel, "PaRDeS."

2. Particularly noteworthy is the Zohar's complex approach to more ecstatic figures, who merited to enter but not exit from the experience of the encounter with divinity—for example, the biblical figures of Nadab and Abihu, or the Companions who died an ecstatic death in the *Idra Rabba* (Zohar 3:144a–b).

3. Zohar 2:99b and see also 2:219b on the verse "Like a hind craving for watercourses" (Ps. 42:2).

4. Mishnah *Yadayim* 3:5.

5. BT *Ḥagigah* 15b.

6. Zohar 3:37b. See Liebes, "Zohar ve-eros," pp. 99–103.

7. Zohar 1:148a.

8. On the earlier gatherings prior to the Idra Rabba, see Liebes, "Messiah of the Zohar," pp. 7–12.

9. Zohar 3:144a.

10. See Liebes, "Messiah of the Zohar," pp. 52–58; Fishbane, *Kiss of God*, pp. 34–39; Maimonides, *The Guide of the Perplexed* 3:51; Hecker, "Kissing Kabbalists."

11. See, for example, *Zohar Ḥadash* 105a.

12. On entering and exiting in peace, see below, pp. 326–39.

13. On wisdom (*ḥokhmah*) in the Bible, see Gordis, *Koheleth*, pp. 16–18.

14. *Zohar Ḥadash*, Song of Songs 62d.

15. *Zohar Ḥadash*, Song of Songs 62a.

16. See Sviri, "Ha-psikhologiyah ha-mistit shel al-Hakim a-Termathi," vol. I, p. 54 ff.; Sviri, *Taste of Hidden Things*, pp. 1–16. See also Baḥya ibn Pakuda, *Ḥovot ha-Levavot*, introduction. See also Diana Lobel, *A Sufi-Jewish Dialogue*.

17. On Shekhinah, see Scholem, *Mystical Shape of the Godhead*, pp. 140–96; Tishby, *Wisdom of the Zohar* 1:371–87; Wolfson, *Speculum That Shines*, pp. 355–68; Wolfson, *Circle in the Square*, pp. 1–28; Green, "Bride, Spouse, Daughter"; Green, "Shekhinah, the Virgin Mary, and the Song of Songs."

18. See below, Chapter 14.

19. On the conditions and prerequisites for contact with Shekhinah, see, for example, Zohar 3:56–57.

20. See Wolfson, *Circle in the Square*, pp. 29–48; Wolfson, *Speculum That Shines*, pp. 336–45. Circumcision and its mythic, symbolic, and political meanings have held an important place in Wolfson's work of the past two decades.

21. See below, Chapter 6.

22. *Zohar Ḥadash* 91–93. See Liebes, "Zikkat ha-Zohar le-erets Yisra'el"; Huss, "Ḥakham adif mi-navi," pp. 132–33; see below p. 21. On the figure of Rashbi as a member of the household exceeding the rank of the servant, see *Zohar Ḥadash* 91–93; Liebes, "Zikkat ha-Zohar le-erets Yisra'el"; Huss, "Ḥakham adif mi-navi," p. 127.

23. See Zohar 1:20b, 178a; see also the story about Tikkun Leil Shavuot, 1:8a.

24. See Zohar 1:246a–247b on Jacob's blessing of Naphtali and Joseph for an interesting discussion of human masculinity and femininity in relation to divinity. On the task of the kabbalists in arousing the passion and jealousy of the blessed Holy One, see Zohar 3:191a. See also *Zohar Ḥadash* 99c.

25. Compare the human being's relationship with Shekhinah in the Zohar with the three types of relationship with the goddess *Shakti* in Tantric and Hindu texts: as maidens and attendants, as hero, or as son to his mother. See Zimmer, *Philosophies of India*, pp. 590–91.

26. On masculinity and femininity, see Wolfson, *Speculum That Shines*, pp. 357–60. See also Wolfson, "Min ve-miniut be-heker ha-kabbalah."

27. Zohar 3:127b–128a, *Idra Rabba*; Zohar 3:288a, *Idra Zuta*.

28. Zohar 3:17b, 20b, 75b. See Zohar on Lamentations, *Zohar Ḥadash*, 91–93.

29. Mopsik, introduction, *Le Zohar: Lamentations*, pp. 7–58.

30. Cordovero, *Tikkunei ha-Zohar im perush OrYakar, Bava Metsia* 4:185. I am grateful to Boaz Huss, from whom I first learned of this passage; and to Bracha Sack, who directed me to its source. See further comments by Cordovero:

> Since the exile and oppression began after the destruction of the House and She-khinah was exiled with the Jewish people, therefore Rabbi Shim'on arose with his Companions to compose this book, in order that through the revelation of secrets the light of *Tiferet* would be revealed, *and there would thus be some rest for Malkhut through uniting* (Heb. *yiḥud) and rectifying* (Heb. *tikkun). And there is no doubt that in our generation, too, when a person engages in this wisdom, he effects great benefit; and Shekhinah dwells upon him personally if his ways are proper. (*Tikkunei ha-Zohar im perush OrYakar, Bava Kamma* 2:102; cited in Sack, *Be-sha'arei ha-kabbalah,* p. 38.)

See also Cordovero, *Tikkunei ha-Zohar im perush OrYakar, Bava Kamma* 3:227, 1:58; Sack, *Be-sha'arei ha-kabbalah,* pp. 40, 45. On the Companions and the Shekhinah, see below, pp. 116–20. On the idea that zoharic exegesis has theurgic power, see Huss, "*Sefer ha-Zohar* as a Canonical, Sacred and Holy Text," pp. 291–92; Huss, "The Anthological Interpretation," p. 7.

31. See Zohar 1:15a, 2:2b, 23a; *Ra'aya Meheimna* 3:124b. In *Ra'aya Meheimna* and *Tikkunei ha-Zohar,* this verse serves a special function as an explicit reference to the world of the Zohar. The various interpretations of the verse have already been the subject of considerable scholarly inquiry; see Wolfson, *Speculum That Shines,* pp. 367–92; Liebes, "Zohar ve-eros," pp. 73–76. On the *maskilim* in the Zohar, *Ra'aya Meheimna,* and *Tikkunei ha-Zohar,* see Giller, *The Enlightened Will Shine,* pp. 21–32.

32. On this passage in the Zohar, see Matt, *Book of Enlightenment,* pp. 30, 226; Wolfson, *Speculum That Shines,* p. 391; Huss, "Ḥakham adif mi-navi," p. 139; Huss, "Hofa'ato shel Sefer ha-Zohar," p. 522. See further below, pp. 269–70.

33. Mishnah *Ḥagigah* 2:1; BT *Ḥagigah* 11b. In Zohar 1:18a, 2:164b, the biblical word *maskilim* is clarified through the zoharic word *sokhletano,* from the root *s-kh-l,* "knowledge," as in Onkelos' ancient Aramaic translation of Exodus 35:31, which renders Heb. *tevunah* as *sokhletano.*

34. BT *Bava Batra* 12a.

35. Zohar 3:35a. According to Wolfson and Huss, there is no question that the Zohar's comments there about the *ḥakham* allude to Rabbi Shim'on. See Wolfson, *Speculum That Shines,* p. 391; Huss, "Ḥakham adif mi-navi," p. 139; Huss, "Hofa'ato shel Sefer ha-Zohar," p. 522.

36. See below, p. 376.

37. Zohar 2:2a.

38. In terms of its literary style, it is difficult to assign this passage with certainty either to the main corpus of the Zohar or to *Tikkunei ha-Zohar.* The passage appears under the heading *Matnitin* ("our Mishnah") and displays similarities with other *matnitin* passages, yet at times it also recalls the style of the *tikkunim.* Liebes has commented on its unique style; see "Zohar ve-eros," p. 74, note 46.

39. Zohar 2:127a.

40. On the "poverty" of Shekhinah, see, for example, Zohar 3:19b; 1:170a. In addi-

tion to the attribute *dal*, the Zohar also refers to Shekhinah as *evyon, ani,* and *misken*—all biblical synonyms for poverty.

41. On this Zohar passage, see Liebes, "Zohar ve-eros," p. 74, note 52.

42. *Shekel ha-Kodesh*, pp. 16–17.

43. Mopsik, introduction to R. Moses de León's *Shekel ha-Kodesh*, pp. 7–8.

44. The style of this passage clearly does not belong to the main literary units of the Zohar and recalls passages in *Ra'aya Meheimna* and *Tikkunei ha-Zohar*. In his book on the latter works, Pinchas Giller has written that the author of these late zoharic compositions, who already related to the Zohar as a canonical work, took the definitions of the *maskilim* as he found them in the Zohar, and applied them in the main in relation to society, authority, and the cosmic order; Giller, *The Enlightened Will Shine*, p. 22. Indeed, as Giller has shown, there are passages, clearly in the style of *Ra'aya Meheimna* and *Tikkunei ha-Zohar*, in which a new ethos of *maskilim* was created. Yet many passages, especially those printed in the *Tikkunim* in the *Zohar Ḥadash*, cannot be definitely attributed to one of the known strata of the Zohar. See, for example, *Zohar Ḥadash* 93–94 (on the Zohar as a written composition); 99c (*maskilim* as *ba'alei sekhel* who know how to nurture the daughter of the king during prayer); 103a (those who know the Cause of Causes through Shekhinah, who represents the boundary of the world of emanation); 105a-c, 106b (the *maskilim* as righteous).

45. See below, Chapter 10.

46. Zohar 1:4a; Matt, Pritzker edn., vol. 1, p. 22.

47. On the intensity of mystical life, see Elior, "Panehah ha-shonot shel ha-ḥerut," especially pp. 47–74. Similar, and perhaps even more daring, reflections on the disdain for moderation, and on the ability to disregard social norms in order to devote one-self entirely to mystical-religious life, can be found in Sufi literature. See, for example, Rumi, *The Essential Rumi*, pp. 104–5, 173–74.

48. This view is presented in a story in which the Companions encounter the hermit who lives with his disciples in the desert throughout the year, aside from the month of Tishrei. In response to Rashbi's question about his lifestyle, the hermit explains that he chooses not to conduct his religious life in the towns and cities—the normative locus of Torah study—but rather, outside the settled areas (*yishuv*), outside the established Jewish communities. It is precisely in the desert, because of the intensity of the oppositions and contrasts found there, that one is able to bring to light new-ancient words of Torah. He claims that it is precisely there, in the non-*yishuv* areas that words of Torah are clarified (*mityashevim*). According to the extreme mystical theology of that hermit, one must go precisely to the harsh, difficult, and dark places. One must be familiar with evil, and through knowing evil, bring it to submission. Elsewhere, according to Rabbi Shim'on, the knowledge of the secret of evil is the patrimony of a select few, even among the mystics (Zohar 2:34b). He who worships God from amid the darkness is able to draw forth from Him the light and the good, and to use this pure light to protect the world from evil. See Zohar 3:47b; Liebes, "Messiah of the Zohar," pp. 16–17; Wolfson, "Light Through Darkness," p. 73. See also Moses de León, *Shekel ha-Kodesh*, p. 38.

49. Cf. Resh Lakish's view regarding he who performs repentance out of love, that his deliberate sins are transformed into merits: BT Yoma 86b.

50. Compare Rumi's poem on Joseph and his capacity to wait; *The Essential Rumi*, pp. 139–40. On Rav Yeisa Sava's praxis of intensifying yearning and waiting, see Zohar 2:62b. See Hecker, *Mystical Bodies, Mystical Meals*, p. 144.

51. See Zohar 2:10a–b. Compare Rumi's poem about the dawn: "The breeze at dawn has secrets to tell you. / Don't go back to sleep"; *Open Secret*, Quatrains 91, p. 7.

52. For a detailed discussion of this homily, see below, pp. 265–68.

53. Compare the image of the dawn in Paul Celan's poem "Death Fugue"; Celan, *Selections*, p. 46.

54. A wonderful modern example can be found in the prayer composed by Hillel Zeitlin immediately after the First World War, "Ḥasdei avot ve-go'el li-vnei vanim," which contains harsh words of rebuke against God on account of the bloodshed throughout the world. Zeitlin concludes three pages of outcry and protest with the following words: "May our eyes behold the King in His beauty!" See Zeitlin, *Al gevul shnei olamot*, pp. 225–28. On Zeitlin, see Green, "Three Warsaw Mystics," pp. 22–36.

55. Translated by T. Carmi, *The Penguin Book of Hebrew Verse*, p. 349.

Chapter 3

1. See Liebes, "Messiah of the Zohar," pp. 1–12, 48–52.

2. BT *Shabbat* 130a.

3. Zohar 1:217a. The image of the "jarful of manna" will be explained below.

4. On the significance of pseudepigraphy in the Zohar, and on the question of where the authors of the Zohar "really" see themselves—in exile or in the Land of Israel—see Liebes, "Zikkat ha-Zohar le-erets Yisra'el."

5. See BT *Sanhedrin* 108a, 110b.

6. See also Moses de León, *Shekel ha-Kodesh*, p. 79.

7. *Rav Metivta* is found in the Zohar portion *Shlaḥ Lekha*, 3:161b–174a. See Wolski and Carmeli, "Those Who Know Have Wings."

8. Midrash Lamentations Rabbah, petiḥtah 33; BT *Ta'anit* 30b. For a parallel to the description of the members of this generation in the Garden of Eden, see *Seder Gan Eden* (version B), Jellinek, *Beit ha-Midrash*, 3:132–40.

9. It is possible that this is a development of the homily in Midrash Numbers Rabbah 16.11. See also BT *Sanhedrin* 110b, which cites the same verse, "Behold I am sending My messenger to clear the way before Me; and the Lord whom you seek shall come to His temple suddenly" (Mal. 3:1, NJPS), but to a different end, namely, that the members of this generation have no portion in the World to Come.

10. Zohar 3:162a–b, 163b.

11. See the famous story of Raba bar Bar Ḥana on the gigantic stature of the dead of the wilderness, BT *Bava Batra* 73b.

12. Rabbinic texts emphasizing the uniqueness of the wilderness generation include: JT *Avodah Zarah* 1:1: "Which generation is most beloved of all the generations? He said to them: The wilderness generation"; Midrash Leviticus Rabbah 13.2: "Rabbi

Shim'on bar Yoḥai opened: The blessed Holy One measured all the nations and did not find a nation worthy of receiving the Torah except for the wilderness generation."

13. Mekhilta, *Beshallaḥ*, at *Zeh eli ve-anveihu* (Exod. 15:2); Midrash Deuteronomy Rabbah 7.8; Song of Songs Rabbah 2 and 3; *Yalkut Shim'oni*, Exodus 16:244. In a lengthy homily on the giving of the Torah at Mt. Sinai, Zohar 2:82a–b expounds the praises of *dor de'ah* and distinguishes between it and the generation of the prophet Ezekiel.

14. On manna in the Zohar, see Hecker, *Mystical Bodies, Mystical Meals*, pp. 82–90, 99–101. On manna and spiritual perception already in Naḥmanides, see Halbertal, *Al derekh ha-emet*, pp. 126–29.

15. Surprisingly, the verse cited by the Zohar is actually about the gathering of quail, which ultimately leads to the incident at Kibroth-hattaavah ("Graves of Lust"; Numbers 11), and not about the gathering of the manna.

16. On the "*omer* of manna" as referring to the Zohar itself, see below, pp. 368–70.

17. Compare the modern poet Bialik's view of the wilderness generation as the first generation of the redemption with his view of Zionism and the early pioneers in his "The Dead of the Desert" (*Metei Midbar*): "We are the brave, last of the enslaved, first to be free! With our own strong hand, our hand alone [and not the hand of God!— M.H.-E.] we tore from our neck the heavy yoke." Bialik, *Selected Poems*, pp. 102–19.

18. According to a rabbinic midrash, Moses died in the desert in order that he might continue to lead his people when they are revived: "Why did Moses die in the desert? In order that the wilderness generation might return and arise through his merit" (*Pesikta Rabbati* 1:3).

19. The context of this passage is a homily on the verse "If the whole community of Israel errs and the matter is hidden from the eyes of the congregation . . ." (Lev. 4:13), which is interpreted by the Zohar as referring to the confused and erroneous state that will prevail when "the matter is hidden from the eyes of the congregation," namely after the death of Rabbi Shim'on.

20. Zohar 1:22a; Matt, Pritzker edn., vol. 1, p. 169.

21. See, for example, Midrash Song of Songs Rabbah 1.

22. See, for example, Midrash Numbers Rabbah 13.

23. BT *Megillah* 11b.

24. *Pesikta de-Rav Kahana* 5.12: "*And Solomon sat on the throne of YHVH* (1 Chron. 29:23)—the moon in its fullness"; Midrash Exodus Rabbah 15.26: "When Solomon arrived, the disk of the moon became full."

25. Zohar 1:223a; Matt, Pritzker edn., vol. 3, p. 339. See also Zohar 2:175a.

26. Mishnah *Yadayim* 3:5. Similarly, the ancient authors of the *Heikhalot* corpus and of the esoteric work *Shiur Komah* placed in the mouth of "he who enters the seventh [highest] chamber" verses from the Song of Songs.

27. See Cohen-Alloro, "Ha-magyah ve-ha-kishuf be-Sefer ha-Zohar."

28. Zohar 1:223b; Matt, Pritzker edn., vol. 3, p. 343. See also *Zohar Ḥadash* 51c–d.

29. It is important to note the relationship between the sefirot *Yesod* and *Tiferet* in the zoharic attitudes toward aspects of masculine gender.

30. *Zohar Ḥadash*, Song of Songs 62–63.

31. *Sefer Shekel ha-Kodesh*, pp. 22–23; Wijnhoven's edition of "Sefer ha-Mishkal," p. 49.

32. On the use of the abstract noun *niḥa* (satisfaction/pleasure) and its erotic contexts in the Zohar, see Liebes, "Messiah of the Zohar," pp. 52–55 and notes.

33. See also Zohar 2:145a.

34. BT *Sanhedrin* 7a.

35. See also Zohar 1:60a–b, 63b.

36. See Liebes, "Ha-Zohar ke-renesans."

37. On the ambivalence surrounding the generation of Rabbi Shim'on, see Liebes, "Messiah of the Zohar," pp. 5–8, 31–34. (In my opinion, the Zohar passage 3:58a cited by Liebes refers not to the generation of Rabbi Shim'on, but rather to the generation that will come after his death and those of his disciples. Rabbi Shim'on's words, which echo the entrance into the vineyard at Yavneh, are in fact in praise of the generation in which a creative enterprise akin to that of the Rabbis of antiquity can transpire, yet are uttered with an awareness that in the future this Torah, too, is destined to be forgotten.) On the manner in which Rabbi Moses Cordovero understood the state of the generation of Rabbi Shim'on, see Sack, *Be-sha'arei ha-kabbalah*, pp. 35–38.

38. See below, pp. 204–6.

39. Zohar 1:225a, 96b. The relationship between the sages of Babylonia and the sages of the Land of Israel receives it most extreme expression in the Zohar commentary on Lamentations: *Zohar Ḥadash* 91a–93d. In this section Rashbi and his circle are not mentioned at all, and the unit is constructed as an exchange of letters between the residents of the Land of Israel residing among the ruins of the sanctuary and the residents of Babylonia already resident in exile for many years. The subject of the epistles is an argument between the two communities as to who is more worthy of expounding the secret/ esoteric meaning of the verses of Lamentations. See Liebes, "Zikkat ha-Zohar le-erets Yisra'el"; Mopsik, introduction, *Le Zohar: Lamentations*; see below, pp. 181–83. See also Huss, "Ḥakham adif mi-navi," p. 133, note 119, on the suggestion that the stammering of the Babylonians recalls the stammering of Moses, who, according to Huss, in the Zohar symbolizes the figure of Rabbi Moses Naḥmanides (Ramban).

40. Huss, "Ḥakham adif mi-navi," pp. 129–33.

41. See above, pp. 31–32.

42. See also Zohar 1:225a.

43. BT *Kiddushin* 66a: "Shim'on ben Shetaḥ restored the Torah to its ancientry [or: antiquity]" (and perhaps the Zohar's authors identified Shim'on ben Shetaḥ with Shim'on bar Yoḥai); BT *Yoma* 69b: "The Men of the Great Assembly restored the crown to its ancientry [or: antiquity]." The present story, about restoring the crown of the divine attributes to its antiquity, is similar to the entire zoharic enterprise, insofar as it constitutes the Rabbis' revolutionary, exegetical reconstruction of the image of God. The rabbis present their homily as if uttered by the prophets Daniel and Jeremiah and the Men of the Great Assembly, yet the entire story is in fact a reflection on the bold, exegetical path of the Rabbis, who reinterpreted the image of God in order that it might still hold meaning for their generation.

44. Zohar 3:228a, 130a. On "antiquity" (*atikut*), see Liebes, "Messiah of the Zohar," pp. 43–52. On the state of consciousness associated with *Atika*, see below, Chapter 14.

45. See Matt, "New-Ancient Words."

46. Zohar 1:92b; Matt, Pritzker edn., vol. 2, p. 85.

47. Zohar 3:22b.

48. Mal. 3:16.

49. Huss, "*Sefer ha-Zohar* as a Canonical, Sacred and Holy Text," pp. 275–307.

Chapter 4

1. See David Greenstein, PhD dissertation.

2. Mishnah *Avot* 3:2, 3:6. BT *Berakhot* 6a. Compare Zohar, *Midrash ha-Ne'elam* 1:116a: "Open your mouth, since *Shekhinah* accompanies us! For whenever people engage in words of Torah, *Shekhinah* comes and joins, especially on the way, since *Shekhinah* appears anticipatingly, preceding those who attain faith in the blessed Holy One" (Matt, Pritzker edn., vol. 2, p. 176). See also Zohar 2:217a; 3:59b.

3. For example, in the story of Kfar Tarsha (Zohar 1:92b–96b), or in the story of the bringing of the rains (Zohar 3:59b–62b).

4. On the centrality of *hitbodedut* (isolation) as a means of attaining mystical experience in the ecstatic Kabbalah, see Idel, *Mystical Experience in Abraham Abulafia*, pp. 7–10, 37–41.

5. See below, pp. 352–64.

Chapter 5

1. Examples of the loci of zoharic stories: On the way—1:157a; 2:155b, 3:200b. In a field—*Idra Rabba*, 3:127b–128a; *Zohar Ḥadash*, Ruth, 84d. Under trees—2:127a. In a cave—1:117b, 230b, 249a; 3:20b. In a house—1:92b; 2:165b. In Rabbi Shim'on's home—*Idra Zuta*, 3:287b; 2:143a; 1:14a.

2. Zohar 3:39a.

3. See Zohar 3:162a–197b; 1:7a; 2:190b among others. In contrast to the absence of the yeshiva in the Zohar's main corpus, the celestial academy is the central locus in the composition *Ra'aya Meheimna*.

4. On the mystical-religious consciousness that views the margins of society as the locus of the living, divine word, see De Certeau, *The Mystic Fable*, p. 13.

5. Zohar 1:219a–b; 2:127a–b; 3:22b.

6. This is not the case in *Midrash ha-Ne'elam*, which is filled with personages known to us from the world of the sages.

7. See Liebes, "Zohar ve-eros," especially pp. 87–103; Liebes, "Ha-Zohar ke-sefer halakhah," pp. 581–605.

8. See Tishby, *Wisdom of the Zohar* 3:1089–1121; Goldreich, "Beirurim bi-r'iyyato ha-atsmit," pp. 459–96. Giller, *Enlightened Will Shine*, pp. 59–74.

9. On the community of Castile at the time of the Zohar's composition, see Baer, "Todros ben Yehudah ha-Levi u-zmano"; Baer, *History of the Jews in Christian Spain*, vol. I, pp. 111–37. On Todros ben Yehudah ha-Levi, see also Shirman, *Ha-shirah ha-Ivrit bi-Sfarad u-ve-Provans* 2:413–18.

In contrast to the Zohar's main corpus, in *Ra'aya Meheimna* and *Tikkunei ha-Zohar* the criticism of Jewish communities' social order and values is far more explicit and venomous. See Baer, "Ha-reka ha-histori"; Scholem, *Kabbalah and Its Symbolism*, pp. 68–70; Tishby, *Wisdom of the Zohar* 3:1089–1121; Gottlieb, *Meḥkarim be-sifrut ha-Kabbalah*, pp. 545–50. On the relationship between the views (in various parts of the Zohar) of the halakhic establishment, see Liebes, "Ha-Zohar ke-sefer halakhah," pp. 597–99; Giller, *The Enlightened Will Shine*, pp. 27–32; Goldreich, "Beirurim bi-r'iyyato ha-atsmit," pp. 476–81.

10. Ta-Shma, *Ha-nigleh she-ba-nistar*, pp. 11–17, 35–40, 50–52.

11. Idel, "Kabbalah and Elites," pp. 5–19; Idel, "PaRDeS," pp. 245–64; Idel, *Kabbalah: New Perspectives*, p. 212–13; Huss, "Ḥakham adif mi-navi," pp. 129–33; Huss, "Hofa'ato shel Sefer ha-Zohar," pp. 32–40.

12. *Zohar Ḥadash*, Lamentations 91–94; Zohar 3:6a, 74a, 297b among others.

13. Unlike in Bialik's poem "Levadi" (By Myself), where the wind has removed everyone from the *beit midrash*, which has lost its relevance, yet Shekhinah remains behind. Bialik, *Selected Poems*, p. 32.

14. This view represents a development of the rabbinic conception as expressed, for example, in BT *Megillah* 29a. See Liebes, "Zohar ve-eros," pp. 104–12. On the manner in which the mystics transform themselves into a sanctuary, see the Zohar's commentary to the Torah portions *Terumah* and *Vayakhel*. See also my article "'Ad atah yoshvim hayinu.'"

15. On the experience of the living word of God residing outside the hegemonic centers, see De Certeau, *The Mystic Fable* 1, pp. 12–13.

16. On the transformation of the status of Shekhinah from a powerful queen to a loving yet powerless companion in exile, see: *Zohar Ḥadash*, Lamentations, 92b.

17. See above, Chapter 1.

18. Cordovero, *Sefer Gerushin*; Sack, *Be-sha'arei ha-kabbalah*, pp. 34–54.

19. Cordovero, *Or Yakar*, 1:58; see Sack, *Be-sha'arei ha-kabbalah*, p. 45, note 65.

Chapter 6

1. For discussion of the nocturnal delight in addition to what is found in this chapter, see below, p. 243.

2. Scholem explored the way in which the Kabbalists' ideas received ritual form, and—of direct relevance for our discussion—the way in which the cosmic-mythic union of male and female received such expression. See Scholem, *Kabbalah and Its Symbolism*, pp. 118–57.

3. BT *Berakhot* 3b–4a.

4. Zohar 2:195b–196a.

5. Ibid.; Zohar 1:92a–b.

6. See BT *Berakhot* 3a; *Sanhedrin* 16a; JT *Berakhot* 5b. In the Zohar, see, for example, 1:157b; 2:67b, 173b; 1:260b (*Hashmatot*).

7. Zohar 1:77b, 82b, 92a, 176b, 178b, 231b; 2:46a; 3:13a, 22a, 148b, 213a. Regarding the creation of the Zohar's myth, note also the influence of Midrash Song of Songs Rabbah 8 on the biblical phrase "sitting in the gardens" (Song 8:13).

8. Zohar 1:17b, 18a, 153b.

9. Zohar 1:178b, 231b. Part of her disappearance is her commingling with the light of the male.

10. Zohar 1:8a; 3:98b, 180a. In terms of mode of conduct, the *tikkun* for the night of the annual Shavuot (Pentecost) festival is not different in its essence from the regular, nightly *tikkun* of the Companions. What is distinct, however, is that the Shavuot homilies relate to the fact that this is a night of participation with Shekhinah, before Her entry—on the morrow, the day of the giving of the Torah—into the wedding canopy with the blessed Holy One; hence the homilies' subject is love.

11. Zohar 1:38a.

12. In rabbinic literature, Leviathan is also associated with the fourth watch. BT *Avodah Zarah* 3b: "In the fourth watch, He sits and sports with Leviathan, as is said: *and Leviathan that you formed to sport with* (Ps. 104:26). R. Nahman the son of Yitshak said, "He sports with His creatures."

13. Zohar 1:38a, 82b.

14. Zohar 2:127b.

15. Zohar 1:38a.

16. *Guide of the Perplexed* 3:51. See Fishbane, *Kiss of God*, pp. 24–30.

17. See Isaac of Acre, *Sefer me'irat einayim*, p. 217; Idel, *Kabbalah: New Perspectives*, p. 51; Fishbane, *Kiss of God*, pp. 24–30.

18. Sviri, *Taste of Hidden Things*, pp. 124–44.

19. On the shaman's ability to participate simultaneously in numerous levels of reality, see Meged, *Sha'arei tikvah ve-sha'arei eimah*, pp. 27–31. See also Aldous Huxley's description of a state of consciousness where the body functions physically while consciousness occupies a different domain; Erickson, "Special Inquiry with Aldous Huxley," pp. 45–71.

20. On the different garments of the soul in the Garden of Eden, see Cohen-Alloro, *Sod ha-malbush*, pp. 50–88.

21. Zohar 1:7a: "At midnight, the blessed Holy One delights in the righteous in the Garden of Eden, and this is the time when human beings delight in Torah."

The souls in the garden also delight in one another, as described in *Rav Metivta*, Zohar 3:167b–168a.

22. Zohar 1:135b. The idea that joining together to study Torah brings about the indwelling of Shekhinah is found already in rabbinic literature. See, for example, Mishnah *Avot* 3:2.

23. For example, regarding *tikkun leil Shavuot*, see Zohar 3:98a, 180a; perhaps also with regard to circumcision, 1:10b. On the importance of ritual washing of the hands, see also *Tsava'at R. Eliezer Hagadol* 10.

24. See below, Chapter 11.

25. See the parallel to this passage, with slight modifications, on 3:303a, *Tosafot*; see also the end of this chapter.

26. Psalm 134 is associated with ritual washing of the hands, a precondition for the priestly raising of the hands. See BT *Sotah* 39a. On the mystical intention that the Zohar attributes to the priestly raising of the hands, see Zohar 3:146a–b; 2:278a (*Tosafot*). See Hecker, *Mystical Bodies, Mystical Meals*, pp. 152.

27. See also the parallels in Zohar 1:136b; 2:67a. See below, pp. 129–31, for a detailed discussion of this passage.

28. Zohar 1:60b: "Come and see: All those offspring of the Garden of Eden issue from Righteous One only when He enters this ark [sefirah *Malkhut*] in a single bond" (Matt, Pritzker edn., vol. 1, p. 347).

29. Zohar 1:4b contains a description of God's delight with the words of Torah uttered by human beings. Elsewhere the delight is portrayed in terms of the playful games between a father and his daughter, a description seemingly less erotic, or at least possessing a different kind of eros, than that between God and His Shekhinah. It should be noted, though, that in many places throughout the Zohar, divine eros crosses the boundaries of prohibited human sexual relations. See Tishby, *Ḥikrei kab-balah u-shluhoteha*, pp. 40–45; Idel, "Perushim le-sod ha-arayyot," p. 89. Regarding kiss-ing, see Hecker, "Kissing Kabbalists," pp. 171–208.

Zohar 2:97a: "There is a palace called the palace of love. . . . the blessed Holy One finds the holy soul there; He goes to meet her and kisses her and embraces her, and raises her up with Him, and delights in her. This is the meaning of *he shall deal with her as with daughters* (Exod. 21:9)—as a father deals with his beloved daughter, in that he kisses her and embraces her and presents her with gifts, so the blessed Holy One deals with the righteous soul every day."

30. See Zohar 3:35b: "Happy are Israel, for the blessed Holy One gave them a holy Torah, the joy of all, the joy of the blessed Holy One, His amble, as is written: *a source of delight* (Prov. 8:30)!" See also 1:60a.

31. For example, Midrash Genesis Rabbah 8; Midrash *Sifra, Beḥukotai* 1.

32. This connection was explicitly made by R. Moses Cordovero, *Shi'ur Komah*, entry for *hillukh*.

33. Midrash *Sifra, Beḥukotai* 1. See also Midrash *Aggadat Bereshit* 23: "*This is the gate of YHVH* (Ps. 118:20); and David [likewise] said, *I will walk before YHVH in the land of the living* (Ps. 116:9)—this is the Garden of Eden. The blessed Holy One, so to speak, ambles with you, as it is written, *I will walk in your midst* (Lev. 26:12)." It is possible that this is the source of the zoharic image of the blessed Holy One's ambling *within* the human being—and not just "with" him.

34. On the concept of *tiyyul* (ambling) in post-zoharic literature, see Liebes, *Sod ha-emunah ha-Shabta'it*, p. 305 and notes. In addition to citing Cordovero's interpre-tation of the term, Liebes also cites later developments associated with the term in Lurianic Kabbalah (*Sefer ha-Gilgulim* 72), where the *tiyyul* is portrayed in an acutely sexual manner.

35. Cordovero, *Shi'ur Komah* 29.

36. Ḥayyim Ben Atar, *Or ha-Ḥayyim*, at Lev. 26:3.

37. According to BT *Ketubot* 62b, the intercourse of the "disciples of the wise" is from Sabbath eve to Sabbath eve.

38. Zohar 2:136b.

39. See Wolfson, "Eunuchs Who Keep the Sabbath," pp. 151–85; Idel, *Kabbalah and Eros*, pp. 206–7, 235.

40. The zoharic Garden of Eden, like the Garden of Eden so humorously and satiri-cally depicted by Itzik Manger, is quintessentially "Jewish" and not "Gentile." See Itzik Manger, *Sippur Gan Eden*.

41. On Torah study as bringing comfort and consolation to God, see Zohar 1:231a; 2:195b–196a. In his study of "Tradition and New Creation in the Ritual of the Kabbalists," Scholem focused in the main on the mourning and consolation associated with the nocturnal arousal, owing to his interest in the development of the ritual of *Tikkunei Ḥatsot* in the Kabbalah of the sixteenth century, which he saw as a ritual response (of cosmic proportions) to the trauma of the expulsion and exile experienced by the Spanish kabbalists. See Scholem, *Kabbalah and Its Symbolism*, pp. 146–53.

42. Zohar 2:46a; 3:13a.

43. On the portion one receives with the souls of the righteous in the Garden of Eden, see also Zohar 2:173b: "When a person arises at that time to engage Torah, he partakes with the righteous in the garden." See further below, p. 243.

44. The connection between the experience of Torah study and sexual intercourse is already found in rabbinic literature. See, for example, BT Eruvin 54b; on study and sexuality, see below, pp. 159–65.

45. Shekhinah delights in the two *tsaddikim* (righteous ones) who arouse her—the lower righteous one causes Her to pour forth Her waters of desire, and the upper righteous one bestows upon Her His waters. "Sabbatical [*Shmita*] dwells constantly between two righteous ones, as it is written, *The righteous will inherit the land* (Ps. 37:29)—Righteous One above, righteous one below. From Righteous One above, She obtains supernal water, from righteous one below, female emits water toward male in consummate desire" (Zohar 1:153b; Matt, Pritzker edn., vol. 2, pp. 356–57).

In the same way, the divine attribute of *Yesod* is also positioned between two females, the sefirah *Malkhut* below and the sefirah *Binah* above (ibid.), and the man who sets out on a journey is positioned between two females, his wife below and Shekhinah above (Zohar 1:50a).

46. Liebes, "Zohar ve-eros," pp. 68–70. On eros and the Zohar, see below, p. 226.

47. BT Ḥagigah 12b; *Avodah Zarah* 3b. In the Zohar, see 1:92a, 194b; 2:57a; 3:213a among others.

48. Zohar 1:92a–b.

49. Examples of the many stories transpiring during the nocturnal study vigil include: 1:92b, 135a, 229b; 2:36b, 173b, 195b, 209a; 3:67a, 193a.

50. On *tikkun ḥatsot* (the midnight vigil) in the Kabbalah, see Idel, *Messianic Mystics*, Appendix 2, pp. 308–20.

51. Zohar 1:77b.

52. Zohar 1:7a.

53. Zohar 1:136b, 76a–b.

54. Zohar 1:82b, 132b–133a, and many more times.

55. Zohar 1:4a. On awaiting dawn, see above, pp. 83–84.

56. See the parallel passage on *Zohar Ḥadash* 53b. The first verse cited by the ancient *ḥasidim* is "O YHVH, You are my God, I will extol You; I will praise Your name, for You have acted wondrously, counsels of old of steadfast faithfulness" (Isa. 25:1), followed by "I praise You for I am awesomely, wondrously made; Your work is wonderful, I know it very well" (Ps. 139:14), and finally, "A river flows from Eden . . ." (Gen. 2:10).

Chapter 7

1. Yechiel Goldberg, "Foolishness of the Wise," pp. 45–46, 69–78.

2. Toward, for example, the host in the story of Kfar Tarsha (Zohar 1:92b), the old man in the *Sava de-Mishpatim* (2:94b), the young mute in a story in the commentary to the Torah portion *Terumah* (2:147a), and the man wandering in the field in Zohar Ruth (*Zohar Ḥadash* 84d).

3. Excluding the story of the encounter between Rashbi and his son Ele'azar with the desert hermit in Zohar 2:183b, where the figure of the old man and the child are a kind of shadow image to Rabbi Shim'on and his son. That hermit is a Rashbi-like figure operating in the desert—the domain of the other side, as opposed to inhabited areas.

4. Zohar 1:7a; Matt, Pritzker edn., vol. 1, p. 43.

5. Presumably the donkeys' behavior echoes the actions of the biblical donkeys in Num. 22:22-35 and in 1 Kings 13:24.

6. Zohar 1:7b; Matt, Pritzker edn., vol. 1, p. 49.

7. 3:265b, 59b, and 221b among others.

8. Zohar 2:97b. The riddle is repeated in the continuation of the story, 104a; part of the solution to the riddle is found in 98a, and perhaps also in the story of Rav Hamnuna Sava in the Introduction to the Zohar. In many other places as well, an "old man" refers to Rashbi and to his manner of expounding Torah.

9. We have here a sophisticated and double allusion, for the "rock" is also Hamnuna Sava himself (3:188a).

10. A similar structure is employed in the story of the wondrous child, *yanuka* (Zohar 3:186a–192a), and in many other stories as well. See below, Chapter 12, note 29.

11. Perhaps the decision to "distribute" wisdom and Torah among all manner of figures, in all kinds of places, is connected to Rabbi Shim'on's words in the famous talmudic story about the entrance to Yavneh. The sages' words give expression to a sober historical perspective: "The Torah is destined to be forgotten among Israel." But Rashbi responds: "Heaven forfend that the Torah will be forgotten among Israel, as is said: *it will never be lost from the mouth of their offspring* (Deut. 31:21)! How then do I interpret *Men shall wander from sea to sea and from north to east to seek the word of the LORD, but they shall not find it* (Amos 8:12)?—That they will not find a clear halakhah or a clear mishnah in one single place!" (BT *Shabbat* 138b). Since Rabbi Shim'on was later chosen to be the Zohar's hero, his world (namely, the future world of the rabbinic Rabbi Shim'on) must portray a state in which the Torah has indeed not been forgotten, and is no longer found in a single place but rather in many places. See Liebes, "Messiah of the Zohar," pp. 5–7.

12. See, for example, Ḥayyim Vital, *Sefer ha-gilgulim*, 65a–b.

13. Zohar 2:23a. On the *maskilim* (the enlightened), see Chapter 2.

14. Zohar 2:99a; Matt, *Book of Enlightenment*, p. 125.

15. On sleep and the sensation of the world to come (or "world that is coming") in the passage to an alternate reality, see Idel's discussion of sensations and feelings in prophetic-mystical experience, in his *Mystical Experience in Abraham Abulafia*, pp. 74–83.

See also the comments by Rabbi Joseph ben Shalom Ashkenazi, a member of the zoharic circle:

> Vision is that which generates terror and fear in the prophet until his feelings and sensations are obliterated, as is said in Daniel, *and I saw this great vision and was drained of strength, my vigor was destroyed, and I could not summon up strength* and *overcome by deep sleep, I lay prostrate on the ground* (Dan. 10:8–9); and then on account of the fear, the senses cease functioning, and the influence flows to the speaking faculty, and it flows on to the imaginative [faculty], and it will seem to him as though he sees the face of a man speaking with voice and wind and speech. (Ashkenazi, *Perush le-parashat Bereshit*, pp. 222–23)

It is possible to interpret the Companions' experience in *Rav Metivta* as the "sleep of prophecy" discussed by Ashkenazi, except that in this case the experience is collective. On the connection between Ashkenazi and the zoharic circle, see Liebes, "How the Zohar was Written," pp. 93–95.

16. BT *Ḥagigah* 14b; JT *Ḥagigah* 9a. For a brief discussion of this story as a touchstone in Jewish mystical articulations, see above, Chapter 2, pp. 63–64. See also Liebes, *Ḥet'o shel Elisha*.

17. Rabbi Joseph ben Shalom Ashkenazi describes a state of mystical experience that perhaps fits the Companions' experiences in *Rav Metivta*. Ashkenazi describes the state of the "sleep of prophecy" as the "obliteration of the senses" while awake, enabling the prophet to attain intensified experiences including levitation:

> The philosophers have already written on the issue of prophecy, saying that it is not improbable that there will be a person to whom matters will appear in his imaginative faculty, comparable to that which appears to the imaginative faculty in a dream. All this [could take place] while someone is awake, and all his senses are obliterated, as the letters of the divine name [stand] in front of his eyes, in the gathered colors. Sometimes, he will hear a voice, a wind, a speech, a thunder, and a noise with all the organs of his hearing sense, and he will see with his imaginative faculty with all the organs of sight, and he will smell with all the organs of smell and he will taste with all the organs of taste, and he will touch with all the organs of touch and he will walk and levitate. All this while the holy letters are in front of his eyes, and its colors are covering it; this is the sleep of prophecy. (Ashkenazi, *Perush le-parashat Bereshit*, p. 223, cited also in Idel, *Kabbalah: New Perspectives*, p. 105 and notes; see also above, note 15.)

18. On *Rav Metivta*, see Scholem, "Mekorotav shel ma'aseh Rav Gaddi'el ha-Tinok," p. 281. See also Wolski and Carmeli, "Those Who Know Have Wings."

Chapter 8

1. Zohar 3:79b. See also 2:95a, 98b (about words of Torah); 3:20a (about the Psalms of David); 3:157a (about the writings of King Solomon); among others.

2. Zohar 3:128a, *Idra Rabba*.

3. Gikatilla, *Gates of Light: Sha'are Orah*, Section 2, 129.

4. On the zoharic secret and its masculine and feminine associations, see Wolfson, "Occultation of the Feminine," pp. 113–54. On the phenomenon of the secret and esotericism in Jewish thought in its medieval cultural and social context, see Halbertal, *Concealment and Revelation*.

5. Azulai, *Moreh be-etsba* 2; *Ma'arekhet sefarim* 2:33. My thanks to my colleague Boaz Huss for drawing my attention to these passages.

6. See Scholem, *Kabbalah and Its Symbolism*, pp. 32–87; Tishby, *Wisdom of the Zohar* 3:1076–121; Idel, "Tefisat ha-Torah," pp. 23–84.

7. Midrash Genesis Rabbah 1.1, 4.

8. BT *Menaḥot* 29b.

9. BT *Eruvin* 54b. See Elon, *From Jerusalem to the Edge of Heaven*, pp. 53–58. See Boyarin, *Carnal Israel*, pp. 134–66.

10. The "doe" of the Zohar (discussed above, Chapter 2) is similar to the beloved in the Song of Songs, and perhaps also to the figure of the doe (the beloved) in medieval poetry—although, in contrast with the Torah, the latter remains unattainable.

11. Zohar 2:99a–b. On *Sava de-Mishpatim*, see above, pp. 48, 68. See also Liebes, "Zohar ve-eros," pp. 87–98; Oron, "'Simeini kha-ḥotam'"; Idel, *Kabbalah: New Perspectives*, 222–34; Wolfson, "Beautiful Maiden Without Eyes"; Giller, "Love and Upheaval"; Yisraeli, *Parshanut ha-sod ve-sod ha-parshanut.*

12. See below, pp. 206–8. See also Idel, *Language, Torah and Hermeneutics*, pp. ix–xvii.

13. On different conceptions of seeing and vision in Jewish literature, see Wolfson, *Speculum That Shines*, which is wholly devoted to this topic; Wolfson, "Beautiful Maiden," pp. 155–203.

14. See below, pp. 222–25.

15. In his introduction to his Torah commentary, Rabbi Moses Naḥmanides (Ramban) describes the Torah as "comprised entirely of the names of the blessed Holy One." According to this conception, there can be no hierarchy of verses, as the manner in which we read the Torah is merely a particular division of its original and ancient form, whereby the writing was continuous without division into words. Thus, in a most essential way, the verse ". . . and Lotan's sister was Timna" (Gen. 36:22) is no less divine than the verse "Hear, O Israel . . ." (Deut. 6:4).

16. Liebes, "Zohar ve-eros," pp. 87–112.

17. Zohar 1:245b. See Liebes, "Messiah of the Zohar," p. 53. On the Kabbalists' transgression of gender boundaries in their role as generators of female waters, see Wolfson, *Circle in the Square*, pp. 110–12.

18. BT *Ta'anit* 8b; *Bava Metsia* 42a; *Bava Batra* 2b.

19. See, for example, the opening to the *Idra Rabba*, 3:128a; on the request to disclose secrets at an appropriate time, see 1:1b; on the caution surrounding disclosure and innovation, see 1:5a.

20. Liebes, "Messiah of the Zohar," pp. 26–34. Wolfson, "Occultation of the Feminine," pp. 113–54.

21. Another prime example is found in *Sava de-Mishpatim*, where the old man vacillates over whether to share the secrets he has accumulated and acquired through great effort with the two young companions.

> The old man wept as before and said to himself, "Old man, old man, how greatly you have toiled to attain these holy words and now you should say them in a single moment!?" [He continues his internal dialogue and says,] "Do not be afraid, old man, for you have joined battle many times with powerful men and you have not been afraid.

Should you now be afraid? Say your words, for the blessed Holy One and the Assembly of Israel are here, and those who are here are worthy." (Zohar 2:98a)

See also Zohar 2:101b.

22. See Wolfson, *Speculum That Shines*, p. 274, notes 13, 14, 339, 388, 396; Wolfson, "Occultation of the Feminine." On the Platonic view of the philosopher-mystic as feminine, see Finkelberg, "Plato's Language of Love."

23. BT *Sukkah* 53a; JT *Sanhedrin* 10:2.

24. On the attitude of Rabbi Shim'on's circle and generation to the reality of the secret, see above, pp. 99–104. See as well Ḥ. Bialik's classic essay "Revealment and Concealment." On the transition from the attitude toward the secret in the time of King David (as author of the Psalms) to the attitude displayed in the days of King Solomon (as author of Song of Songs), see *Zohar Ḥadash* 62d.

25. See Liebes, "Zohar ve-eros, p. 70.

26. Shimon Lavi, *Ketem Paz* 1:210a. See Huss, *Al adnei paz*, pp. 58–59.

27. On the manner in which the Zohar's relationship with the Torah (as exposing the dynamic worlds of divinity) becomes for later kabbalists the basis for their relationship with the Zohar itself, see Idel, *Kabbalah: New Perspectives*, pp. 231–33.

28. *Matnita di-lan* (our Mishnah) is a literary, renaissance expression. It refers to collected statements of foundational values in the Zohar, like those appearing in *Sifra de-Tseni'uta*, which constitutes a kind of Mishnah for the Zohar. Similarly the *Matnitin* (our Mishnah) literature in the Zohar, as its name suggests, constitutes the Mishnaic foundation for the zoharic Talmud. See Gottlieb, *Meḥkarim*, pp. 163–214. The term *Matnita di-lan* also distinguishes its referent from all other Mishnahs (as did "the Mishnah"—that is, of Rabbi Yehudah ha-Nasi), depicting its teaching as distinctive. It is "our" Mishnah, that is, of the initiates of the palace, the zoharic circle. The reflexive expression defines the group's self-image: like the tannaim who have their Mishnah, so we—who continue their creative enterprise—have our Mishnah. On the term's meaning, see further Matt, "Matnita di-lan," pp. 123–45.

29. See, for example, Zohar 2:147a.

30. See Zohar 3:61b, 62a.

31. On the Zohar's ambivalence regarding the disclosure of secrets, see Liebes, "Messiah of the Zohar," pp. 26–48.

32. Zohar 3:79a.

33. Zohar 3:60b; and throughout the homilies in the *Idra Rabba*.

34. See Liebes, "Messiah of the Zohar," pp. 12–48.

35. See Liebes, "Messiah of the Zohar," pp. 23–26.

36. This verse is expounded in the Zohar (2:87a) against anyone who says words of Torah that he did not receive from his teacher.

37. Zohar 2:79a. See also 3:57b.

38. See below, pp. 209–17; see also Zohar 1:121a, 77a.

39. Huss, "Ḥakham adif mi-navi," pp. 132–33.

40. To account for the Zohar's distinctions among Companions by their locale, David E. S. Stein (personal communication) has suggested another explanation: psychological splitting, fantasy, and creation of an alter ego. That is, through their writing, the zoharic

circle of authors allowed their "superhero" characters—Rabbi Shimon's circle—a freedom regarding the Land of Israel that they themselves only partly felt, while projecting *their own* reservations onto the figures of the Babylonian Companions. This approach enabled the zoharic circle—who did not come to live in the land of Israel—to reckon with their own Diaspora consciousness. (In contrast, Stein suggests, Ramban does not seem like a good candidate to be a model for the Babylonian Companions, for his consciousness of the Land of Israel was actually very strong: he ultimately came to the land of Israel.)

41. On this passage and the meaning of *psellos*, see Liebes, "Zikkat ha-Zohar le-erets Yisra'el," p. 36, note 25; Huss, "Ḥakham adif mi-navi," p. 132. The Babylonians are not alone in fearing to open their mouths despite the fact that they have received secrets. Rabbi Shim'on describes the generation of King Solomon in the same way, in order to distinguish it from the generation in which he, Rashbi, abides. On the "stammerers" of Solomon's generation, see Zohar 2:149a. See above, p. 98 and notes there.

42. On the Babylonians, see Zohar 1:225a. On the Zohar's attitude towards Babylonia and its Torah, see Liebes, "Zikkat ha-Zohar le-erets Yisra'el."

43. Zohar 1:94b.

44. Zohar 1:95b.

45. See, for example, the story about another "zoharic" village, the village of Ramin, appearing in the Zohar's commentary to the Torah portion *Noaḥ*, 1:63a–64b. See also the story of the encounter between Rashbi and the desert hermits, 2:183b.

46. See above, p. 49.

47. Like Moses' wish in the story of Eldad and Medad (Num. 11:29).

48. On oppositional stories in the Zohar, see Meroz, "'Va-ani lo hayiti sham?'" and also "The Path of Silence."

49. The zoharic figure of Joseph serves as a symbol for the balance between withholding and bestowing. See Zohar 1:208a; see as well at the opening of the *Idra Rabba*, 3:127b–128a. On disclosure and concealment in relation to the verse that appears in our story, "Do not withhold good from one who deserves it" (Prov. 3:27), see 2:98a, 1:96b.

50. Citing Prov. 25:11, "*Like apples of gold in settings of silver filigree is a word spoken in right circumstances*," Rabbi Samuel ibn Tibbon of Provence defines the revelation of secrets as the expansion of the space around the silver filigrees covering the apples of gold. If we borrow his imagery and apply it to the world of the Zohar, it emerges that apples of gold *unadorned* by filigrees of silver are considered undesirable. The apples of gold, the world of the secret, require the filigrees of silver in order to preserve their erotic quality. On the esotericism of Ibn Tibbon, see Halbertal, *Concealment and Revelation*, pp. 105–13.

Chapter 9

1. On this topic, see Wolfson, *Speculum That Shines*, pp. 326–92.

2. Midrash Song of Songs Rabbah 1; Midrash Leviticus Rabbah 16.4.

3. Zohar 3:73a.

4. BT *Bava Batra* 15a. We also find this idea in Maimonides' allegorical interpretation of the story of the Garden of Eden (*Guide of the Perplexed* 2:30). There are, however, allegorical texts where parts of the biblical text stand for parts of another system without reducing the original text to a simple schema and without transforming the *nimshal* (ref-

erent) to an excessively detailed language no longer resonant with the original; for example in the allegories of the Church Fathers to the Song of Songs, and in the allegories of Philo of Alexandria.

5. Idel, *Kabbalah: New Perspectives*, pp. 200–249.

6. Cordovero, *Pardes rimmonim, sha'ar ha-oti'ot* 1.

7. On the structures of classical rabbinic homilies, see Heinemann, *Darkhei Ha-Aggadah*, pp. 1–62; Frankel, *Midrash ve-aggadah*; Mack, *Midrash ha-aggadah*, pp. 50–59.

8. On the kabbalistic homily, see Gruenwald, "Ha-metsi'ut ha-midrashit," pp. 255–98.

9. Idel, *Kabbalah: New Perspectives*, pp. 222–34.

10. Zohar 1:1b.

11. Zohar 2:140a.

12. Idel, "He'arot rishoniot," p. 775.

13. *Zohar Ḥadash* 85b.

14. Zohar 2:140a. See above, p. 54.

15. Eitan Fishbane, "Tears of Disclosure," pp. 25–47.

16. For translation and discussion, see above, pp. 168-71.

17. Zohar 3:204b.

18. Zohar 3:21a.

19. It should be noted here that in rabbinic interpretations of the verses of the Song of Songs, alongside the tendency to highlight and develop the erotics of the composition, we also find the opposite tendency of de-eroticization of the verses. On eroticization as a hermeneutical tool, see Idel, *Kabbalah: New Perspectives*, p. 223.

20. Hollenback's comments on the softening or circumscription of ordinary vision and sense perception so as to make space for alternate conceptions are particularly apt in this regard:

One usually sees the aura or the mystic light only if one has disengaged oneself from the process of physical sense perception and awakened a latent trans-sensory faculty of perception that normally remains unmanifest as long as the mind is preoccupied with processing information that comes into it from the imagination and the five senses. (Hollenback, *Mysticism*, p. 66)

21. See Liebes, "Zohar ve-eros," pp. 70–72.

22. See, for example, Zohar 3:20a–23a (the story of the disclosure of the deeper meaning of "If the whole community of Israel has erred"; Lev. 4:13); 3:61b–62a (the secret of "While the king was on his couch, my nard gave forth its fragrance"; Song 1:12); 3:157a–b (the interpretation of "For in respect of the fate of man and the fate of beast, they have one and the same fate"; Eccles. 3:19).

23. See below, pp. 321–29.

24. See, for example, Zohar 2:126a.

25. See, for example, Zohar 3:59b.

26. Zohar 1:92bff; see the detailed discussion of this story above, pp. 183–88.

27. Zohar 2:198a–201a.

28. Zohar 3:59b–62a.

29. Zohar 1:8a.

30. Zohar 3:127b–145a.

31. On the collective event known as the Idra Rabba, see Liebes, "Messiah of the Zohar," pp. 12–48.

32. R. Moses Cordovero, who dedicated his life to reading the Zohar, describes in his commentary the manner of the genesis of zoharic innovation:

> R. Shim'on and his companions did not say that which they had already received. . . . And how were they different from the other companions of the generation? Indeed the matter is that they would begin [studying] a verse, and in their righteousness, by virtue of their wisdom, the holy spirit would dwell among them. While elaborating on words of Torah, through that which had already been said, little by little they would draw down until the innovation of the verse was innovated in their intellect . . . and they would engender an innovation in Torah, *ḥiddush Torah*. (Cordovero, *Or Yakar* 9:99)

See Sack, *Be-sha'arei ha-kabbalah*, pp. 45–46.

33. Midrash Song of Songs Rabbah 1; Midrash Leviticus Rabbah 16.4.

34. See Midrash *Tanḥuma, Ki Tissa* 18.

35. As in the Old Man's comments in *Sava de-Mishpatim*, 2:95a.

36. See below, pp. 245–49, for the full text of this homily and discussion.

37. Zohar 3:134b.

38. Zohar 3:161b. See below, pp. 150–53.

39. Zohar 3:144a.

40. See Liebes, "Messiah of the Zohar," pp. 63–65.

41. See above, pp. 118–20.

42. See the parallel text on 1:197b and see below, pp. 184–85. See also Zohar 3:88a.

43. I wish to thank my jazz musician friend Steve Peskoff for riffing with me on this interlude.

Chapter 10

1. On the voice of calling and the heavenly herald see Liebes, "Zohar ve-eros," p. 76, note 62.

2. As my teacher Yehuda Liebes pointed out to me, the word *he'arah* has its origin in Tibbonite Hebrew, as a translation of the Arabic word *tanbih*, from the root *n-b-h*, "note."

3. In this chapter, I focus not only on the literary layers called *guf ha-Zohar* (the main corpus of the Zohar), but also *Matnitin* and *Tosefta*.

4. On the "implied author," see Even, *Milon munaḥei ha-sipporet*, p. 80.

5. See Wolfson, *Circle in the Square*, p. 81 and notes; Idel, *Kabbalah: New Perspectives*, pp. 207–10.

6. See Tishby, *Wisdom of the Zohar* 2:677–722.

7. On the importance in zoharic literature of the verse "A river issues from Eden to water the garden," see below, Chapter 11.

8. See Altmann, "*Homo Imago Dei*," pp. 235–59; Lorberbaum, *Tselem Elohim*, pp. 228–60.

9. See Mopsik, "Body of Engenderment."

10. On the Torah in Kabbalah, see Scholem, *Kabbalah and Its Symbolism*, pp. 32–86; Tishby, *Wisdom of the Zohar* 3:1077–121; Idel, "Tefisat ha-Torah"; Wolfson, *Circle in the Square*, pp. 1–28.

11. On how different conceptions of Torah generate different modes of exegesis, see Idel, "Infinities of Torah," pp. 141–58; idem, "He'arot rishoniyot al ha-parshanut ha-kabbalit le-sugehah," pp. 773–84; idem, *Kabbalah: New Perspectives*, pp. 208–10.

12. See Meroz, "Zoharic Narratives and their Adaptations."

13. A banner example is found in the section *Sava de-Mishpatim*, where the old man experiences the verses as if they are approaching him as warriors on the battlefield, and he is unsure whether he will be able to endure them. The battle is in fact the labor of esoteric exegesis. See Zohar 2:109a–110b.

14. On the verse "Let the simple enter here . . . !" as the seductive call of the Torah, see also 1:193a; 2:99a. Surprisingly, as Liebes has noted, the words "let the simple enter here" are said in the Bible both by Wisdom (Prov. 9:4) and by the "seductress woman of folly," whose seductions lead to the depths of Sheol (Prov. 9:16). See Liebes, "Zohar ve-eros," p. 97, note 186.

15. BT *Ḥagigah* 12b. See Liebes, *Ḥet'o shel Elisha*, pp. 126–29.

16. The call to abandon the material blessings of this world and to walk the path of divine light is in fact a genre unto itself. Two beautiful examples of such calls to develop one's mystical identity are the letter of Pseudo-Dionysus to Timothy (see Liebes, "Dionisiyut ve-Yahudut"); and in the twentieth century, between the two world wars, the stirring words of Hillel Zeitlin: "The voice of God calls out to every man in every place at every time: Leave, O Man, Leave! . . . Go and seek out the distant land, the supernal land, the land of heaven. . . . go forth to yourself, to the root of your supernal soul. . . . that which was said to Abraham is said continuously to all the people of the world, but their eyes are closed and their ears sealed, or as the Zohar says, "Woe to those who have sleep in their sockets . . ." (Zeitlin, *Sifran shel yeḥidim*, pp. 25–28). On Zeitlin see Schatz, "Darko shel Hillel Zeitlin"; Bar-sela, *Bein sa'ar li-dmamah*; Green, "Three Warsaw Mystics," pp. 22–36.

17. Ps. 115:4–8. See also the use of this verse in *Tikkunei Zohar, tikkun* 69, 114a.

18. On *Matnitin* and *Tosefta* in the Zohar, see Gottlieb, "Ma'amrei ha-Matnitin ve-ha-Tosefta she-ba-Zohar," *Meḥkarim be-sifrut ha-Kabbalah*, pp. 163–214; Matt, "Matnita di-lan," pp. 123–45; Pedaya, *Ha-mar'eh ve-ha-dibbur*, pp. 120–33, where she suggests that we view the *Matnitin* in the Zohar as texts reflecting an ecstatic practice derived from ancient esoteric traditions of the *Heikhalot* literature.

19. Mishnah *Avot* 6:2.

20. Maimonides, *Mishneh Torah*, Book of Knowledge, Lore of Repentance 3.4.

21. It is possible that the concept "consciousness" as we use it today is a modern consolidation of the concepts heart, soul, and spirit; and perhaps it constitutes a parallel to the zoharic term *sokhletano* (see above, Chapter 2, note 33).

22. Zohar 3:13a.

23. On the exegesis of Song of Songs, see Green, "Song of Songs."

24. See also Zohar 1:62a, 61b.

25. See above, pp. 81–84.

26. Zohar 1:227a.

27. For example, as said by the old man in the opening to the parable of the maiden in *Sava de-Mishpatim*: "Human beings are so confused in their minds! They do not see the way of truth in Torah. Torah calls out to them every day, in love, but they

do not want to turn their heads' (2:99a; Matt, *Book of Enlightenment*, p. 123). Perhaps the meaning is that Torah coos like a dove, as in the story in BT *Berakhot* 3a: "I heard a *bat kol* (heavenly voice) cooing like a dove, saying: Woe to the children on account of whose sins I destroyed My house, burnt My sanctuary, and exiled My children among the nations!" Similarly: "Torah stands calling out to human beings to engage her, strive for her, but no one bends an ear!" (Zohar 1:134b; Matt, Pritzker edn., vol. 2, p. 258). See also 1:224a, 134b, 227a; 2:99a; 3:57b, 80a.

28. On humans' future recompense for their deeds, see Rabbi Akiva's comments in Mishnah *Avot* 3:14–16; and in the Zohar, 3:57b, 58a.

29. As is the Zohar's way, even the biblical story of Jacob's awakening (Gen. 28:16) receives an erotic interpretation, namely, his awakening to the presence of the female dimension of divinity in the world. See 1:147a–150b.

30. "The Hymn of the Pearl," transl. Hans Jonas; in Jonas, *Gnostic Religion*, pp. 112–29. On sleep, see MacRae, "Sleep and Awakening in Gnostic Texts."

31. See Jonas, *Gnostic Religion*, pp. 68–75: "We are dealing here, as in the whole group of metaphors of sleeping, not with a mythological detail, a mere episode in the narrative, but with a fundamental feature of existence in the world. . . . men in general are 'asleep' in the world." See also Pagels, *Gnostic Gospels*; Couliano, *The Tree of Gnosis*.

32. The opening of the *Idra Rabba*, 3:127b.

33. Similarly, at the heart of the Buddhist worldview we find the experience of awakening, from which the name Buddhism is derived. (The word for "Buddhism" in Sanskrit also means "awakening." The Buddha is the "awakened one," and from the root B.U.D.H are derived the words for numerous concepts relating to intelligence and consciousness.) In Buddhism we also find the view that a veil of slumber or illusion lies spread over consciousness. See Zimmer, *Philosophies of India*, pp. 1–14, 464–72; Humphreys, *Buddhism*, pp. 15–16; Yoshinori, *Buddhist Spirituality*, pp. xv, 6–7. Likewise in Hinduism, from which Buddhism is derived, we find that the sage considers as sleep what most of humanity considers as a state of wakefulness. For example: "What is night for all beings is the time of awakening for the self-controlled, and the time of awakening for all beings is night for the introspective sage." (*Bhagavad-Gita* 2:69)

34. The herald calls for an awakening whose purpose is to arouse pleasure, a quintessentially erotic arousal. See, for example, Zohar 2:89a, 173b, 154b.

35. Song of Songs 2:7, 3:5, 8:4; transl. NJPS.

36. Midrash *Meḥilta, masehta de-shira* 3.

37. See Hollenback, *Mysticism*, pp. 40–47.

38. See, for example, Zohar 3:199a; 2:137b.

39. BT *Yoma* 54b. On the verbal root *'-r-h* (ערה) in rabbinic Hebrew, see Ezrahi, "Shenayyim keruvim," pp. 19–20 and notes.

40. See 3:58b. The spiritual development of the Jewish male is described in the Zohar as an awakening that comes in stages, and it has ritual circumcision as its prerequisite; see 3:91b. Wolfson has shown the connection between being ritually circumcised and the ability to have a vision of the divine. In this zoharic passage, circumcision awakens and bestows the celestial spirit on a man. See Wolfson, *Circle in the Square*, pp. 29–48.

41. Zohar 1:181b; Matt, Pritzker edn., vol. 3, pp. 100–101, modified.

42. See Idel, "Radical Hermeneutics," especially pp. 165–68; Idel, "Non-linguistic Infinities." Idel writes of "aggressive" hermeneutical approaches, with the yardstick for aggression being the extent to which the simple meaning (*peshat*) of the verse is obliterated. The extent of obliteration or "aggression" depends upon the basic attitude toward the status of the canonical text, and on the extent of the desire or obligation to preserve its wholeness. Idel distinguishes between the modes of interpretation of the ecstatic kabbalists (who maintain a particularly tense attitude toward the canonical text, and thus sometimes engage in its "obliteration") and theosophical kabbalists (for whom the sacred text constitutes a "starting point for contemplation, material to be penetrated without obliterating its basic structure"). Idel, *Kabbalah: New Perspectives*, p. 208. The Companions of the Zohar apply a range of different hermeneutical techniques to Scripture and sometimes even interpret it in a manner far removed from their simple meaning; yet from their own perspective and in terms of their own self-image and conception of the Torah, their actions are not aggressive. On the contrary, under their loving gaze the text is not obliterated, but rather is progressively enriched and constructed through the exposure of previously concealed layers.

43. *Mishkan ha-Edut*, Ms. Berlin 193 (Qu. Or. 883), folio 51a–b, as cited by Scholem in *Major Trends*, p. 396 (note 151). (Translation is based on Scholem.)

44. See Wolfson, *Book of the Pomegranate*, p. 1 (Hebrew section). Charles Mopsik cites this passage in his important remarks about R. Moses de León as a prophet and kabbalist, in the introduction to his edition of de León's *Shekel ha-Kodesh*. See his discussion, pp. 6–8.

45. Other examples of his use of the language of awakening and arousal include: *Shekel ha-Kodesh*, pp. 19, 20, 36, 38, 48, 79; *Sefer ha-Rimmon*, on nearly every page; "She'elot u-tshuvot le-Rabbi Moshe de Leon be-inyanei kabbalah," in Tishby, *Ḥikrei ha-kabbalah u-shluḥoteha*, pp. 44–45; *Sefer ha-Mishkal*, p. 62. (In comparison with his other works, *Sefer ha-Mishkal* contains far fewer uses of these verbs.)

46. One foundation of this myth of restoring the male and female to a face-to-face state is the combination of two stories about the cherubim in the holy of holies. The first tells how the cherubim would face one another as long as Israel performed the will of God, but would separate and face away from one another when Israel sinned (BT *Bava Batra* 99a). The second describes the cherubim as male and female engaged in sexual union (BT *Yoma* 54a–b). See Scholem, *Mystical Shape of the Godhead*, pp. 140–97; Tishby, *Wisdom of the Zohar* 1:298–302, 371–87; Idel, "Dimuyyim u-ma'asim miniyyim ba-kabbalah"; Idel, *Kabbalah: New Perspectives*, pp. 128–36; Ezrahi, "Shenayyim keruvim."

47. Zohar 1:245b. On this passage see Liebes, "Messiah of the Zohar," p. 53.

48. Zohar 2:95b.

49. For example, the splitting of the Sea (Exodus 14) is considered as breaking this law, and as an instance of arousal from above not stimulated by the arousal below. According to the zoharic story about the splitting of the Sea (a myth that was extensively developed in the Kabbalah of Isaac Luria), amid the silence and lack of active arousal below, light from the depths of *Atika*, from the crown of the sefirotic world, flowed forth, inundating all the worlds, bringing about a change in the laws of nature and thus splitting the sea. See Zohar 2:52b.

50. Zohar 1:86b; Matt, Pritzker edn., vol. 2, p. 53. See also 1:88a: "*I am my beloved's and his desire is for me* (Song 7:11). They have already established that through an arousal below arises an arousal above, for nothing arouses above until something arouses below" (Matt, Pritzker edn., vol. 2, p. 61). See also Zohar 1:35a, 77b, 244a; 2:135b; among others.

51. See Liebes, "Zohar ve-eros," pp. 87–112.

52. Zohar 3:164a.

53. See Wolfson, "Forms of Visionary Ascent"; Wolfson, *Speculum That Shines*, pp. 326–92.

54. The eyes that they open are mainly those of the soul; and sometimes these are opened only when the eyes of flesh are closed. See 2:23b and see below, pp. 268–71. Perhaps the highest degree is the ability to integrate the sensual eye of flesh with the soul's eye so as to see all, in the words of the Zohar, as "one thing."

55. Similar to the expression "all ears," which designates complete attention.

Chapter 11

1. The Zohar shows interest also in other verses with present continuous verbs. "All the streams flow into the sea, yet the sea is never full" (Eccles. 1:7) is expounded by the Zohar in terms of the continuous flow of the rivers of divine bounty into the "sea," namely, the sefirah *Malkhut*. And the verse "And your people, all of them righteous, shall forever inherit the land" (Isa. 60:21) serves as a code verse; it is expounded many times as signifying the ever-present possibility of "inheriting" (attaining) the feminine divine attribute and quality, which is termed "land."

2. See, for example, 1:33b: "until it reaches that river which flows and issues, whose waters never cease." See also 2:1a; 3:4a. The combination "flows and issues" is derived from a combination of the verse from Daniel with our verse from Genesis. The combination of these verses is present already in Midrash *Pirkei de-Rabbi Eli'ezer* 12: "But did not a river flow and issue from Eden to water the garden, as is said: *And a river issues from Eden to water the garden?*"

3. Genesis Rabbah 15.2.

4. See Abrams, *Rabbi Asher ben David*, p. 75 (Ms Moscow, Ginzburg 321, folio 56b); see also the other variants cited on p. 199. After this passage, which R. Asher introduces with the words "from a Kabbalistic tradition [that has been transmitted to me]," he begins a section that expounds the word "Eden" with the words, "in my opinion." We can therefore assume that the reading of our verse as an illustration of the continual dissemination of the divine plenty among the attributes comes to him as an existing esoteric tradition, although I have been unable to find the source. In his commentary on the Torah, Rabbi Menaḥem Recanati quotes in Hebrew, without citing the source, the passage from the *Thirteen Attributes*, between two Zohar passages. In other words, he had received the tradition of the Hebrew version and not the zoharic paraphrase. See Recanati on Gen. 10:2. On other passages from the writings of R. Asher ben David cited by Recanati, see Abrams, *Rabbi Asher ben David*, pp. 274–78. See also the citation, with no indication of source, in *Mar'ot ha-tsov'ot* by Rabbi David ben Judah he-Ḥasid; *The Book of Mirrors*, pp. 128–29 (Hebrew text).

5. Abrams, *Rabbi Asher ben David*, p. 199–200 (Ms. New York, 1609, folio 73a).

6. Zohar 3:69b. On the verbal root *n-h-r* as "light" in the Bible, see Isa. 60:5, Ps. 34:6. See Kushner, *The River of Light*.

7. Zohar 2:210b.

8. Zohar 3:289b, 290a, *Idra Zuta*.

9. "But we have learned in our concealed Mishnah: When *yod* unites with *he*, then this verse is fulfilled: *A river issues from Eden to water the garden* (Gen. 2:10). Do not say: 'when they unite,' but rather: 'they unite' literally!" (Zohar 1:95b; Matt, Pritzker edn., vol. 2, pp. 105–6). Compare 3:4a.

10. Zohar 3:65b.

11. Zohar 1:82b, 208a.

12. R. Moses Cordovero makes an important observation about the fluidity of gender in kabbalistic symbols depending on the context. According to him, in light of the syntax of our verse, the river is female and represents the sefirah *Binah*: if the river issues from Eden, and if Eden symbolizes *Hokhmah*, then the river must be the sefirah connected with *Hokhmah*, namely the mother, *Binah*. This, he writes, is a contextual definition: "And behold, we cannot associate the mother with *Binah* if [she] is not united with the father, *Hokhmah*; for by virtue of *Hokhmah*, which pours forth bounty, *Binah* is called a receiving female. And if there is no *Hokhmah*, male, father, then there is no *Binah*, mother, female." On transformations in the gender of symbols in theosophical Kabbalah, see Liebes, "How the Zohar Was Written"; Wolfson, "Crossing Gender Boundaries in Kabbalistic Ritual and Myth," in *Circle in the Square*, pp. 79–121.

13. *Pirkei de-Rabbi Eli'ezer* 21; Zohar 1:35b, Matt, Pritzker edn., vol. 1, pp. 223–24. As Yehuda Liebes pointed out to me, the connection between garden and woman may originate from the similarity of Greek *gyne* (woman) to Hebrew *gan* (garden), as in the homily in Midrash Genesis Rabbah 18.4.

14. See Idel, *Kabbalah: New Perspectives*, pp. 200–49; Idel, "He'arot rishoniyot," p. 773, note 2.

15. On the dynamism of symbols in the Zohar, see Liebes, "Zohar ve-eros."

16. R. Moses de León, *Shekel ha-Kodesh*, p. 56; see also p. 40. On the centrality of this verse for de León, see also Wijnhoven's edition of *Sefer ha-Mishkal* (*Sefer Nefesh ha-Hakhamah*), 4a, 13b, 20b, 22a–b.

17. On this verse, see Liebes, "Zohar ve-eros," pp. 70–80; Wolfson, "Forms of Visionary Ascent"; Wolfson, *Speculum That Shines*, pp. 356–57, 383–92. See above, pp. 75–80.

18. On the words *nahar* and *nahara* as designating light, see also 3:69b.

19. Zohar 1:34a; Matt, Pritzker edn., vol. 1, p. 211, adapted. On the connection between *nahar di-nur* and the Milky Way, see *Milon ben Yehudah* (1958), entry for *nahar*, p. 3557. See also Zohar 1:33b; 2:246a.

20. See also 1:32a.

21. See below, pp. 230, 259, 275–76.

22. Midrash Leviticus Rabbah (Vilna edn.) 34.15. The parallel version of this midrash connects the Garden of Eden with the End of Days: "*You shall be like a watered garden*—this is the Garden of Eden; *like a spring whose waters do not fail*—like the spring which in the future will flow from the holy of holies, as is said: *In that day fresh water shall flow from Jerusalem* (Zechariah 14:8)." (Leviticus Rabbah [Margaliot edn.] 34.15)

23. The Zohar's conception of the World to Come as a dimension located outside of time is similar to R. Moses Maimonides' conception in his *Mishneh Torah*, Lore of Repentance 8.8:

> The sages did not use the expression "the World to Come" with the intention of imply- ing that [this realm] does not exist at present, or that the present realm will be destroyed and then that realm [the World to Come] will come into being. The matter is not so. Rather, the World to Come exists and is present, as is said: *How great is the good that You have hidden . . . which You have made . . .* (Ps. 31:20). Rather it is called the World to Come only because that life comes to a human being after life in this world in which we exist, as souls in bodies. This [realm of existence] is presented to all humanity at first.

While the World to Come of Maimonides is indeed a dimension of being that exists simultaneously alongside ordinary, earthly reality, it is not described in a dynamic way as flowing into human reality—as we find in the Zohar. According to Maimonides, corpo- real existence prevents the experience of the World to Come, which for him is a reality accessible only to the soul, and thus bodily death is a precondition for any experience of this dimension. In the Zohar, on the other hand, the quest is precisely to experience the flow of the divine river also during bodily life. Rabbi Moses Naḥmanides (Ramban) meanwhile disagreed explicitly with Maimonides on this matter and understood the World to Come as a reality that comes in temporal terms after this world. See *Kitvei ha-Ramban, Sha'ar ha-gemul*, pp. 299–311.

24. Zohar 3:290b (*Idra Zuta*). On this same page, Rabbi Shim'on thrice mentions the continuous, unceasing nature of the river that issues from Eden as being the knowl- edge that shines in his heart, which before his death he seeks to impart to his disciples so that they too may radiate in perfection.

25. Zohar 2:83a, Matt, Pritzker edn., vol. 4, p. 461. See also Zohar 2:90a.

26. On the value of studying at night, see BT *Berakhot* 3b; *Avodah Zarah* 3b. On the blessed Holy One's delight with the souls who learn Torah from midnight till dawn, see above, Chapter 6.

27. On the river as a symbol for God's song, and on the human song that ascends from the river of song that issues from Eden, see Zohar 2:4a, 18b, 54a.

28. Cf. Abraham Abulafia's description of prophetic experience: "Afterward, if he is worthy, the spirit of the living God will dwell upon him . . . and he will feel as if his whole body, from tip to toe, were anointed with the unction of oil." Cited from *Sefer ḥayyei olam ha-ba* in Idel, *Studies in Ecstatic Kabbalah*, p. 15.

29. See above, Chapter 6.

30. From his intensive study of the Zohar, Rabbi Isaac Luria understood homilies of this kind as a mystical praxis, whereby the one engaged in prayer unites, in his thought, with the depths from which the river issues and flows: "The intention is that in his prayer man must cause his thought to ascend to the place of the watering of the depth of the well that issues and flows to *Ze'eir Anpin*, by virtue of the supernal path that en- ters the depth of *Binah*; and this is the supernal point of Zion in *Binah*." *Sha'ar ma'amrei Rashbi, perush sifra di-tsni'uta*, 28d. In this description, "the point of Zion" is a sexual symbol and the "raising of thought" plays a part in the erotic union of the supernal path that enters the depth of *Binah* and causes the river to flow.

31. This activity itself is a praxis whose telos is emotional intensification and mystical experience. See above, pp. 197–99. On this story, see Liebes, "Zohar ve-eros," p. 109.

32. The process by which the divine dimensions of the human being (R. Shim'on) are revealed greatly affects the possibility for the mystics to participate in, and come in contact with, the divine. The more that the proximity, similarity, and identity between human beings and God is clarified, the more apparent is the possibility of human participation in the divine—and the participation of the divine in humanity.

33. The source of these homilies is Midrash Song of Songs Rabbah 1.55.

34. On the import of this word, see above, p. 173–76.

35. For other commentaries on this verse, see Zohar 1:30a; 2:226b.

36. For analysis of the *Idra Zuta*, see Liebes, "Messiah of the Zohar," pp. 63–74.

37. On the connection between *botsina* (lamp/luminary) and "mouth" in the Zohar, see Liebes, "Zohar ve-eros," pp. 105–6. On consciousness as "river" and "light" in the writings of Philo, see Niehoff, "What Is in a Name?" Compare the comments made by R. Isaac Luria about the plenty (*shefa*) that flowed through him all his life: "Whenever I open my mouth to say to you some secret of Torah, the plenty wells up inside me like an overflowing river, and I seek all manner of strategies so as to open for you a small, fine conduit, so that you will be able to bear it. For if I will give you too much, you will forfeit everything, like a baby who chokes from an excess of milk that comes to him all at once" (Benayahu, *Toledot ha-Ari*, 10:164). It is interesting to reflect on this experience of Isaac Luria as a basis for his conception of *tsimtsum* (contraction/withholding) as necessary for the creation of sustainable worlds.

38. On the nocturnal delight, see above, Chapter 6.

39. For a parallel, see 3:303a, *Tosafot*. See above, pp. 144–45; below, pp. 261, 286.

40. Liebes, "Zohar ve-eros," pp. 67–80.

41. Moses de León, *Shekel ha-Kodesh*, p. 26.

Chapter 12

1. See Idel, *Kabbalah: New Perspectives*, pp. 35–38.

2. Cordovero, *Shi'ur Komah*, entry for "Torah," 13b.

3. On light as the imagery for describing the divine world, and the symbolism of light in the description of divinity and mystical experience, see Wolfson, *Speculum That Shines*, esp. pp. 270–81; Idel, "Perush al ha-kenisah le-Pardes," pp. 32–45.

4. Tishby, *Wisdom of the Zohar* 1:274. On the history of conceptions of light in pre-Zoharic Kabbalah and on the way in which Abraham Abulafia saw light as characteristic of the prophecy among the sefirotic kabbalists, see Idel, *Mystical Experience in Abraham Abulafia*, pp. 77–83. See Cordovero's summary of the subject of light and its manifestations in the world of the sefirot in his book *Pardes rimmonim, sha'ar erkei ha-kinuyyim*, entry "light," and also in *sha'ar ha-tsahtsahot*.

5. Midrash *Tanhuma, Beha'alotekha* 7; see also *Midrash Tehillim* 22:11. See also Sack, "Mashal gimmel ha-orot."

6. BT *Hagigah* 12a.

7. Midrash Genesis Rabbah 3, 6, 41; BT *Hagigah* 12a. On the light seen by the fetus in utero, see BT *Niddah* 30b. On the qualities of the light of the first day of Creation

and its incarnations among Adam, Moses, David, and the righteous, and on the eye's visionary capacity, see Zohar 1:31–32.

8. *Sefer ha-Bahir*, ed. Abrams, §§ 1, 12, 17, 97–99, 106, 131 (cited in Zohar 1:264a, *Hashmatot*). According to the *Bahir*, the light that remains after its concealment is the Torah's light, secreted away for those who guard her.

9. On revelatory experience and light among the kabbalists of Provence and Gerona, see Pedaya, "Aḥuzim ba-dibbur," pp. 591–96.

10. See Scholem, "Concept of Kavvanah"; *Origins of the Kabbalah*, pp. 331–35.

11. Solomon Ibn Gabirol, *Keter Malkhut*; Judah Halevi, *Kuzari* 4:15.

12. Hollenback dedicates an interesting chapter to clarifying the centrality of light in mystical experience—Hollenback, *Mysticism*, pp. 56–74.

13. Zohar 3:165b; 3:129b, *Idra Rabba*.

14. *Shekel ha-Kodesh*, p. 16.

15. Rabbi Joseph ben Shalom Ashkenazi, *Perush le-parashat Bereshit*, p. 49.

16. Joseph ben Shalom Ashkenazi, Commentary on *Sefer Yetzirah* 4b.

17. For example, the many descriptions in which the Companions merit a glimpse of the upper worlds suffused with light. In a story that appears in the Introduction to the Zohar (1:4a), we are told of Rabbi Ḥiyya, who fasts forty days and then forty more in order to see Rabbi Shim'on in the upper world, at the end of which he merits to see both Rabbi Shim'on and his son El'azar in a vision. The entire vision is saturated with lights shining more brilliantly than the light of the sun. This revelation combines experiences of sight and sound.

18. Zohar 1:52b.

19. On the body radiating light during mystical experience, see Hollenback, *Mysticism*, pp. 60–74.

20. Midrash Exodus Rabbah 1; see Zohar 2:11a; 3:187b. The light that served Moses throughout the three months of his concealment is the hidden light that returned and shone upon him at Mt. Sinai (Zohar 1:31b–32a).

21. It is the writing of the Torah or the Song of Moses that bestowed upon him the splendor of his face: Midrash Deuteronomy Rabbah 3; Midrash Exodus Rabbah 47. See Rabbi Ḥayyim Ben Atar's *Or ha-ḥayyim* on Exod. 34:35: "In R. Meir's scroll was written 'garments of light' [as opposed to garments of skin]; similarly the skin of Moses' face became light." In his commentary to Exod. 5:22, Rabbenu Baḥya ben Asher distinguishes between divine light, the light of *ḥokhmah*, and sensed light, like that experienced by Moses.

22. Ibn Ezra, (Long) Commentary on the Torah, at Exod. 34:29 (transl. NJPS).

23. *Midrash Tehillim* 72.

24. As quoted in Gottlieb, *Meḥkarim be-sifrut ha-Kabbalah*, p. 156. Gikatilla reads the verse from Job contrary to the simple meaning, where light reveals secrets. For Gikatilla, engaging with secrets and mysteries is what engenders light.

25. *Zohar Ḥadash*, Terumah, 42a–b. In this story, Rabbi Shim'on declares that the book given by the angels to Enoch from among the branches of the Tree of Life, containing knowledge of the ways of the blessed Holy One, is hidden and present among the Companions. In other words, the Companions' esoteric lore includes the knowl-

edge of how to shine with the divine light, and how to ascend to humanity's divine source.

26. See below, pp. 305–8.

27. Zohar 3: 143b. See above, pp. 45–47.

28. Rabbi Reḥumai, in Zohar 1:11a; Matt, Pritzker edn., vol. 1, p. 76. On Rabbi Shim'on as a source of light, see above, pp. 36–37. In dozens of passages, light appears as the key epithet for him, such as 1:4a, 156a, 197b; 2:114a; 3:159a. On the word *botsina* (lamp, luminary) and its different meanings and inflections in the Zohar, see Liebes, *Perakim be-milon Sefer ha-Zohar*, pp. 136–67.

29. *Shekel ha-Kodesh*, p. 57. The Zohar contains a parallel to this conception of the human being—as a wick with oil, in which and from which burns the flame of the soul, and of the human as a wick for which Shekhinah is the flame—in the story of the miraculous child (*yanuka*) in the Zohar's commentary to the Torah portion *Balak*, 3:187a.

30. On the union (or intercourse) of the souls of the righteous, the intercourse between the male and the female in the Garden of Eden after midnight, and the souls of converts born from this light-filled union, see Zohar 3:167b, 168a. On this homily in its entirety, see above pp. 136–38, 144–45, 250–51; below, p. 286.

31. See Yehuda Liebes' fascinating remarks about *zohar* as eros and creativity in "Zohar ve-eros," pp. 73–80, 85–86.

32. Regarding when the composition began being called *Sefer ha-Zohar* (Book of Radiance), see Huss, "Hofa'ato shel Sefer ha-Zohar."

33. On this dependence between the inner divine light and the capacity to see the divine light, see Wolfson, *Speculum That Shines*, p. 272. The same circular structure is found in a collection of homilies on "*The enlightened will shine like the radiance of the sky*," in *Zohar Ḥadash, Tikkunim*, 103d–105d. In terms of literary style, these passages lie between the main corpus of the Zohar and the classic style of *Tikkunei Zohar*. According to this description, contemplation of secrets with the eye of knowledge requires radiance, while radiance is produced through the contemplation of secrets. The Torah's radiance is produced through the innovations of the enlightened and is a dynamic garment, a kind of divine armor, which bestows upon them the capacity to travel without fear through the divine world. The quest to become radiant receives explicit expression in *Tikkunei Zohar*, a later layer within the zoharic corpus. See below, pp. 376–79.

34. Liebes, "Zohar ve-eros," p. 75.

35. In the Cremona edition of the Zohar, the word *zohar* in this homily is enlarged, and the sentence that follows is set at a distance, in order to highlight its special status. This is also the case in Ms. JTS 1771.

36. Zohar 2:2a; see above, pp. 237–39.

37. Zohar ibid.; Matt, Pritzker edn., vol. 4, p. 2.

38. Elsewhere in the Zohar, in a homily expounding the occasion of Joseph's disclosure to his brothers, this verse is interpreted as referring to the sefirah *Yesod*. See Zohar 1:208a.

39. Zohar 1:4a. On this expression as an epithet of the Companions, see above, pp. 81–84.

40. Zohar 2:140a.

41. The idea of tending to the small light in order to merit the great light appears in Midrash *Tanhuma, Tetsaveh*, 4, in a homily on the lights of the Temple: "If you light the lamps, I will surely illuminate you from the great light in the future, as is said: *For YHVH shall be for you an everlasting light* (Isa. 60:19).

42. Zohar 1:51a; Matt, Pritzker edn., vol. 1, p. 284. See also Zohar 1:83b.

43. On the dawn, see above, pp. 125, 143–44. On the connection between the lower (black) light and the upper (white) light, see 1:12a, 77b, 83b; 2:213b.

44. Zohar 2:52a; Matt, Pritzker edn., vol. 4, p. 259.

45. See Hollenback, *Mysticism*, pp. 56–74.

46. See above, pp. 37–38.

47. Zohar 3:34a. See also 2:149a; 3:88a.

48. See above, pp. 233–35 and notes there, and p. 251.

49. The Zohar reworks rabbinic homilies about the "thread of grace" that flows down onto those who learn Torah at night (BT *Berakhot* 3b) and about the concealed light (BT *Ḥagigah* 12a; Midrash *Tanna de-Bei Eliyahu Zuta* 21), which are here transformed into a thread that flows forth from the great divine light from which the world is sustained.

50. See the parallel passage in R. Moses de León, *Shekel ha-Kodesh*, pp. 96–97, and notes there. On the praxis of rolling the closed eyeball, see Wolfson, *Speculum That Shines*, pp. 380–83; see also Matt's notes in his translation of this passage, *Zohar: The Book of Enlightenment*, pp. 242–44. See also Liebes, *Perakim be-milon Sefer ha-Zohar*, entry *gilgula*, pp. 291, 293, 316.

51. See also 1:43a, 97a. On Rashbi and Moses, see above, pp. 37–38, and see Huss, "Hakham adif mi-navi," pp. 109–14.

52. Zohar 1:52b; 2:52b.

53. Zohar 3:128b, *Idra Rabba*: "From the illumination of this whiteness, the righteous inherit the world that is coming." See 3:135b.

54. On the act of *tikkun* in the *Idra*, see Liebes, "Messiah of the Zohar," pp. 55–74.

55. Zohar 3:129b. Compare Gikatilla's portrayal in his book *Sha'arei Tsedek* of the relations between the solitary eye, the sefirah *Keter*, and the two eyes of *Ḥokhmah* and *Binah*, who are like doves "bathing in supernal milk and whiteness." See Gottlieb, *Meḥkarim be-sifrut ha-kabbalah*, "sha'arei tsedek," pp. 144, 157, 160: "Know that the first of all lights is white, and it absorbs all the colors."

56. "All white" is also a description of semen. See, for example, 3:296b, *Idra Zuta*.

57. Zohar 2:122b.

58. This desire for white, associated both with the desire for perfection (eros) as well as death (thanatos), receives expression in Allen Afterman's mystical poem "Desire for White": "Everything, its open mouth / lipless / its gaze cloudless / everything, its one desire / soundless / desire, of the inner colors of white." Afterman, *Kabbalah and Consciousness*, p. 113.

59. Jeremiah 17:13.

60. Isaiah 11:9; Zechariah 14:8. See Haviva Pedaya's fascinating discussion about the story of water at the time of the redemption, "Temurot be-kodesh ha-kodashim";

Pedaya, "Mayyim nikre'u ḥayyim"; see also her discussion of the imagery of water in the writings of the kabbalists of Provence and Gerona and in Jewish Sufism, "Aḥuzim ba-dibbur," pp. 596–607.

61. Mishnah *Yoma* 8:9. On images of God as water in late antiquity, see also Philo's view: Niehoff, "What Is in a Name?"

62. See *Sefer ha-Bahir*, ed. Abrams, §§ 4, 15, 85, 105 among others.

63. See above, pp. 229ff.

64. Zohar 3:69b. See Tishby, *Wisdom of the Zohar* 1:272, 274.

65. See Zohar 2:142b on the soul's descent into the body through the mystery of *and satisfy your soul with sparkling flashes* (Isaiah 58:11).

66. See Zohar 1:92a–b; see above, pp. 139, 243; see also 1:162a.

67. In numerous places throughout the Zohar, *mayyim rabbim* (the mighty waters) is interpreted as the hidden depths of divinity, and the prayer of the "faithful one" is precisely to experience the rushing of divinity flowing from the depths. See, for example 1:31a; 2:146b; 3:54b.

68. The Mishnaic description of the water libation as well as the other ceremonies and rituals of Sukkot is understood by the Zohar as the drawing down in deed (*be-uvda*), and not only in word (*be-milah*), of the flow of divine bounty into the world. See 3:31b.

69. This passage is of interest also in terms of the relations it engenders between *Tiferet* and *Yesod*, and between masculinity and sexuality. On the rain of blessings that comes from the union of the blessed Holy One and His Shekhinah when man guards the "sign of the covenant" (ritual circumcision), see 1:189b.

70. The root ענג (*'oneg*) appears also in Psalms (37:4, 37:11) and in Job (22:26, 27:10) in the context of man's relationship with God. *'Oneg* and *ta'anug* are also associated in Biblical language with the experience of luxury and delicacy. See, for example, Deut. 28:54, 56; Jer. 6:2.

71. See "the luxuries of commoners" (Eccles. 2:8) and "palaces of pleasure" (Isa. 13:22).

72. This epithet derives from the verse "If you call the Sabbath 'delight'" (Isa. 58:13). See Midrash *Otiyot de Rabbi Akiva*, version b: "Sabbath—one-sixtieth of the World to Come, in which you delight in the delight of rest, as is said: *Then you will delight in YHVH.*"

73. Midrash *Pesikta Rabbati* 36. See also *Midrash Tehillim* to Psalms 149, on the delight of the righteous in the Garden of Eden.

74. See, for example, Midrash *Kallah Rabbati* 8:1; Midrash *Derekh Erets Zuta* 5:1.

75. See, for example, JT *Shabbat* 60b.

76. *Sefer Yetsirah* 2:4.

77. *Sefer ha-Bahir*, ed. Abrams, p. 145, § 48; p. 143, § 45.

78. See Pedaya, "Aḥuzim ba-dibbur," pp. 589, 592–96.

79. See Idel, *Mystical Experience in Abraham Abulafia*, pp. 184–90. On the experience of being washed or anointed as the sensation of mystical pleasure, see: "And you shall feel in yourself an additional spirit arousing you and passing over your entire body and causing you pleasure, and it shall seem to you as if balm has been placed upon you,

from your head to your feet, one or more times, and you shall rejoice and enjoy it very much." From *Ozar Eden Ganuz*, cited in Idel, p. 188. "And it shall appear to him as if his entire body, from his head to his feet, had been anointed with anointing oil." From *Ḥayyei ha-olam ha-ba*, p. 57, cited in Idel, p. 128.

80. See also 3:104a.

81. As expressed in an eighteenth-century commentary on the Prophets and the Writings, *Metsudat Tsiyon*, on Ps. 90:17 and Zech. 11:7: *no'am* is linguistically connected with pleasantness, sweetness, and love. As Yehuda Liebes has remarked to me, *ne'imim* is the permanent epithet for the gods in the pre-Israelite Near Eastern literature of Ugarit.

82. Hollenback, *Mysticism*, pp. 40–55.

83. See, for example, Patanjali, Yoga Sutra, I.17, II.41, II.42.

84. On "path" versus "way," see above, pp. 118–20, 202. See also 2:31b.

85. Another example of the soul's experience of the *no'am YHVH* is in the section *Rav Metivta*, where Rashbi and the Companions visit the celestial worlds. In the entrance to the inner chambers, when the veils are removed one by one, the *no'am YHVH* is revealed in the Hall of Love (3:171b).

86. It is the *no'am YHVH* that causes the souls to radiate, as Rabbi Abba learned from the miraculous book he found in a cave in the desert (*Zohar Ḥadash* 53d). See also Zohar 2:127a on the *no'am* in the experience of sitting in the palanquin, namely, the lower Garden of Eden.

87. See above, pp. 121ff.

88. On the symbolism of crown and crowning, see Green's excellent study, *Keter*.

89. On the experience of male contemplation of the masculinity of divinity, see Wolfson, *Speculum That Shines*, pp. 326–97.

90. Zohar 2:57b, 58a.

91. For a description of the *no'am* as a quality of *Atika Kadisha* that flows and spreads among the divine grades below, see 3:161b, where the flow is from *Atika Kadisha* to the brain, and from the brain to the heart.

92. See above, pp. 233ff.

93. See also Zohar 2:127a.

94. R. Abraham Isaac Kook, "Bein nevu'ah le-halakhah." Translation from Bokser, *Abraham Isaac Kook*, pp. 377–78.

95. On the phenomenon of *devekut* in Jewish literature, see Idel, *Kabbalah: New Perspectives*, pp. 38–58; Idel, *R. Menaḥem Recanati*, pp. 125–41.

96. See above, pp. 229–31.

97. For example, these two verses appear together in the opening of the Zohar's commentary to the Torah portion *Vayeḥi* (1:216a); upon departing the Idra Rabba (3:144b); and also 3:298b.

98. See, for example, *Zohar Ḥadash* 53b; 1:185a; 2:123a, 220b; 3:26b, 288b.

99. Zohar 2:87b. Similarly, Israel's cleaving to the Holy Name accounts for the proximity in essence and name between God (Elohim) and Israel (Yisra'el); 3:138b, 129a.

100. On the expression *gufa di-malka*, see Yehuda Liebes, *Perakim be-milon Sefer ha-*

Zohar, entry for *gufa*, pp. 226–27. As Liebes suggests, *gufa di-malka* may have been a mythologization of the rabbinic expression *gufei torah*; ibid., p. 173.

101. *Zohar Ḥadash*, Genesis, 1d. On *devekut* in the sense of intercourse, as in the Zohar's translation of Potiphar's wife's words "Lie with me!" as "Cleave to me!" see 1:190b; *Zohar Ḥadash* 59a.

102. Zohar 1:51b; Matt, Pritzker edn., vol. 1, p. 285.

103. See Zohar 1:216a; 2:86a. See Wolfson, *Circle in the Square*, pp. 29–48.

104. Zohar 1:84b; Matt, Pritzker edn., vol. 2, p. 38. See also 3:9b.

105. See 1:204a, 207b. See also 1:50b for an important discussion about the possibilities of cleaving to God, or more particularly the feminine aspect of God, which is fire, without being consumed.

106. Zohar 3:92b.

107. Zohar 3:45b.

108. Zohar 3:107a. See discussion pp. 341–46.

109. See Idel, *Kabbalah: New Perspectives*, pp. 43–45.

110. See Fishbane, *Kiss of God*; Wirshubski, *Sheloshah perakim*, pp. 14–22.

111. Weeping in the Zohar comes usually as a response to mystical experience and not in preparation for it. See Idel, *Kabbalah: New Perspectives*, pp. 75–88. The most ecstatic weeping in the Zohar is perhaps Rabbi Shim'on's love-filled ode to the Torah; 3:166b, *Rav Metivta*.

112. See above, pp. 65–66. See also Liebes, "Messiah of the Zohar," pp. 52–55 and notes.

113. See also the famous liturgical poem by Yannai, "Va-yhi be-ḥatsi ha-lailah," which appears in the Passover Haggadah.

114. *Avot de-Rabbi Natan* (B) 13. See also the parallel text in *Pirkei de-Rabbi Eli'ezer* 2.

115. Zohar 2:105b; Matt, *Book of Enlightenment*, p. 125.

116. On the paradoxical nature of mystical language, see below, Chapter 15.

117. In the story of Kfar Tarsha, which appears in the Zohar's commentary to the Torah portion *Lekh Lekha*, we also find a description of the loss of the sense of time as one of the characteristics of the collective mystical experience attained by the entire group. On this story, see above, pp. 183–88.

118. On Rashbi's comparisons between himself and Moses, see above, pp. 44–47. See also Huss, "Ḥakham adif mi-navi," pp. 103–25.

119. See Ludwig, "Altered States of Consciousness," pp. 13–14; Shanon, *Antipodes of the Mind*, pp. 305–14; Huxley, *Doors of Perception*, p. 25.

120. A similar description is found in the unit *Rav Metivta*, where we read of a mystical state extending seven days that was devoid of a sense of "this world"; Zohar 3:164a.

121. Zohar 1:224b.

122. Zohar 2:127b.

123. Zohar 1:142b; 2:44a.

124. Zohar 2:12a.

125. *Idra Rabba*: Zohar 3:133a, 137b–138a.

126. On smelling the words of Torah, see 1:4b. The blessed Holy One inhales the

aroma of the good deeds of the souls of the righteous (2:173b). See *Zohar Ḥadash*, Song of Songs 64a–65a for an important mythical midrash on smell and fragrance.

127. Zohar 3:162a. Perhaps this idea was taken from the description of the Messiah in Isaiah 11:3: "He shall sense [literally, smell] the truth by his reverence for YHVH and not judge by what his eyes behold, nor decide by what his ears perceive."

128. BT *Shabbat* 33–34.

129. On fire in Jewish mystical literature see Elior, "Paneyah ha-shonot shel ha-ḥerut," pp. 60–61. On fire as characteristic of descriptions of mystical experience across the world see Deikman, "Deautomatization and the Mystic Experience," pp. 24–25.

130. BT *Ḥagigah* 14b.

131. See Midrash Song of Songs Rabbah 1.11 on *Your cheeks are comely with plaited wreaths, your neck with strings of ḥaruzim, jewels* [or: beads] (Song of Songs 1:10), which expounds the descent of the heavenly fire as deriving from the bead-stringing activity of the sages. See also Midrash Leviticus Rabbah 16.4. See also Liebes, *Ḥet'o shel Elisha*, pp. 107–9.

132. Zohar 3:134b. During the Idra Zuta, the heavenly fire that descends is also a fire of judgment expelling those who are not worthy of the occasion; 3:287b.

133. Zohar 1:94b.

134. Exod. 34:29–35.

135. Num. 6:24–26.

136. Midrash Leviticus Rabbah 1.1. There the discussion is about prophecy, and about the connection between prophets and angels.

137. See, for example, the description of the transformation of Enoch into an angel, in Schäfer, *Synopse zur Hekhalot-Literatur*, 19.

138. *Avot de-Rabbi Natan* (B) 13.

139. Zohar 1:94b; Matt, Pritzker edn., vol. 2, p. 98.

140. See Midrash Ecclesiastes Rabbah 8; *Midrash Shmu'el* 16. According to *Pesikta de-Rav Kahana* 4, at the giving of the Torah at Mt. Sinai, the entire nation merited facial radiance due to the illumination of Shekhinah upon them.

141. Zohar 2:15a.

142. See above, pp. 75–80, 261–65. Boaz Huss has suggested that the phenomenon of facial radiance is the meaning that the Zohar bestows upon the verse "And the enlightened will shine like the radiance of the sky." He has highlighted the fact that Ibn Ezra already described Moses' shining face as the illumination of the sky's radiance. He further suggested that such radiance has its origin in the divine light reflected in the "speculum that shines" (*ispaklarya ha-me'irah*), from which both the face of Moses and Rashbi shone. Huss concludes that the *zohar* (radiance) in Sefer ha-Zohar is the light of the "speculum that shines," reflected in the faces of the mystics worthy of its contemplation. See "Ḥakham adif mi-navi," pp. 113–14.

143. As Yehuda Liebes has observed, this midrash, like others in *Zohar Ḥadash*, is similar in style to the writings of the kabbalist Joseph Angelet and his circle, thus deriving from a later stratum of zoharic literature. See Liebes, "Ha-shabta'ut u-gvulot ha-dat," p. 10, note 57.

144. See also 1:218a.

Chapter 13

1. Bergson, *Creative Evolution*, pp. 3–10, 52–53. See also Kolakowski, *Bergson*, pp. 2–4.

2. Bergson, *Creative Evolution*, pp. 97–108; see also pp. 276–77: "So that all life, animal and vegetable, seems in its essence like an effort to accumulate energy and then to let flow into flexible channels, changeable in shape, at the end of which it will accomplish infinitely varied kinds of work. That is what the vital impetus passing through matter would fain to do all at once."

3. Ibid., pp. 53–54.

4. Bergson, *Creative Evolution*, pp. 53–54, 218–20. See also Kolakowski, *Bergson*, pp. 25–26.

5. Bergson, *Creative Evolution*, p. 195.

6. Ibid., p. 292.

7. Ibid., pp. 218–20:

Let us seek, in the depth of our experience, the point where we feel ourselves most intimately within our own life. It is into pure duration that we can then plunge back, a duration in which the past, always moving on, is swelling unceasingly with a present that is absolutely new. . . . Rare indeed are the moments when we are self possessed to this extent: it is then that our actions are truly free. And even at these moments we do not completely possess ourselves. Our feeling of duration, I should say the actual coinciding of ourself with itself, admits of degree. But the more the feeling is deep and the coincidence complete, the more the life in which it replaces us absorbs intellectuality by transcending it. . . . Now our intellect does undoubtedly grasp the real moments of real duration after they are past; we do so by reconstituting the new state of consciousness out of a series of views taken of it from the outside, each of which resembles as much as possible something already known; in this sense we may say that the state of consciousness contains intellectuality implicitly. Yet the state of consciousness overflows the intellect; it is indeed incommensurable with the intellect, being itself indivisible and new. Now let us relax the strain, let us interrupt the effort to crowd as much as possible of the past into the present. If the relaxation were complete, there would no longer be either memory or will—which amounts to saying that, in fact, we never do fall into this absolute passivity, any more than we can make ourselves absolutely free. But, in the limit we get a glimpse of an existence made of a present which recommences unceasingly—devoid of real duration, nothing but the instantaneous which dies and is reborn again endlessly.

8. We can also draw inspiration from Bergson's conception of language and its ability to express varied levels of reality. Despite being part of the intellect and constructed from a system of abstract signs whose purpose is to categorize, divide, and conceptualize—rather than capture the unique and singular—Bergson saw in human language a phenomenon capable of overcoming, to a certain degree, its limitations. It is able to break through to a different—non-Platonic—understanding of reality. See Kolakowski, *Bergson*, p. 18. On the inspirational connections with the materiality of language in the poetic context, see Bergson, *Creative Evolution*, pp. 281–82. On the modes in which linguistic processes operate vis-à-vis processes that relate to things in and of themselves

in a state of free consciousness that is not bound to automatic habit, see *Creative Evolution*, pp. 201–2.

9. On different types of ecstasy in religious experience, see Pedaya, "Aḥuzim ba-dibbur." Note that in certain parts of the Zohar (for example, in *Rav Metivta* and in parts of the *Idrot*), we are dealing with what the Companions experienced in their bodies in another dimension of reality.

10. Sharma, "Ecstasy."

11. Ibid., p.14. Sharma advocates an anti-reductionist position in employing this term so as not to miss out on the rich discussions of ecstasy found in a range of disciplines—history, anthropology, psychology, chemistry, comparative religion, etc. On ecstasy, see also Zimmer, *Philosophies of India*, pp. 435–41, 560–63.

12. Scholem, *Major Trends*, p. 124.

13. Ibid., pp. 138–43.

14. Idel, *Kabbalah: New Perspectives*, p. xi.

15. See Wolfson, *Speculum That Shines*, pp. 329–31; Wolfson, "Forms of Visionary Ascent," p. 211.

16. Pedaya, "Aḥuzim be-dibbur," pp. 567, 588. See also her comments on integrated purposes in mystical experience, pp. 609–10.

17. See, for example, Abulafia's letter to R. Yehudah Salmon, quoted in Idel, *Mystical Experience in Abraham Abulafia*, pp. 77, 83.

18. See Sharma, "Ecstasy."

19. See, for example, the story about the bringing of rain in the Zohar's commentary to *Aḥarei Mot*, 3:62a (see above, pp. 245–49); and the story of Kfar Tarsha in the commentary to *Lekh Lekha*, 1:94b. Ecstasy, culminating ultimately in death, is described in the story of the death of three participants in the Idra Rabba, and of course also in the account of Rabbi Shim'on's death in the *Idra Zuta*.

20. Pedaya, "Aḥuzim be-dibbur," pp. 575, 588.

21. For example, in the description of mystical experience in the story of the bringing of rain; see above, note 19.

22. See above, pp. 279-90.

23. See, for example, the description of the entrance to the sixth chamber in Heikhalot literature in Schäfer, ed., *Synopse zur Hekhalot-Literatur*, pp. 170, 172.

24. Idel, *Mystical Experience in Abraham Abulafia*, pp. 74–77, 119–21.

25. See above, pp. 209–15.

26. On these positions regarding prophecy, see Efrat, *Ha-filosofiyah ha-Ivrit ha-atikah*, pp. 11–21.

27. Midrash *Mekhilta de-Rabbi Yishma'el, Yitro,* 4.

28. To the extent that Rabbi Akiva was chastised "for making the Shekhinah profane"—BT *Ḥagigah* 14a. At the same time, Rabbi Akiva is the one whose relationship with God is described as a relationship between a lover and his beloved, and about him "Draw me after you, let us run! The king has brought me into his chambers. Let us delight and rejoice in your love" (Song of Songs 1:4) is expounded, BT *Ḥagigah* 15b.

29. For example, in the story in the Zohar's commentary to *Aḥarei Mot*, 3:62a, and

also in the *Idra Zuta* in the account of Rashbi's death. These descriptions display a tension between incarnation and deification. Rashbi is at once the actualization of a divine attribute in the world as well as the most perfect human being who attains a level of identification with the divine attribute. See Liebes, "Myth vs. Symbol," pp. 212–19.

30. I prefer the term "contained" over the term "normal" employed by Max Kadushin to describe rabbinic mysticism. Kadushin extensively discussed the concept "normal mysticism," which he saw as a determinative characteristic of the Jewish religion in general, as well as its mystical elements in particular. My main concern with his suggestion is that according to his definition, it is difficult to distinguish between mysticism and non-mysticism. If all Jewish religious life is defined as "normal mysticism," then how exactly are unique religious phenomena to be identified and defined? The rabbis found ways to distinguish between religion and "normal" religious experience on the one hand, and persons and events in which more intense and unique encounters with the divine transpired on the other. Descriptions of the *benei aliyah* (the elect), the *ḥasidim* (pietists), *anshei ma'aseh* (miracle workers), and those who entered the *pardes* (divine orchard) furnish us with numerous examples of such encounters. See Kadushin, *The Rabbinic Mind*. See also Holtz, *Be-olam ha-maḥshavah shel Ḥazal*, pp. 173–233; Lorberbaum, *Tselem Elohim*, p. 23.

31. The concept of "containment" or "holding" as employed in the writings of the psychoanalyst Donald Winnicott is of much value in this context. *Containment* refers to the experience of an infant whose intense, boundaryless emotions are shaped by the mother through her embrace, actions, and facial expressions. Through the mother's behavior, the infant is able to live these experiences without being overwhelmed. See Winnicott, "The Theory of Parent-Infant Relationship," pp. 585–95; Abrom, *The Language of Winnicott*, pp. 183–89.

Similarly helpful are the paired concepts "container-contained" in the thought of the psychoanalyst Wilfred Bion. For Bion, these terms refer to something internal to a person: what constitutes the foundational structure of the psyche and the processes of thought, rather than to interpersonal relations. The *container* is the conceptual, personal, or social quality in which the *contained*, namely, ideas or persons, are able to find the space for their implementation, holding, or clarification. Bion characterizes the relations between God and the world, as well as the relations between the mystic and society, within this container-contained dynamic. See Symington, *Clinical Thinking of Wilfred Bion*, pp. 50–58.

32. Zohar 2:128a.

33. On the expression "restoring the Torah to her antiquity," see above, pp. 102–4; and below, p. 351.

34. See above, pp. 296–300.

35. Zohar 2:10a. On David and his sorrow regarding the coming of the morning and his obligations to the affairs of state, see BT *Berakhot* 3b.

36. On the differences in the experience of studying Torah during the day and during the night, see the Zohar's homilies on "By day YHVH commanded His grace, and by night His song is with me" (Psalms 42:9), 1:82b, 92a, 178b; 2:18b, 46a, 149a; 3:65a, among others. See above, p. 143.

37. A prime example is the homily that concludes the ecstatic event in the story of the bringing of rain in *Aḥarei Mot*. See above, pp. 245–49.

38. Idel, *Mystical Experience in Abraham Abulafia*, pp. 6–7, 9–10.

39. See above, pp. 190–91.

40. Idel, remarks made in the seminar "Mistikah ve-Kabbalah: hadgarot ve-gishot," Hebrew University, 1986.

41. *Shekel ha-Kodesh*, introduction, pp. 6–8.

42. *Perush ha-Merkavah*, p. 58. See also *Zohar Ḥadash* 37c–38a.

43. See also 3:16b, 74a. See 2:177b (*Sifra de-Tseni'uta*) for a description of the mystical sin of separating *Ḥokhmah* from *Binah*, and the *yud* from the *hei* of the tetragrammaton. See Wolfson's interesting comments on the secret and concealment in their feminine aspect in the Kabbalah and in the Zohar: Wolfson, "Occultation of the Feminine."

44. Zohar 2:66b. Liebes, "Messiah of the Zohar," pp. 27–28; Wolfson, *Speculum That Shines*, pp. 336–45.

45. Zohar 3:15a.

46. Zohar 3:204b. See above, pp. 168–71.

47. Zohar 3:44b.

48. Zohar 3:62a. See above, pp. 248–49.

49. Tishby, *Ḥikrei kabbalah u-shluḥoteha, She'elot u-tshuvot le-Rabbi Moshe de Leon be-inyanei Kabbalah*, p. 55, citing BT *Bava Batra* 12a. On de León and prophecy, see Mopsik, introduction to R. Moses de León's *Shekel ha-Kodesh*, pp. 6–8.

Chapter 14

1. The Zohar itself does not tend to employ the technical terminology of kabbalistic language; it seldom names the sefirot by their chief designations. Nevertheless, we use the sefirotic structure here as a shorthand way to speak with a degree of abstraction about the states of consciousness.

2. On Abraham Abulafia's influence on Joseph Gikatilla regarding his treatment of the sefirot in an ascending order from *Malkhut*, see Moshe Idel's "Historical Introduction" in Gikatilla, *Gates of Light*. For her part, Haviva Pedaya writes: "The different components of mystical experience do not always exist in a ladder of ascension, but rather can be described as different springs whose source lies in the sense of expansion" ("Aḥuzim be-dibbur," p. 610).

3. Shulman, *Perakim be-shirah ha-hodit*, pp. 105–15.

4. Masters and Houston, *Varieties of Psychedelic Experience*, p. 308. See also Cousins, *Christ of the 21st Century*, pp. 35–40, who employs and tests this model in his exploration of the religious-mystical worldview of contemporary Christianity. For additional research that seeks to characterize the conditions for generating states of consciousness (including mystical experience) different from ordinary states of wakefulness, see Ludwig, "Altered States of Consciousness," pp. 9–22; Deikman, "Deautomatization and the Mystic Experience," pp. 23–43.

5. I find a poetic description of this state in two poems by the Israeli poet Dahlia Ravikovitch, "Delight" and "You surely remember." See Ravikovitch, *Kol ha-shirim ad koh*. (For translations, see *Hovering at a Low Altitude: The Poetry of Dahlia Ravikovitch*,

transl. Chana Bloch and Chana Kronfeld; W.W. Norton, forthcoming.) See Huxley, *Doors of Perception.*

6. On the relations between *Ze'eir Anpin, Arikh Anpin,* and *Nukba,* see Liebes, "Messiah of the Zohar," esp. pp. 43–48.

7. Zohar 3:129a, *Idra Rabba.* Rabbi Isaac Luria, who later developed the zoharic myth in extraordinary detail as well as its map of mystical consciousness, likewise recognized that "the righteous are in *Ze'eir Anpin,*" and that their quest is to behold the countenance of *Arikh Anpin.* See his *Sha'ar ma'amrei Rashbi, perush sifra de-tsni'uta* 2, 26c. His description of the mystics in relation to the three manifestations of God present during the course of the Sabbath—namely, Shekhinah on the eve of Shabbat, *Atika Kadisha* in the morning, and *Ze'eir Anpin in the afternoon*—is found in the songs that he composed for the Sabbath meals. See Liebes, "Zemirot le-seudot Shabbat," pp. 540–55.

8. See Liebes, "Messiah of the Zohar," pp. 44–45.

9. Zohar 1:209a–b. See Hellner-Eshed, "Nefesh ha-kanah ba-zohar," pp. 98–116.

10. Zohar 2:52b.

11. See Zohar 2:122b; 3:128b, 129b, 130a, 136b. See also 3:288a, *Idra Zuta.*

12. To my mind, something of White Light Consciousness can be found in the Israeli poet Zelda's images of dreams in her poem "Be-nahar ha-sheinah," *Shirei Zelda,* p. 146.

13. On the Torah of *Atika* as the Torah both of the World to Come and of the messianic era, see Liebes, "Messiah of the Zohar," pp. 43–52.

14. See above, pp. 283–90. This state comprises the third and fourth categories of consciousness described by Masters and Houston; see above, p. ••.

Chapter 15

1. Idel, *Kabbalah: New Perspectives,* pp. 218–32.

2. My thanks to Michal Govrin for explicating this idea.

3. William James places ineffability at the heart of his definition of mystical states: "The handiest of the marks by which I classify a state of mind as mystical is negative. The subject of it immediately says that it defies expression, that no adequate report of its contents can be given in words" (James, *Varieties of Religious Experience,* p. 380). Of particular interest is his contention that the communication of mystical experience is possible only among those who have merited such an unmediated experience. (This is not the case for the zoharic circle, which sees itself as part of an "imagined community" of the faithful, the mystics across the generations, who are able to communicate their experience.)

See Michael Sells' insightful remarks on the deconstructive quality of mystical, apophatic language (in contrast to cataphatic language) in his discussion of negative, mystical language: Sells, *Mystical Languages of Unsaying,* pp. 1–13. According to Sells, the dilemma of transcendence engenders three main types of response: (a) silence; (b) the distinction between the divine as it is in itself and the divine as it is in the world, in order to distinguish between that which is capable of being expressed and that which cannot; and (c) the decision not to resolve the dilemma of transcendence by distinguishing two types of divinity, but rather to internalize the paradoxical, irresolvable question, the aporia, such that in place of silence, it engenders a new discourse. In the context of our discussion, the performative aspect of such discourse is most important; negative or paradoxical language engenders among the reader or speaker an experience and not merely discursive understanding (ibid, p. 10). See Michael Sells, "Bewildered Tongue."

Michel de Certeau defines the paradoxical singularity of mystical experience in that it always comprises both the hidden and the revealed. In his opinion, critical analysis that dismisses mystical language as lacking acuity and as verbose in its imagery—will leave the researcher with only a collection of trivial details about various individuals and groups. The researcher must pay close attention to what mystics say of their experiences, and to their personal perception of the facts of the experience. See DeCerteau, "Mysticism," pp. 16–17.

In a more humorous vein, my teacher Prof. Ewert Cousins once joked that if there were to be a cocktail party for all the mystics of the world, the room would be divided into two camps: on one side all the cataphists would assemble, speaking and laughing with one another; while on the other side, the apophists would stand in profound somberness. There is no doubt as to where the Companions of the Zohar would congregate in such an assembly.

4. See, for example, Zohar 1:1b. See above, pp. 331–32; below, p. 358ff.

5. See Tishby, *Wisdom of the Zohar* 1:292–94, 424–26.

6. See, for example, Zohar 1:246b, 74a.

7. See above, p. 340ff.

8. Zohar 1:2a–b and see Liebes, "Zohar ve-eros," pp. 67–68.

9. See R. Moses Cordovero's commentary to this passage, *Or yakar* 1:16–17.

10. On this homily, see Wolfson, *Circle in the Square*, pp. 104–5.

11. See Cordovero, *Or Yakar* 1:16–17.

12. This homily nicely illustrates Wolfson's contention that the purpose of theosophical speculation is not merely to recognize the knowable aspects of divinity, but rather is a practical means to attain ecstatic experience, which, at its peak, can culminate in *devekut* or union. See Wolfson, "Forms of Visionary Ascent," p. 211.

13. See above, pp. 168–71.

14. See above, pp. 150–53. Compare the zoharic parable of the maiden in the palace. There, as the intimacy grows, so too the capacity to speak and reveal secrets—even if in the context of the parable, the secrets are entirely those of the beloved and not the lover! See above, pp. 160–64.

15. Zohar 1:245a; Matt, Pritzker edn., vol. 3, p. 500.

16. Zohar 3:79a.

17. Pedaya, "Aḥuzim be-dibbur," pp. 580–81.

18. On the paradoxical nature of mystical language see, Sells, *Mystical Languages of Unsaying*. In his chapter on Plotinus, Sells describes the genesis of paradox in mystical language as follows: "Real contradictions arise when the limited referential function of language encounters a rigorously apophatic notion of the unlimited" (Sells, *Mystical Languages of Unsaying*, p. 21; and introduction, pp. 3–4). In the Zohar's description of mystical experience, the paradoxical is deeply enmeshed in Ezekiel's description of the

vision of God. There, the creatures are described as "dashing to and fro" (*ratso va-shov*; 1:14), which the Zohar construes as expressing an experience that cannot be grasped in a static state, insofar as its essence is continuously dynamic and thus it is unable to be fathomed by ordinary human consciousness (3:288b, *Idra Zuta*).

19. See Zohar 1:16b; 3:164b.

20. See, for example, Zohar 1:103b, on the soul's activity in the body and God's manifestation in the world; and 3:134b on the expansion of *Atika*.

21. See Zohar 3:128a regarding the presence of the Most Ancient of Ancients. Similarly, see 1:16a, "broke through and did not break through" as a description of the emergence of *Ein Sof* from its aura; *Zohar Ḥadash* 39c, "shine and do not shine." Perhaps also the paradoxical language in the old man's riddle in *Sava de-Mishpatim* (2:95a) is itself an indication of the kind of reality to which the old man is attuned, as well as the mystical riddles in *Rav Metivta* (3:162b).

22. See, for example, Zohar 3:128a.

23. Zohar 3:131b.

Chapter 16

1. Boaz Huss has explored this question, and what follows is based in part on his research. See Huss, "Hofa'ato shel Sefer ha-Zohar," pp. 516–23.

2. On the Book of Adam and the Book of Enoch, see Idel, "Enoch is Metatron." On the Book of Adam in the Zohar, see 1:37b, 55a–b, 58b, 76a; 2:70a, 131a, 143b, 181a, 197a, 275b; 3:68b. On the Book of Enoch, see 1:13a, 37b, 55a–b, 58b; 2:55a, 100a, 105b, 180b, 192b, 217a, 277a; 3:10b, 236a, 240a, 248b.

3. See, for example, Zohar 1:37a. See Wineman, *Mystic Tales from the Zohar*, pp. 33–52.

4. *Zohar Ḥadash* 42d.

5. Zohar 3:303b. Interestingly, in rabbinic literature it is Rabbi Abba who is from Akko. And perhaps we have here an allusion to R. Isaac of Acre, the author of *Me'irat einayim*, who was associated with the Zohar's promulgation.

6. In its biblical context, this verse is not connected with the manna at all, but rather with the quail, the overindulgence in which led to the story of *Kivrot ha-Ta'avah* (Graves of Lust).

7. On his suggestion (and subsequent reservations) that the concealed jar of manna alludes to *Sifra de-Tseni'uta* (Book of Concealment), see Liebes, "How the Zohar was Written," pp. 200–201, note 58. See also Huss's suggestion that the omer's worth of manna refers to one of the Zohar's units: "Hofa'ato shel Sefer ha-Zohar," p. 518.

8. See Goldreich, "Beirurim bi-r'iyyato ha-atsmit," pp. 465–96.

9. See Lieberman, *Hellenism in Jewish Palestine*, pp. 83–99, and especially p. 84 note 9 and sources there.

10. Arguments and quarrels surrounding the "true legacy" of the teacher are a central theme in all religions and sects. Of particular relevance in this context is the example of the struggle surrounding the recording of the teachings of Isaac Luria, and the way in which R. Ḥayyim Vital so strenuously sought to emphasize his exclusive right as the legitimate heir of the Ari to record the oral teachings of his master, and not any other version by Luria's other disciples. His comments and dreams appearing in *Sefer*

ha-Ḥezyonot, whether consciously or unconsciously, are tantamount to the invention of the myth of his authority.

11. As Boaz Huss has noted, despite the fact that from this description it would seem that Rabbi Abba wrote a text which includes Rashbi's words in the *Idra Zuta*, the fact that this account is in the third person suggests a distinction between Rabbi Abba's text and the text of the *Idra Zuta* that has reached us. Huss, "Hofa'ato shel Sefer ha-Zohar," p. 519.

12. Zohar 3:296b; Matt, *Book of Enlightenment*, p. 187.

13. See Huss, ibid.

14. See Liebes, "Messiah of the Zohar," p. 35.

15. Zohar 2:123b.

16. Huss, "Hofa'ato shel Sefer ha-Zohar," p. 521; on the tradition that Elijah revealed the secrets of the Zohar, found in the main in *Ra'aya Meheimna* and *Tikkunei Zohar*, see p. 530. According to Huss, this tradition was directed against the claim, prevalent among the disciples of the Rashba (Solomon ibn Adret of Barcelona), that Elijah had revealed himself to the first kabbalists (ibid., p. 538).

17. Zohar 3:166b. On the word *aḥmata* ("satchel"), see Liebes, "Shimmushan shel millim be-Sefer ha-Zohar," pp. 17–18. See also Huss, "Hofa'ato shel Sefer ha-Zohar," p. 16, note 58.

18. Liebes, "Zohar ve-eros," p. 85.

19. Matt, *Book of Enlightenment*, pp. 30, 226.

20. Ibid, p. 243. See also Huss, "Ḥakham adif mi-navi," p. 139.

21. On this entire passage and the interpretation of this verse, see above, pp. 75–80. On this verse, see Zohar 1:16a; 2:2a, 23a; *Ra'aya Meheimna* 3:124b; and above, pp. 237–38, 261–62.

22. Boaz Huss has suggested that the Zohar's comment about "the wise one who contemplates by himself, from himself, words that others cannot mouth" (echoing Mishnah *Ḥagigah* 2:1, regarding one who is worthy of being taught the secrets of the chariot: "only if he is wise and understands by himself") alludes to Rabbi Shim'on. According to Huss, such a comment, which reflects the self-consciousness of the Zohar's authors, is directed against the view of Rabbi Moses Naḥmanides (Ramban), who claimed that human beings are unable to understand such matters by themselves unless they have received them from a teacher. Huss, "Ḥakham adif mi-navi," p. 139.

23. See Huss, "Hofa'ato shel Sefer ha-Zohar," pp. 529–32.

24. See also *Zohar Ḥadash, Tikkunei Zohar*, 103d.

25. On questions surrounding the status of the Zohar as a book, and on the attempt to trace the manner of its distribution until its printing, see Abrams, "Eimatai ḥubberah ha-hakdamah"; Abrams, "Critical and Post-Critical Textual Scholarship," pp. 59–65; El-kayam, "Ha-Zohar ha-Kadosh shel Shabbetai Tsvi."

26. See Huss, "Hofa'ato shel Sefer ha-Zohar," pp. 507–42; Huss, "*Sefer ha-Zohar* as a Canonical, Sacred and Holy Text."

Bibliography

Abrams, Daniel. "Critical and Post-Critical Textual Scholarship of Jewish Mystical Literature." *Kabbalah* 1 (1996): 17–71.

———. "Eimatai ḥubberah ha-hakdamah le-Sefer ha-Zohar?" *Asufot* 8 (1994): 211–26.

Abrom, Jan. *The Language of Winnicott*. London: Karnac Books, 1996.

Abulafia, Abraham. *Sefer ḥayyei olam ha-ba*. Jerusalem: A. Gross (private edition), 1998.

Afterman, Allen. *Kabbalah and Consciousness*. Riverdale-on-Hudson, NY: Sheep Meadow Press, 1992.

Altmann, Alexander. "*Homo Imago Dei* in Jewish and Christian Theology." *Journal of Religion* 48 (1968): 235–59.

Asher ben David. *Rabbi Asher ben David: Kol ketavav ve-iyyunim be-kabbalato*. Edited by Daniel Abrams. Los Angeles: Cherub Press, 1996.

Ashkenazi, Joseph ben Shalom. *Commentary on Sefer Yetzirah* (attributed to R. Abraham b. David of Posquieres).

———. *Perush le-parashat Bereshit le-Rabbi Yoseph ben Shalom Ashkenazi*. Edited by Moshe Hallamish. Jerusalem: Magnes Press, 1984.

Ashlag, Yehudah. *The Zohar with the Sulam commentary of Yehudah Ashlag*. Edited and compiled by Michael Berg. New York: Kabbalah Centre International, 2003.

Azulai, Ḥayyim Joseph David. *Moreh be-etsba*. Jerusalem: Ahavat Shalom, 1980.

———. *Shem ha-gedolim (Ma'arekhet sefarim)*. Jerusalem: n.p., 1967.

Baer, Yitzhak. "Ha-reka ha-histori shel ha-Ra'aya Meheimna." *Zion* 5 (1940): 1–44. Reprinted in *Mehkarim u-masot be-toldot Am Yisrael*. Vol. II, 306–48. Jerusalem, 1986.

———. *A History of the Jews in Christian Spain*. 2 vols. Translated by Louis Schoffman. Philadelphia: Jewish Publication Society, 1978.

———. "Todros ben Yehudah ha-Levi u-zmano." *Zion* 2 (1937): 19–55. Reprinted in *Mehkarim u-masot be-toldot Am Yisrael*. Vol. II, 269–305. Jerusalem, 1986.

Bahya ibn Pakuda, *Ḥovot ha-Levavot* (Duties of the Heart). Translated by Moses Hyamson. Jerusalem: Bloch, 1945; reprinted 1965.

Bhagavad-Gita, translated by Juan Mascaro. New York: Penguin, 1980.

Bar-Sela, Shraga. *Bein sa'ar li-dmamah: Ḥayyav u-mishnato shel Hillel Zeitlin*. Tel-Aviv: Ha-kibbutz Ha-me'uchad, 1999.

Ben Atar, Ḥayyim ben Moshe. *Sefer or ha-Ḥayyim: Al ha-Torah*. Jerusalem: Horev, 2003.

Ben Yisrael, Yehoshua Avraham. *Ge'ulat Yisra'el ha-shalem*. Pietrekov: Mordechai Tzederbaum, 1913.

Benayahu, Meir ben Yitzhak Nissim, ed. *Sefer Toledot ha-Ari*. Jerusalem: Machon Ben Zvi, 1967.

Bergson, Henri. *Creative Evolution*. Translated by Arthur Mitchell. 1911. Reprint, New York: The Modern Library, 1944.

Bialik, Ḥayyim Naḥman. *Revealment and Concealment: Five Essays*. Translated by Jacob Sloan. Jerusalem: Ibis Editions, 2000.

———. *Selected Poems*. Bilingual edition, translated by Ruth Nevo. Jerusalem: Dvir and *The Jerusalem Post*, 1981.

Boyarin, Daniel. *Carnal Israel: Reading Sex in Talmudic Culture*. Berkeley: University of California Press, 1993.

Carmi, T. *The Penguin Book of Hebrew Verse*. London: Penguin Books, 1981.

Celan, Paul. *Selections*, edited by Pierre Joris. Berkeley: University of California Press, 2005.

Cohen-Alloro, Dorit. "Ha-magyah ve-ha-kishuf be-Sefer ha-Zohar." PhD diss., Hebrew University, 1989.

———. *Sod ha-malbush u-mar'eh ha-mal'akh be-Sefer ha-Zohar*. Jerusalem: Hebrew University, 1987.

Cordovero, Moses. *Pardes Rimmonim*. Munkacs: Kahana and Fried, 1906. Reprint, Jerusalem: Mordechai Etyah, 1962.

———. "Or yakar" commentary. In *Sefer ha-Zohar im perush Or Yakar*. Jerusalem: Ahuzat Yisrael, 1962–1981.

———. *Sefer Gerushin*. Jerusalem, 1962.

———. *Shi'ur komah*. Jerusalem, no date.

Couliano, Ioan, P. *The Tree of Gnosis: Gnostic Mythology from Early Christianity to Modern Nihilism*. New York: HarperCollins, 1992.

Cousins, Ewert H. *Christ of the 21st Century*. Rockport, MA: Element, 1992.

David ben Judah he-Ḥasid. *The Book of Mirrors: Sefer Mar'ot ha-Zove'ot*. Edited by Daniel Matt. Chico, CA: Scholars Press, 1982, pp. 128–29 [Hebrew text].

De Certeau, Michel. *The Mystic Fable*. Translated by Michael B. Smith. Chicago: University of Chicago Press, 1992.

———. "Mysticism." Translated by Marsanne Brammer. *Diacritics* 22, no. 2 (Summer 1992): 11–25.

Deikman, Arthur J. "Deautomatization and the Mystic Experience." In *Altered States of Consciousness: A Book of Readings*, edited by Charles T. Tart, 23–43. New York: John Wiley & Sons, 1969.

Efrat, Israel. *Ha-filosofiyah ha-Ivrit ha-atikah*. Tel-Aviv: Dvir, 1965.

Elior, Rachel. *Heikhalot Zutarti*. In *Jerusalem Studies in Jewish Thought*, supplement I. Jerusalem: Magnes Press, 1982.

———. *Jewish Mysticism: The Infinite Expression of Freedom*. Translated by Yudith Nave and Arthur B. Millman. Portland, OR: Littman Library of Jewish Civilization, 2007. Originally published as "Panehah ha-shonot shel ha-herut" (*Alpaim* 15 [1998]: 9–119).

Elkayam, Avraham. "Ha-Zohar ha-Kadosh shel Shabbetai Tsvi." *Kabbalah* 3 (1998): 345–87.

Elon, Ari. *From Jerusalem to the Edge of Heaven: Meditations on the Soul of Israel.* Translated by Tikva Frymer-Kensky. Philadelphia: Jewish Publication Society, 1996.

Erickson, Milton H. "Special Inquiry with Aldous Huxley." In *Altered States of Consciousness: A Book of Readings,* edited by Charles T. Tart, 45–71. New York: John Wiley & Sons, 1969.

Even, Yosef. *Milon munaḥei ha-sipporet,* Jerusalem: Akademon, 1978.

Ezrahi, Ohad. "Shenayyim keruvim." In *Ha-yashan yehaddesh ve-he-ḥadash yitkaddesh,* edited by Yitschak Hayut-Man and Ohad Ezrahi, 5–97. Jerusalem: Hay-Or, 1997.

Finkelberg, Margalit. "Plato's Language of Love and the Female." *Harvard Theological Review* 90, no. 3 (1997): 231–61.

Fishbane, Eitan P. "Tears of Disclosure: The Role of Weeping in Zoharic Narrative." *Journal of Jewish Thought & Philosophy* 11, no. 1 (2002): 25–47.

Fishbane, Michael. *The Kiss of God: Spiritual and Mystical Death in Judaism.* Seattle: University of Washington Press, 1994.

Frankel, Yonah. *Midrash ve-aggadah.* Tel Aviv: Ha-universita Ha-ptuḥa, 1996.

Garb, Yoni. "Paths of Power." *Journal of Religion* 78 (1998): 593–601.

Gikatilla, Joseph. *Gates of Light: Sha'are Orah.* Translated by Avi Weinstein. San Francisco: HarperCollins, 1994.

———. *Sha'arei Tsedeq.* Cracow: Fischer and Deutscher, 1881.

Giller, Pinchas. *The Enlightened Will Shine: Symbolization and Theurgy in the Later Strata of the Zohar.* Albany: State University of New York Press, 1993.

———. "Love and Upheaval in the Zohar's *Sabba de-Mishpatim.*" *The Journal of Jewish Thought and Philosophy* 7 (1997), pp. 1–30.

Goldberg, Yechiel Shalom. "The Foolishness of the Wise and the Wisdom of Fools in Spanish Kabbalah: An Inquiry into the Taxonomy of the Wise Fool." *Journal for the Study of Sephardic and Mizrahi Jewry* 1, no. 2 (October–November 2007): 42–78.

Goldreich, Amos. "Beirurim bi-r'iyyato ha-atsmit shel ba'al Tikkunei ha-Zohar." In *Massu'ot,* edited by Michal Oron and Amos Goldreich, 459–96. Jerusalem: Mosad Bialik, 1994.

Gordis, Robert. *Koheleth: The Man and His World: A Study of Ecclesiastes.* New York: Schocken Books, 1968.

Gottlieb, Efraim. *Meḥkarim be-sifrut ha-Kabbalah.* Edited by Joseph Hacker. Tel Aviv: Tel Aviv University, 1976.

Green, Arthur. "Bride, Spouse, Daughter: Images of the Feminine in Classical Jewish Sources." In *On Being a Jewish Feminist: A Reader,* edited by Susannah Heschel, 248–60. New York: Schocken, 1983.

———. *Keter: The Crown of God in Early Jewish Mysticism.* Princeton, NJ: Princeton University Press, 1997.

———. "Shekhinah, the Virgin Mary, and the Song of Songs." *AJS Review* 26, no. 1 (2002): 1–52.

———. "The Song of Songs in Early Jewish Mysticism," *Orim: A Jewish Journal at Yale* 2 (1987), pp. 49–63.

———. "Three Warsaw Mystics." In *Rivka Schatz-Uffenheimer Memorial, Volume II*, edited by Rachel Elior and Joseph Dan, 1–58. Jerusalem: Hebrew University, 1996.

———. "The *Ẕaddiq* as *Axis Mundi* in Later Judaism." In *Essential Papers on Kabbalah*, edited by Lawrence Fine, 291–314. New York University Press, 1995.

———. "The Zohar: Jewish Mysticism in Medieval Spain." In *An Introduction to the Medieval Mystics of Europe*, edited by Paul E. Szarmach, 97–134. Albany: State University of New York Press, 1984.

Greenstein, David. *Aimless Pilgrimage: The Quotidian Utopia of the Zohar*. PhD diss., New York University, 2003.

Gruenwald, Ithamar. "Ha-metsi'ut ha-midrashit: Mi-derashot ḥazal li-drashot ha-mekubbalim." In *Sefer ha-Zohar ve-doro* (*Meḥkerei Yerushalayim be-Mahashevet Yisra'el* 8 [1989]), edited by Joseph Dan, 255–98. Jerusalem: Hebrew University, 1989.

Halbertal, Moshe. *Al derekh ha-emet: ha-Ramban vi-yetsiratah shel masoret*. Jerusalem: Hartmann Institute, 2006.

———. *Concealment and Revelation: Esotericism in Jewish Thought and Its Philosophical Implications*. Translated by Jackie Feldman. Princeton, NJ: Princeton University Press, 2007. Originally published as *Seter ve-giluy: ha-sod u-gvulotav be-masoret ha-Yehudit bi-ymei ha-beinayim* (Jerusalem: Yeriot, 2001).

Halevi, Judah. *The Kuzari: In Defense of the Despised Faith*, translated by N. Daniel Korobkin. Northvale, NJ: Jason Aronson, 1998.

Halperin, David. *The Faces of The Chariot*. Tübingen: J. C. B. Mohr, 1988.

Hecker, Joel. "Kissing Kabbalists: Hierarchy, Reciprocity and Equality." In *Love—Ideal and Real—in the Jewish Tradition from the Hebrew Bible to Modern Times*, edited by Leonard J. Greenspoon, Ronald A. Simkins, and Jean A. Cahan, 171–208. Omaha, NE: Creighton University Press, 2008.

———. *Mystical Bodies, Mystical Meals: Eating and Embodiment in Medieval Kabbalah*. Detroit: Wayne State University Press, 2005.

Heinemann, Isaak. *Darkhei Ha-Aggadah*. Jerusalem: Magnes Press, 1970.

Hellner-Eshed, Melila. "'Ad atah yoshvim hayinu be-tsel Ets ha-Ḥayyim be-Gan ha-Eden.'" *De'ot* 8 (July 2000): 18–21.

———. "Nefesh ha-kanah ba-Zohar." *Elu V'elu* 4 (1997): 98–116.

Henikh, Gershon, ed. *Tsavva'at Rabbi Eli'ezer (Orḥot Ḥayyim)*. Warshaw: Meir Halter, 1891. Reprint, Bene-Berak: Agudat Ḥasidei Radzyn, 1990.

Hollenback, Jess. *Mysticism: Experience, Response and Empowerment*. University Park, PA: Penn State Press, 1996.

Holtz, Abraham. *Be-olam ha-maḥshavah shel Ḥazal: Be-ikvot mishnato shel Max Kadushin*. Tel-Aviv: Sifriyat Ha-poalim, 1979.

Humphreys, Christmas. *Buddhism*. London: Penguin Books, 1962.

Huss, Boaz. *Al adnei paz: Ha-kabbalah shel R. Shim'on Ibn Lavi*. Jerusalem: Magnes Press, 1990.

———. "The Anthological Interpretation: The Emergence of Anthologies of Zohar Commentaries in the Seventeenth Century." *Prooftexts* 19 (1999): 1–19.

———. "Ḥakham adif mi-navi: R. Shim'on bar Yoḥai u-Mosheh Rabbenu ba-Zohar." *Kabbalah* 4 (1999): 103–39.

———. "Hofa'ato shel Sefer ha-Zohar." *Tarbiz* 70 (2001): 507–42.

———. "*Sefer ha-Zohar* as a Canonical, Sacred and Holy Text: Changing Perspectives of the Book of Splendor between the Thirteenth and Eighteenth Centuries." *Journal of Jewish Thought and Philosophy* 7 (1998): 257–307.

Huxley, Aldous. *The Doors of Perception*. London: Chatto & Windus, 1954.

Ibn Gabirol, Solomon. *Keter Malkhut*, edited by J.A. Zindman. Jerusalem: Mossad Harav Kook, 1957.

Idel, Moshe. *Absorbing Perfections: Kabbalah & Interpretation*. New Haven: Yale University Press, 2002.

———. "Dimuyyim u-ma'asim miniyyim ba-kabbalah." *Zmanim* 42 (1992): 31–39.

———. "Enoch is Metatron." *Immanuel* 24 / 25 (1990): 220–40.

———. *Hasidism: Between Ecstasy and Magic*. Albany: State University of New York Press, 1995.

———. "He'arot rishoniyot al ha-parshanut ha-kabbalit le-sugehah." In *Sefer ha-yovel le-Mordechai Breuer*, edited by Moshe Bar Asher, 773–84. Jerusalem: Akademon, 1992.

———. "An Historical Introduction." In *Gates of Light: Sha'are Orah*, by Joseph Gikatilla, xxiii–xxxiv. San Francisco: HarperCollins, 1994.

———. "Infinities of Torah in Kabbalah." In *Midrash and Literature*, edited by Geoffrey H. Hartman and Sanford Budick, 141–58. New Haven: Yale University Press, 1986.

———. "Kabbalah and Elites in Thirteenth-Century Spain." *Mediterranean Historical Review* 9 (1994), pp. 5–19.

———. *Kabbalah and Eros*. New Haven: Yale University Press, 2005.

———. *Kabbalah: New Perspectives*. New Haven: Yale University Press, 1988.

———. *Language, Torah and Hermeneutics in Abraham Abulafia*. Translated by Menachem Kallus. Albany: State University of New York Press, 1989.

———. *Messianic Mystics*. New Haven: Yale University Press, 1998.

———. "Models of Learning in Jewish Mysticism." Lecture presented to the Advanced Studies Institute, Hebrew University, Jerusalem, Summer 1998.

———. *The Mystical Experience in Abraham Abulafia*. Translated from the Hebrew by Jonathan Chipman. Albany: State University of New York Press, 1988.

———. "Non-linguistic Infinities and Interpretation in Later Jewish Mysticism." *The Jerusalem Review* 2 (1997/8): 209–31.

———. "PaRDeS: Some Reflections on Kabbalistic Hermeneutics." In *Death, Ecstasy, and Other Worldly Journeys*, edited by John J. Collins and Michael Fishbane, 245–64. Albany: State University of New York Press, 1995.

———. "Perush al ha-kenisah le-Pardes be-reshit ha-kabbalah." *Mahanayim* 6 (1994): 32–45.

———. "Perushim le-sod ha-arayyot be-reshit ha-kabbalah." *Kabbalah* 12 (2004): 89–199.

———. *R. Menaḥem Recanati ha-Mekubbal*. Vol. 1. Jerusalem: Schocken, 1998.

———. "Radical Hermeneutics: From Ancient to Medieval, and Modern

Hermeneutics." In *Ermeneutica e critica*, 165–201. Roma: Academia nazionale dei lincei, 1998.

———. *Studies in Ecstatic Kabbalah.* Albany: State University of New York Press, 1988.

———. "Tefisat ha-Torah be-sifrut ha-Heikhalot ve-gilguleha ba-Kabbalah." *Meḥkerei Yerushalayim be-Maḥashevet Yisra'el* 1 (1981): 23–84.

Isaac ben Samuel of Acre. *Sefer me'irat einayim.* Critical edition, by Amos Goldreich. Jerusalem: Akademon, 1981.

Jacobs, Louis. *Holy Living: Saints and Saintliness in Judaism.* Northvale, NJ: Jason Aronson, 1990.

James, William. *The Varieties of Religious Experience: A Study in Human Nature.* 1902. Reprint, New York: Collier Books, 1974.

Jellinek, Adolph, ed. *Beit ha-Midrash.* 3rd ed. 6 vols. In vol. 2. Jerusalem: Wahrmann Books, 1967.

Jonas, Hans. *The Gnostic Religion.* Boston: Beacon Press, 1963.

Kadari, Menaḥem Z. A. *Dikduk ha-lashon ha-Aramit shel ha-Zohar.* Jerusalem: Kiryath Sefer, 1971.

Kadushin, Max. *The Rabbinic Mind.* New York: Bloch, 1952.

Kolakowski, Leszek. *Bergson.* New York: Oxford University Press, 1985.

Kook, Abraham Isaac. *Abraham Isaac Kook: The Lights of Penitence, The Moral Principles, Lights of Holiness, Letters, Essays, and Poems.* Translated by Ben Zion Bokser. New York: Paulist Press, 1978.

———. "Bein nevu'ah le-halakhah," in *Orot ha-kodesh* 4:402. Jerusalem: Mosad Harav Kook.

Kushner, Lawrence. *The River of Light: Spirituality, Judaism, and the Evolution of Consciousness.* San Francisco: Rossel Books, 1981.

Lavi, Shimon. *Sefer Ketem Paz.* Jerusalem: Hahavat Shalom, 1981.

de León, Moses ben Shem Tov. *Perush ha-Merkavah.* Edited by Asi-Farber Ginat. Edited for publication by Daniel Abrams. Los Angeles: Cherub Press, 1998.

———. *Sefer Shekel ha-Kodesh.* Edited by Charles Mopsik. Los Angeles: Cherub Press, 1996.

Lieberman, Saul. *Hellenism in Jewish Palestine: Studies in the Literary Transmission, Beliefs and Manners of Palestine in the I Century B.C.E.-IV Century C.E.* 2nd ed. New York: Jewish Theological Seminary of America, 1962.

Liebes, Yehuda. "Christian Influences on the Zohar." In Liebes, *Studies in the Zohar* (see below), 139–61, 228–44.

———. "Diyonisiyut ve-Yahadut," *Hadarim* 13 (1999): 66–68.

———. "Ha-mashiaḥ shel ha-Zohar: Li-dmuto ha-meshiḥit shel Rabbi Shim'on bar Yoḥai." In *Ha-ra'yon ha-meshiḥi be-Yisra'el*, edited by Shemuel Re'em, 87–236. Jerusalem: Israel Academy of Sciences and Humanities, 1982.

———. "The Messiah of the Zohar." Translation of portions of "Ha-mashiaḥ shel ha-Zohar" (see above). In Liebes, *Studies in the Zohar* (see below), 1–84, 163–93.

———. "Ha-Zohar ke-renesans." *Da'at* 46 (2001): 5–11.

———. "Ha-Zohar ke-sefer halakhah." *Tarbiz* 64 (1995): 581–605.

———. *Ḥet'o shel Elisha.* Jerusalem: Akademon, 1990.

———. "How the Zohar Was Written." In Liebes, *Studies in the Zohar* (see below), 85–183, 194–227.

———. "Myth vs. Symbol in the Zohar and in Lurianic Kabbalah." Translated by Eli Lederhandler. In *Essential Papers on Kabbalah*, edited by Lawrence Fine, 212–42. New York University Press, 1995.

———. *Perakim be-milon Sefer ha-Zohar*. Jerusalem: Hebrew University, 1977.

———. "Shabta'ut u-gvulot ha-dat," *Mehkerei Yerushalayim be-Mahashevet Yisra'el* 16–17 (2001): 1–21.

———. "Shimmushan shel millim be-Sefer ha-Zohar." In *R. Efraim Gottlieb Z"l: Hartsa'ah le-zikhro . . .*, 17–19. Jerusalem: Hebrew University, 1974.

———. *Sod ha-emunah ha-Shabta'it*. Jerusalem: Mosad Bialik, 1991.

———. *Studies in the Zohar*. Translated by Arnold Schwartz, Stephanie Nakache, and Penina Peli. Albany: State University of New York Press, 1993.

———. "Zemirot le-seudot Shabbat she-yiysed ha-Ari ha-kadosh." *Molad*, new series, 4 (1972): 540–55.

———. "Zikkat ha-Zohar le-erets Yisra'el." In *Tsiyyon ve-tsiyyonut be-kerev Yehudei Sefarad ve-ha-Mizrah*, edited by W. Zeev Harvey et al., 31–44. Jerusalem: Misgav Yerushalayim, 2002.

———. "Zohar ve-eros." *Alpayim* 9 (1994): 67–119.

———. "Zohar and Tiqqunei Zohar: From Renaissance to Revolution." *Te'uda* 21–22 (2007): 251–301.

Lobel, Diana. *A Sufi-Jewish Dialogue: Philosophy and Mysticism in Bahya ibn Paquda's Duties of the Heart*. University of Pennsylvania Press, 2006.

Lorberbaum, Yair. *Tselem Elohim: Halakhah ve-aggadah*. Jerusalem: Schocken, 2004.

Ludwig, Arnold M. "Altered States of Consciousness." In *Altered States of Consciousness: A Book of Readings*, edited by Charles T. Tart, 9–22. New York: John Wiley & Sons, 1969.

Luria, Isaac. *Sha'ar ma'amrei Rashbi*. Jerusalem: Defus Lewi, 1898.

Mack, Hananel. *Midrash ha-aggadah*. Tel Aviv: Misrad Ha-bitachon Ha-hotsa'ah La-or, 1989.

MacRae, George "Sleep and Awakening in Gnostic Texts." In *Le origini dello gnosticismo*, edited by U. Bianchi, 496–507. Leiden: E. J. Brill, 1967.

Maimonides, Moses. *The Guide of the Perplexed*. Translated by Shlomo Pines. Chicago: University of Chicago Press, 1978.

———. *Mishneh Torah*. Schlusinger, 1947.

Manger, Itzik. *Sippur Gan Eden*. Tel Aviv: Am Oved, 1982.

Margolin, Ron. *Mikdash Adam*. Jerusalem: Magnes Press, 2005.

Masters, R. E. L. and Jean Houston. *The Varieties of Psychedelic Experience*. New York: Holt, Rinehart & Winston, 1966.

Matt, Daniel C., trans. 2nd ed. *The Essential Kabbalah: The Heart of Jewish Mysticism*. San Francisco: HarperSanFrancisco, 1995.

———. "Matnita di-lan: Tekhnikah shel hiddush be-Sefer ha-Zohar." In *Sefer ha-Zohar ve-doro (Mehkerei Yerushalayim be-Mahashevet Yisra'el* 8 [1989]), edited by Joseph Dan, 123–45. Jerusalem: Hebrew University, 1989.

————. "New-Ancient Words: The Aura of Secrecy in the *Zohar*." In *Gershom Scholem's 'Major Trends in Jewish Mysticism': 50 Years After*, edited by Peter Schäfer and Joseph Dan, 181–207. Tübingen: Mohr Siebeck, 1993.

————, trans. and ed. *Zohar: The Book of Enlightenment*. New York: Paulist Press, 1983.

————, trans. and ed. *The Zohar: Pritzker Edition*. 4 vols. Stanford: Stanford University Press, 2004–2007.

Meged, Naḥum. *Sha'arei tikvah ve-sha'arei eimah*. Tel Aviv: Modan, 1998.

Merkur, Daniel. "Unitive Experience and the State of Trance." In *Mystical Union and Monotheistic Faith*, edited by Moshe Idel and Bernard McGinn. 125–153. New York: Macmillan, 1989.

Meroz, Ronit. "Der Aufbau des Buches Sohar" [Al mivneihu ha-mekori shel Sefer ha-Zohar; On the original structure of the Zohar; lecture delivered in Hebrew at the World Congress of Jewish Studies, 1997]. *PaRDeS: Zeitschrift der Vereinigung für jüdischen Studien* e.V., II (2005): 16–36.

————. "The Path of Silence: An Unknown Story from a *Zohar* Manuscript," *The European Journal of Jewish Studies*, 1, no. 2 (2008), pp. 319–42.

————. "'Va-ani lo hayiti sham?': Kuvlanotav shel Rashbi al pi sippur Zohari lo yadu'a." *Tarbiz* 71 (2002): 163–93.

————. "Zoharic Narratives and their Adaptations." *Hispania Judaica Bulletin* 3 (2000): 3–63.

Mopsik, Charles. "The Body of Engenderment in the Hebrew Bible, the Rabbinic Tradition and the Kabbalah." In *Fragments for a History of the Human Body*, edited by Michel Feher with Ramona Naddaff and Nadia Tazi, 48–73. New York: Zone, 1989.

————, trans. and ed. *Le Zohar*. 4 vols. Lagrasse: Verdier, 1981–1996.

————, trans. and ed. *Le Zohar: Lamentations*. Lagrasse: Verdier, 2000.

Naḥmanides, Moses. *Sha'ar ha-gemul*. In *Kitvei Ramban*, edited by Chaim D. Chavel. Jerusalem: Mossad ha-Rav Kook, 1963.

Niehoff, Maren. "What Is in a Name? Philo's Mystical Philosophy of Language." *Jewish Studies Quarterly* 2 (1995): 220–52.

O'Flaherty, Wendy Doniger. *Sexual Metaphors and Animal Symbols in Indian Mythology*. Delhi: Motilal Banarsidass, 1981.

Oron, Michal. "Me-omanut ha-derush shel ba'al ha-Zohar." In *Sefer ha-Zohar ve-doro* (*Meḥkerei Yerushalayim be-Maḥashevet Yisra'el* 8 [1989]), edited by Joseph Dan, 299–310. Jerusalem: Hebrew University, 1989.

————. "'Simeini kha-ḥotam al libbekha': Iyyunim ba-poetikah shel ba'al ha-Zohar be-farashat 'Sava de-Mishpatim.'" In *Massu'ot: Meḥkarim be-sifrut ha-kabbalah . . . mukdashim le-zikhro shel Prof. Efrayim Gottlieb Z"l*, edited by Michal Oron and Amos Goldreich, 1–24. Jerusalem: Mosad Bialik, 1994.

Pagels, Elaine. *The Gnostic Gospels*. New York: Random House, 1979.

Patanjali. *Patanjali's Yoga Sutras: with the Commentary of Vyasa and the Gloss of Vachaspati Misra*. Translated by Rama Prasada. New Delhi: Munshiram Manoharlal, 1995.

Pechter, Mordechai. "Between Night and Day." *Jerusalem Studies in Jewish Thought* 8 (1989): 311–46.

Pedaya, Haviva. "Aḥuzim ba-dibbur: Li-vruro shel ha-defus ha-mitpa'el etsel rishonei ha-mekubbalim." *Tarbiz* 65 (1996): 565–636.

———. *Ha-mar'eh ve-ha-dibbur: Iyyun be-tivah shel havayat ha-hitgalut ba-mistorin ha-Yhudi.* Los Angeles: Cherub Press, 2002.

———. "Mayyim nikre'u ḥayyim." In *Gog u-Magog. Avodat ma'abadah* (program for a play for the Israel Festival). Jerusalem, 1994.

———. "Temurot be-kodesh ha-kodashim min ha-shulayim el ha-merkaz." *Mada'ei ha-Yahadut* 37 (1997): 53–110.

Ravikovitch, Dahlia. *Kol ha-shirim ad koh.* Tel-Aviv: Ha-kibbutz Ha-Me'uchad, 1995.

Recanati, Menaḥem. *Perush al ha-Torah.* Jerusalem: M. Atia, 1961.

Rumi [Maulana Jalal a-Din Rumi]. *The Essential Rumi.* Translated by Coleman Barks with John Moyne. San Francisco: Harper, 1995.

———. *Open Secret: Versions of Rumi.* Translated by John Moyne and Coleman Barks. Boston: Shambhala, 1999.

Sack, Bracha. *Be-sha'arei ha-kabbalah shel Rabbi Mosheh Kordo'iero* [Cordovero]. Beer-Sheva: Ben-Gurion University of the Negev Press, 1995.

———. "Mashal gimmel ha-orot be-Sefer Ayelet Ahavim le-Rabbi Shelomo Alkabets." In *Studies in Jewish Religious and Intellectual History, Presented to Alexander Altmann on the Occasion of His Seventieth Birthday*, edited by Siegfried Stein and Raphael Loewe, 53–61. Tuscaloosa: University of Alabama Press, 1979.

Schäfer, Peter, ed. *Synopse zur Hekhalot-Literatur.* Tübingen: J. C. B. Mohr, 1981.

Schatz, Rivka. "Darko shel Hillel Zeitlin el ha-mistikah ha-Yehudit." *Kivvunim* 3 (1979): 81–91.

Scholem, Gershom. "The Concept of Kavvanah In Early Kabbalah." In *Studies in Jewish Thought: An Anthology of German Jewish Scholarship*, edited by Alfred Jospe, 162–75. Detroit: Wayne State University Press, 1981.

———. *Major Trends in Jewish Mysticism*, 3rd rev. edn. New York: Schocken, 1954.

———. "Mekorotav shel ma'aseh Rav Gaddi'el ha-Tinok." In *Devarim be-go: Pirkei morashah u-thiyah* [Explications and Implications: Writings on Jewish Heritage and Renaissance], edited by Avraham Shapira, 270–83. 2nd ed. 2 vols. Tel Aviv: Am Oved, 1976.

———. *On the Kabbalah and Its Symbolism.* Translated by Ralph Manheim. New York: Schocken, 1969.

———. *On the Mystical Shape of the Godhead: Basic Concepts in the Kabbalah.* Translated from the German by Joachim Neugroschel; edited and revised by Jonathan Chipman. New York: Schocken, 1991.

———. *Origins of the Kabbalah.* Philadelphia: Jewish Publication Society, 1987.

———. *Reshit ha-kabbalah ve-Sefer ha-Bahir: Hartsa'otav shel Prof. Gershom Sholem.* Edited by Rivka Shatz. Jerusalem: Hebrew University, 1979.

———. *Zohar: The Book of Splendor: Basic Readings from the Kabbalah.* New York: Schocken, 1949.

Sefer ha-Bahir [The Book Bahir: An Edition Based on the Earliest Manuscripts]. Edited by Daniel Abrams. Los Angeles: Cherub Press, 1994.

Sells, Michael A. "Bewildered Tongue: The Semantics of Mystical Union in Islam." In *Mystical Union and Monotheistic Faith*, edited by Moshe Idel and Bernard McGinn, 87–124. Macmillan, 1989.

———. *Mystical Languages of Unsaying*. Chicago: University of Chicago Press, 1994.

Shanon, Benny. *The Antipodes of the Mind: Charting the Phenomenology of the Ayahuasca Experience*. Oxford: Oxford University Press, 2002.

Sharma, Arvind. "Ecstasy." In *Encyclopedia of Religion*, edited by Mircea Eliade, 5:11–17. New York: Macmillan, 1987.

Shirman, Haim. *Ha-shirah ha-Ivrit bi-Sfarad U-ve-Provans*. Jerusalem: Mosad Bialik, 1961.

Shulman, David. *Perakim be-shirah ha-hodit*. Tel Aviv: Universitah Meshuderet, 1986.

Sontag, Susan. *Against Interpretation, and Other Essays*. New York: Dell, 1966.

Sviri, Sara. "Ha-psikhologiyah ha-mistit shel al-Hakim a-Termathi," PhD diss., Tel Aviv University, 1979.

———. *The Taste of Hidden Things*. Inverness, CA: The Golden Sufi Center, 1997.

Symington, Joan and Neville Symington. *The Clinical Thinking of Wilfred Bion*. London: Routledge, 1996.

Ta-Shma, Israel M. *Ha-nigleh she-ba-nistar*. 2nd ed. Tel Aviv: Ha-kibbutz Ha-me'uchad, 2001.

Tene, Naomi. "Darkhei itsuv ha-sippur be-Sefer ha-Zohar." PhD diss., Bar-Ilan University, 1992.

Tishby, Isaiah. *Hikrei ha-kabbalah u-shluhoteha*. Vol. 1. Jerusalem: Magnes Press, 1982.

Tishby, Isaiah and Fischel Lachower. *The Wisdom of the Zohar*. English translation by David Goldstein. Oxford: Oxford University Press, 1989.

Urbach, Ephraim E. "Ha-masoret al torat ha-sod bi-tkufat ha-Tannaim." In *Mehkarim be-kabbalah u-ve-toledot ha-datot*, 1–28. Jerusalem: Magnes Press, 1968.

Vital, Hayyim. *Sefer ha-gilgulim*. Amsterdam: David Ben Menachem Man, 1774.

———. *Sefer ha-Hezyonot*. Edited by Aaron Eshkoli. Jerusalem: Mossad ha-Rav Kook, 1954.

Wijnhoven, Jochanan. "Sefer ha-Mishkal: Text and Study." PhD diss., Brandeis University, 1964.

Wineman, Aryeh. *Mystic Tales from the Zohar: Translation and Commentary*. Princeton, NJ: Princeton University Press, 1998.

Winnicott, Donald. "The Theory of the Parent-Infant Relationship." *International Journal of Psychoanalysis* 41 (1960): 585–95.

Wirshubski, Chaim. *Sheloshah perakim be-toledot ha-kabbalah ha-Notsrit*. Jerusalem: Mosad Bialik, 1975.

Wolfson, Elliot R. "Beautiful Maiden Without Eyes: *Peshat* and *Sod* in Zoharic Hermeneutics." In *The Midrashic Imagination: Jewish Exegesis, Thought and History*, edited by Michael Fishbane, 155–203. Albany: State University of New York Press, 1993.

———. *The Book of the Pomegranate: Moses De León's Sefer Ha-Rimmon*. Atlanta: Scholars Press, 1988.

———. *Circle in the Square: Studies in the Use of Gender in Kabbalistic Symbolism*. Albany: State University of New York Press, 1995.

————. "Dimui anthropomorphi ve-ha-symbolica shel ha-otiyot be-Sefer ha-Zohar." In *Ha-kenes ha-bein le'umi le-toldot ha-mystica ha-yahadut*, Vol. 3, *Sefer ha-zohar ve-doro*, edited by Joseph Dan, 147–81. Jerusalem: Hebrew University, 1989.

————. "Eunuchs Who Keep the Sabbath: Becoming Male and the Ascetic Ideal in Thirteenth-Century Jewish Mysticism." In *Becoming Male in the Middle Ages*, edited by Jeffrey J. Cohen and Bonnie Wheeler, 151–85. New York: Garland Publishing, 1997.

————. "Forms of Visionary Ascent as Ecstatic Experience in Zoharic Literature." In *Gershom Scholem's 'Major Trends in Jewish Mysticism': 50 Years After*, edited by Peter Schäfer and Joseph Dan, 209–35. Tübingen: Mohr Siebeck, 1993.

————. "Hai Gaon's Letter and Commentary on *Aleynu*: Further Evidence of Moses de León's Pseudepigraphic Activity." *Jewish Quarterly Review* 81 (1991): 365–410.

————. "The Hermeneutics of Visionary Experience: Revelation and Interpretation in the *Zohar*." *Religion* 18 (1988): 311–45.

————. "Left Contained in the Right: A Study in Zoharic Hermeneutics." *AJS Review* 11 (1986): 27–52.

————. "Letter Symbolism and Merkavah Imagery in the *Zohar*." In *Alei Shefer: Studies in the Literature of Jewish Thought Presented to Rabbi Dr. Alexandre Safran*, edited by Moshe Hallamish, 195–236. Ramat Gan: Bar-Ilan University, 1990.

————. "Light Through Darkness: The Ideal of Human Perfection in the *Zohar*." *Harvard Theological Review* 81 (1988): 73–95.

————. "Min ve-miniut be-ḥeker ha-kabbalah" [Gender and Heresy in the Study of Kabbalah]. *Kabbalah* 6 (2001): 231–62.

————. "Occultation of the Feminine and the Body of Secrecy in Medieval Kabbalah." In *Rending the Veil: Concealment and Revelation of Secrets in the History of Religions,* edited by Elliot R. Wolfson, 113–54. New York: Seven Bridges Press, 1999.

————. *Through a Speculum That Shines: Vision and Imagination in Medieval Jewish Mysticism*. Princeton, NJ: Princeton University Press, 1994.

Wolski, Nathan and Carmeli, Merav. "Those Who Know Have Wings: Celestial Journeys with the Masters of the Academy." *Kabbalah* 16 (2007): 83–114.

Yisraeli, Oded. *Parshanut ha-sod ve-sod ha-parshanut: Megammot midrashiyyot ve-hermenoitiyyot be-"Sava de-Mishpatim" she-ba-Zohar*. Los Angeles: Cherub Press, 2005.

Yoshinori, Takeuchi, ed. *Buddhist Spirituality: Indian, Southeast Asian, Tibetan, and Early Chinese*, Vol. 1. New York: Crossroads, 1993.

Zeitlin, Hillel. *Al gevul shenei olamot*. Tel Aviv: Yavneh, 1965.

————. *Be-pardes ha-ḥasidut ve-ha-kabbalah*. Tel Aviv: Yavneh, 1982.

————. *Sifran shel yeḥidim*. Jerusalem: Mossad Harav Kook, 1979.

Zelda [Zelda Schneersohn Mishkovsky]. *Shirei Zelda*. Tel Aviv: Ha-kibbutz Ha-me'uchad, 1985.

Zimmer, Heinrich. *Philosophies of India*. New York: Pantheon Books and Princeton University Press, 1951.

Index of Names and Book Titles

Index of Subjects and Terms

Index of Works Quoted

ZOHAR

RABBINIC LITERATURE

MEDIEVAL JEWISH SOURCES